INTERVIEWING

SAGE BENCHMARKS IN SOCIAL RESEARCH METHODS

INTERVIEWING

VOLUME I

EDITED BY
Nigel Fielding

SAGE Publications
London • Thousand Oaks • New Delhi

Introduction and editorial arrangement © Nigel Fielding, 2003

First published 2003

All rights reserved. No part of this publication may be reproduced, stored in a retrieval system, transmitted or utilized in any form or by any means, electronic, mechanical, photocopying, recording or otherwise, without permission in writing from the Publishers.

Every effort has been made to trace all the copyright holders of the material reprinted herein, but if any have been inadvertently overlooked the publishers will be pleased to make the necessary arrangements at the first opportunity.

SAGE Publications Ltd
6 Bonhill Street
London EC2A 4PU

SAGE Publications Inc
2455 Teller Road
Thousand Oaks, California 91320

SAGE Publications India Pvt Ltd
32, M-Block Market
Greater Kailash
New Delhi 110 048

British Library Cataloguing in Publication Data

A catalogue record for this book is available
from the British Library

ISBN 0-7619-7339-7 (set of four volumes)

Library of Congress Control Number: 2002105448

Typeset in Berthold Baskerville by The Bardwell Press, Oxford, England
Printed in Great Britain at the Cambridge University Press, Cambridge, England

CONTENTS

VOLUME I

Appendix of Sources   I
Editor's Introduction: Hearing the Social   IX

PART ONE
EPISTEMOLOGICAL AND DISCIPLINARY PERSPECTIVES ON THE INTERVIEW

Introduction   3
1. Of Sociology and the Interview   *Mark Benney & Everett C. Hughes*   5
2. Interviewing for Organizational Research   *William F. Whyte*   13
3. Merton and Methodology   *Aage B. Sørenson*   30
4. Finding the Common Denominator: A Phenomenological Critique of Life History Method   *Gelya Frank*   35
5. Biography and the Social Sciences   *Franco Ferrarotti*   58

PART TWO
VARIETIES OF RESEARCH INTERVIEWS: TYPES AND MODES

Introduction   77

Section One
Comparing Types of Research Interviews

6. Methods of Interviewing   *E. S. Bogardus*   83
7. The Controversy Over Detailed Interviews: An Offer for Negotiation   *Paul F. Lazarsfeld*   90
8. Understanding the Standardized/Non-Standardized Interviewing Controversy   *Paul Beatty*   109
9. Does Conversational Interviewing Reduce Survey Measurement Error?   *Michael F. Schober & Frederick G. Conrad*   124
10. Theorizing the Interview   *Ray Pawson*   151

Section Two
Individual Interviews

11. Dimensions of the Depth Interview   *Raymond L. Gorden*   170

Section Three
Survey Interviews

12. Artifacts are in the Mind of the Beholder   *Howard Schuman*   180
13. Interactional Troubles in Face-to-Face Survey Interviews
    Lucy Suchman & Brigitte Jordan   191

Section Four
Focussed Interviews

14. The Focused Interview   *Robert K. Merton & Patricia L. Kendall*   232
15. The Focussed Interview and Focus Groups: Continuities and
    Discontinuities   *Robert K. Merton*   261

Section Five
Group Discussions

16. The Group Interview   *E. S. Bogardus*   277
17. Studying Intergroup Relations Embedded in Organizations
    Clayton P. Alderfer & Ken K. Smith   286

Section Six
Focus Groups

18. Focus Groups   *David L. Morgan*   323
19. The Methodology of Focus Groups: The Importance of
    Interaction Between Research Participants   *Jenny Kitzinger*   347
20. Focus Groups and Ethnography
    Michael Agar & James MacDonald   365

VOLUME II

PART TWO
VARIETIES OF RESEARCH INTERVIEWS: TYPES AND MODES
(continued)

Section Seven
Cognitive Interviewing

21. Enhancement of Eyewitness Memory with the Cognitive Interview
    *R. Edward Geiselman, Ronald P. Fisher, David P. MacKinnon
    & Heidi L. Holland*   3

Section Eight
Life History Interviews

22. Interviewing for Life-History Material   *Ruth Shonle Cavan*   19
23. Doing Life Histories   *Annabel Faraday & Kenneth Plummer*   33
24. Social Genealogies Commented On and Compared: An Instrument for Observing Social Mobility Processes in the 'Longue Durée'
    Daniel Bertaux   55

Section Nine
Biographical Interpretive Method

25. Eliciting Narrative Through the In-Depth Interview
    Wendy Hollway & Tony Jefferson   77

Section Ten
Telephone and Computer-Assisted Interviewing

26. Telephone Interviews in Social Research: Some Methodological Considerations   *Charles A. Ibsen & John A. Ballweg*   95
27. The Effect of Computer-Assisted Interviewing on Data Quality: A Review   *Edith D. de Leeuw, Joop J. Hox & Ger Snijkers*   106

Section Eleven
Online Interviewing

28. E-mail: A Qualitative Research Medium for Interviewing?
    Craig D. Murray & Judith Sixsmith   128

Section Twelve
Feminist Interviewing Methods

29. Feminist Perspectives on Empowering Research Methodologies
    Patti Lather   149
30. A Feminist, Qualitative Methodology: A Study of Women
    with Breast Cancer   *Anne S. Kasper*   168

PART THREE
DESIGNING INTERVIEW-BASED RESEARCH

Introduction   187

Section One
Access, Sampling and Informed Consent

31. Informed Consent and Survey Response: A Summary of the
    Empirical Literature   *Eleanor Singer*   193
32. Interviewing Undocumented Immigrants: Methodological
    Reflections Based on Fieldwork in Mexico and the U.S.
    Wayne A. Cornelius   209

Section Two
Question Types and Question Formulation

33. Reducing Response Error in Surveys   *Seymour Sudman*   231
34. The Open and Closed Question
    Howard Schuman & Stanley Presser   268
35. A Decade of Questions   *Nora Cate Schaeffer*   296
36. Acquiescence and Recency Response-Order Effects in
    Interview Surveys   *McKee J. McClendon*   310

Section Three
Question Wording Problems and Using Vignettes

37. Strong Arguments and Weak Evidence: The Open/Closed
    Questioning Controversy of the 1940s   *Jean M. Converse*   345
38. How to Ask Questions About Drinking and Sex: Response
    Effects in Measuring Consumer Behavior
    Ed Blair, Seymour Sudman, Norman M. Bradburn & Carol Stocking   360
39. The Reliability of Recall Data: A Literature Review   *Shirley Dex*   372
40. The Vignette Technique in Survey Research   *Janet Finch*   398

VOLUME III

PART THREE
DESIGNING INTERVIEW-BASED RESEARCH
(continued)

Section Four
Recording and Transcription

41. Tape Recorded Interviews in Social Research *Rue Bucher, Charles E. Fritz & E. L. Quarantelli*	3
42. Representing Discourse: The Rhetoric of Transcription *Elliot G. Mishler*	12

PART FOUR
CONDUCTING INTERVIEW-BASED RESEARCH

Introduction	41

Section One
Interview Technique, Probing and Prompting

43. Field Methods and Techniques: A Note on Interviewing Tactics *Howard S. Becker*	45
44. A Research Note on Experimentation in Interviewing *Arnold M. Rose*	49
45. Probing: A Dangerous Practice in Social Surveys? *William Foddy*	52

Section Two
Co-Producing Interview Data and Rapport

46. The Uncooperative Interviewee *Lee Sigelman*	65
47. Collaborative Interviewing and Interactive Research *Barbara Laslett & Rhona Rapoport*	74
48. The Life Study: On Mutual Recognition and the Subjective Inquiry *Thomas J. Cottle*	88
49. Women's Life Stories and Reciprocal Ethnography as Feminist and Emergent *Elaine J. Lawless*	100
50. Interviewing Style and Respondent Behavior: An Experimental Study of the Survey-Interview *Wie Dijkstra*	124
51. Questions for the Ethnographer: A Critical Examination of the Role of the Interview in Fieldwork *Charles L. Briggs*	144

PART FIVE
FIELD RELATIONS IN INTERVIEW-BASED RESEARCH

Introduction   171

Section One
Sensitive Topics and Respondents' Welfare

52. White-Knuckle Research: Emotional Dynamics in Fieldwork with Racist Activists   *Kathleen M. Blee*   175
53. Data Collection in Dangerous Neighborhoods: Lessons From a Survey of Public Housing Residents in Chicago
Victoria Gwiasda, Nina Taluc & Susan J. Popkin   193

Section Two
Power Relations, Gender Relations and Ethics

54. Hired Hand Research   *Julius A. Roth*   208
55. Respondents' Intrusion upon the Situation: The Problem of Interviewing Subjects with Special Qualities
James K. Skipper, Jr. & Charles H. McCaghy   223
56. Talking and Listening from Women's Standpoint: Feminist Strategies for Interviewing and Analysis   *Marjorie L. DeVault*   230
57. Interviewing Women: Issues of Friendship, Vulnerability, and Power   *Pamela Cotterill*   256
58. Self-Deception and Self-Discovery in Fieldwork
Arlene Kaplan Daniels   275

PART SIX
INTERVIEWERS: CHARACTERISTICS AND QUALITIES

Introduction   295

Section One
Gender

59. When Gender Is Not Enough: Women Interviewing Women
Catherine Kohler Riessman   301

Section Two
Interviewer Training and Interviewer Cheating

60. Analysis of the Interviewer's Behavior
Barbara S. Dohrenwend & Stephen A. Richardson   331

61. The Cheater Problem in Polling   *Leo P. Crespi*   340
62. The Observers Observed: French Survey Researchers at Work
    Jean Peneff   352

Section Three
Interviewing Special Respondents: Elites, 'Deviants', Children, Minorities and the Vulnerable

63. Interviewing an Ultra-Elite   *Harriet Zuckerman*   373
64. "Surely You're Not in This Just to be Helpful": Access, Rapport, and Interviews in Three Studies of Elites   *Susan A. Ostrander*   389

VOLUME IV

PART SIX
INTERVIEWERS: CHARACTERISTICS AND QUALITIES
(continued)

Section Three
Interviewing Special Respondents: Elites, 'Deviants', Children, Minorities and the Vulnerable
(continued)

65. Interviewing Homosexuals   *Maurice Leznoff*   3
66. On Reaching Out-of-School, Hard-to-Reach Youth: Notes on Data-Gathering   *Elmer Luchterhand & Leonard Weller*   8
67. The Use of Depth Interviewing with Vulnerable Subjects: Lessons From a Research Study of Parents with Learning Difficulties   *Tim Booth & Wendy Booth*   15

Section Four
Interviewer Effects

68. Age and Sex in the Interview
    Mark Benney, David Riesman & Shirley A. Star   34
69. The Effect of Interviewer's Gender on the Interviewing Process: A Comparative Enquiry   *Maureen Padfield & Ian Procter*   48
70. The Effects of Black and White Interviewers on Black Responses in 1968   *Howard Schuman & Jean M. Converse*   59
71. Interviewer Variability: A Review of the Problem   *Martin Collins*   83

PART SEVEN
ANALYSING INTERVIEW DATA

Introduction 103

Section One
Analytic Perspectives on the Interview:
Grounded Theory, Micro-Analysis, Ethnomethodology, the Accounts Perspective, Hermeneutics and Postmodernism

72. Grounded Theory Research: Procedures, Canons, and Evaluative Criteria *Juliet Corbin & Anselm Strauss* 107
73. Interpreting Discourse: Coherence and the Analysis of Ethnographic Interviews *Michael Agar & Jerry R. Hobbs* 125
74. Doing Data: The Local Organization of a Sociological Interview *Stephen Hester & David Francis* 158
75. The Spoken and the Unspoken: A Hermeneutic Approach to Understanding the Cultural Viewpoints that Underlie Consumers' Expressed Meanings
    Craig J. Thompson, Howard R. Pollio & William B. Locander 177
76. Ghostwriting Research: Positioning the Researcher in the Interview Text *Carl Rhodes* 216

Section Two
Problems in Analysing Interviews

77. Asking Questions (and Listening to Answers): A Review of some Sociological Precedents and Problems *Irwin Deutscher* 231
78. The Sociological Significance of Ambivalence: An Example from Adoption Research *Katarina Wegar* 246
79. Problems of Editing "First-Person" Sociology *Bob Blauner* 262
80. The 1,000-Page Question *Steinar Kvale* 279

Section Three
Interviews in Multiple-Method Research

81. The Informant in Quantitative Research *Donald T. Campbell* 288
82. Participant Observation and Interviewing: A Comparison *Howard S. Becker & Blanche Geer* 294
83. Comment on "Participant Observation and Interviewing: A Comparison" *Martin Trow* 305

PART EIGHT
BIAS, CULTURAL TRANSLATION, VALIDITY AND RELIABILITY

Introduction   315

Section One
Bias, Cultural Translation and Social Desirability

84. Contagious Bias in the Interview: A Methodological Note
    Stuart A. Rice   319
85. Multilingual Interviewing in Israel   *Haim Blanc*   322
86. The Worst Place and the Best Face
    Catherine E. Ross & John Mirowsky   329
87. An Investigation of Interview Method, Threat and Response
    Distortion   *William Locander, Seymour Sudman & Norman Bradburn*   336

Section Two
Validity and Reliability

88. "How Do You Know If the Informant is Telling the Truth?"
    John P. Dean & William Foote Whyte   350
89. The Reliability and Validity of Interview Data Obtained from
    59 Narcotic Drug Addicts   *John C. Ball*   360
90. Coding Reliability and Validity of Interview Data
    Kathleen S. Crittenden & Richard J. Hill   367
91. Interviews, Surveys, and the Problem of Ecological Validity
    Aaron V. Cicourel   378
92. The Place of Inter-Rater Reliability in Qualitative Research:
    An Empirical Study
    David Armstrong, Ann Gosling, John Weinman & Theresa Marteau   392

Appendix of Sources

1. "Of Sociology and the Interview," *Mark Benney & Everett C. Hughes*
   American Journal of Sociology, vol. 62, no. 2, 1956, pp. 137–142

2. "Interviewing for Organizational Research," *William F. Whyte*
   Human Organization, vol. 12, no. 2, 1953, pp. 15–22

3. "Merton and Methodology," *Aage B. Sørenson*
   Contemporary Sociology, vol. 20, no. 4, 1991, pp. 516–519

4. "Finding the Common Denominator: A Phenomenological Critique of Life History Method," *Gelya Frank*
   Ethos, vol. 7, no. 1, 1979, pp. 68–94

5. "Biography and the Social Sciences," *Franco Ferrarotti*
   Social Research, vol. 50, no. 1, 1983, pp. 57–80

6. "Methods of Interviewing," *E. S. Bogardus*
   Journal of Applied Sociology, vol. 9, 1924, pp. 456–467

7. "The Controversy Over Detailed Interviews: An Offer for Negotiation," *Paul F. Lazarsfeld*
   Public Opinion Quarterly, vol. 8, 1944, pp. 38–60

8. "Understanding the Standardized/Non-Standardized Interviewing Controversy," *Paul Beatty*
   Journal of Official Statistics, vol. 11, no. 2, 1995, pp. 147–160

9. "Does Conversational Interviewing Reduce Survey Measurement Error?," *Michael F. Schober & Frederick G. Conrad*
   Public Opinion Quarterly, vol. 61, 1997, pp. 576–602

10. "Theorizing the Interview," *Ray Pawson*
    British Journal of Sociology, vol. 47, no. 2, 1996, pp. 295–314

11. "Dimensions of the Depth Interview," *Raymond L. Gorden*
    American Journal of Sociology, vol. 62, 1956, pp. 158–164

APPENDIX OF SOURCES

12. "Artifacts are in the Mind of the Beholder," *Howard Schuman*
    American Sociologist, vol. 17, 1982, pp. 21–28

13. "Interactional Troubles in Face-to-Face Survey Interviews," *Lucy Suchman & Brigitte Jordan*
    Journal of the American Statistical Association, vol. 85, no. 409, 1990, pp. 232–253

14. "The Focused Interview," *Robert K. Merton & Patricia L. Kendall*
    American Journal of Sociology, vol. 51, 1946, pp. 541–457

15. "The Focussed Interview and Focus Groups: Continuities and Discontinuities," *Robert K. Merton*
    Public Opinion Quarterly, vol. 51, no. 4, 1987, pp. 550–566

16. "The Group Interview," *E. S. Bogardus*
    Journal of Applied Sociology, vol. 10, 1926, pp. 372–382

17. "Studying Intergroup Relations Embedded in Organizations," *Clayton P. Alderfer & Ken K. Smith*
    Administrative Science Quarterly, vol. 27, no. 1, 1982, pp. 35–65

18. "Focus Groups," *David L. Morgan*
    Annual Review of Sociology, vol. 22, 1996, pp. 129–152

19. "The Methodology of Focus Groups: The Importance of Interaction Between Research Participants" *Jenny Kitzinger*
    Sociology of Health and Illness, vol. 16, no. 1, 1994, pp. 103–121

20. "Focus Groups and Ethnography," *Michael Agar & James MacDonald*
    Human Organization, vol. 54, no. 1, 1995, 78–86

21. "Enhancement of Eyewitness Memory with the Cognitive Interview," *R. Edward Geiselman, Ronald P. Fisher, David P. MacKinnon & Heidi L. Holland*
    American Journal of Psychology, vol. 99, no. 3, 1986, pp. 385–401

22. "Interviewing for Life-History Material," *Ruth Shonle Cavan*
    American Journal of Sociology, vol. 35, 1929, pp. 100–115

23. "Doing Life Histories," *Annabel Faraday & Kenneth Plummer*
    Sociological Review, vol. 27, no. 4. 1979, pp. 773–798

24. "Social Genealogies Commented On and Compared: An Instrument for Observing Social Mobility Processes in the 'Longue Durée'," *Daniel Bertaux*
    Current Sociology, vol. 43, nos. 2–3, 1995, pp. 69–88

25. "Eliciting Narrative Through the In-Depth Interview," *Wendy Hollway & Tony Jefferson*
    Qualitative Inquiry, vol. 3, no. 1, 1997, pp. 53–70

26. "Telephone Interviews in Social Research: Some Methodological Considerations," *Charles A. Ibsen & John A. Ballweg*
    Quality and Quantity, vol. 8, 1974, pp. 181–192

27. "The Effect of Computer-Assisted Interviewing on Data Quality: A Review," *Edith D. de Leeuw, Joop J. Hox & Ger Snijkers*
    Journal of the Market Research Society, vol. 37, 1995, pp. 325–344

28. "E-mail: A Qualitative Research Medium for Interviewing?," *Craig D. Murray & Judith Sixsmith*
    International Journal for Social Research Methodology, vol. 1, no. 2, 1998, pp. 102–121

29. "Feminist Perspectives on Empowering Research Methodologies," *Patti Lather*
    Women Studies International Forum, vol. 11, no. 6, 1988, pp. 569–581

30. "A Feminist, Qualitative Methodology: A Study of Women with Breast Cancer," *Anne S. Kasper*
    Qualitative Sociology, vol. 17, no. 3, 1994, pp. 263–281

31. "Informed Consent and Survey Response: A Summary of the Empirical Literature," *Eleanor Singer*
    Journal of Official Statistics, vol. 9, no. 2, 1993, pp. 361–375

32. "Interviewing Undocumented Immigrants: Methodological Reflections Based on Fieldwork in Mexico and the U.S.," *Wayne A. Cornelius*
    International Migration Review, vol. 16, no. 2, 1982, pp. 378–404

33. "Reducing Response Error in Surveys," *Seymour Sudman*
    The Statistician, vol. 29, no. 4, 1980, pp. 237–274

34. "The Open and Closed Question," *Howard Schuman & Stanley Presser*
    American Sociological Review, vol. 44, 1979, pp. 692–712

35. "A Decade of Questions," *Nora Cate Schaeffer*
    Journal of Official Statistics, vol. 11, no. 1, 1995, pp. 79–92

36. "Acquiescence and Recency Response-Order Effects in Interview Surveys," *McKee J. McClendon*
    Sociological Methods & Research, vol. 20, no. 1, 1991, 60–103

37. "Strong Arguments and Weak Evidence: The Open/Closed Questioning Controversy of the 1940s," *Jean M. Converse*
    Public Opinion Quarterly, vol. 48, 1984, pp. 267–282

38. "How to Ask Questions About Drinking and Sex: Response Effects in Measuring Consumer Behavior," *Ed Blair, Seymour Sudman, Norman M. Bradburn & Carol Stocking*
Journal of Marketing Research, vol. 14, no. 3, 1977, pp. 316–321

39. "The Reliability of Recall Data: A Literature Review," *Shirley Dex*
Bulletin de Méthodologie Sociologique, vol. 49, 1995, pp. 58–89

40. "The Vignette Technique in Survey Research," *Janet Finch*
Sociology, vol. 21, no. 1, 1987, pp. 105–114

41. "Tape Recorded Interviews in Social Research," *Rue Bucher, Charles E. Fritz & E. L. Quarantelli*
American Sociological Review, vol. 21, 1956, pp. 359–364

42. "Representing Discourse: The Rhetoric of Transcription," *Elliot G. Mishler*
Journal of Narrative and Life History, vol. 1, no. 4, 1991, pp. 255–280

43. "Field Methods and Techniques: A Note on Interviewing Tactics," *Howard S. Becker*
Human Organization, vol. 12, no. 4, 1954, pp. 31–32

44. "A Research Note on Experimentation in Interviewing," *Arnold M. Rose*
American Journal of Sociology, vol. 51, 1945, pp. 143–44

45. "Probing: A Dangerous Practice in Social Surveys?," *William Foddy*
Quality & Quantity, vol. 29, no. 1, 1995, pp. 73–86

46. "The Uncooperative Interviewee," *Lee Sigelman*
Quality and Quantity, 16, 1982, pp. 345–353

47. "Collaborative Interviewing and Interactive Research," *Barbara Laslett & Rhona Rapoport*
Journal of Marriage and the Family, vol. 37, 1975, pp. 968–977

48. "The Life Study: On Mutual Recognition and the Subjective Inquiry," *Thomas J. Cottle*
Urban Life and Culture, vol. 2, no. 3, 1973, pp. 344–360

49. "Women's Life Stories and Reciprocal Ethnography as Feminist and Emergent," *Elaine J. Lawless*
Journal of Folklore Research, vol. 28, 1991, pp. 35–60

50. "Interviewing Style and Respondent Behavior: An Experimental Study of the Survey-Interview," *Wie Dijkstra*
Sociological Methods & Research, vol. 16, no. 2, 1987, pp. 309–334

APPENDIX OF SOURCES   V

51. "Questions for the Ethnographer: A Critical Examination of the Role of the Interview in Fieldwork," *Charles L. Briggs*
   Semiotica, vol. 46, 1983, pp. 233–261

52. "White-Knuckle Research: Emotional Dynamics in Fieldwork with Racist Activists," *Kathleen M. Blee*
   Qualitative Sociology, vol. 21, no. 4, 1998, pp. 381–399

53. "Data Collection in Dangerous Neighborhoods: Lessons From a Survey of Public Housing Residents in Chicago," *Victoria Gwiasda, Nina Taluc & Susan J. Popkin*
   Evaluation Review, vol. 21, no. 1, 1997, pp. 77–93

54. "Hired Hand Research," *Julius A. Roth*
   American Sociologist, vol. 1, no. 4, 1966, pp. 190–196

55. "Respondents' Intrusion upon the Situation: The Problem of Interviewing Subjects with Special Qualities," *James K. Skipper, Jr. & Charles H. McCaghy*
   Sociological Quarterly, vol. 13, 1972, pp. 237–243

56. "Talking and Listening from Women's Standpoint: Feminist Strategies for Interviewing and Analysis," *Marjorie L. DeVault*
   Social Problems, vol. 37, no. 1, 1990, pp. 96–116

57. "Interviewing Women: Issues of Friendship, Vulnerability, and Power," *Pamela Cotterill*
   Women's Studies International Forum, vol. 15, nos. 5–6, 1992, pp. 593–606

58. "Self-Deception and Self-Discovery in Fieldwork," *Arlene Kaplan Daniels*
   Qualitative Sociology, vol. 6, 1983, pp. 195–214

59. "When Gender Is Not Enough: Women Interviewing Women," *Catherine Kohler Riessman*
   Gender and Society, vol. 1, no. 2, 1987, pp. 172–207

60. "Analysis of the Interviewer's Behavior," *Barbara S. Dohrenwend & Stephen A. Richardson*
   Human Organization, vol. 15, no. 2, 1956, pp. 29–32

61. "The Cheater Problem in Polling," *Leo P. Crespi*
   Public Opinion Quarterly, vol. 10, 1946, pp. 431–445

62. "The Observers Observed: French Survey Researchers at Work," *Jean Peneff*
   Social Problems, vol. 35, 1988, pp. 520–535

63. "Interviewing an Ultra-Elite," *Harriet Zuckerman*
   Public Opinion Quarterly, vol. 36, no. 2, 1972, pp. 159–175

64. ""Surely You're Not in This Just to be Helpful": Access, Rapport, and Interviews in Three Studies of Elites," *Susan A. Ostrander*
   Journal of Contemporary Ethnography, vol. 22, 1993, pp. 7–27

65. "Interviewing Homosexuals," *Maurice Leznoff*
   American Journal of Sociology, vol. 62, 1956, pp. 202–204

66. "On Reaching Out-of-School, Hard-to-Reach Youth: Notes on Data-Gathering," *Elmer Luchterhand & Leonard Weller*
   Adolescence, vol. 14, no. 56, 1979, pp. 747–753

67. "The Use of Depth Interviewing with Vulnerable Subjects: Lessons From a Research Study of Parents with Learning Difficulties," *Tim Booth & Wendy Booth*
   Social Science and Medicine, vol. 34, no. 3, 1994, pp. 415–424

68. "Age and Sex in the Interview," *Mark Benney, David Riesman & Shirley A. Star*
   American Journal of Sociology, vol. 62, 1956, pp. 143–152

69. "The Effect of Interviewer's Gender on the Interviewing Process: A Comparative Enquiry," *Maureen Padfield & Ian Procter*
   Sociology, vol. 30, no. 2, 1996, pp. 355–366

70. "The Effects of Black and White Interviewers on Black Responses in 1968," *Howard Schuman & Jean M. Converse*
   Public Opinion Quarterly, vol. 35, 1971, pp. 44–68

71. "Interviewer Variability: A Review of the Problem," *Martin Collins*
   Journal of the Market Research Society, vol. 22, no. 2, 1980, pp. 77–95

72. "Grounded Theory Research: Procedures, Canons, and Evaluative Criteria," *Juliet Corbin & Anselm Strauss*
   Qualitative Sociology, vol. 13, 1990, pp. 3–21

73. "Interpreting Discourse: Coherence and the Analysis of Ethnographic Interviews," *Michael Agar & Jerry R. Hobbs*
   Discourse Processes, vol. 5, 1982, pp. 1–32

74. "Doing Data: The Local Organization of a Sociological Interview," *Stephen Hester & David Francis*
   British Journal of Sociology, vol. 45, no. 4, 1994, pp. 675–695

75. "The Spoken and the Unspoken: A Hermeneutic Approach to Understanding the Cultural Viewpoints that Underlie Consumers' Expressed Meanings," *Craig J. Thompson, Howard R. Pollio & William B. Locander*
   Journal of Consumer Research, vol. 21, no. 3, 1994, pp. 432–452

APPENDIX OF SOURCES   VII

76. "Ghostwriting Research: Positioning the Researcher in the Interview Text," *Carl Rhodes*
    Qualitative Inquiry, vol. 6, no. 4, 2000, pp. 511–525

77. "Asking Questions (and Listening to Answers): A Review of some Sociological Precedents and Problems," *Irwin Deutscher*
    Sociological Focus, vol. 3, no. 2, 1969/1970, pp. 13–32

78. "The Sociological Significance of Ambivalence: An Example from Adoption Research," *Katarina Wegar*
    Qualitative Sociology, vol. 15, no. 1, 1992, pp. 87–103

79. "Problems of Editing 'First-Person' Sociology," *Bob Blauner*
    Qualitative Sociology, vol. 10, no. 1, 1987, pp. 46–64

80. "The 1,000-Page Question," *Steinar Kvale*
    Qualitative Inquiry, vol. 2, no. 3, 1996, pp. 275–284

81. "The Informant in Quantitative Research," *Donald T. Campbell*
    American Journal of Sociology, vol. 60, no. 4, 1955, pp. 339–342

82. "Participant Observation and Interviewing: A Comparison," *Howard S. Becker & Blanche Geer*
    Human Organization, vol. 16, 1957, pp. 28–32

83. "Comment on 'Participant Observation and Interviewing: A Comparison'," *Martin Trow*
    Human Organization, vol. 16, 1957, pp. 33–35

84. "Contagious Bias in the Interview: A Methodological Note," *Stuart A. Rice*
    American Journal of Sociology, vol. 35, 1929, pp. 420–423

85. "Multilingual Interviewing in Israel," *Haim Blanc*
    American Journal Sociology, vol. 62, 1956, pp. 205–209

86. "The Worst Place and the Best Face," *Catherine E. Ross & John Mirowsky*
    Social Forces, vol. 62, no. 2, 1983, pp. 529–536

87. "An Investigation of Interview Method, Threat and Response Distortion," *William Locander, Seymour Sudman & Norman Bradburn*
    Journal of the American Statistical Association, vol. 71, no. 354, 1976, pp. 269–275

88. "'How Do You Know If the Informant is Telling the Truth?'," *John P. Dean & William Foote Whyte*
    Human Organization, vol. 17, 1958, pp. 34–38

89. "The Reliability and Validity of Interview Data Obtained from 59 Narcotic Drug Addicts," *John C. Ball*
American Journal of Sociology, vol. 72, 1967, pp. 650–654

90. "Coding Reliability and Validity of Interview Data," *Kathleen S. Crittenden & Richard J. Hill*
American Sociological Review, vol. 36, 1971, pp. 1073–1080

91. "Interviews, Surveys, and the Problem of Ecological Validity," *Aaron V. Cicourel*
American Sociologist, vol. 17, 1982, pp. 11–20

92. "The Place of Inter-Rater Reliability in Qualitative Research: An Empirical Study," *David Armstrong, Ann Gosling, John Weinman & Theresa Marteau*
Sociology, vol. 31, no. 3, 1997, pp. 597–606

Editor's Introduction: Hearing the Social

Nigel Fielding

When Sage's Chris Rojek approached me with the idea of collecting together a set of classic articles on interviews in social research I was intrigued and daunted. I've used interviews in all my empirical research, in studies of extremist politics, communes, the occupational socialisation of lawyers, probation officers and police, the conduct of child abuse investigations, the problems of community policing, and courtroom legal discourse. Latterly, somewhat incestuously, I've been studying the professional practice of social researchers, particularly their use of information technology, and again I've been conducting interviews and group discussions. I enjoy interviewing because I find it natural. I've always asked lots of questions. I seem to be drawn to the gaps in argument, the missing evidence, the withheld motive. My questions are often my best shot at capturing the object of interest itself, and my musings about the answers have both spurred the analysis and stimulated thinking about how we know what we think we know. So when Chris Rojek broached this project I had some questions for him. In particular, whatever do we mean by 'classic'?

In the present context 'classic' is clearly a term referring to quality. But in a post-modern, self-aware, overheated world, surely what is 'quality' is so contested as to be hopelessly problematic? Well no, actually. In any age, of any *weltanschauung*, quality stands out. Quality is an idea that we have not heard before, and that stimulates us to change our thinking to embrace or (at least) accommodate it. That, then, is my Occam's razor for this collection.

It had to be a pretty sharp razor, too. I have had to be highly selective, even in a collection stretching to four volumes and over 90 articles. Note that last word. The set comprises only *articles* published in journals (mostly sociology, social science, research methodology and psychology journals). It does not include extracts from books. I would be the first to say that many classics of interviewing have been published in book form. This includes a core of original treatments, and a larger group of textbooks which convey their principles and findings to a wider readership. But books are relatively accessible. If researchers must have one of the core original treatments and it is not in their library, it is merely a matter of ordering it from the bookstore or inter-library loan. This cannot so easily be said of the classic journal articles.

As a prominent – perhaps the dominant – social research tool, the methodological literature on interviewing reaches back to the earliest days of the social, behavioural and political sciences. Many journals from that period have long ceased publication. Some of the libraries that took the journals have been lost to war, political upheavals or university reorganisations. Many more of the journals bearing key texts were – and are – of very limited circulation. Latterly the much-remarked proliferation of academic journals has defeated the budget of even the best-endowed libraries. Indeed, my own university, founded in the 1960s, has a modern, IT-intensive library, but my trawl for articles for this set rapidly overtook its collection and taxed our interlibrary loan budget beyond the limit, so I spent much time on the motorways and railways travelling to other libraries. In short, it is harder to get sight of classic articles than of classics published in other media. With the worldwide growth of higher education, too, there are new universities and related institutions constantly springing into being, and established institutions are broadening their programmes.

Readers may by now be asking some questions of their own. For example, as well as that 'quality' criterion, and excluding all but journal articles, what else has Fielding done by way of selection? For one thing, the set does not include articles published in electronic media. These media are accessible online. Also, an element of the selection process has involved citation analysis, and online material has not been available sufficiently long to index its significance by reliable citation measures. Another element of selection is that the collection is confined to articles published in the English language. For much of their history, social and behavioural research have been dominated by the Anglo-American literature (with the accent decidedly on the second half of that hyphenation), and English is the predominant 'language of science'.[1] This does not mean that the articles are solely authored by people whose first language is English. Far from it. I am conscious that there are debatable assumptions here, and I expect that in future we will have cause to re-evaluate both the criteria relating to online publication and to English language publication, but as it stands these choices seem realistic.

So, my Occam's Razor may be sharp but its blade is not altogether straight. I simply hope it is not distorted. Wright Mills (1959) enjoined us to make clear our allegiances. To my personal sense of how I recognise a 'classic' and what constitutes 'quality', I bring the perspectives of a (primarily) qualitative researcher educated on both sides of the Atlantic, whose social science education began in 1964 (in US secondary schools) and continued in a formal sense until 1977 (the award of my PhD at the London School of Economics). While I became aware of the debate about relativism in my undergraduate sociology degree, perhaps more than contemporary students I construe problems of subjectivity as 'quality control' issues rather than proof that no concrete knowledge of the social world is possible.

In the realm of theory I am oriented to symbolic interactionism. That commitment is important, but I've never felt that sociology has the answer to all the interesting problems society confronts, and I've participated in much multi-disciplinary research. As a result I have not confined the selection of articles to those in sociology journals. I am largely an empirical researcher rather than a theorist, and most of my substantive work has been in criminal justice, particularly policing, although my first sustained project was a participant observation study of the racialist National Front political party, an experience which has given me an abiding scepticism about rigid codes of ethical research practice. As a methodologist, I have been largely concerned with interviewing (Fielding and Thomas, 2001), multiple-method research (Fielding and Fielding, 1986; Fielding and Schreier, 2001) and the social research applications of information technology (Fielding and Lee, 1991, 1998). I need hardly rehearse that all selection involves bias, and perhaps these autobiographical details convey a few of mine. It is entirely inescapable that my selection of 'classics' may not be the next person's. I merely hope that a good proportion of what I have chosen corresponds with what other reasonably informed methodologists would choose.

I mentioned that the set includes over 90 articles. The first was published in 1924 and the most recent in 2000. To compile the base from which I selected, I employed database searches, bibliometric analyses, my own reading lists, annotations of sources read over the years, sets of papers from methodology conferences, and conversations with other researchers and methodologists. The initial catalogue resulting from this came to 546 items. The first sift, which included de-selecting all non-journal sources and performing citation analysis on the remainder, reduced the number to 430 articles. The next sift involved me reading the 430 articles and annotating them on various criteria. I then made the final selection.

Before I leave the topic, I should say that 'classic' does not mean 'old'. Some classics are indeed vintage (and it has been fascinating to see just how much contemporary concerns were presaged in early contributions) but others are recent. I will shortly begin a tour of the organisation of the set, which is based on a processual conception of the stages of interview research. I have attempted to include articles that lend insight into each of these stages and, where there has been debate, to indicate its flavour by including articles representing the different positions. This means that the processual organisation is crosscut by a thematic organisation, and that some topics are more extensively represented than others. The set includes articles on as wide a range as possible of types of interview. There are, for example, contributions relating to interviews used to collect data for quantitative research (e.g., survey interviewing) as well as for qualitative research (in its numerous forms), and both one-to-one and group interviewing are addressed.

Interviewing assumes that we can understand the social world by listening to talk and interpreting what is said. Interpersonal skill is involved: we are familiar with the idea that some people are 'good listeners'. Also a skill is being thoughtful about what one has heard. From a researcher's perspective, this means being good at interpretation, drawing on an analytic sensitivity to see the theoretical in the empirical.

Within this framework is great variation. The survey interviewer employs uniform 'methods of administration' and highly structured 'research instruments'. The qualitative interviewer employs a flexible style, and a degree of structure bound more by the implicit rules of conversation than any rules of research method. Using these approaches, and their many variants, is a matter of fitness for purpose. The survey researcher's style addresses the interview as an information-gathering exercise on the basis that respondents can appropriately act as informants about the topic. The qualitative researcher's style reflects an interest in more ineffable matters, knowledge of which is co-constructed with interviewees.

In the survey approach, we assume the existence of tangible objects of knowledge in the social world, so that our purpose is to 'mine' them (Kvale 1996) using means which encourage accurate and full responses. In the qualitative approach we pursue conceptual phenomena which are situationally-embedded, unstable and endlessly re-negotiated. Our purpose is to understand processes – inherently slippery and contingent, because dynamic – from a standpoint within them. We might think of the interview as an island in a flowing river. We seek means to make it as accommodating of reflection as possible while recognising that what is reflected is constantly changing. We help our respondents onto its banks but to clamber up they must grasp our hands.

That is, in placing our particular method on this particular occasion somewhere in the variant range of structure, we recognise that our work is a co-construction and yet that it is inescapably *our* work. The terms 'non-standardised' and 'unstructured' are misnomers, because there is always some structure when we embark on conversation for a purpose (indeed, purposeless talk is, by definition, babble). We must then decide what degree of structure is appropriate to our purpose, and while we may seek a structure meaningful to interviewees and which minimises our interventions, structure will always be there. That is not to say it will be consistent; perceived structure has always to be monitored in performance and assessed in analysis (Chamberlain and Thompson, 1997).

As my earlier reference to selection as bias may suggest, it is generally recognised nowadays that there are few corners of the social world about which we can claim objective knowledge. Our knowledge is always situated – in our biography, our circumstances, our allegiances and interests. The tour of the organisation of this set can begin from that point. All reasoning depends on a theory of knowledge. The collection represents a range of approaches to the foundations of the interview. From a special issue of *American*

Journal of Sociology on interviewing, Benney and Hughes [1][2] profile its importance in the discipline of sociology, discussing the participants' roles and issues relating to interview communication. For Whyte [2], single interviews have no meaning on their own, acquiring meaning only as part of a corpus, an argument he develops in the course of considering the uses for which interview data are and are not best suited. The need to integrate method with theory and empirical information is a theme continued in Sorensen's [3] brief but illuminating account of Merton's approach to the 'focussed interview'. From the standpoint of phenomenology, Frank [4] offers us the life history interview as text, exploring whether such work can be regarded as 'scientific'. For Ferrarotti [5] life history provides a corrective to the versions of history organised around the doings of the powerful. He compares this critical approach with the understandings formulated by positivist and quantitative analyses, arguing that generalized accounts can be built up from the subjective and the particular. The articles in this section illustrate how different schools of thought embrace different epistemologies, emphasising different criteria of adequacy or validity, a set of contrasts we maintain throughout.

There are many varieties of research interview. The field is aided by the widely-used typology which distinguishes interviews by their degree of 'standardization', the extent to which they are 'structured'. Comparing types of interview – standardized, semi-standardized and non-standardized interviews – starts our section exploring this variety. Bogardus [6] considers different kinds of non-research interviews conducted in various professions, comparing and contrasting interviews by such people as doctors with research interviews. Lazarsfeld [7] is seminal in the debate over standardization which even by the 1940s had sharply divided the methodology field. In Beatty's [8] account, the divisions still endured some 50 years later, although in the intervening years there had been ebbs and flows in the relative status of standardized and nonstandardized approaches. These changes in status largely related to our developing understanding of the nature of communication in the interview.

Schober and Conrad [9] make the important contribution that both standardised and nonstandardised approaches are valid but under different circumstances. When respondents are clear both about the ideas about which they are being interviewed, and how these fit their own experiences, the standardised method excels, but when these conditions are not satisfied the nonstandardised approach is best. For Pawson [10] the methodological polarization into standardised ('structured') and nonstandardised ('unstructured') camps is not helpful. Drawing on a realist theory of knowledge he emphasises the theoretical objectives of interviewing and shows how this approach can inform interview design.

With a more refined sense of the power and limits of the 'standardization typology' in mind we now consider the numerous different modes of interview. We first encounter the individual interview (in US usage, the 'one-on-one' interview, for more delicate UK usage, the 'one-to-one' interview), in Gorden's classic account [11] of the depth interview. Gorden emphasises the nature of communication in such interviewing and highlights the social psychological processes at work.

In many respects the survey interview is a distinctive form, marked by more widely-accepted conventions than the depth interview mode (although later contributions reveal substantial, if seldom-acknowledged, similarities in fieldwork). Schuman [12] shows the survey interview's origin in two instinctive human actions – asking questions, and using samples of opinion as a basis for inference. The whimsical style of the piece, based on a fictitious (or is he?) interactionist drawn to survey technique, conveys much in a few pages. Regular conversation displays informal but influential conventions which need to be taken into account in research design, as Suchman and Jordan [13] argue in what might be taken as a subversive article, a critique of the survey interview, but one nevertheless published in the *Journal of the American Statistical Association*. In the course of their critique these authors do an excellent job of profiling the nature of survey interviews, and I have included the response articles by other methodologists and the authors' 'rejoinder'.

A landmark in interview methodology was Merton and Kendall's [14] 'focussed interview', discussed earlier in Sorensen [3] and represented here by the early *American Sociological Review* account and a later reflection by Merton [15] after elements of the method were taken up in the familiar research tool called the 'focus group'. Not all interviewing is done in one-to-one mode but there are important contrasts to consider between interviewing individuals and group interviews. The fundamentals are explained by Bogardus [16], and Alderfer and Smith [17] consider ways that the essence of group discussions relate to social psychological processes of interaction and group dynamics. With these points in mind we can address the increasingly ubiquitous 'focus group', the variant of group interview which draws (broadly) on Merton's principles for focussed interviews. From Morgan [18], a leading authority on focus group method, we include an overview specifying its distinctive features and procedures, while Kitzinger [19] highlights the group dynamic aspect, presenting ways to lead groups and maximise interaction. Describing the focus group as somewhere between a chaired meeting and a conversation, Agar and MacDonald [20] substantiate a key point made by both previous articles, that insight depends on comparing focus group data to information from other sources.

To an extent the modes we have so far considered are generic. That is, they are broad, and subsume a range of practice. The 'cognitive interview' is a specialised mode drawing on cognitive psychology to address respondents' problems in recalling traumatic or long-past events. Initially psychology was concerned with how its findings could be used in the legal context, then emphasis shifted to demonstrating that criminal justice system assumptions about witness recall were flawed. Finally psychologists realised that, if eyewitness memory was prone to error, psychological techniques might facilitate memory retrieval. Geiselman, Fisher, MacKinnon and Holland [21] adapted findings from the experimental literature to an interview strategy that improved recall and is also useable in applied research.

Life history interviewing is a long-established method particularly important in social history and anthropology but which also finds application in sociology and social psychology. It is a demanding method for both respondents and researchers, aiming for great depth and to recover experiences across the life course. To illustrate the enduring relevance of themes remarked on early in the practice of the method we include Cavan [22], while to examine the practicalities and the research relationships involved we include Faraday and Plummer [23]; and to show the subtle and powerful analytic work possible we have Bertaux [24]. The Biographical Interpretive Method interview might be regarded as a branch of life history. It emerged from techniques developed to address the special circumstances of interviews with survivors of Nazi oppression. Having a psychotherapeutic grounding and orientation to handling sensitive topics, the method is insightfully portrayed by Hollway and Jefferson [25].

New communication technologies increasingly find application in social research. Their particularities make for distinct interviewing modes. Telephone interviewing is an instance. The telephone's usefulness to researchers was long restricted by the class-based nature of telephone ownership. This is now less significant, and cost-effectiveness relative to field interviews has advanced its use. Methodological research comparing it with other modes is reported by Ibsen and Ballweg [26]. Another technology which has increasingly influenced interview practice is the computer. The emergence of computer-assisted interviews has prompted a methodological literature which is reviewed by de Leeuw and her colleagues [27]. As computer networking has progressed, online interviews and focus groups have emerged as a further technologically-based mode of interviewing. Murray and Sixsmith [28] offer a useful appraisal of their scope.

Some argue that feminist method has a particular affinity for the interview. This rich source of methodological discussion features at several points in these volumes. Feminist interviewing forms our last distinct mode of interviewing, with Lather's [29] discussion of contrasting feminist studies, from which she extracts links between feminist principles and given interviewing practices. Kasper's [30] study of female cancer-sufferers offers an especially clear discussion of the strengths and difficulties involved in feminist interviewing.

The next stage of our tour takes in the design of interview-based research. One of the first issues is drawing the sample and gaining access to those selected. The complexities of sampling and access are well-considered by Cornelius [32] in his account of researching 'illegal' immigrants to the United States. When requesting interviews, researchers must offer an introduction about the research and it is usually necessary for ethical and legal reasons to seek respondents' 'informed consent', as considered by Singer [31].

Some modes involve elaborate instruments while others may involve posing only one question (as did Kasper) or an interaction which does not seem to involve asking questions at all. But even if they are implicit, it is hard to imagine an interview which does not involve asking questions. Question construction is a major topic of methodological attention. Bradburn and Sudman's book (1974) assessing measurement error reported that the largest response effects do not come from interviewers or respondents but from the interview schedule and its perceived context, prompting research on question wording and sequence effects.

We first tackle question types and the effects of question formulation. Sudman's [33] masterly discussion treats question types and formulation as means to reduce error in response to survey interviews. Much hangs by whether we use 'open' or 'closed' questions; Schuman and Presser's [34] is the classic account. For a useful summary of the detailed effects of different question formulations we include Schaeffer [35]. Particular preoccupations have been with respondents' tendency to agree and with question order effects. Collaboration between methodologists and cognitive psychologists has produced an understanding of these, using a stage model of questioning and answering. McClendon [36] offers an account of what has been found and an insight into the reasons for the effects.

There are many ins-and-outs in designing good questions, and question-construction intimately affects our data. From Converse [37] we learn that institutional 'politics' affect question design and preferences for particular types of question wording. One question-construction issue of which most people are aware is the biassed or 'loaded' question, addressed by Blair *et al* [38] in relation to asking sensitive questions. Also a challenge is when we ask respondents to report upon past experiences. Retrospective questions raise important concerns about memory and cognition, one of several features Dex [39] identifies in her review of the problems of 'recall data'. Some interview designs include non-conventional questioning techniques, of which the most prominent is the vignette, the presentation of an elaborated story to which the respondent is asked to react. Finch [40] is the classic contribution.

Having designed the research instrument, researchers must consider how to capture the responses made to it. We did not always have cheap, reliable means of audio-recording. From the early days of tape recording Bucher, Fritz and Quarantelli [41] identify the issues relating to technical means of data capture. Converting recorded data to text on the page, as a step towards analysis, is no trivial background activity. As Mishler's [42] fine and subtle account illuminates, practical transcription decisions pre-figure analysis.

We have now chosen our interview mode, designed our research instrument and decided how to record the data. Assuming we have gained access, introduced our interview, and received consent, we can begin interviewing. People use interviewing because it has advantages relative to other methods of tackling their subject. Realising these advantages depends on the quality of communication, and a large influence is the researcher's interviewing technique. We include Becker's [43] early contribution on tactics for getting at the 'reality' of attitude and action. When initial questions do not succeed we may employ probes and prompts to seek elaborated responses. These techniques are much-debated; some condemn prompting altogether. Like Becker, Rose [44] explores the effects of different tactics, leading him to discuss the nature of spontaneous probing, a matter Foddy [45] pursues.

Producing interview data is now recognised as a collaborative accomplishment rather than the mechanical extraction of uncontaminated 'data' from the respondent as if one were plucking fruit from a tree. Although there are many studies of refusal to participate Sigelman [46] offers a rare discussion about people who agree but prove unforthcoming. Laslett and Rapoport [47] is a seminal contribution on securing cooperation by working with respondents, making them feel party to the interview rather than merely a research 'subject'. They commend important, but demanding, refinements of technique. With a similar objective, Cottle [48] takes a very different approach, blurring the distinction between interview and participant observation and seeking to make research encounters into ongoing relationships rather than one-off data collection occasions. Between these extremes is Lawless's [49] procedure, which she sees as particularly suited to feminist research, in which interviews are mixed with 'dialogic' sessions where the researcher is just another participant in the discourse and the analysis is explicitly debated by all the participants. These imaginative variations raise questions about the effects of interview style, into which Dijkstra [50] offers insight. That innovative techniques may not overcome all barriers to communication is the subject of Briggs' [51] elegant semiotic analysis of interview communication.

Interview interaction fundamentally affects the data available for analysis. The practice of interviewing can prompt anxieties, nuances and sensitivities for which textbooks do not prepare us. A particular concern is when we interview about sensitive topics. In 'risk society', which is increasingly concerned to manage every sort of risk, and where science and social organization regularly spawn new challenges, respondents are asked questions about an ever-increasing range of topics that are sensitive, either because they are intrusive (e.g., the profoundly personal questions of AIDS research) or raise disturbing possibilities (eg., terrorism). Blee [52] considers the 'emotional dynamics' that arise in interviewing on sensitive topics and, because her subject was violent racists, the implications of emotional dynamics for interviewers' personal security. Some of the technical, tactical and practical means for protecting the rights, personal security and welfare of interviewers are considered in Gwiasda, Taluc and Popkin's [53] account of fieldwork in an inner city ghetto.

While not all interview research is sensitive, all interview research does depend on the relationship between researcher and researched. Power is an important dimension. Linking Gwiasda *et al*'s account of fieldworker protection and the power relations of interviewing is Roth's [54] argument that when we weigh the quality of interview data we must remember the circumstances of those who went into the field to collect it. While researchers can manifestly or subtly oppress the researched, researchers can also be exploited and oppressed. Pursuing the subtleties of interviewers' relations with interviewees, we encounter Skipper and McCaghy's [55] account of an (attempted) interview with a striptease artiste. Few social science articles can be described as hilarious, but in my view this has to be one. There is a serious core, though. The authors detail means to manage the problems of interviewing those engaged in 'deviant behaviour' and parallels to other topics where similar problems may occur.

Gender is a prominent aspect of the power dimension of interviewer/respondent relationships. Devault's [56] widely-cited article shows how interviewers can use their own experiences to better interpret what respondents say and manage their performance of interviews. Although gender is her central reference point, Devault's insights can be extended across other social dividing lines, such as ethnicity or age. While some feminists have followed Oakley (1981) in arguing that 'women interviewing women' intrinsically achieve rapport and insight, Cotterill [57] takes issue with this. She notes other social divisions that identity of gender may not overcome, and shows how these other sources of social power influence interview interaction.

We might take the articles on power relations and the nuances of gendered power relations as saying that the more obvious divisions within interviewing practice – interviewer/interviewee, research manager/fieldworker/respondent, male/female – do not work in the straightforward way we expect. If so, rather than the interviewer's demographic or status characteristics, what may influence what is achieved in the field may be far more individual qualities. This is the tenor of Daniels' [58] wry and self-revealing discussion of her long experience as an interviewer. Perhaps particular qualities and characteristics help interviewers manage fieldwork. We therefore further examine the influence of interviewer characteristics, beginning with Kohler Riessman's [59] discussion of the precise way that identity of gender failed to overcome the effect of ethnicity in her research. But another interviewer characteristic, competence, has nothing to do with gender or ethnicity.

Attention to shortcuts and procedural deviations can help us to anticipate problems and recognise when the assumptions of particular interview modes are unrealistic. Dohrenwend and Richardson's [60] account of interviewer competence is directed to training and refinement of technique through practice. Like Roth, Crespi's [61] account of cheating by interviewers locates the problem in working conditions. Peneff [62] takes an illuminating tack, arguing that rather than 'cheating' we ought to see deviation from standardised practice as attempts by interviewers to accommodate the research subject's situation. This revealing study takes the lid off survey practice and by doing so builds bridges between proponents of standardised and non-standardised approaches.

Interviewing special populations also affects field relations. The substantial literature is represented here by contributions on interviewing elites, 'deviants', children and the vulnerable. Social scientists have long been interested in elites. Status differentials between researcher and researched, confidentiality, manipulation and candour are among the issues. Zuckerman [63] offers methodological pointers for dealing with respondents whose status exceeds the interviewer's, in her case, Nobel Laureates. Ostrander's [64] comprehensive account includes warnings about how elite respondents can threaten the interviewer's interests and even their livelihood.

Although the category 'deviant' is increasingly contested, studies of this and other marginal populations – for whom being researched may be particularly consequential – call for special measures to protect research subjects. While the situation has changed considerably, we can still learn from Leznoff's [65] discussion of researching homosexuals at a time when homosexuality was more unambiguously 'deviant' than it is now. Special considerations of protection, comprehension and recall apply when interviewing children, as discussed by Luchterhand and Weller [66]. The Booths' [67] study of parents with learning difficulties explores complex ethical and methodological considerations which arise in interviewing the vulnerable: the mentally ill, those with physical disabilities, and the socially inadequate.

We now see that 'interviewer effects' – characteristics, qualities and behaviour of interviewers – influence the data that are collected. Interviewer matching, where characteristics like gender or race are matched to the respondent, is often commended. An early account of interviewer effects is given by Benney, Riesman and Star [68], and a particularly clear example of gender-of-interviewer effects is offered by Padfield and Procter [69].

Seminal research, and indeed the very topic of 'interviewer effects', came from the USA, whose character as an 'immigrant society', and transition from segregationism through a 'melting pot' ideology to multi-culturalism, stimulated strong concern with the race of interviewers and respondents. Schuman and Converse [70] draw on this tradition in assessing the effects of race on interview response. But we should not lose sight of our earlier observation that, while demographic characteristics have effects, so does the individual interviewer's performance, a matter systematically tackled in Collins' [71] account of the performance of different interviewers.

By now we have a grasp of the design, procedures and conduct of interviews, and things that affect the quality and character of the data. It is time to step back from fieldwork and consider what to do with the data that have been collected. The variety of types and modes is matched by many different perspectives on the status of interview data. The range runs from those who take interview data as unproblematic factual reports on the social world through those for whom interview data represent artful signs of the co-production of the appearance of an interview while lacking any reality outside the context of their production. Of the many analytic perspectives, we focus on grounded theory, micro-analysis and ethnomethodology, the accounts perspective, hermeneutics and postmodernism.

A key step in much analysis is classification or 'coding' of data. This is an important move in managing the data, manipulating it according to an analytic strategy and weighing the evidence for the analysis. Corbin and Strauss [72] profile the essential canons of the grounded theory approach to data management, coding and data analysis. For Agar and Hobbs [73], the quality of the analysis reflects its 'coherence'. They divide 'coherence' into several forms, showing how inferences in respect of each may be warranted as a basis for systematic, detailed and secure analyses. Also a species of micro-analysis is the perspective associated with ethnomethodology, represented by Hester and Francis's [74] dissection of an interview with an educational psychologist, revealing how his account of his work reflects practices employed in the interview to elicit the account.

Hermeneutics is one of the longest-established approaches to the analysis of encultured meanings. Thompson, Pollio and Locander [75] apply the tool of the 'hermeneutic circle' to the interpretation of consumer accounts of preferences. From postmodernism we take Rhodes' [76] rendering of the way that researchers are inscribed in the phenomenon under analysis, employing the metaphor of the interviewer as 'ghostwriter' of the interviewee's script.

Analysis of interview data negotiates problems of context, subjectivity, perspective and scope. Meaning-structures are culturally-nuanced and obscured. Deutscher [77] shows how problems revolving around ambiguities of language are encountered even when interviewing in our own culture, strongly connecting with Wegar's [78] account of how ambivalence, reflecting the 'dilemmatic' nature of human thought, is neglected in interpreting interview talk. These concerns also manifest in editing interview data, as in Blauner's [79] account of his work on texts where respondents' words were minimally-edited but selection and interpretation still weighed heavily. Pointing out that analysis begins even before the interview, Kvale [80] emphasises the importance of research design and a critical angle on the 'empiristic' assumptions behind much interview practice.

The contested character of data is not an issue confined to interview data. Some see the best response in comparing results from different methods on the basis that the strengths of one may compensate weaknesses of the other(s). Multiple-method research raises the relationship between interviewing and other methods. Campbell's [81] classic study of morale in submarine crews offers an endorsement of the interview by a researcher associated with a strongly positivist approach; the study led Campbell to change his estimation of qualitative research overnight. This contrasts with Becker and Geer's [82] critical comparison of interviews with participant observation, a matter provoking Trow's [83] trenchant response.

The uncertain status of interview data is the focus of a section conveying problems of bias, cross-cultural interviewing, and the 'social desirability' phenomenon. Rice [84] offers the classic epitome of biassed interviewing and expounds some necessary principles to control it. From Blanc [85] we learn of the deep problems of interviewing in another culture, and that commonsense, not technical prescription, is the best response. A major obstacle is the 'social desirability' phenomenon, where respondents form an impression of the socially acceptable, preferred response and feed interviewers what they think interviewers want to hear. Ross and Mirowsky [86] show how the phenomenon operates, with a kind of shadow-boxing between interviewer and interviewee in which situated meaning escapes from view. In a study from the survey tradition, Locander, Sudman and Bradburn [87] specify the workings of such bias and consider means of minimising it.

This brings us to the final theme of our set: the validity and reliability of interview data. Dean and Whyte [88] offer a 'new' perspective in an old article. They take the stance that there is no 'real' or underlying view, and consider the trade-off between objective and subjective. Ball [89] shows, though, that we can expect certain kinds of data to be accurately reported even by respondents with good reason to distort their account. Crittenden and Hill [90] tackle a fundamental issue — whether different researchers would similarly code the same data. They demonstrate the conditions under which they do and do not. Cicourel [91] suggests that reliability and validity reflect deeper problems than the need for better code definitions and training. These problems reflect invalid epistemological assumptions about interview interaction. However, Armstrong and his colleagues [92] demonstrate that, even in work with unstructured data, different researchers identify similar themes, though also signalling the individual perspectives we all bring to analytic work.

Having toured the collection, it is only necessary to remark on its organisation. The set is laid out in eight parts: "Epistemological and Disciplinary Perspectives on the Interview"; "Varieties of Research Interviews: Types and Modes"; "Designing Interview-Based Research"; "Conducting Interview-Based Research"; "Field Relations in Interview-Based Research"; "Interviewers: Characteristics and Qualities"; "Analyzing Interview Data"; and "Bias, Cultural Translation, Validity and Reliability". Each part begins with a brief introduction summarising the key papers and other relevant articles which readers may wish to be aware of as supplementary literature. It only remains for me to express the hope that these articles will inform a long and insightful practice of interviewing, this most accessible and widely-practised of social research methods.

Notes

1. Readers may note that the volumes mix US and British spellings. In the interests of accuracy, spellings are consistent with the original sources.
2. Refers to the article number in this collection.

References

Bradburn, N. and S. Sudman (1974) *Response Effects in Surveys: A Review and Synthesis*, Chicago: Aldine.
Chamberlain, M. and P. Thompson (1997) 'Genre and Narrative in Life Stories', in M. Chamberlain and P. Thompson, eds., *Narrative and Genre*, London: Routledge.
Fielding, N. and J. Fielding (1986) *Linking Data*, Beverly Hills, CA: Sage.

Fielding, N. and R. Lee, eds., (1991) *Using Computers in Qualitative Research*, London: Sage.

Fielding, N. and R. Lee (1998) *Computer Analysis and Qualitative Research*, London: Sage.

Fielding, N. and M. Schreier, eds., (2001) 'Qualitative and Quantitative Research: Conjunctions and Divergences', Special Issue of *Forum Qualitative Sozialforschung/ Forum: Qualitative Social Research*, 2(1) [On-line Journal].

Fielding, N. and H. Thomas (2001) 'Qualitative Interviewing', in G.N. Gilbert, ed., *Researching Social Life* (second edition), London: Sage.

Kvale, S. (1996) *InterViews: An Introduction to Qualitative Research Interviewing*, London: Sage.

Oakley, A. (1981) 'Interviewing Women: A Contradiction in Terms', in H. Roberts, ed., *Doing Feminist Research*, London: Routledge and Kegan Paul.

Wright Mills, C. (1959) *The Sociological Imagination*, New York: Oxford University Press.

PART ONE
EPISTEMOLOGICAL AND DISCIPLINARY
PERSPECTIVES ON THE INTERVIEW

PART ONE

Epistemological and Disciplinary Perspectives on the Interview

Nigel Fielding

Benney and Hughes's [1][†] introduction to an *American Journal of Sociology* special issue captures themes in sociology's approach to research interviews. They note interviewing's importance in sociology, discussing interviewer roles and how the need for comparability of data between interviews affects communication. Identifying the need for a relationship of equality between interviewer and respondent, they anticipate later perspectives when they recognise that one can only say both parties behave as if they are equals for the duration of the interview. For Whyte [2] no single interview stands alone, having meaning only in terms of other interviews and observations. Whyte considers the work for which unstructured interviewing is and is not best-suited, emphasising elicitation of accounts of process.

Sorensen's [3] discussion of Merton's approach to integrating theory, method and empirical research places the 'focused interview' in Merton's epistemological agenda. For Merton the point of researching causes and effects is not to identify causal effects but to determine what those effects mean. Research tells a story showing why observed relationships come into being.

Despite his contemporary association with positivism and structural-functionalist theory, Merton's ideas find resonance in a different tradition, phenomenology. Here the interview is practised as a 'life history'. For Frank [4] the life history is a collaborative text involving the consciousness of investigators as well as subjects. We always approach life histories, like biographies, with the question of how the subject compares to ourselves. Frank considers whether life histories can be appropriate to a social analysis that considers itself scientific, and the problem of describing a 'life', 'a person' and 'the self' in a way that reflects the subject's experience.

Although Ferrarotti [5] contrasts life history more harshly than does Frank against quantitative and positivist approaches, he places a critical realist burden on the method's role in the discipline of social history. He sees life history as 'history from below', a corrective to elite versions, and a means to connect individual biography with the global, structural characteristics of lived historical situations. Historians' traditional biographical methods prefer secondary materials as being more 'objective' but Ferrarotti insists that we restore 'primary materials and their explosive subjectivity'. He maintains that there can be a science of the particular and the subjective which nevertheless arrives at a knowledge of the general. To do this researchers must find the mediations between individuals, their groups and their context.

We may note subsidiary references not appearing in this collection. Interviews have been important methods in sociology and psychology from the first. Laswell (1939) sought to bridge these disciplines' perspectives, highlighting Freud's 'insight interview'. Noting that it originated psychological concepts like trait, reaction, personality and culture, Laswell argues that insight interviews prompt more intensive methods of social observation. It was a means in the discovery of culture, helping respondents better see themselves, unlike survey methods.

Readers interested in applied psychological research interviews should note Reynolds and Gutman (1988), which explains how market researchers use them. Reynolds and Gutman focus on linkage (or 'laddering') between product attributes, the consequences of these attributes for consumers, and the personal values these consequences reinforce. Their technique creates cognitive maps of consumer choice, with laddering done by directed probes based on distinctions mentioned by respondents. The interviewer manipulates the interview to make it seem unstructured while maximising control. Resulting data are scored numerically. Sociology and psychology are not the only social sciences interested in interviews. While we do not think of economics as much engaged in fieldwork, Piore (1979) profiles the interview's role and benefits in a discipline not usually associated with such methods.

Note

†. Refers to the article number in this collection.

References

Laswell, H. (1939) 'The Contributions of Freud's Insight Interview to the Social Sciences', *American Journal of Sociology*, 45, 375–390.
Piore, M. (1979) 'Qualitative research in economics', *Administration Science Quarterly*, 24(4), 560–569.
Reynolds, T. and J. Gutman (1988) 'Laddering Theory, Method, Analysis and Interpretation', *Journal of Advertising Research*, 28(1), 11–31.

1

Of Sociology and the Interview

Mark Benney & Everett C. Hughes

Sociology has become the science of the interview, and that in two senses. In the first sense the interview has become the favored digging tool of a large army of sociologists. The several branches of social study are distinguished from one another perhaps more by their predilection for certain kinds of data and certain instruments for digging them up than by their logic. While the essential features of human society have probably varied within fairly narrow limits in all times and places where men lived, certain of these features can be more effectively observed in direct contact with living people. Others may perhaps be best seen through the eyes of men who left documents behind them. Sociologists have become mainly students of living people. Some, to be sure, do still study documents. Some observe people in *situ*; others experiment on them and look at them literally *in vitro*. But, by and large, the sociologist of North America, and in a slightly less degree in other countries has become an interviewer. The interview is his tool; his works bear the marks of it.

Interviews are of many kinds. Some sociologists like them standardized and so formulated that they can be "administered" to large groups of people. This can be done only among large homogeneous populations not too unlike the investigator himself in culture. Where languages are too diverse, where common values are too few, where the fear of talking to strangers is too great, there the interview based on a standardized questionnaire calling for a few standardized answers may not be applicable. Those who venture into such situations may have to invent new modes of interviewing. Some of the articles which follow deal with problems of large-scale standardized interviews; others tell of the peculiar problems of interviewing special kinds of people.

In the second sense sociology is the science of the interview in a more essential way. The subject matter of sociology is interaction. Conversation of

---

Source: *American Journal of Sociology*, vol. 62, no. 2, 1956, pp. 137–142.

verbal and other gestures is an almost constant activity of human beings. The main business of sociology is to gain systematic knowledge of social rhetoric; to gain the knowledge, we must become skilled in the rhetoric itself. Every conversation has its own balance of revelation and concealment of thoughts and intentions: only under very unusual circumstances is talk so completely expository that every word can be taken at face value. The model of such exposition is the exchange of information among scientists. Each is pledged to tell all he knows of the subject in terms whose meanings are strictly denoted. Every member of any society knows from early childhood a number of such model situations and the appropriate modes of rhetoric. He knows them so well, in fact, that he can improvise new ones and can play at the game of keeping others guessing just what rhetoric he is using. We mention these subtleties of social rhetoric and social interaction, not to spin out analysis of them, but to sharpen the point that the interview, as itself a form of social rhetoric, is not merely a tool of sociology but a part of its very subject matter. When one is learning about the interview, he is adding to sociological knowledge itself. Perhaps the essence of the method of any science is the application, in quest of new knowledge, of what is already known of that science. This is certainly true of sociology; what we learn of social interaction – of the modes of social rhetoric – we apply in getting new knowledge about the same subject.

But the interview is still more than tool and object of study. It is the art of sociological sociability, the game which we play for the pleasure of savoring its subtleties. It is our flirtation with life, our eternal affair, played hard and to win, but played with that detachment and amusement which give us, win or lose, the spirit to rise up and interview again and again.

The interview is, of course, merely one of the many ways in which two people talk to each other. There are other ways. About a year ago Miss Margaret Truman was employed on Ed Murrow's "Person to Person" television show to interview her parents in their home, and the event proved to be a notable exercise in multiple role-playing. As a daughter, Miss Truman asked the kinds of questions that any daughter might ask of a parent: "Dad, how is the book coming?" As interviewer, she asked questions that bore the unmistakable stamp of the newspaperman: "So many people want to know what you do to relax, inasmuch as you don't fish, hunt, or play golf." And at the end of the interview she achieved a nice convergence of the two roles by asking, as interviewer, her parents' views about herself, as daughter. Now Miss Truman is by way of being both a professional daughter and a professional interviewer, and the happy idea that she should act in the one role in a situation and with people where the other role is conventionally to be expected takes us right to the center of our concern.

If we look at the variety of ways in which people in our culture meet together and talk, we will be struck not only by the range of expectations which subsume unique, particular encounters under a rubric of reciprocal roles but also by the different degrees of self-involvement that inform the playing of different roles. Much attention has been given to the range of intensity with which the individual plays his roles; much less attention has been paid to the degree of *expected* intensity. It is clear enough that along with more or less specific expectations of the appropriate behavior in a given role go other expectations about the degree of self-involvement. The general expectation is that Miss Truman should be more involved in the role of daughter than of interviewer; and certainly she managed to underline the family ties by very frequent use of such terms of address as "Dad" and "Mommie" and also by occasionally prefacing a question with the phrase, "Ed Murrow wanted me to ask...." These differences of expected intensity are to some extent codified for us in such terms as "commandment," "law," "rule," "standard," "convention," "fashion." At the upper limits of intensity there is a total prescription of alternative roles – the priest must never be a lover, the citizen must never be a traitor: only minimal distinction is expected between the self and the role. At the lower limit there is still the expectation that, when roles conflict, the resolution shall favor one role rather than another – but, by their very semantics, such terms as "convention" or "fashion" operate in areas of life where ethical neutrality is acceptable and ambivalence frequent. Thus, Miss Truman could abandon the role of interviewer for that of daughter without our feeling that violence has been done to our ethos; she could not, if the two roles conflicted, abandon the role of daughter so easily.

The role of the interviewer, then, is one governed by conventions rather than by standards, rules, or laws; it is a role that is relatively lightly held, even by professionals, and may be abandoned in favor of certain alternative roles if the occasion arises. *What* alternative roles is another matter. The interview is a relatively new kind of encounter in the history of human relations, and the older models of encounter – parent–child, male–female, rich–poor, foolish–wise – carry role definitions much better articulated and more exigent. The interviewer will be constantly tempted, if the other party falls back on one of these older models, to reciprocate – tempted and excused. For, unlike most other encounters, the interview is a role-playing situation in which one person is much more an expert than the other, and, while the conventions governing the interviewer's behavior are already beginning, in some professional circles, to harden into standards, the conventions governing the informant's behavior are much less clearly articulated and known. Viditch and Bensman, discussing this aspect of the interview, give examples of the respondent's insecurity in his role: "In a difficult joint interview between a husband and wife, which required them to discuss certain problems, respondents would remind their spouses of failures to fulfil the instruction to 'discuss' with the remark that 'this is not what they wanted!' When couples failed to fulfil the instructions and saw that they had failed, they frequently apologized for their 'ignorance' or ineptitude."[1] Of course there is an enormous amount of preparatory socialization in the respondent role – in schools and jobs, through the mass media – and more and more of the potential respondents of the Western world are readied for the rap of the clipboard on the door. (In some places, perhaps, overreadied. There was a charming story in the London *News of the World* recently about a political canvasser who liked to demonstrate, on the backsides of young suburban mothers, how they could check the urge to delinquency in their offspring. During the ensuing prosecution it was suggested that the ladies had become, through their experiences with interviewers, so docile as subjects of experiments that they were surprised at nothing.) Probably the most intensive presocialization of respondents runs in roughly the social strata from which interviewers themselves are drawn – the middle, urban, higher-educated groups, while at the top and bottom – though for different reasons – the appropriate role of the informant is apparently much less known. At the moment it is enough to say that where the parties to an interview are unsure of their appropriate roles they are likely to have recourse to other, more firmly delineated social roles that will turn the encounter into one where they feel more at home.

Two conventions characterize most interviews and seem to give this particular mode of personal encounter its uniqueness: these are the conventions of *equality* and *comparability*.

The view that information obtained under stress is likely to be unreliable is not universal, even in our own culture, as "third degree" practices by the police and some popular techniques of cross-examination in the law courts indicate. But in the research interview, at least – and we can regard this as archetypal – the assumption is general that information is the more valid the more freely given. Such an assumption stresses the voluntary character of the interview as a relationship freely and willingly entered into by the respondent; it suggests a certain promissory or contractual element. But if the interview is thought of as a kind of implicit contract between the two parties, it is obvious that the interviewer gains the respondent's time, attention, and whatever information he has to offer, but what the respondent gets is less apparent. A great many people enjoy being interviewed, almost regardless of subject, and one must assume, from the lack of tangible rewards offered, that the advantages must be totally subjective. Here Theodore Caplow's suggestion, in his article in this issue, that the interview profits as a communication device from the contrast it offers to conversation in less formal situations might satisfy us until further evidence is available: that by offering a program of discussion, and an assurance that information offered will not be challenged or resisted, self-expression is facilitated to an unusual degree and that this is inherently satisfying. In this sense, then, the interview is an understanding between the two parties that, in return for allowing the interviewer to direct their communication, the informant is assured that he will not meet with denial, contradiction, competition, or other harassment. As with all contractual relations, the fiction or convention of equality must govern the situation. Whatever actual inequalities of sex, status, intelligence, expertness, or physique exist between the parties should be muted. Interviewing-training consists very largely of making interviewers aware of the kinds of social inequalities with which respondents are likely to be concerned and of teaching them how to minimize them. This is most important, perhaps, if the respondent is likely to see himself as inferior in some respect to the interviewer, and certainly this has been the most closely studied aspect of interviewer effect.

But what happens when, as increasingly happens, a run-of-the-mill, middle-class interviewer encounters a member of some financial, intellectual, or political elite? Our own impression is that such respondents contrive to re-establish equality in the interview by addressing themselves subjectively, not to the actual interviewer, but to the study director or even his sponsor. The different subjective uses to which respondents put these ghostly figures is something that might very profitably be looked into; certainly, people of superior status are more aware of them, and make more use of them, than others.

Evidently such a view of the interview has much in common with Simmel's view of sociability. Both in the interview as seen here and in the sociable gathering as seen by Simmel the convention of equality is a formal necessity and is achieved by excluding from immediate awareness all those attributes of the individual, subjective and objective, which make for inequalities in everyday life. But, as Simmel stresses, the objects of a sociable gathering can be achieved only within a given social stratum – "sociability among members of very different social strata often is inconsistent and painful."[2] The muting of minor social inequalities, such as age, sex, wealth, erudition, and fame, can be accomplished only by the physical elimination of the grosser subcultural differences. But the interview was designed to provide a bridge for communicating between the social strata precisely of the kind that sociability cannot provide (if it could, interviewing would be unnecessary). And this fact brings out another important difference between the interview as practiced and the sociable gathering as seen by Simmel – in the handling of affect. The identifications which bring people together easily in sociable gatherings are primarily established on an emotional basis, and, as Simmel stresses, any affective expression which runs counter to these emotional bonds is suppressed: it is, says Simmel, the essential function of *tact* "to draw the limits, which result from the claims of others, of the individual's impulses, ego-stresses, and intellectual and material desires."[3] The only emotional expression tolerable in the sociable gathering is that which heightens the emotional bonds already established within the group. Psychologically, however, exclusion from these shared affective responses constitutes social inequality; and, if equality in the interview is to be established, it must at bottom be achieved by the interviewer's encouraging and accepting the affect as well as the information the respondent offers. (Hence the growing emphasis on "rapport" in the technical manuals dealing with the interview.) The problem of establishing equality in the interview, then, depends on the expression rather than the suppression of affective responses, on some encouragement of the private, idiosyncratic, and subjective dimensions of at least one of the personalities involved. True, the interview *tends* toward the form of the sociable conversation, in that, once the interviewer has been "cued" to the level of discourse a given respondent is capable of, and has adapted himself to it, communication is expected to approximate that which would take place between actual equals, so that the information carried away is assumed to be such as a man might give when talking freely to a friend. Thus students of the dynamics of interviewing find that there is in general an early release of affect, followed by a more equable flow of information.

Interviewing, then, is distinguished by the operations of the convention that both parties to the encounter are equals, at least for the purposes and duration of the encounter. But there is another important characteristic of the interview which serves to differentiate it from other modes of human interaction – the convention of *comparability*. The first operates primarily for the advantage of the respondent; the second, for the advantage of the interviewer and his employers. They are not completely compatible conventions, and the latent conflict between them is always threatening to become manifest.

Regarded as an information-gathering tool, the interview is designed to minimize the local, concrete, immediate circumstances of the particular encounter – including the respective personalities of the participants – and to emphasize only those aspects that can be kept general enough and demonstrable enough to be counted. As an encounter between these two particular people the typical interview has no meaning; it is conceived in a framework of other, comparable meetings between other couples, each recorded in such fashion that elements of communication in common can be easily isolated from more idiosyncratic qualities. However vaguely this is conceived by the actual participants, it is the needs of the statistician rather than of the people involved directly that determine much, not only the content of communication but its form as well. Obviously, this convention conflicts with the psychological requirements for equality of affective interchange, and one can observe various attempts to resolve the problem, from interviewing in groups to interviewing in depth. At its most obvious the convention of comparability produces the "standardized" interview, where the whole weight of the encounter is placed on the order and formulation of the questions asked and little freedom is permitted to the interviewer to adjust the statistician's needs to the particular encounter. The statistician, indeed, seldom uses *all* the material collected; few reports, apparently, make use of more than 30 or 40 per cent of the information collected. But less obtrusively it enters into almost all interviewing, even psychiatric interviewing, as the possibilities of statistical manipulation of "data" force themselves on the attention of research-minded practitioners. Here technological advances such as the tape recorder are hastening the process – directly, by making available for comparison transcripts of psychiatric interviews hitherto unobtainable and, indirectly, by exposing more clearly to colleagues those purely personal and private (or "distorting" and "biasing") observations and interpretations which the practitioner brings into the interview with him. The very displacement of the older words "session" or "consultation" by the modern word "interview," to describe what passes between the psychiatrist and his patient, is a semantic recognition of this spread of the convention of comparability.

All this amounts to a definition of the interview as a relationship between two people where both parties behave as though they are of equal status for its duration, whether or not this is actually so; and where, also, both behave as though their encounter had meaning only in relation to a good many other such encounters. Obviously, this is not an exhaustive definition of any interview; it leaves out any reference to the exchange and recording of information, to the probability that the parties involved are strangers, and to the transitory nature of the encounter and the relationship. In any formal definition of the interview these elements must have a place.

A relationship governed by the conventions just discussed can occur, it is clear, only in a particular cultural climate; and such a climate is a fairly new thing in the history of the human race. Anthropologists have long realized – if not always clearly – that the transitory interview, held with respondents who do not share their view of the encounter, is an unreliable source of information in itself. It is not until they have been in the society long enough to fit into one of its better-defined roles that they can "tap" a valid communication system and hear the kind of messages that the others in the culture hear. Equally, the climate which makes widespread interviewing possible in the West today is itself relatively novel. A century ago, when Mayhew pioneered in the survey by interviewing "some thousands of the humbler classes of society," the social distance between his readers and his subjects, though they largely lived in the same city, was such that he could best conceptualize his undertaking as an ethnological inquiry, seeking to establish that "we, like the Kaffirs, Fellahs and Finns, are surrounded by wandering hordes – the 'Sonquas' and the 'Fingoes' of this country." Mayhew was a newspaperman, and his survey was first published in a London newspaper. This fact serves to remind us that interviewing as we know it today was an invention of the mass-communications industry and, as a mode of human encounter, has much the same boundaries. On the other hand, the interview has become something very like a medium of mass communication in its own right, and one, on the whole, with less frivolous and banal concerns than related media. One might even make the point that newspapers, movies, radio, and television have been encouraged to pursue their primrose paths by delegating to the survey researchers and their interviewers most of the more serious functions of social communication. If this is so, the interviewer has ousted the publicist by virtue of the convention of comparability, and the ideological and social shifts which have made it possible for individuals willingly to populate the statistician's cells become as worthy of study as, say, the spread of literacy.

We can trace the spread of this convention from the time it was a radical idea in the mind of Jeremy Bentham and a few of his disciples until it became a habit of thought of all but the very top and bottom segments of our society.

In like fashion we trace the growth of the convention of equality from the ideas of John Locke and his disciples to its almost total permeation of the American scene. To chart such changes in the way people relate themselves to one another is the historian's job rather than the sociologist's, and it is one requiring volumes rather than pages. But even a brief review of the course of such changes will lead to a sharper sense of the novelty and significance of the interview as a mode of human relationship and will perhaps aid in assessing its limits and potentialities in the future.

Notes

1. A. Viditch and J. Bensman, "The Validity of Field Data," *Human Organization,* XIII, No. 1 (spring, 1954), 20–27.
2. Kurt Wolff (trans.), *The Sociology of Georg Simmel* (Glencoe, Ill.: Free Press, 1950), p. 47.
3. *Ibid.,* p. 45.

2

Interviewing for Organizational Research

William F. Whyte

To many people, the methods we use in human relations research seem very mysterious. For example, suppose we say that in our studies we interview people. A natural answer to that statement is that lots of people interview: a newspaperman interviews; a psychologist interviews; a political scientist interviews; and so on.

What is there distinctive about our interviewing methods? This is not a question of trying to prove that human relations methods are better than other methods. It is simply a question of providing an adequate description of the methods that we use.

I find I have difficulty in describing our interviewing methods in general terms. At least, when I do so the ideas do not seem to get across very well to students. No doubt this is partly because one can learn to interview only by interviewing; but I think there are other problems involved also.

In the first place, I think that even the names given to our interviewing methods are highly misleading: one method is often called "non-directive" or "unstructured." Actually, it is neither, as we shall seek to show in this article.

Secondly, I think we can only explain the interviewing method adequately through examining actual case examples. "Actual" examples mean verbatim records of everything that was said and done by interviewer and informant in a given case. It does not mean that the notes were typed up or dictated later by the interviewer on the basis of his memory This sort of record, which we generally use in research, may cover with reasonable accuracy the data we have elicited from the informant, but considerable experience in comparing tape recordings with memory recordings of even skilled interviewers has convinced me that memory recording so telescopes the actual interviewing process that it is of little value in demonstrating the nature of this process.

Source: *Human Organization*, vol. 12, no. 2, 1953, pp. 15–22.

For my purposes, then, there is no substitute for a recording of an actual interview. One will be presented in the following pages for purposes of discussion. This is not presented as an ideal interview. In fact, certain mistakes will be pointed out. It simply has the value of being a full record of a particular interview where few such records are currently available. Nor do I claim that all people in human relations or social anthropology interview in this general pattern, or should so do. I think important similarities will be found, but there will be important differences, also. The work currently being done at Cornell University by Stephen A. Richardson and his associates, in analyzing the field research training process, certainly shows that there is no such thing as *the* good research interview. There will be important differences according to the purpose of the interviewer, the nature of the situation, the nature of the interviewer-informant relationship, and the personalities of the two individuals. Only when we have examined more verbatim transcripts will we be able to speak with more authority upon the interviewing process.

This is simply a sample of one type of field research interview. The sample is then used for a very preliminary analysis of the human relations research interviewing process. In order for the following interview to be understandable, certain background information must first be presented. I made the interview in the Spring of 1952, during a one-day visit to the Chicago plant of Inland Steel Container Company, a steel fabricating plant engaged in the manufacture of pails and barrels. In 1951, I had published a book *Pattern for Industrial Peace* – that described and analyzed the evolution of union–management relations in this plant. The book aimed to explain the extraordinary change that had taken place – from a situation of extreme conflict to one of very cordial relations.

My aim here, insofar as such a brief visit allowed, was to catch up with developments in union–management relations that had taken place since I had last been in the plant. Before the following interview took place, I had talked with Robert Novy, vice president in charge of production for this and two other plants, and Edward Grosscup, plant manager. After the interview in question, I also interviewed the then president of the local union, Edward Kohlheim.

The interviews were held in the management conference room of the plant. In each case, I explained the tape-recording equipment as simply a convenience to myself, and then went ahead with the interview. At the time, I had no intention of using any of the interviews verbatim, since such interview material is regarded as confidential in our research; I have since obtained the permission of the informant in this case to reproduce the record.

This is an interview with Columbus Gary, now president of the local of the United Steel Workers of America in this plant. At the time of the interview, he was vice president of the union and chairman of its grievance committee. It is the function of the grievance committee to raise protests to management concerning alleged violations of the contract, and to bring up other problems raised by the membership. The steward is the departmental representative on grievances. In this case, there was a grievance man at the next higher level, representing all the departments on a particular floor. In charge of this activity, the chairman of the grievance committee in steelworker locals occupies a position comparable in importance to that of the president of the local union. Gary, in this case, is a man of long service with the company, and has had broad experience throughout the periods of conflict and cooperation.

Gary was neither a complete stranger to me nor a close acquaintance. I had interviewed him only once during the course of the study, but my book had been published in the meantime. This event was celebrated in Chicago, with the company holding a public meeting and presenting copies of the book to every worker in the plant. Since the book apparently shows both union and management officials in a very favorable light, I had no problem of rapport in dealing with Gary. This is important to note, for there is considerable difference in the interviewer's procedure where he undertakes his interviews in a situation where he is unknown and under some natural suspicion.[1]

Columbus Gary, then was willing to tell me anything I wanted to know. What, then, did I want to know?

The portion of the following verbatim interview covered 27 minutes. Each speech is numbered so that we can refer more readily to parts of the interview in the discussion to follow.

The reader should be warned that, at first, he will not understand everything that Gary is saying, since he discusses same rather complicated problems. In this the reader is at no disadvantage, compared with the interviewer. I was at first quite confused concerning the situations described. Most of this interview involves a process of clarifying Gary's original statements so that eventually a relatively clear, step-by-step account of social process emerges.

Interview With Columbus Gary

1. *Whyte*: ... I'm trying to catch up on things that have happened since I was last here to study this case. That was back in 1950. I think probably the best thing to start would be if you could give your own impressions as to how things are going now, compared to the past. Do you think things are getting better or worse, or staying about the same?

2. *Gary*: Well, now, things are quite a bit different now, because in the past we used to have a lot of written grievances, we had to have, and now I think we only have one written grievance that's been written in the last year and a half, I think. It means that things would have to be getting better otherwise you would have more grievances written up. We used to have from one to 10 a week. We used to have a grievance meeting once a week. It had to be held because we had so many things pending that were piled up, so we had to meet every week, and sometimes we'd have a meeting in between. You had a

grievance meeting scheduled each week, a two-hour meeting, and then you had to have other meetings in the week, too. Now, in a grievance meeting you take up these grievances that you have – from one to 10 a week that was written up that nobody could do anything about. Such grievances as that, you had one in the last two years, so naturally, as I said, our relations here from those things are much better than they used to be. I mean, if we have a problem, you can call whoever you want to talk to, the superintendent, the plant manager, or whoever you figure that it's in their hands, and you tell them the problem you want to see them about, and you get it ironed out from there. Therefore, you save a lot of grievance and a lot of writing that you don't have to do, and that means satisfaction to both parties. They give us that opportunity to do, and I think it worked out very nicely. Our relationships are much better than what it used to be. Otherwise you couldn't settle things that way.

3. *Whyte*: That's interesting. You mean that it isn't that you don't have problems, but you take them up and talk them over before you write them up, is that it?

4. *Gary*: That's right. And whatever the case may be, you get it settled right there and then. Before, you used to take them up and talk about them, and then you had to write them up, and they would drag along for a week, and another week, and a month before you could settle them, and when you have them you have a meeting every week. You had a long string of grievances, because the one that you had last week wasn't settled. I mean, you'd take them up to the foreman, and then he'd go to his supervisor, and then you'd go to the personnel office. You go over them this week, and then you have some pending because the personnel office, the personnel managers, they couldn't do nothing. And as to the things that come up there, he would have to take them to his boss, and that means that when this meeting is over with, you have to wait until next week before you could get it settled. So all those grievances and things don't happen like that now. When you've got a problem, if it needs immediate attention, that's what it gets. You call the fellow that you figure is able to give you the information you want. So I think the relationships are much better than what they used to be. We still have our problems, but you can get right down to them, all the way up to top management. You sit right down and iron them out right there and then.

5. *Whyte*: That's very interesting. I wonder if you could give me an example of a problem that came up recently, or not so recently, that would illustrate how you handled it sort of informally without writing it down.

6. *Gary*: Well, I don't know that I could give you a problem that we had, to the satisfaction of both parties, that I don't know whether you could have had a grievance, but it would've created a big problem if we hadn't have did it that way. I mean, we was working on the pail department. We've got two lines there, one main line, and one that makes oil containers on it, and the oil container business was very slow two or three days a week. But on the main line, where you make the Number 8s, they run six days a week. So what they

wanted to do is to bring this line in at 10 o'clock – this oil line that didn't have much work to do – and they could work from 10 until 4:30 on their line, and from 4:30 to 6:30 they could go over to the main line and work on that on Number 8. Therefore, it would give this oil line there five days, and the main line would work five days, too. So when this was put out, well, the people were very much upset about it. That was Friday. He said, "You come on in at 10 o'clock Monday." Well, everybody was very much upset about it – "Why do you change our hours that way?" So I got ahold of Mr. Grosscup. I called him and I told him to give me a chance to talk with the people. "You leave them as they are until I have this meeting. I'll have the meeting the first thing Monday. I could explain it to them so that nobody would have no misunderstanding why these things are being done." He called off the changing of this shift. He let them stay that way. Monday, I had a meeting with the whole department, and I went into detail of how come this had to be done, that it wouldn't only benefit the company, it would benefit them, too. I mean, the company would save time-and-a-half on Saturday on a few people, but therefore you've got another few people still to give three days a week that would get five days, so I thought it was better that still you get the handful of people that get time-and-a-half on the six days. You've got another whole line who didn't get but two or three days, would get the whole five days. When I got through explaining to them, they were very agreeable, and I came back and I told Mr. Grosscup. So that following Monday he changed the shift at 10 o'clock and everybody worked out all right. So it all depends on how you do it. He could have just said, "O.K., I'm just going to do it that way. You go ahead on and come in." Well, everybody would have been upset, and then you'd have problems on your hands because this fellow shoved it down your throat. When you give us a chance to let everybody know what was going on, why it works out very nicely. He postponed it for a week until I got a chance to tell my people and I explained it to them. After I explained it to them, they were very much satisfied and it worked out real nice. Now, that's some of the things you do without writing them up, and you save a lot of problems in your department.

7. *Whyte*: That's a good example. I wonder if you could give me a little more detail about the beginning of it. Did Mr. Grosscup first tell you about it? How did you first find out?

8. *Gary*: Well, he told me. Usually, in the last six months, when orders and steel have been kind of slack, we would go up, probably once a week, and ask him how this was going to be working for the next week. He would give you as much as maybe a week or a week and a half or two weeks in advance on how the orders were coming in, which he didn't have to do, but it was helpful to us. We could tell our people how they were going to work and everything. So, this particular time, he told us that this line was very slow, but "I've got one line that's in the same department that were working six days, and you've got another line that's only working two and three days," and how he was going to do it. Well, I couldn't tell him not to, I mean,

because that's the right (management has) of operating the plant. But the minute I find out that people object to just coming out and tell them, well, "you come in at 10 o'clock Monday," and "you go from line to line," then I told him to hold up on the change until I got a chance – because he went into detail with me how come he wanted to do it, and why, and how it would be helpful to management. I know, because he wouldn't have to pay time-and-a-half for that order that they could get out through the week. In the meantime, you had people that were working two and three days a week would get five days, so both sides got benefits by it. So he explained that to me, what he was going to do. I didn't have to tell the people unless they were becoming upset about it. When I see that, when he told them what they were going to do and they wasn't satisfied, then I told him to hold off and he did. So that's how I've got to push nobody because we talked it over before he told his foremen what to do.

9. *Whyte*: I see. He first explained it to you and you went to the people on the job to tell them about it, but then you saw that they didn't understand it.

10. *Gary*: That's right, because you have to go by one, and if you just tell this one, and you figure this one will tell somebody else, they either will add something or take something away. I mean, when it gets to the last one, you wouldn't hardly know it yourself if you heard it again. So I thought it would be better to have a meeting with them, and then you could tell them all at the same time, and there would be nobody have no misunderstanding. If they had any questions to ask they could ask me and I could tell them. That's why when he first told me about it, and you just told the people what they were going to do, so they got upset. And when I heard some of it, it wasn't like it was supposed to be, so I knew right then it was going to create a problem. So instead of doing that, he postponed it for another week, and I imagine if it was going to create a problem we still could have worked out something so everybody worked out all right just the same. But anyhow, he didn't carry his own program out like he had set up, due to the fact that it was going to create a problem in the plant.

11. *Whyte*: That's an interesting one. I was talking with Mr. Grosscup and Mr. Novy, and they mentioned a case that you could surely tell me more about – and the details – as I'm not too clear about it. I guess it was in the punch-press department that the girls had some system of rotating the jobs. What do they call them, the floating girls?

12. *Gary*: Yeah, you have a line in the punch press where everybody has their job, they've got the same job every day. Then you have quite a few jobs on the floor. I mean, that they don't run all the time, just depending on what items you've got to run. Well, those, you call them the flow girls, and they used to have – nobody'd know what they were going to do and you didn't have no first-come-first-serve. I mean, if I had been there a little longer than you, and here's a job open here that I figured might not last but a couple hours, but if I wait, here's one that's going to start at 10 o'clock, it probably would last all day, and if I had the seniority, I would skip the first one and

know I was going to take this job. I'd wait a couple of hours and I could get what I wanted. That would mean that the fellow with the seniority would get the benefit of the doubt at all times, and the fellow who didn't have much seniority, he would be the fellow that gets pushed around. And we didn't think that was fair, that that should be done, because we want all the people to be treated fair in this plant. So we did work out a system where he would start at the top of his seniority list to assign his job, whatever he had open. I mean, he could give him the best one, that's what he had then, and when that run out, if it run out at 11 o'clock, or 2 o'clock, what else he had available he would give him then; but then the other fellow that didn't have anything, if he run out of a job before the younger person got their job, then he probably would loan that one out sometime, until he'd get something open, and then he would assign that one. That way, we worked it out so everybody would be satisfied. I mean, you wouldn't have to take it, you might be smart, you'd come in and you get with somebody, say the thing only runs such and such a job, but it ain't going to come on 'till 10.30 and will last all day. But here's a job that's only got about five or six hours – pretty good job, too – but it isn't as good as that one. Well, you would, according to your seniority, that is, you say, "No, I don't want it. Give it to somebody else," and that would mean the younger fellow would get pushed around at all times. We didn't think that was fair, and I told them to – you could start off at your seniority list, the job that you had available in the morning, sign them all to it, and then whatever job run out first, wherever you had open, then you would sign up for it, and that way everybody would get a good share of whatever that he had. It worked out real nice, and it's still working in the punch-press department.

13. *Whyte*: Now, let me see if I understand it. These jobs would be better or worse according to what? The incentive rate? Or ...

14. *Gary*: That's right. I mean, a certain job that you could make more on. You'd probably make about the same money, but it would be a harder job. You'd have to work a little harder to make the same amount of money. So, I mean, if I got most of the seniority, I would try to pick something that's easy. So, in order to treat everybody fair – well, whatever you've got in the morning, that's assigned to them. Then, if this runs out, whatever he'd have come up later, then he would get that, and nobody would come over and talk, "I'm older than you. My job run out and I'll go over and take yours." I mean, he just doesn't do it like that. I mean, if my job run out today, then if he doesn't have something for me to do, I'll probably go on to another department or something like that. In that way, the only time the older fellow with seniority takes somebody else's job is when his job is eliminated altogether, and then he'd have to go to the next best place. But if it just run out for the day, the time being, then he doesn't take anybody else's job, just because he's older than someone else.

15. *Whyte*: Do the people in the department pretty well agree among themselves as to how they rate the jobs, which job is more desirable than the other?

16. *Gary:* Oh, yeah, when you were going to set this up, you got the people together and you chose that job: one, two, three. I mean, this is the best job, this number one. You let them say which one it should be, so when they are assigned to those jobs, then you don't have no come-back. You tell them what you're going to set up. You know, which one is going to be one, two, three, four, like that, and then you go according to seniority, and then you let them decide "Well, yes, this will be one, this will be two," etcetera. Everybody in the department knows that when this job is running, it goes to the one with the most seniority. This is number one, the next down the line is number two. We don't do that ourselves. We let the people decide, too, because they are the ones that have to work with it.

17. *Whyte:* I see. But if, say, I have top seniority and job number one, but even though I know it's only going to last a couple of hours, and job number two would then come on for the whole day, still I take number one, is that right?

18. *Gary:* That's right, yeah. And you let them say which one is number one and number two, and so on, because if you just left them open like that, they didn't know this was going to last all day, I would take this as number one; even though I'm the number one fellow, I would take the number two job instead of number one. But you let them decide now, because you don't know which one is going to run all day, and you let them decide one, two, three, four, how they're going to be. Then you assign them accordingly, and if it runs out, well, you find the next best thing that you can. Maybe your job lasts all day today, and half-day tomorrow. Maybe mine don't. But the next day it might be vice-versa. But you still assign them, one, two, three, four.

19. *Whyte:* I see. Well, that's very interesting. I understand what you worked out, but I don't understand just the steps that you took. I mean, how did it first come to you that there was a problem here that something ought to be done about?

20. *Gary:* Well, I used to take the attitude that – I tried to go by union policy. We set up a rule and regulation which we should govern ourselves by, and you put it into the department where people are working, and if you deviate from that a little bit, as long as everybody concerned was satisfied I didn't bother with it. But if you deviate from what should be done and create a problem, then I come into it. And when I use my seniority to take advantage of every job in the department, then I say that we're wrong. I mean, because it creates a problem, because a young fellow, he will always get kicked around. If this job, then, was the best one when it was running good, the one with the most seniority wanted it. If you figured that it wasn't going to last quite all day, and wanted another that would last all day, then he would wait and take that one, and we didn't think that was fair when you're jumping around and around. So we figured we'd line up something that was going to be beneficial to everybody, that everybody would get his share. Because you have the most seniority I didn't think you should gather up everything, just because you happened to have a little bit more seniority than I.

21. *Whyte*: I understand that, but now, you mean that people came to you with …

22. *Gary*: Oh, yes, that's why we got into this thing, because they come to us, we complained. The foreman in the department, he would take his lists home some nights and try to figure out something how to keep down confusion. But it would still create a problem because the other people with the most seniority, they would try to take advantage of it. He tried to work something out, and every day I would have the same thing. I would go down there and try to help him straighten it out, and it just got so every day I went to the punch-press department, trying to help them line something up that would be beneficial to everybody. I thought, instead of doing that, you could bring it upstairs here, and we would sit down at the table, and we would work out how we would do it, and then we would go back to the people and have a meeting with them and let them name the one, two, three jobs.

23. *Whyte*: All right, you came upstairs. Who do you mean came up?

24. *Gary*: Ob, we met with the management. We got the supervisor and Mr. Grosscup, and whoever else that he had that he wanted to bring in, and the foreman, and the shop steward in the department.

25. *Whyte*: You and the shop steward on the union side, and Mr. Grosscup and Mr. Evans and the foreman. Then you talked about this, and then how did that develop?

26. *Gary*: Well, we talked about how it had been doing, how people had been taking advantage of it. It created a problem to the younger fellows down the line. I mean, he would use his seniority to take the best one today because he figured he was going to work all day. Tomorrow maybe the worst job in the department was going to work all day. He would use his seniority to take all. Well, naturally, that means the younger fellow would be pushed around at all times. And it would create a problem, which it was. It was creating quite a headache down there. You didn't do this overnight, because you had to figure out how you could do it so you don't hurt anybody. Everybody would get just about the same break.

27. *Whyte*: Did you have one discussion with the management, then you worked out this plan?

28. *Gary*: Well, the way we done it, I got the steward and the grievance man on that particular floor, and we went into how this ought to be done, and then when we got to management we recommended how it should be done.

29. *Whyte*: Oh, I see.

30. *Gary*: And they went along with our recommendation. Now, sometimes we recommend something and they have something better. Then we accept that. The same thing with them. They recommend something and we have something better. They use ours. We're not stubborn on either side. I mean, if they bring up something and we've got something that will work out better to all concerned, better than what they offer, then they'll use it. And the same thing, if we've got something in mind that we want to use and we

get to talking about it, they bring up something where this will work better, and you see that it would work better. That's O.K. Then we use that.

31. *Whyte*: I see. So you had a meeting with the grievance man, the steward, and you. Among the three of you, you worked out this general idea how it should be done. Then you proposed it to management, and they accepted it.

32. *Gary*: They accepted it. They instructed the foremen how to apply it, and then we put it in writing. We put a provision in there that it's subject to changes, department changes, and working condition changes due to certain orders that comes in. If that happens, then we could come back and talk about it again. As long as conditions exist as is, this will be it.

33. *Whyte*: I see.

34. *Gary*: And then, after you got it decided, we'll work it this way, but we won't name the job. We only set up how we would work one, two, three, by seniority, but we wouldn't name the job. Then we got the people together and we told them how we were going to do it, how we were going to assign people from the floor on these jobs: one, two, three, four, down the line. Now, you name the job which you think should be number one, and they name the number one, and number two, and number three.

35. *Whyte*: Do they all pretty well agree how they make the number one, two, three?

36. *Gary*: They pretty well all agree. We didn't have very much – they talked about it, which ones should be the first second and third, until everybody agreed which should be the first, second, and third due to the past performance. There were some changes. When I explained it to them, they said, "If this condition changes, we'll go back and change it to something else. But, as long as the condition exists as is, then we'll do it like this."

37. *Whyte*: That's very good. Now, was this a union departmental meeting?

38. *Gary*: Yeah, just for the department only. Such things as this, we don't take it up in a regular membership meeting because you are bored in other departments. The whole meeting was something that just concerned a few people in the department, so we just have a department meeting only.

39. *Whyte*: Yeah, well who was at the department meeting for the union officers?

40. *Gary*: Well, the stewards, the grievance man from that floor, and myself …

41. *Whyte*: And you conducted the meeting?

42. *Gary*: That's right. I conducted the meeting because I am the chairman of all grievances. It makes no difference where they come from, the grievance should come by me.

43. *Whyte*: You're both vice president and grievance chairman?

44. *Gary*: And chairman of the grievance committee.

45. *Whyte*: I see. So then you're in all of the departmental meetings?

46. *Gary*: That's right. I mean, if they just want to have a department meeting, sometimes they just have a department meeting. You don't have a

problem, but you just have a scheduled meeting as a routine. These I don't care! I don't attend a meeting like that unless I'm requested.

47. *Whyte*: I see.

48. *Gary*: If they've got a problem or anything they want ironed out, then I do attend.

49. *Whyte*: I see. Well, does the president sometimes attend those meetings too, or …

50. *Gary*: Oh, yeah. He can attend any meeting, just as I do. I mean, without request, because he is the president of the local. A president is quite busy because you have other things to attend to, and as long as you don't need him, you can get along without him, you try to let him avoid some of those things. So that's why he doesn't attend every department meeting.

51. *Whyte*: Well, how do you find this business of having the regular departmental meetings? Are people pretty much interested?

52. *Gary*: Very much, because you bring them up-to-date on a lot of things, and you usually have them once a month. It don't have to be in the department, but you can tell what happens in other departments. I mean, it can be working conditions or certain things like that, that you can bring up and explain to the others. Most of the time, you don't have a problem when you have a department meeting. When you have a problem like they had in the punch-press, you don't wait 'til your regular department meeting once a month. What you do is call a special meeting, as I did for the pail assembly when they had their problem. I called a meeting and thrashed this out right there and then.

53. *Whyte*: Well, I suppose there, when there is a special problem up, you get quite a lot of the people out, do you?

54. *Gary*: Oh yes, then you get just about everybody in the department.

55. *Whyte*: But at a routine meeting …

56. *Gary*: Well, just so many attend all the time.

57. *Whyte*: About 20 percent?

58. *Gary*: Well, you get more than that. You get sometimes 50 percent at just a regular departmental meeting. Of course, usually they don't last long. Maybe 45 minutes up to an hour. Sometimes half an hour, just the routine meeting.

59. *Whyte*: Just at the end of the work day?

60. *Gary*: Yeah, when your shift is over with. That's about 4:45, as soon as they get out. They get off at 4:30, you give them 15 minutes to get there, and maybe 5:15 or 5:30 it's all over. So they don't mind attending because they don't have to go no place. They come right by the office from work, so they just stop by. It's very convenient for them.

* * *

Commentary

I had already heard from Novy and Grosscup concerning interesting developments in the pail-assembly and punch-press departments. However, I did not wish to start the interview by asking Gary about either of those situations because, first, I wanted to get an idea of what he considered important. Therefore, I began with a rather general question. This led him to express himself largely in terms of the sentiments he felt regarding the relationship.

When he had had a chance to express his sentiments here, I sought at once to move from sentiments to specific interpersonal events. This was done in (5) by asking him to illustrate what he meant. This prompted Gary to bring out the pail assembly story voluntarily. Gary then gives a general idea of the nature of the problem and what was done about it, but note that he does not give a step-by-step account. In (7) I seek to get him to start at the beginning and give the steps. Thus prompted, in (8) and (10) Gary fills in some of these steps. Note, however, that this topic could have been pursued further with profit. It is clear that Grosscup informed Gary regarding the proposed change in the department, but it is not clear whether it was Gary or someone in management who first gave the information to the workers. This particular step would require further checking. Note, also, that I failed to establish the time of the events.

In (11) I change the subject and ask him to comment upon the situation in the punch-press department that I had heard about. This is apparently a complicated situation that takes a good deal of explaining. Gary begins in (12) by telling what the situation was, and then telling what the solution to the problem was. Note that he omits completely any account of the social process whereby the problem came to his attention, and went through several interpersonal steps towards its solution. I note this omission, but first seek to get certain technical details filled in.

In (13) I raise a question, but then make the mistake of giving one possible answer to that question. This is probably quite a common error in interviewing: presenting a leading question instead of a question with the possible answers completely open.

We continue to work on the technical side of the problem in (13) through (18).

In (19) I make an effort to get him to tell me the steps whereby the changes were made. The question apparently is not understood, for Gary simply restates the problem. Only after another prod does he, in (22), begin to mention some actual instances of behavior. He mentions bringing the problem "upstairs here" – apparently a reference to the room in which we are sitting. So the site of the conference is at least located, but no people are yet in it. (23) represents an attempt to find out who the people were. (27) represents another attempt to fill in details of behavior, and note that it brings out a conference with steward, grievance man, and grievance chairman, that took place before the "upstairs" conference Gary has been talking about. This was, of course, a very essential step in the process.

In (31) I review some of the steps, as I understand them, to check whether my understanding is correct. Gary nods assent (not shown in the transcript, of course) and continues with the next steps. By now, Gary apparently realizes that I am interested in getting the steps in the process clarified, so he continues in (34) and (36), indicating how he brought the agreement with management to the workers. But, as yet, it is not clear which people were involved or where the meeting was held. (37) represents an attempt to get at this information. We find in (38) that it was a meeting for all workers in the department, but we don't yet know who was there representing the union officers. (39) is directed at this point. In (41) I come up with an interruption and also a leading question. The interruption is perhaps of some importance because there may have been other union officers present that Gary was going to mention. Perhaps the president was there, for example. The leading question was probably not a serious error, although the question could just as well have been put in neutral form.

(43) through (48) clarifies Gary's position in these departmental meetings.

(49) raises the question of the relation of the president to these meetings. The relation of president to grievance chairman is important in any steelworker local, and seemed particularly worthy of notice here, since I had been informed that the president, vice president, and grievance chairman were running against each other for president of the local in the election that was to take place a few weeks hence. However, this theme was elaborated upon in a section of the interview that is not reported here.

The discussion from (51) to the end represents an effort to get some more information regarding the departmental meetings and the part they play in the union-management relationship. The discussion establishes when and where the meetings take place but, beyond that, it is of little value. It would be important to know how many people attend regular and how many attend special department meetings, but an interview is a very poor instrument for this sort of information.

The Nature of Human Relations Research Interview

As we compare this case with the rules for the non-directive or counseling interview, as given by Roethlisberger and Dickson,[2] we note important similarities and also important differences. First, let us note the similarities.

According to the non-directive school, the interviewer should concentrate on listening. He is not to talk except to get the informant to express himself more fully. In this case, Gary was speaking approximately seven-eighths of the time, so the interviewer was listening all right. My participation was designed to do more than get him to express himself fully, as will be indicated below.

The interviewer is directed not to interrupt the informant. I sought to follow this rule, but violated it once. How serious was this breach? In this case, little if anything seems to have been lost. Regarding interruptions, the main questions are these: Do they antagonize or upset the informant? Do they make for a "choppy" interview by keeping the informant down to short statements on which he has no opportunity to elaborate? Do they throw the informant off the track just when he is warming up to some important point?

Without question, interruptions can give rise to any or all of these results. On the other hand, there are various kinds of interruptions. We have examined transcripts where the interruptions seemed to have no such consequences. The point is that the purpose of the interview and not the rule itself should be borne in mind. It may even be important for researchers to learn to interrupt *gracefully*. We sometimes encounter informants who are so garrulous and rapid in speech that we will never get from them some of the information we need if we are unwilling to interrupt. Such was not the case with Columbus Gary. But, on the other hand, it should be clear that the single interruption did not have serious adverse consequences.

The interviewer is directed not to argue, and to avoid passing moral judgments upon what the informant is saying. These rules seem to fit this case well enough.

The interviewer is advised to restate what has been said from time to time and present it to the informant for comment. This interview contains frequent restatements which seem helpful in testing the interviewer's understanding and in getting the informant to give further details.

So far, then, I was following the rules of non-directive or unstructured interviewing, but that was not the whole story. While I talked only one-eighth of the time, I was working hard to structure the interview along definite lines that I had in mind.

That does not mean that I had a number of specific questions to which I required answers. Nor does it mean that I wanted comments only on situations that I raised for discussion. I was glad to begin by encouraging the informant to discuss events and situations that seemed important to him. But note the nature of this discussion.

As I saw it, Gary's sentiments regarding the union–management relationship were more or less incidental to the inquiry. I knew they would come out anyway as he discussed events, so right at the outset I sought to move him from a statement of sentiments to an account of interpersonal events. I was interested not only in what happened at a particular time, but in how that event related to others that took place before and afterwards. For all these events I wanted answers to the question: Who did what when, with whom, and where? – the question which, according to Eliot Chapple, all field researchers need to be asking.

Note that the answers to this question do not come out very readily, even though the informant is quite willing to give full details. I do not believe this is a deficiency in the informant. He seemed to me an unusually good informant. He simply had a tendency, which is probably natural to most of us, to state a problem and then jump to an account of the decision that was made in the solution of the problem. In such an account we have the substance without the social process. We don't know how the problem came to the attention of the person concerned, or any of the steps leading to the action that was considered to solve the problem. The interviewer needs to learn to recognize the difference between a statement of substance and an account of process, so that he can move the informant from one to the other. In most cases, as in this one, it will take more than one question or statement to get a reasonably full account of process. Even here, important steps in the process could have been clarified further, but it should be evident that the interview did go far beyond the original statement of the substance and solution of the problem.

The Interview in the Context of Research

No single interview stands alone. It has meaning to the researcher only in terms of other interviews and observations. While it was not possible to follow up on this particular interview at the time it was made, it may help to explain the uses of interviewing if we were to assume that time and interest were available to make a full-scale study of the union-management situation in this plant. How, in such a case, would we build upon the Gary interview?

In the first place, we would want to interview other people who are mentioned as having played prominent roles in the situations Gary describes. As we got them to give an account of the situations, other important details would be fitted in. For example, we would get information on events within management that might not have been known to Gary. (Such follow-up interviews would, of course, have brought up other situations that we would have wanted to explore, also.)

On the management side, we would certainly want to interview at least Grosscup, the plant manager, Evans, his assistant, and the foremen in the two departments. It might be particularly interesting to interview the foremen, for their role is unclear in the Gary account. We might be inclined to wonder whether the prominent role played by the union in these departments has undermined the role of the foreman.

On the union side, we would want to get accounts from the stewards, the grievance man, and the president of the local. We would also want to interview at least a sample of the workers in these departments in order to try to trace out their relations with each other, the foreman, the steward, and other union and management officers.

There is much more to be done, even with Columbus Gary himself. Note that this interview gives only an account of certain outstanding events in his recent experience in union-management relations. This could be very misleading. We don't know whether these events are representative of the way in which union and management people work together, or whether they are the exceptional and spectacular developments that make a particular impression upon the individual. For this reason, we would want to place these particular events into a context formed by the pattern of interpersonal contacts that Gary experiences regularly. For example, how often during the week does he see and talk to Ed Grosscup? And when they get together, does Gary call on Grosscup or does Grosscup call in Gary? We would want the same sort of contact information for Gary's interactions with Evans, the foremen, the stewards, grievance men, and other union officers, and any others with whom there is any frequency of interaction. Only thus would we be able to build up a picture of the social system in action.

In the case of neither department did I establish the time period of the events. Looking for examples of "the way you do things now," that deficiency is not important. However, if this interview had been part of a systematic and continuing study of the social system, then establishing the time for these events would be essential in enabling us to relate them to other events.

Although much important information can be obtained along the lines indicated here, it is necessary also to recognize the limitations of the interviewing method. There are some sorts of information that cannot adequately be elicited through this means. Meetings or conferences represent one example. Whenever more than two people get together to discuss some problem, the informant is unlikely to be able to give a very accurate picture of what took place. He may remember, to some extent, who said what, and he will probably have some idea of the nature of the problem that brought the group together, and of the decision that was reached. But just how this decision was evolved, few informants will be able to report adequately. Furthermore, when it is a question of the attendance at a relatively large meeting, few informants will report accurately. This is likely to be particularly true in the case of organizations such as unions, where it is thought to be very desirable and important to have a large turnout. Without any desire to falsify the situation, the informant is likely to think of the average turnout in terms of the largest number of people he remembers at a meeting, and so on.

Thus, for certain sorts of data there is no substitute for observation. The interview is particularly designed to get at accounts of interpersonal events taking place through time, and at contacts having certain frequencies.

I have not emphasized the importance of the human relations interview for getting at expressions of sentiments. These come out in the interview to be sure, but they should be considered rather as incidental to the purpose of the interview. If we are really primarily concerned with getting at expressions of sentiments, then we will find that the questionnaire survey that can be administered rapidly to a large population is a much more efficient instrument. On the other hand, the questionnaire is very ill-adapted to getting at accounts of interpersonal events. It is here that the interview is the indispensable method.

Notes

1. Burleigh B. Gardner and William F. Whyte, "Methods for the Study of Human Relations in Industry," *American Sociological Review*, October, 1946.

2. Fritz J. Roethlisberger and W.J. Dickinson, *Management and the Worker*, Harvard University Press, 1939, pp. 270–291.

3

Merton and Methodology

Aage B. Sørenson

We commonly see methodology as consisting of rules for knowing about the world and techniques for obtaining information about the world. Robert K. Merton has made contributions to both of these areas of sociological methodology, but these contributions have not made Merton a recognized methodologist. His contribution to technique is to procedures for interviewing: how to conduct an unstructured but focussed interview. These interview techniques are not widely known or appreciated by sociologists. Merton's most well-known contribution to the rules for knowing the world is two essays about the relation between theory and empirical research. These essays say a number of useful things, but they have not made Merton a recognized philosopher of sociology, probably because they do not make pronouncements about the superiority of any particular methodology – quantitative, qualitative, or interpretive. The essays, therefore, do not contribute to the standard arsenal of arguments in current *methodenstreiten*, arguments that are de rigueur for those who wish to be recognized as philosophical methodologists.

Despite Merton's lack of recognition as a methodologist, both of the methodological contributions mentioned have recently received attention. The manual of problems and procedures for *The Focused Interview* by Merton, Fiske, and Kendall has appeared in a second edition (the first edition appeared in 1956). Merton's two essays on the relation between theory and research (in *Social Theory and Social Structure*) form the topic of two essays, by Hubert M. Blalock, Jr., and Mark Gould, in the most recent volume about Merton, *Robert K. Merton: Consensus and Controversy*.

Merton's association and collaboration with Paul Lazarsfeld produced the most successful integration of social research and social theory in the history of sociology. Unfortunately, the two essays by Blalock and Gould do not try to characterize the nature of this integration or what we can learn about methodology from the research done at Columbia University in the 1940s and '50s. Perhaps unexpectedly, given its apparent nature as a manual, *The Focused Interview* does provide some insights into the nature of the integration.

The last decades have seen a clear tendency for sociologists to specialize as theorists, methodologists, or researchers. There are separate journals for these activities, and separate prestige hierarchies. Ideally, the same person occupies the three roles, but usually this is not the case. Furthermore, the different occupants of the three roles interact little and not very freely.

In the language of sociometry, the three roles form a triad. In this triad asymmetric ties connect methodologists and theorists to researchers, but there are no ties in the other direction or between theorists and methodology. Methodologists tell researchers about the proper procedures and techniques, but use most of their time telling each other about the latest inventions in statistics and econometrics (if they are quantitative methodologists) or in philosophy (if they are qualitative methodologists). Methodologists use research as examples for applications of techniques, but do not use research to discover things. Similarly, recognized theorists rarely use theory to discover things. Theorists tell researchers about the importance of theory, but not which ideas are interesting for empirical research. Mostly they tell each other which theory is superior or, even better, which theory about theory is the best. Researchers, being on the receiving end of all this advice, prudently avoid calling their ideas "theory" or their actual practices "methods." In this organization of modern sociology, Merton is a theorist.

Calling Merton a specialist in theory is like characterizing the Taj Mahal as a tomb: it is not incorrect, but it is far from the whole story. Merton is one of the few who master all three roles in the triad. This facilitates communication among the roles. In particular, research and evidence bear on theory in Merton's work, while methodology becomes not merely technique or philosophy but a codification of procedures for research designed to make discoveries about the world. *The Focused Interview* provides the evidence for this characterization of Merton. It also provides the account – in the introduction to the second edition – of the origin of the happy combination of theory, methods, and research that is Merton's sociology.

In one of the most spectacular instances of downward occupational mobility ever recorded in academia, Robert Merton, in 1941, left a full professorship at Tulane University for an assistant professorship at Columbia University. At Columbia he joined Paul Lazarsfeld; Lazarsfeld was the methodologist, Merton to be the theorist. A student of Sorokin, who is willing to experience downward occupational mobility, should be unwilling to let the prescribed division of labor interfere with scholarship. So in contrast to another famous theory – methods pair – Parsons and Stouffer at Harvard – Merton soon began to collaborate with Paul Lazarsfeld. The collaboration began around something apparently quite mundane: the development of interview techniques to better understand the recorded audience responses of radio morale programs. It was a collaboration that went on to inspire and produce some of the best sociology ever made.

In his account of the origin, Merton tells about how he was invited by Lazarsfeld to observe a session testing audience responses to radio programs designed to help increase support for the war effort. The research on their effectiveness was sponsored by a federal agency called the Office for Facts and Figures (in an interesting metamorphosis this office later became the Voice of America). Lazarsfeld had designed a way to record positive and negative responses to programs by having the audience press red and green buttons. The cumulative recordings from a session gave a measure of audience reaction, or overall program effect, but no clue as to why these effects came about. In the session that Merton observed, one of Lazarsfeld's assistants interviewed the participants about their reactions. When Merton criticized the manner in which these interviews were conducted, Lazarsfeld co-opted Merton into developing better procedures for these interviews. The result is *The Focused Interview*. A much longer story about this product of Lazarsfeld and Merton's first encounter and the subsequent fate of the manual is told with Mertonian elegance and wit in the introduction to *The Focused Interview*. Only fools will attempt to paraphrase such tales. Sociologists desiring education should acquire *The Focused Interview* for its introduction, even if they have no interest in interviewing.

The purpose of the focussed interview is to analyze and interpret reactions to an attempt of persuasion by a radio or film message. The content of the message is first coded into variables that are the exogenous variables for the analysis. The dependent variable is the registered positive or negative reaction during exposure to the message. Correlating the variables created in the content analysis with the audience reactions establishes the link between cause and effect. However, establishing the relationship does not establish how and why the effects come about. The focussed interview is designed to accomplish this by ascertaining the respondents' definitions of the situations presented by the message.

The focussed interview's strategy is to base the interview on hypotheses about how effects are derived from the content analysis of the message. These hypotheses are then tested and elaborated on in the interviews. Merton *et al.* formulate four criteria for how the interviews best explain observed audience reactions: range, specificity, depth, and personal context. In more conventional methodological language, the intervening variables identified in the interviews have variation, precision, validity, and no spurious correlation with unmeasured background variables. The manual provides numerous suggestions, with illustrative examples, for how these criteria can be achieved. The manual further includes suggestions for how the procedures can be modified in group interviews. It concludes with a discussion of a set of very practical problems, such as how to get started and how to cope with interruptions.

The apparent purpose of the research using this technique is very practical: explanations of audience reactions are used to improve the effectiveness of the message. Successful focussed interviews produce more effective propaganda, advertising, and entertainment. Sociologists have shown very little interest[1] in these matters in the last thirty years; the manual of procedures for the focussed interview has largely been used outside academia, in advertisement agencies and the like. The procedures spawned so-called focus groups for the testing of audience reaction – a development recorded with amusement by Merton, who at first was unaware of the link between focus groups and the focussed interview.

The Focused Interview is more than a manual for improving propaganda and advertisement. It is also a codification of procedures for developing theory from analysis of patterns of evidence. The theory consists of ideas about why certain situations presented by mass media produce certain responses. These ideas are developed at length in Merton's book on mass persuasion and in the essay with Lazarsfeld on the same topic in *Social Theory and Social Structure*. However, the general strategy is not limited to mass media research. Perhaps the most persuasive use of this strategy for constructing theory is the development of reference group theory by Merton and Alice Rossi (1957). Their essay may be conceived of as an application of the principles of the focussed interview to the analysis of Stouffer's findings from *The American Soldier*. By developing arguments about why certain effects or patterns of findings are produced, Merton and Rossi produce one of the most important pieces of sociological theory. Merton's other work provides numerous examples of this strategy of developing ideas by arguing with evidence.

The many examples in Merton's work of developing theoretical arguments grounded in evidence certainly constitute one of his most important contributions to sociology. This strategy makes Merton the contemporary sociological theorist with the most significant impact on empirical research. Unfortunately, codification of this strategy is never attempted, by Merton or by others, outside *The Focused Interview*. The mass-media context for this codification is probably too removed from current sociological concerns for it to have an impact.

Nothing about the value of Merton's method for theory construction is to be found in the two essays on the matter in *Robert K. Merton: Consensus and Controversy*. Blalock's essay takes as point of departure Merton's argument that progress in sociology derives from formulating empirically grounded middle-range theories. Blalock accepts this well-known advice as sound. He then surveys our progress toward realizing the program. He finds that the program has run into difficulties caused by the existence of too many causal variables connected by too many causal influences and by measurement problems. Econometric models, LISREL, and other sophisticated tools all will help overcome these difficulties, but much needs to be done. Other problems include micro-macro problems and the fragmentation of sociology. Despite all these problems, Blalock finds that some progress has been made; his main example of progress is status attainment research.

It is ironic to see status attainment research as an example of progress in the context of Merton's methodology. The research clearly represents a major advance in technique and in developing empirical generalizations. However, it is also the major example of a large body of quantitative research primarily concerned with establishing causal effects without worrying about what the effects mean. The irony of seeing status attainment research as the mark of progress in the direction proposed by Merton is, of course, that it was exactly the need to understand how effects come about that motivated the development of the focussed interview and other empirical analysis by Merton. The main defect of status attainment research, and of much of the quantitative labor market research that has followed it, is that theory formulation is seen as a matter of choosing variables and not as a matter of developing and sustaining an argument about why observed relationships come into being. The problem is lack of attention to the need of research to tell a story that makes us understand better what we observe. In other words, the problem is lack of attention to the problem dealt with in *The Focused Interview*.

Gould's essay has nothing to do with empirical research, but it is a nicely developed argument in favor of grand theory. This is theory about theory. Several other essays in *Robert K. Merton: Consensus and Controversy* deal with the same theme. None deals with the excitement of confronting ideas with evidence. That is a shame. Perhaps the next book about Merton will improve on the characterization of Robert K. Merton by making that excitement a more important theme.

Note

1. An interesting and important exception is the use of focussed interviews by Knodel *et al.* (1987).

References

Knodel, John E., Apichat Chamratrithirong, and Nibhon Debavalya. 1987, *Thailand's Reproducrive Revolution: Rapid Fertility Decline in a Third World Setting*. Madison: University of Wisconsin Press.

Merton, Robert K. and Alice S. Rossi. 1957. "Contributions to the Theory of Reference Group Behavior." Pp. 225–80 in *Social Theory and Social Structure*, by Robert K, Merton. Glencoe, IL: Free Press.

4

Finding the Common Denominator: A Phenomenological Critique of Life History Method

Gelya Frank

Introduction

There appears to be a renewed if not accelerating interest in qualitative methods in the social sciences. This interest raises again the questions examined by Dollard (1935), Allport (1942), Kluckhohn (1945), and Langness (1965) about the use of personal documents for social science research. An article by Honigmann (1976) surveys the literature on qualitative methods and characterizes the qualitative approach as one relying not only on the observer's professional training and conceptual orientation but also on that observer's personal skills and resources for understanding. Honigmann's article, with roots apparently in the philosophy of Wilhelm Dilthey, offers an interesting theoretical complement to the discussion by Nash and Wintrob (1972) on the emergence of selfconsciousness in anthropology as a historical event.

Along with the turn to qualitative methods, some discussion has focused on the potential for phenomenological philosophy to provide the social sciences with a qualitative approach that might allow verbal and written data to be analyzed in all their complexity and that might permit the essential reality of cultural objects to shine through verbal descriptions. Working primarily with first-person accounts, Goffman (1963) treats the question of how stigmatized individuals maintain consistent relations with their consociates when interacting face to face. Relying on interviews and observations of a single case, Garfinkel (1967a) addresses the problem of how an intersexed person can maintain identity in a society that permits an individual to have one gender only. Bogdan (1974) deals with disparities between a life of a transsexual as

Source: *Ethos*, vol. 7, no. 1, 1979, pp. 68–94.

described by the subject and as documented in official reports. He also (1977) addresses the issue of describing the subjective states of individuals in an oppressed population, this time the mentally retarded. Bogdan and Taylor (1976) deal with the world as experienced by a mentally retarded person through that person's own reports. Watson (1976), with reference to a Guajiro woman's oral account, attempts a list of categories on which to ground an anthropological life history from a phenomenological perspective. He argues that understanding is itself a legitimate use for life history data and that hermeneutics, the branch of phenomenology that concerns textual analysis, provides a key. Recent philosophical sources for a hermeneutic or interpretative social science include Gadamer (1975), Ricoeur (1976), and Kockelmans (1976).

Because of confusion about what phenomenology is and about the methods appropriate to it, it is useful to review the development of the phenomenological movement briefly. The publication in 1913 of Husserl's *Ideen zu einer reinen Phänomenologie und phänomenologischen Philosophie* served to launch the phenomenological movement not as a school or a system but as a group of practitioners committed to putting philosophy on intuitive grounds (Shimomissé 1977). Spiegelberg (1960) provides a comprehensive introduction to the key figures in the movement, while Dallmayr (1973) traces the development of phenomenological influences on social science in the United States and Europe. In the United States, phenomenology has entered sociology largely through the theoretical descriptions of Alfred Schutz, whose significance can be discerned in Cicourel (1964), Garfinkel (1967b), Goffman (1959, 1967, 1974), Psathas (1973), and Turner (1974), among others. The term "phenomenon" was introduced in philosophy just before Hegel and reappears in the work of several neo-Kantians, including Max Weber. While some works that draw on sources other than Husserl and those close to him present themselves as phenomenological – for example, Bogdan and Taylor (1975), whose approach derives from Weber – I will try to use the term in its specialized sense.

This article aims at an approach to life history that deals with its essential elements, since it is with essences that phenomenology is concerned. It is necessary therefore to take into full consideration (1) that the life history is a text or document and (2) that unlike the autobiography with which it is frequently grouped, the life history is a collaboration involving the consciousness of the investigator as well as the subject. The problem of whether life histories can be appropriate to a social analysis that considers itself scientific will also be treated, as well as the problem of describing "a life," "a person," and "the self" in a way that reflects the subject's actual experience.

The Place of Life History in Anthropological Science

The attempt to find a scientific use for the life history has been broached in a number of ways. DuBois (1944) applied psychoanalytic theories to the interpretation of informants' behavior, dreams, and performance on projective tests. Simmons (1942) suggested that the assemblage of personal data in his life history of a Hopi could be used to formulate generalizations about the culture and to test theories about individual behavior with respect to culture. Leighton and Leighton (1949) produced a scientific life study of a Navaho by considering the individual as a psychobiological entity within networks of material and symbolic relations. The concepts used in the analysis of this life history are defined precisely, and the entire text is structured as an internal system of references to the informant's account, the investigators' field notes, and outside sources. The work by Leighton and Leighton stands out as one of the most thorough life histories ever produced and, from the standpoint of the investigators, one of the most honest in pointing out the gaps in the data. Of course there have been other scientific life histories employing other methods (Langness 1965). Much depends upon the current definition of science when considering which among the more recent life histories is "scientific" rather than simply systematic and insightful (Erikson 1962, 1969; Hughes 1974; Mandelbaum 1973; Spradley 1969). Some analyses are constructed to authenticate or explicate primary sources for the life history text (Lurie 1971; Nabokov 1967; Opler 1969). For the purposes of this paper, I am not including these historical and ethnographic reconstructions as analyses of the life history. I am also, for convenience, excluding those works, many of them excellent, that use life histories to develop or illustrate a more general analysis of cultures (Allport, Bruner, and Jandorf 1955; Kennedy 1977; Landes 1971: Mohanti 1974; Moore 1973: Roy 1975).

A truly comprehensive list of the life histories, autobiographies, and other personal documents either written by anthropologists or used by them would show a preponderance of works that are only briefly set in cultural or historical context or not analyzed at all. This tendency was noted both by Kluckhohn (1945) and by Langness (1965) in their reviews of the literature and remains a feature of professional life histories (Barton 1963; Winter 1959), as well as popular ones (Lame Deer and Erdoes 1972; Rosengarten 1975). Very recent interest in the life history has provided a body of methodological recommendations (Angrosino 1976; Bogdan 1977; Crapanzano 1977; Earlix 1977; Jung 1972, 1973; Mandelbaum 1973; Myerhoff 1975, 1977; Progoff 1975; Watson 1970, 1976; White 1974).

What is it that has led investigators and readers to expect that a life history speaks for itself and that the material is self-evident? A recent article relying on case material elicited from a mentally retarded person can illustrate this presumption:

> Ed's story stands by itself as a rich source of understanding. We will resist the temptation to analyze it and reflect on what it tells us about Ed. Our position is that at times and to a much greater extent than we do now, we must listen to people who have been labeled retarded with the idea of finding out about ourselves, our society, and the nature of the label (Bogdan and Taylor 1976:51).

I want to suggest that it is the presumed self-evidence of life history materials that has stood in the way of their easy acceptance for social science research.

Ethnomethodology, a phenomenological sociology, has shown how the social sciences have taken on a language and a body of techniques with which practitioners establish that their work is professional by producing findings that differ from the understanding of social behavior that a lay person could offer (Garfinkel 1967b; Turner 1974). Life history documents stand so close to the prescientific world view that the professional attitude of social scientists seems to be to reject them outright. Characteristically, a scientific procedure relies on models that represent the original (Ruddock 1972), often by reducing the thing described to an abstraction based on part of the whole and then treating that abstraction as if real (Shimomissé 1977). Most anthropologists, if questioned directly, would certainly acknowledge that a life history is only a selected sample of a person's experiences, but it is rare that any systematic attempt has been made to indicate the kind of material that has been included as against the kind of material that has not. It would be difficult, then, for the life history document to be considered a scientific model of the subject's life in the same sense that a kinship diagram can be considered a model of a village's actual marriage relationships. In practice, the life history has been treated as a direct representation of the informant's life, as something almost equivalent to the informant's life, and insufficient attention has been directed toward the precise ways in which the life history is limited as a resource for making inferences about the subject's actual experience.

This is a paradox. The use of the life history for scientific purposes demands analysis and abstraction. However, the self-evidence of the life history makes it difficult even to conceive of ways to analyze it. Many life histories have been acknowledged as literary documents that can impart the feel of a culture better than more conventional ethnographic descriptions. Simone de Beauvoir's admiration for the works of Oscar Lewis on this basis is not unique (De Beauvoir 1975:153). But the questions have not yet been examined as to how the communication of this feel is accomplished, or what this feel is, and why it is such a persuasive agent in communicating an unfamiliar reality. It is exactly the self-evident quality of the life history that needs to be examined now, along with what it is that gives the life history its special ability to impart another life and, by extension, another way of life.

Finding the Person in the Life History: The Natural Attitude

Langness (1964, 1965) has suggested that the life history provides the social sciences with a common denominator for data and theory. Although each of the social sciences may take a different domain for analysis or employ specialized procedures, all describe events that depend on the behavior over time of individual persons. Further, as noted in the Foreword, "in one sense much of what any cultural anthropologist collects in the field and on which he bases his professional monographs is biographical in character" (Langness 1965:vi). Locating the individual person's life as a cross section in space and time, the life history offers a relatively unspecialized technique for collecting materials relevant to any set of concerns about human existence in society.

Langness did not elaborate on his point about the life history as a common denominator, nor has anyone else taken it up. However, the perspective from which it comes is not entirely new or unorthodox. Sapir wrote that all behavioral qualities thought to characterize the behavior of groups depend on the interaction of individual persons for their reality (Sapir 1951:515). Goldenweiser, just before Kroeber's article on the superorganic in cultural analysis, argued that the biographical individual (the family) transcended the biological, the psychological, and the civilizational matrix (Goldenweiser 1916).

Because of the obvious comparability of the life history with the life of any reader, whether social scientist or not, I would like to suggest that the life history may be a common denominator in a still more fundamental way. In the back of the reader's mind, the reader's own life provides the most immediate and natural framework for sifting through the reported experiences of the life history subject. The material may always be read in such a way as to provide an answer to the question: "In what way is this person like, or unlike, myself?" At some level of awareness, biographies are probably read, absorbed, and even judged in contrast with the reader's own life, a contrast that can account for the tremendous accessibility and popularity of life histories for readers at every level of intellectual training.

The common denominator afforded by the life history is an appeal to the person, the whole person, below or prior to anthropological issues or other specialized concerns. I am suggesting that generalizations about the life course or the life cycle based on the life history represent a secondary layer of meaning (Van Gennep 1960; Buhler and Massarik 1968; Erikson 1968; Neugarten 1968; Sheehy 1976). More primary is the connection made by the reader through identification (transference) in the psychological sense used by Freud and empathy as a phenomenon described by Scheler (1954) and Stein (1970), fleshing out the character in the story with appropriate feelings, when the reader's own experience permits this positive identification to take place.

While this primary act of readership has not been demonstrated empirically, its existence can not only be noted through introspection but derived from work already describing how our minds operate when we are having experiences that we recognize as our own and when we are understanding another person. A review of this philosophical and anthropological evidence may help clarify the contention that everyone, when reading a biography, uses the question of the subject's similarity to self as an interpretive frame.

Consciousness has been taken to consist of inner thoughts rather than the entire situation that gives structure and meaning to the individual's existence, perception, understanding, and actions. Classical psychology assumes a distinction between mind and body, following the Augustinian view of the person, in which the soul – later identified with the mind – enters the animal body to make it human. Merleau-Ponty (1945) argued the counter view that mind and body are a unity that cannot be described separately as if they were ordinary objects in the material world. He offers as an example the mental patient described by Glebe and Goldstein who could not locate a point on his body where the experimenters touched him with a ruler but could easily brush a mosquito from the place on his body where it happened to light (Merleau-Ponty 1945:119–129). His illness consisted of an inability willfully to abstract and reorganize elements of his behavior that continued to function normally when bound in context. To imitate a salute, the patient had to put himself totally in the posture of a military officer, like Helen Keller trying to comprehend what her father did when reading by putting on his spectacles, sitting in his armchair, and propping papers in front of her face (Keller 1902:14).

It follows that our mind is situated in our body in ways far more pervasive than indicated by the empirical sciences. It is not only that our brain is located in our head but that the body is the habitual point of departure for all our perceptions. Our conventional view of any object, from a house to a nebula, depends on a human viewer with human sensory capacities (Merleau-Ponty 1945:494; Von Uexkull 1957). Even further, our body is always calculated into any figure–ground relationship as a tacit third term:

> When I say that an object is *on* a table, I always mentally put myself either in the table or in the object, and I apply to them a category which theoretically fits the relationship of my body to external objects. Stripped of this anthropological association, the word *on* is indistinguishable from the word "under" or the word "beside" (Merleau-Ponty 1962:101).

Our presence in relation to objects is always from the standpoint "here," whether we are in motion or at rest. "Here" is the orientation point of the self, the "zero position" (Stein 1970). This appears to hold not only in spatial and temporal relationships but in psychological and social ones. Every society has been shown by ethnology to have a system of kinship relations that can be conceptualized as a network spreading out in time and space from a single self. Relatives are reckoned as "close" or "distant," and there exists universally what has been called, in reference to the Gahuku-Gama, a "distributive" recognition of moral obligation (Read 1955:257). Moral responsibility is acknowledged along a continuum of distance, so that those closer to Ego are entitled to stricter ethical behavior.

The Christian ethic of universal moral responsibility in Western culture may appear an exception, but in practice moral responsibility is distributive here too. For example, parents are expected to feed their children before giving charity to orphans.

We each operate from a "here" position in relation to others, calculating social relations in spatial metaphors. The "here" position is constituted by a shifting collage of meanings. This changing collage is our "identity." When we say that we understand another person, we temporarily take over what we perceive of that person's identity. For an instant we abandon our own position "here" and go over to the other person's position, taking it in and making it our own. This is what I think was meant by G. H. Mead (1934) when he characterized intelligent social interaction as putting oneself in the role of the other person by taking on the attitudes of the "generalized other." This relocation in the other's position is always an illusion, however, never fully accomplished because of the structure of the knowing self. Traditionally it has been the literary artist whose business it has been to document such leaps of consciousness. But even here the leap is asymptotic: the closeness with which the other's consciousness is assumed serves to highlight the impossibility of ever reaching that position completely or of abandoning one's own.

There has been an assumption that the life history can be something like a sample of a person's existence such that a reader might infer things about the whole person from the parts revealed in the document. Such a view tends to direct attention away from the very real constructive work that takes place when the living person produces a finite document through the intercession of the author, editor, interviewer, translator, or investigator. The usual aim in life history work has been to record the subject's literal narrative, often by hand (Kluckhohn 1948) if not on tape (Lewis 1961, 1964, 1966). Especially in taped narratives, which tend toward longer documents, the conversational elements are edited out along with repetitions and other passages deemed unimportant, ambiguous, or contradictory to some general pattern that the author perceives. Thus the life history has usually been produced in an archival manner, as a primary document of a life, and for this reason has frequently been treated as an autobiography rather than as a document produced by collaboration. Since primary data must not be adulterated, any analysis has tended to come after the document has been recorded and edited. When the analysis has drawn from psychological protocols, the life history has been treated as something like an absent person. When no analysis has been appended to the text, the life history has been presented as a document that can be understood for itself in its own terms, because every reader already has a sense of how to understand another person.

In *Zulu Woman*, a life history written not by an anthropologist but by a lay person, the author's attitude toward her subject expresses the natural attitude of readers toward biography, which I have sketched above. Reyher compares the subject of her life history with her own life, with her own understandings about life, and with those of her personal contemporaries:

> What did Zulu women do? How did they manage lifelong marriage? Were they happy? Was polygamy, as my sophisticated friends assured me, a natural state of man? Was it possible to love with one's body freely and easily, capturing the spirit and taming it to its primary

needs? Didn't Zulu women get notions, too? Were the heart and soul of a primitive women different from mine, or those of the women I knew? (Reyher 1948:xii).

Here the life history is treated as a subject, as a person. Whatever material is available in the life history will be taken as the evidence for answering the questions the author has posed. Yet this person is not totally another person with a set of experiences that might not even be within the author's power to imagine. Rather the subject becomes a kind of alter ego, which is slipped on and off as each point of understanding about the life of the subject is accomplished. This is not a process of identification that temporarily annihilates the reader's self, as sometimes happens in watching films or in reading novels, but a process of point-by-point affirmation, which I am suggesting takes place when understanding someone else.

In contrast, social scientists have located their analyses of life histories somewhere else than in the everyday process by which the investigator or the reader understands the subject of the biography. In *Baba of Karo*, written by an anthropologist, the author proposes that this life history's value lies in its usefulness as raw data in answering questions unique to social science:

> ... as a record of Hausa life it is unique in the detail, the time-span, the variety of aspects and events, and above all in its immediacy; but it is significant also to the social anthropologist with structural interests as a documentation of the extent to which, and the precise way in which, structure governs and shapes an individual life. A great deal has recently been written on a variety of postulated relationships between "culture" and "personality"; this record will have served a useful function if it suggests ways in which the individual's life process and its relations to the social structure can be studied in greater detail with a diachronic perspective (Smith 1954: 14).

What the social science approach to life history has in common with the natural attitude is that it too treats the material as though questions about the actual person can be answered from it.

If authors and readers of life histories do tend to make sense of the document as if it were a whole person, several issues should be considered critically. Among them, we might try to assess whether the life history represents the life of another individual in the way we think it does. Does it represent actual experiences, and are our inferences about the subject's experiences well founded? We might begin by trying to examine our expectations about what *a person* is as we attempt to understand other lives. This inquiry is a necessary part of life history work from more than one theoretical position. Following the requirements of empirical science, we seek to define the person in order to examine it from a culture-free perspective. Or, looking toward an interpretative social science, we seek to uncover the influence of our own understandings about persons upon our study of lives since we ourselves are situated in a particular social world in time and space.

The Constitution of the Person

It might be expected that a working principle of anthropological life histories would be to consider the subject's preunderstanding of "a person" and "a self" when eliciting self-related material. However, Hallowell (1955) pointed out the absence of any such categories in the Human Relations Area Files (as distinct from the categories of Personality and Soul) and in the literature in general. Such research as has been done on the concept of the person or the individual in the West and elsewhere points to the plasticity of the person historically and contextually. The context may be as immediate as the linguistic cues that call for structured answers in conversation (Linde 1978; Wolfson 1976) or as embracing as the entire cultural system of known things and procedures for making new things meaningful (Geertz 1973a).

Hallowell refers to the preliminary work by Mauss (1938) that looked at the development of the individual self as a social entity in the West, in several societies then called primitive, and in the traditions of India and China. Zuni kinship terms recorded by Cushing designated rank and status, while totem names represented a limited number of personages identified with portions of the body of a mythical beast that correspond to social position. In addition, secret societies conferred a limited set of titles on individual members. Mauss concluded that the individual Zuni's identity existed totally as a clan personage except for a separate ceremonial identity when using fraternity titles and masks. Boas' notes on the Kwakiutl similarly indicate that names carried definite social status within family, clan, and secret society, although the names of nobles additionally changed with age and its concomitant responsibilities, while commoners' names remained the same. From this Mauss hypothesized that the role filled by the individual in primitive societies is that of a personage who performs sacred rituals by which the life of the clan is organized.

In the West the Romans probably borrowed the word *persona* from the Etruscans, who used it in connection with their masques or ancestral rites. The word may have had an alternative Latin origin (Allport 1937:25–29) or an earlier Greek derivation, but according to Mauss the Romans gave the concept of person the sense that is our own today. The Latin *persona* implies a quality fundamental in law, not merely a fact of social organization as expressed in ritual, distinguishing free men (those having legitimate ancestors) from slaves (Krader 1968). The Stoic idea of personal morality and voluntary ethics added to the Latin legal concept the sense of consciousness, autonomy, and responsibility. To this ethical person, Christianity infused a metaphysical base, leaving us with a notion of the person that is fundamentally Augustine's: a person is that animal that has a soul, rational, individual, and indivisible.

The self as a psychological entity is a relatively recent development of the person but had roots in earlier philosophy and theology. It was debated until the late eighteenth century whether individuals possessed free will and whether the soul was a substance. Descartes, and even more Spinoza, demonstrated that the soul was not material but noetic. The sectarian movements brought out the equation of the self with consciousness and the person with the self. Neither Hume nor Kant declared the self a fundamental category of consciousness, but Fichte argued that all consciousness was an act of the self, thereby creating a foundation for the social sciences that take the self as their object.

Since Mauss was interested in the legal and ritual status of the person rather than the psychology of the conscious personality, he did not elaborate his position that every human being has at some time had the sense of oneself as a spiritual and corporeal unity. He did not examine possible cultural differences in this reflexive sense of "self," differences that might be anticipated by the plasticity of the person in other respects. Hallowell (1955) took up this problem where Mauss left off and proposed that anthropologists consider the "behavioral environment" in which a cross-cultural subject's psychological perspective is constituted. One essential element of the behavioral environment proposed by Hallowell is the "spatiotemporal orientation," which illuminates life history data since it is by this orientation that a self is recognized and maintained over a life span:

> If we wish to postulate a sense of self-continuity as a generic human trait, a culturally constituted temporal orientation must be assumed a necessary condition. This seems to be a reasonable hypothesis in view of the fact that self-identification would have no functional value in the operation of a human social order if, at the same time, it was not given a temporal dimension. *Who* I am, both to myself and others, would have no stability. It would make it impossible to assume that patterns of interpersonal relations could operate in terms of a continuing personnel (Hallowell 1955:95).

A person whose identity is not continuous cannot be morally responsible, while all societies depend on the individual's taking responsibility for his or her own acts in order for the society to function. Hence Hallowell suggests that it can be deduced that psychopathological states that alter the maintenance of personal identity are considered abnormal in every society. He offers the example of an Ojibwa account in which the narrator was able to locate in waking consciousness something seen in a dream, implying a spatial contiguity of the dreamscape with local geography. He also relates the story of a low-caste Hindu woman who successfully pleaded with the family of a deceased Brahmin to be allowed to die on his funeral pyre because she had been married to him in a former existence. Both examples illustrate violations of Western notions of the temporal and spatial boundaries on personal existence in cultural contexts where such experiences are normative. Hallowell referred to his paper as "phenomenological" but without wanting to invoke all the implications of that term. It is his interest in the cultural constitution of time and space in the individual's consciousness that makes his use of the term appropriate. More recently Kenny (n.d.) writes that the concept of the self in New Guinea is "an adequate positivist metaphysics mapping the phenomenology of consciousness which, in its turn, is rooted in social life."

Geertz (1973b) writes that in Bali the linear temporal aspects of personal existence are underplayed in favor of the social relations that take place generation after generation, framed by the life span of an idealized individual:

> In the well-lit world of everyday life, the purely personal part of an individual's cultural definition, that which in the context of the immediate consociate community is most fully and completely his, and his alone, is highly muted. And with it are muted the more idiosyncratic, merely biographical, and consequently, transient aspects of his existence as a human being (what, in our more egoistic framework, we call his "personality") in favor of some rather more typical, highly conventionalized, and, consequently, enduring ones (Geertz 1973b:370).

The Balinese employ six different classes of appellations for individuals. The same individual may be referred to as "Father-of," "First Child," "Village Chief," and so on, but the individual's uniquely personal name, often a nonsense syllable, will almost never be used. Some individuals become so immersed in their role as public figures that their occupational title as political or spiritual leader eclipses reference to the other aspects of their social existence. Geertz suggests that we, focusing on psychological traits as the core of personal identity, would say that they have sacrificed their true selves to their role while they, focusing on social position, would say that their role is essential to their true selves. The Balinese example would seem, by way of contrast, to frame the person at present in the West as a self-motivated actor rather than, say, an agent of forces outside personal consciousness.

This quality of the Western self may be a recent development, despite ideas we may have inherited from the Renaissance about what the Greeks were like as individuals (Burckhardt 1943). Using Aristotle's text for the *Poetics* (335 B.C.), Jones (1962) writes that Aristotle never contemplated a "tragic hero" as the focus of drama, since for him tragedy was an imitation not of human beings but of action and life. Character translates as "that which reveals a moral choice." In orienting to character, the modern reader anticipates not the workings of plot, which is meant to imitate Fate, but the revelation of personal consciousness:

> ... because he the reader has inherited – from Socratic–Platonic, Euripidean, Jewish, Roman, Christian, humanist and Romantic sources – an

image of the human self and its working which he accepts for a universal "*donnée*" of life, and never questions ... we see action issuing from a solitary focus of consciousness – secret, inward, interesting – and in which the status of action must always be adjectival: action qualifies, it tells us things we want to know about the individual promoting it; the life of action is our ceaseless, animating consideration of the state of affairs "inside" him who acts, without which action is empty and trivial, an effluvium (Jones 1962:32–33).

But a character in the Aristotelian sense is one who reveals the significance of a situation through the decisive execution of an action. The parallel between Aristotle's sense of the character and of the person appears in his ethical treatises, in which he says that the good for the individual is that which is being sought by the individual's nature or is the fulfillment of the individual's function (Kerfred 1967:162) rather than that, say, which is consciously chosen as good by the individual.

The difficulty of studying persons without examining our preunderstandings and theirs should be clear, as well as that of constructing a stable positive definition of "a person" even within a single culture or society. Recalling a book he read as a boy in which the childhood of famous men was recounted, Sartre (1966) points out the reflexive, ex post facto sense we make of individual destiny:

...the author made a point of constantly inserting allusions to their future greatness, or recalling casually, by means of a detail, their most famous works or deeds, of contriving his accounts so artfully that it was impossible to understand the most trivial incident without relating it to subsequent events. He introduced into the tumult of everyday life a great, fabulous silence which transfigured everything: the future. A certain Sanzio was dying to see the Pope; he was so eager that he was taken to the public square one day when the Pope was due to pass by. The youngster turned pale and stared. Finally, someone said to him: "I suppose you're satisfied, Raffaello. Did you at least take a good look at our Holy Father?" But the boy replied with a wild look: "What Holy Father? All I saw was colors!" (Sartre 1966: 127).

In complicity with the author, the young Sartre read the life of those children "as God had conceived them: starting at the end."

The child who may grow into a famous or extraordinary person may say and do things that have no relevance to a future identity as a public figure. The biography tends to scramble the significance of that life, reading it backward and filling in evidence that proves that the final verdict is the true and correct one. Isn't this, though, the way we tend to view any life, linking selected past events in an order that reveals who that person "really" is – a sample of past behavior that is taken as representative, a generalization based on a theme? This is not to assert that, in the case of the painter Raphael or in Sartre's own life, there was not a unique orientation that linked the child with the future accomplishments. The theme may reflect an actuality, but it is still a selected strand, a construct, a partial image, a model with the limitations on inference of a model, no less in this Western folk text than in our sociology and psychology texts.

We seem to have a sense in the West that, in addition to the presence of causal relationship linking events in a person's life, a person develops into a different being than he or she is as a child. Rousseau is acknowledged as introducing the idea of psychic maturation as an integral element of personhood in *Émile* (1762), in which he writes that every individual has two births, one into physical existence and one, after a crisis, into life (Van den Berg 1964:25). Aries (1962) has shown that the idea of childhood has not always been with us. While a distinction between children and adults was present in the classical period, none was recognized in the Middle Ages or even until very recently in certain socioeconomic classes (Ariès 1962:411–412).

We also have the sense that each person has an inner self, which is distinct from a public self whose acts are conditioned by external considerations. Van den Berg credits Rousseau's *Confessions* (1781), rather than the confessions of Augustine (A.D. 397), with opening up the description of the solitary inner self as a literary form. Perhaps it could be said that the introduction of a form for introspection expanded the faculty that might introspect: Joyce used as much space in *Ulysses* (1919) to relate the internal experiences of half a day as Rousseau used to recount the story of half his life (Van den Berg 1964:232). In attempting to find out whether non-Western subjects experience their thoughts and feelings as we do, we might only learn that once they are encouraged to introspect, an "inner" self will be constructed, that self that we are most in touch with today and value most highly.

No a priori description of a person could ever be expected adequately to predict the contents of a biography in Western cultures. How much more should this be true for cultures we know less about? What we may need to know right now in life history work is more about the way persons construct versions of themselves to present to us, as Crapanzano (1977) suggests and Linde (1978) attempts. We might also pay closer attention to the relationship between the investigator and the subject, to the sociolinguistic structure of the elicitation, and to the manner of delivery, in making out what we perceive to be the content of the life history. It may mean that we will have to analyze in depth a brief interaction (Myerhoff 1977), where in more conventional life histories a decade might be glossed.

The Life History as a Document of Interaction

A phenomenological critique of life history work or the study of lives can operate in at least two ways, which should be distinguished if confusion is to be avoided. First, it can be claimed that any life history "is" phenomenological because it presents a highly complex set of authentic relationships in the subject's experience, even if filtered through the investigator's reports or shaped by the elicitation and recording. The investigator may decide to make of the recorded text a historical example (Nabokov 1967) or a psychological one (Hughes 1974), but the text as a whole remains as an indefinite but rich source of experience for the reader. This tendency to treat the text as a whole, in which the textual nature is taken for granted and not analyzed, constitutes what I described earlier as treating the text as a person. The text falls into the background as a neutral tool or medium for the "phenomena" (the events of a person's life as experienced) to shine through. Autobiographical texts appear to offer a truer experience of the subject's life (Laye 1954), a direct outpouring of consciousness, but here too certain conventions are invoked to structure the narrative (Earle 1972; Misch 1951; Olney 1972, n.d.; Starobinski 1971). Nevertheless, both life histories and autobiographies, when they do not reduce the experience of the subject to abstractions but simply describe what is there for the reporting subject, will resemble the subject's experiences – say, in terms of a succession of experiences related to career or to family life – and may in fact come very close to providing the reader with an "inside" to the subject's experience.

A second way in which the life history or the study of lives may be considered phenomenological is in the hermeneutic sense: acknowledging the life history as a document, its genesis from other documents, and its dependence upon interpretation. The reader's interpretation will be based on assumptions only possibly shared by the subject and the investigator, since frequently life history texts attempt to make understood things that are difficult to communicate interpersonally as well as cross-culturally. Crapanzano (1977) points out that as personal history is variously objectified into the case history, the life history, the biography, and the autobiography, the forms themselves are presumptions that might be an alien construct for the subject, possibly causing him or her an alienating *prise de conscience*. If there is a lack of shared assumptions between the investigator and the subject, there will almost certainly be misinterpretations by the investigator that will be passed on to the reader, and the life history will fail to do what it purports to do, that is, render an account of the subject's actual experiences.

When an account of career choice was elicited among seven middle-class American professionals, the life story that each offered followed the narrative form as a speech event described by Labov, incorporating an evaluation of the experiences recounted (Linde 1978). Experiences are presumed to have occurred sequentially in the order related, and a body of causality by earlier events is presupposed when considering later events in the narrative. The subject tries to make coherent any elements of the narrative that seem discontinuous, supporting the expectation of a single motivated life grounded in a flow of related circumstance, while preserving the requirement that, as a story, the life story come to a point, a feature of narrative elsewhere investigated (Polanyi n.d.).

The life history investigator as well as the subject may do work to make the informant's account a rich, chronological, multithematic but pointed, coherent, continuous, ego-centered structure. The unspecialized life history technique is not only a method but a form:

> Since there is no common agreement yet as to what life histories should be like when the study of personality development is the objective, and since there was no satisfactory model to follow at the time, it was decided to make the initial investigation exploratory in "dragnet" fashion and gather data on any and every topic that appeared to be significantly related to the individual's growth and development. If the first objective was to be a life history, then it seemed that the dominating interests of the individual, in the order in which they were experienced, should determine the presentation of material and regulate the general proportion of space and emphasis on each item. The ideal objective was to mirror the developing personality in such accuracy and detail, and so frame it in its environment, society, and culture, that the reader in moving through the pages might "see" the infant emerge from conception, grow into manhood, and play his adult role, and might come to understand to a certain degree how it happened and if possible how it felt (Simmons 1942: 3).

The life history may be thought of as a process that blends together the consciousness of the investigator and the subject, perhaps to the point where it is not possible to disentangle them. In *From Anxiety to Method in the Behavioral Sciences*, Devereux (1967) gives examples from thirty years of experience in observing the ways in which an investigator's personal reactions (countertransference) to a subject affect the formulation of research problems and methods. Rush (1977) makes the same point and amply demonstrates it with regard to Freud himself and his theories regarding female patients' accounts of father–daughter incest. Wagner (1975) suggests that anthropologists outright invent the realities they describe. If, as suggested earlier in this paper, the investigator relies in a primary way on personal resources in understanding the subject of the life history as another person, then in some sense the life history may represent a personal portrait of the investigator as well. This portrait would take the form of a shadow biography, a negative image, for which the missing text could be found in the investigator's private thoughts, interview questions, field notes, dreams, and letters home. Many life histories are presented as an autobiography told to an investigator. This loose concept of autobiography has been stretched to apply even to edited and translated accounts by more than one person, as in Lewis' *The Children of Sanchez* (1961), presented as "the autobiography of a family" rather than, say, a collection of autobiographies within a family. Can a family have an autobiography in the same sense that a people can have a history? And, if so, would it consist of the separate members' accounts?

Perhaps one feature of the anthropological life history as compared with Western biography has been a refusal to turn the rewoven narrative into discourse toward a single point, although certain structures are observed – such as documenting puberty and marriage. In contrast, say, with accounts of transformation such as Augustine's *Confessions* or modern variants (Eareckson 1976; Haley 1966), the life history has tended to permit various kinds of readings, depending on the anticipated points of concern. The life history maintains its generality, its quality as a textured body of material from which threads can be untangled and rewoven by the investigator or reader. This generality and lack of pointedness have supported the sense of the life history as a person. How the material is elicited and recorded, though, may influence the selection of certain data by the subject.

One claim Lewis made for the technique of taping and transcribing life stories is that "with the aid of the tape recorder, unskilled, uneducated, and even illiterate persons can talk about themselves and relate their observations and experiences in an uninhibited, spontaneous, and natural manner" (Lewis 1961:xii). The life history project, however, itself provides an *occasion* for interaction, an occasion structured by the degree of formality of the interview, its understood purpose, the length of the project and its setting, the respectively perceived role and status of the interviewer and subject, the exchange of money and services, the interviewer's and the subject's motives for undertaking the work, and their conception of the task. I do not want to suggest that life history materials elicited using Lewis' techniques, which have been adopted by others (Krueger 1973) or parallel the work done by others (Terkel 1974), are faulty, more biased than information elicited using other techniques, or less meaningful. What I do want to point out is that, while a life is formed around the meanings an individual develops to connect experiences, the story of a life is not a fait accompli of consciousness but is a form that emerges in discourse with another or with oneself. I would suggest that very few individuals formulate a complete autobiography in their heads, carrying their complete life story intact from beginning to end. If they do, I would suggest that it changes when they decide to write it down or share it with someone they are talking to. Linde shows that even short accounts of career choice will vary with circumstances. Further, in anthropological life history work, tacit negotiations continually occur regarding the purpose of the project, the subject's right to privacy, the investigator's power to demand information, mutual claims for time and services, and the relevance of particular kinds of information. It may even be said that the conventions of discourse frame the story as much as the story, presumed intact in the subject's mind, governs what will be disclosed.

Since speech does not exist independently of the social situation in which it occurs and since the interview is a socially defined speech event with its own conventions for behavior, Wolfson (1976) points out that it is "interview speech" that we are often studying when we think it is conversational narrative as it naturally occurs. Further, Wolfson's research with speakers of

United States English indicates that the free, nondirective techniques that anthropologists frequently use may be confusing for the speaker and may even be taken by the subject to indicate the investigator's incompetence to conduct research, since the conventions of a proper interview are not being observed. If the subject considers the investigator incompetent, it is not unlikely that the subject will exercise more than ordinary discretion in making disclosures.

A comparable situation exists with regard to the transmission over time of oral texts. With respect to the telling of oral histories of whole groups to Western investigators, Vansina (1965) suggests that the testimony is no more than a mirage of the reality it describes:

> The initial informant in an oral tradition gives, either consciously or unconsciously, a distorted account of what has really happened, because he sees only some aspects of it, and places his own interpretation on what he has seen. His testimony is stamped by his personality, coloured by his private interests, and set within the framework of reference provided by the cultural values of the society he belongs to. This initial testimony then undergoes alterations and distortions at the hands of all other informants in the chain of transmission, down to and including the very last one, all of them being influenced by the same factors as the first: their private interests and the interests of the society they belong to, the cultural values of that society, and their own individual personalities (Vansina 1965:76).

Factors such as the presence of an audience or the participation of the informant in a group testimony rather than a personal one can determine that certain subjects will be glossed over by Kuba informants, since mention may only be made of things that would have the approval of everyone present. Vansina warns that an investigator must also be aware that the expression of satisfaction or dissatisfaction with the testimony will incline the informant to slant the testimony to suit what the field-worker's wishes are perceived to be.

Hymes (1973) also demonstrates the personalistic shaping of oral texts by informants, so much so that he advocates applying the concept of authorship and literature in the Western sense to such accounts. It is worth reproducing a footnote in which the reshaping of an account according to the changing life experiences of the informant is referred to. The informant, an Eyak of Alaska, was interviewed in 1932 and again in the 1960s:

> After being widowed and re-marrying amongst the Tlingits, Anna's stories of intermarriage and displacement become much more meaningful. The groundhog man and wolf woman are extremely poignant, taking on several more layers of meaning ...
>
> As I have thought and thought in recent years about the way she tells these stories, I come to an even greater appreciation of the artistic

and philosophical merit of Anna's storytelling, of her own personal tragedy, and her understanding of the tragedy of the Eyak people, and of the nature of human history, as only an Eyak (or maybe an Irishman) could see it (Michael Krauss, personal communication, 30 August 1973) (Hymes 1973:8).

Both Vansina and Hymes offer evidence, then, for the design of oral accounts not only for particular hearers but for particular occasions as well. If these features apply to traditional, patterned oral texts that are not self-referential by design, it would seem essential to consider their presence in personal accounts that draw from the fluidity of everyday life itself.

Conclusion

Introductions to anthropological fieldwork stress the importance of establishing rapport, which the investigator recognizes as feeling free to ask an informant questions, expecting a truthful response. We assume that there is such a thing as a truthful response and compose ethnographies to a great extent from information elicited from subjects and taken as true accounts of real things. When this assumption and practice have been looked at critically by anthropologists, a dualistic world of "emics" and "etics" has been hypothesized (Harris 1968), and the reliability of informants has been questioned (Edgerton 1970).

This article presents a phenomenological consideration of the life history and has suggested that the investigator's influence is always embedded in materials gleaned from interviews, blurring the distinction between "subjective" and "objective" realities. However, we do tend to collect information about other persons as if there is a world that is always there, available to every investigator in the same way, and susceptible to being positively described. This "as if" may be a fiction.

Mintz (1973) wrote: "The investigator must do his best to make clear what he thinks *he* is like so that readers may better judge his interpretation of the life of another." Personal resources used by the investigator to formulate questions, structure situations, and come to understandings are themselves part of the data (Watson 1976). While the investigator's involvement should be made explicit, programmatic self-descriptions by the investigator should be treated no less critically than self-descriptions by the subject. The situational reportage used by Wilson (1974) in *Oscar*, his study of an eccentric Carib, seems to strike a fine balance.

Speaking somewhat metaphorically, the life history can be considered a double autobiography, since it is to the investigator's personal experiences that the subject's accounts are first referred. A question underlying life history work generically is: How is it possible to know or understand another person? Many researchers are now consciously drawing on their own selves through autobiographical writing (Richardson 1975), opening insights into the process of selfconstruction that are not available when an investigator's object in producing a life history text is primarily to listen and record. The use of the investigator's self as a resource for understanding parallels the classical requirement that a psychoanalyst be analyzed, not to cure the analyst so much as to open up the workings of his or her own mind as one sharing general properties with all minds. The critical approach to self-description proposed in this article differs from psychoanalysis by suspending the assumption that each person can be described as an organic unity of traits and tendencies. Bracketing "the person" in this way exposes the way personal accounts are situated in interaction and the way we make sense of words and behavior when understanding others.

References

Allport, G. 1937. *Personality: A Psychological Interpretation.* Holt.
——. 1942. *The Use of Personal Documents in Psychological Science.* Social Science Research Council.
Allport, G. W., J. S. Bruner, and E. M. Jandorff. 1955. Personality under Social Catastrophe: Ninety Life Histories of the Nazi Revolution, *Personality in Nature, Society, and Culture* (C. Kluckhohn and H. A. Murray, eds.), pp. 436–455. Alfred A. Knopf.
Angrosino, M. V. 1976. The Use of Autobiography as "Life History": The Case of Albert Gomes. *Ethos* 4:133–154.
Ariès, P. 1962. *Centuries of Childhood: A Social History of Family Life* (Robert Baldick, trans.). Vintage Books.
Barton, R. F. 1963. *Autobiographies of Three Pagans in the Philippines.* Introduction by Nancy Oestreich Lurie. University Books.
Bogdan, R. 1974. *Being Different: The Autobiography of Jane Fry.* John Wiley and Sons.
——. 1977. Voices: First Person Life Histories as a Method of Studying "Retardation." Paper presented at the 101st annual convention of the American Association on Mental Retardation, New Orleans.
Bogdan, R., and S. J. Taylor. 1975. *Introduction to Qualitative Research Methods: A Phenomenological Approach to the Social Sciences.* John Wiley and Sons.
——. 1976. The Judged, Not the Judges: An Insider's View of Mental Retardation. *American Psychologist* 31:47–52.
Bühler, C., and F. Massarik, eds. 1968. *The Course of Human Life.* Springer.
Burckhardt, J. 1943. *The Civilization of the Renaissance in Italy.* Phaidon Press (original 1860).
Cicourel, A. V. 1964. *Method and Measurement in Sociology.* Free Press.
Crapanzano, V. 1977. The Life History in Anthropological Field Work. *Anthropology and Humanism Quarterly* 2(2–3): 3–7.
Dallmayr, F. R. 1973. Phenomenology and Social Science: An Overview and Appraisal, *Explorations in Phenomenology* (D. Carr and E. S. Casey, eds.), pp. 133–166. Martinus Nijhoff.
De Beauvoir, S. 1975. *All Said and Done.* Warner Books.
Devereux, G. 1967. *From Anxiety to Method in the Behavioral Sciences.* Mouton.
Dollard, J. 1935. *Criteria for the Life History.* Social Science Research Council.

DuBois, C. 1944. *The People of Alor.* University of Minnesota Press.
Eareckson, J. 1976. *Joni: The Unforgettable Story of a Young Woman's Struggle Against Quadraplegia and Depression.* World Wide Publications.
Earl, W. 1972. *The Autobiographical Consciousness: A Philosophical Inquiry into Existence.* Quadrangle.
Earlix, D. A. 1977. Life-History in Social Gerontology: Its Validity and Use. Ph.D. dissertation, Department of Sociology, University of Southern California.
Edgerton, R. B. 1970. Method in Psychological Anthropology, *A Handbook of Method in Cultural Anthropology* (R. Naroll and R. Cohen, eds.), pp. 338–352. Natural History Press.
Erikson, E. H. 1962. *Young Man Luther: A Study in Psychoanalysis and History.* Norton.
———. 1968. Life Cycle. *International Encyclopedia of the Social Sciences,* Vol. 9:286–292.
———. 1969. *Gandhi's Truth: On the Origins of Militant Nonviolence.* Norton.
Gadamer, H.-G. 1975. *Truth and Method.* Seabury Press.
Garfinkel, H. 1967a. Passing and the Managed Achievement of Sex Status in an "Intersexed" Person: Part 1, *Studies in Ethnomethodology,* pp. 116–185. Prentice-Hall.
———. 1967b. *Studies in Ethnomethodology.* Prentice-Hall.
Geertz, C. 1973a. Thick Description: Toward an Interpretive Theory of Culture, *The Interpretation of Cultures,* pp. 3–30. Basic Books.
———. 1973b. Person, Time, and Conduct in Bali, *The Interpretation of Cultures,* pp. 360–411. Basic Books.
Goffman, E. 1959. *The Presentation of Self in Everyday Life.* Doubleday.
———. 1963. *Stigma: Notes on the Management of Spoiled Identity.* Prentice-Hall.
———. 1967. *Interaction Ritual: Essays on Face-to-Face Behavior.* Anchor Books.
———. 1974. *Frame Analysis: An Essay on the Organization of Experience.* Harper and Row.
Goldenweiser, A. 1916. Sociological Terminology in Ethnology. *American Anthropologist* 18:348–357.
Haley, A., ed. 1966. The Autobiography of Malcolm X (with the assistance of Alex Haley). Grove Press.
Hallowell, A. I. 1955. The Self and Its Behavioral Environment, *Culture and Experience,* pp. 75–110. University of Pennsylvania Press.
Harris, M. 1968. *The Rise of Anthropological Theory: A History of Theories of Culture.* Thomas Y. Crowell.
Honigmann, J. J. 1976. The Personal Approach in Cultural Anthropological Research. *Current Anthropology* 17:243–261.
Hughes, C. C. 1974. *Eskimo Boyhood: An Autobiography in Psychosocial Perspective.* University Press of Kentucky.
Husserl, E. 1962. *Ideas: General Introduction to Pure Phenomenology.* (W. R. Boyce Gibson, trans.). Collier Books (original 1913).
Hymes, D. 1973. An Ethnographic Perspective. *New Literary History* 5(1):186–201.
Jones, J. 1962. *On Aristotle and Greek Tragedy.* Oxford University Press.
Jung, J. 1972. Autobiographies of College Students as a Teaching and Research Tool in the Study of Personality Development. *American Psychologist* 27:779–783.
———. 1973. Using Student Autobiographies to Teach Personality in High School. *Behavioral and Social Science Teacher* 1(1):51–54.
Keller, H. 1902. *The Story of My Life.* Grosset and Dunlap.
Kennedy, J. G. 1977. *Struggle for Change in a Nubian Community: An Individual in Society and History* (with the assistance of Hussein M. Fahim). Mayfield.
Kenny, M. G. n.d. *The Concept of the Self in New Guinea* (unpublished manuscript).
Kerfred, G. B. 1967. Aristotle. *The Encyclopedia of Philosophy* 1:151–162. Macmillan.

Kluckhohn, C. 1945. The Personal Document in Anthropological Science, *The Use of Personal Documents in History, Anthropology, and Sociology* (L. Gottschalk *et al.*, eds.). Social Science Research Council.

——. 1948. A Navaho Personal Document with a Brief Paretian Analysis, *Personal Character and Cultural Milieu* (D. G. Haring, ed.). Syracuse University Press.

Kockelmans, J. J. 1976. Toward an Interpretative or Hermeneutic Social Science. *Graduate Faculty Philosophy Journal* 5(1):73–96.

Krader, L. 1968. Person and Collectivity: A Problem in the Dialectic of Anthropology. *Transactions of the New York Academy of Science* (series II) 30:856–862.

Krueger S. 1973. *The Whole Works: The Autobiography of a Young American Couple.* Vintage Books.

Lame Deer, J. (Fire), and R. Erdoes. 1972. *Lame Deer: Seeker of Visions.* Touchstone Books.

Landes, R. 1971. *The Ojibwa Woman.* W. W. Norton.

Langness, L. L. 1964. Biography: A Common Denominator. Paper presented to Section H, American Association for the Advancement of Science, Montreal, December.

——. 1965. *The Life History in Anthropological Science.* Holt, Rinehart and Winston.

Laye, C. 1954. *The Dark Child: The Autobiography of an African Boy.* Farrar, Straus and Giroux.

Leighton, A. H., and D. C. Leighton. 1949. Gregorio, The Hand–Trembler: A Psychobiological Personality Study of a Navaho Indian. *Papers of the Peabody Museum* XL(1).

Lewis, O. 1961. *The Children of Sanchez: Autobiography of a Mexican Family.* Vintage Books.

——. 1964. *Pedro Martinez: A Mexican Peasant and His Family.* Vintage Books.

——. 1966. *La Vida: A Puerto Rican Family in the Culture of Poverty – San Juan and New York.* Vintage Books.

Linde, C. 1978. *The Creation of Coherence in Life Stories* (unpublished manuscript). Structural Semantics Co., P.O. Box 5612, Santa Monica, CA 90405.

Lurie, N. O., ed. 1971. *Mountain Wolf Woman, Sister of Crashing Thunder: The Autobiography of a Winnebago Indian.* University of Michigan Press.

Mandelbaum, D. G. 1973. The Study of Life History: Gandhi. *Current Anthropology* 14:177–206.

Mauss, M. 1938. Une catégorie de l'esprit humain: la notion de personne celle de "moi." *Journal of the Royal Anthropological Institute* LXVIII:263–281.

Mead, G. H. 1934. *Mind, Self and Society: From the Standpoint of a Social Behaviorist.* University of Chicago Press.

Merleau-Ponty, M. 1945. *Phénoménologie de la perception.* Librarie Gallimard.

——. 1962. *Phenomenology of Perception* (Colin Smith, trans.). Routledge and Kegan Paul.

Mintz, S. W. 1973. Comment on The Study of Life History: Gandhi, by David G. Mandelbaum. *Current Anthropology* 14:200.

Misch, G. 1951. *A History of Autobiography in Antiquity* (E. W. Dickes, trans.). Harvard University Press (original 1907).

Mohanti, P. 1974. *My Village, My Life: Portrait of an Indian Village.* Praeger.

Moore, A. 1973. *Life Cycles in Atchalán: The Diverse Careers of Certain Guatemalans.* Teachers College Press.

Myerhoff, B. 1975. Life History as Integration: Personal Myth and Aging. Paper presented at 10th International Congress of Gerontology, Jerusalem, June.

——. 1977. A Symbol Perfected in Death: Continuity and Ritual in the Life and Death of an Elderly Jew, *Life's Career: Aging.* Sage Press.

Nabokov, P. 1967. *Two Leggings: The Making of a Crow Warrior.* Thomas Y. Crowell.
Nash, D., and R. Wintrob, 1972. The Emergence of Self-Consciousness in Ethnography. *Current Anthropology* 13:527–542.
Neugarten, B. L., ed. 1968. *Middle Age and Aging: A Reader in Social Psychology.* University of Chicago Press.
Olney, J. 1972. *Metaphors of Self: The Meaning of Autobiography.* Princeton University Press.
———. n.d. *Autos* Bios* Graphein* (unpublished manuscript).
Opler, M. E. 1969. *Apache Odyssey: A Journey between Two Worlds.* Holt, Rinehart and Winston.
Polanyi, L. n.d. So What's the Point? *Semiotica* (forthcoming).
Progoff, I. 1975. *At a Journal Workshop: The Basic Text and Guide for Using the Intensive Journal.* Dialogue House Library.
Psathas, G., ed. 1973. *Phenomenological Sociology: Issues and Applications.* John Wiley and Sons.
Read, K. E. 1955. Morality and the Concept of the Person among the Gahuku-Gama. *Oceania* XXV(4):233–282.
Reyher, R. 1948. *Zulu Woman.* Columbia University Press.
Richardson, M. 1975. Anthropologist – the Myth Teller. *American Ethnologist* 2:517–533.
Ricoeur, P. 1976. *Interpretation Theory: Discourse and the Surplus of Meaning.* Texas Christian University Press.
Rosengarten, T. 1975. *All God's Dangers: The Life of Nate Shaw.* Avon Books.
Roy, M. 1975. *Bengali Women.* University of Chicago Press.
Ruddock, R., ed. 1972. *The Need for Models, Six Approaches to the Person.* Routledge and Kegan Paul.
Rush, F. 1977. The Freudian Cover-Up: The Sexual Abuse of Children. *Chrysalis* 1(1):31–45.
Sapir, E. 1951. *Selected Writings of Edward Sapir in Language, Culture and Personality* (D. G. Mandelbaum, ed.). University of California Press.
Sartre, J.-P. 1966. *The Words.* Fawcett.
Scheler, M. 1954. *The Nature of Sympathy* (Peter Heath, trans.). Routledge and Kegan Paul (original 1912).
Sheehy, G. 1976. *Passages: Predictable Crises of Adult Life.* E. P. Dutton.
Shimomissé, E. 1977. Philosophy and Phenomenological Intuition. *Analecta Husserliana, The Yearbook of Phenomenological Research* (A.-T. Tymieniecka, ed.).
Simmons, L. W., ed. 1942. *Sun Chief: The Autobiography of a Hopi Indian.* Yale University Press.
Smith, M. F. 1954. *Baba of Karo.* Faber.
Spiegelberg, H. 1960. *The Phenomenological Movement: A Historical Introduction.* Martinus Nijhoff.
Spradley, J. P. 1969. *Guests Never Leave Hungry: The Autobiography of James Sewid, a Kwakiutl Indian.* Yale University Press.
Starobinski J. 1971. The Style of Autobiography, *Literary Style, A Symposium* (S. B. Chatman, ed.), pp. 285–296. Oxford University Press.
Stein, E. 1970. *On the Problem of Empathy* (Waltraut Stein, trans.). Martinus Nijhoff (original 1917).
Terkel, S. 1974. *Working: People Talk about What They Do All Day and How They Feel about What They Do.* Avon Books.
Turner, R., ed. 1974. *Ethnomethodology.* Penguin Education.

Van Den Berg, J.M. 1964. *The Changing Nature of Man: Introduction to a Historical Psychology*. Dell.

Van Gennep, A. 1960. *The Rites of Passage*. University of Chicago Press.

Vansina, J. 1965. *Oral Tradition: A Study of Historical Methodology* (H.M. Wright, trans.). Aldine.

Von Uexkull, J. 1957. A Stroll through the Worlds of Animals and Men: A Picture Book of Invisible Worlds, *Instinctive Behavior: The Development of a Modern Concept* (Clair H. Schiller, trans. and ed.), pp. 5–80. International Universities Press (original 1934).

Wagner, R. 1975. *The Invention of Culture*. Prentice-Hall.

Watson, L. C. 1970. Self and Ideal in a Guajiro Life History. *Acta Ethnologica et Linguistica* (Engelbert Stiglmayr, ed.), No. 21, Series Americana 5.

———. 1976. Understanding a Life History as a Subjective Document: Hermeneutical and Phenomenological Perspectives. *Ethos* 4:95–131.

White, R. W. 1974. Teaching Personality through Life Histories. *Teaching of Psychology* 1(2):69–71.

Wilson, P. J. 1974. *Oscar: An Inquiry into the Nature of Sanity*. Vintage Books.

Winter, E. H. 1959. *Beyond the Mountains of the Moon: The Lives of Four Africans*. University of Illinois Press.

Wolfson, N. 1976. Speech Events and Natural Speech: Some Implications for Sociolinguistic Methodology. *Language in Society* 5(2):189–209.

5

Biography and the Social Sciences

Franco Ferrarotti

Is it not amazing, and in some ways simply wonderful, that in the culture most profoundly imbued with historicism there should have been born its most subtle and fatal critic? Certainly, Friedrich Nietzsche is a critic constantly hanging by the thread of contradiction, as any real critic should be, since he belongs by temperament and training to the race of tightrope walkers.

History is simultaneously useful and damaging. This duplicity suggested the title of a youthful, basic work by Nietzsche.[1] He starts his argument by noting the qualitative difference between animals and man – both "natural beings." Animal behavior is placidly repetitive and mechanical, set in motion only by natural instincts and thus without reflection or history. Human behavior is also inspired by instincts but by goals as well and is thus teleological. That is to say, man sets himself a goal, reflects critically on himself, accumulates memories, and on the basis of collective memory is able to formulate the meaning of his own decisions and evaluate them. The animal has only nature, while man has nature and history.

But what history? History is commonly understood as *historia rerum gestarum*, the history of deeds accomplished, of political leaders and their undertakings. However, according to Nietzsche, *an excess of history prevents the making of history.* Historical action, or action which breaks with the everyday and opens up new possibilities, is practicable only when it is not held up by a paralyzing excess of "historical sense." Hence, paradoxically, there is in historical action an initial ahistorical moment – even an antihistorical one – of which only someone deeply rooted in history is capable. In other words, only someone so certain of his own historical background as to represent it and translate it from reflex consciousness into a powerful natural instinct can formulate without pathos or uncertainty the decisions from which new historical phases are born. In this

---

Source: *Social Research*, vol. 50, no. 1, 1983, pp. 57–80.

sense, therefore, history is important as the collective memory of the past, critical awareness of the present, and operative premise for the future.

From men of action we move to the beings who "preserve and revere," to *antiquarian history*. History becomes in this way not only the history of great events and monuments, elite history, or historical history, but also history as the *collective memory of the everyday*.

> All that is small and limited, mouldy and obsolete, gains a worth and inviolability of its own from the conservative and reverent soul of the antiquary migrating into it, and building a secret nest there. The history of his town becomes the history of himself; he looks on the walls, the turreted gate, the town council, the fair, as an illustrated diary of his youth, and sees himself in it all – his strength, industry, desire, reason, faults and follies. "Here one could live," he says, "as one can live here now – and will go on living; for we are tough folk, and will not be uprooted in the night." And so, with his "we," he surveys the marvellous individual life of the past and identifies himself with the spirit of the house, the family and the city.[2]

With extraordinary insight, Nietzsche here presents the essential elements of cultural anthropology and social history or even, as may be expressed polemically, of history from below. This means that history is no longer conceived of restrictively as the sequence of great events, battles, treaties, dynastic marriages and so forth but rather as the cumulative result of the networks of relations into which, day after day, human groups enter of necessity. Individuals are destined to remain unknown, but together they make up the living substance, the real sociological "flesh" of the historical process. There comes to mind the ironic question of Bertolt Brecht: Who really built the pyramids? The pharaohs who gave them their names or the thousands of workers who carried the sand and the stones on their backs? Clearly, not all this basic framework can come into Nietzsche's essentially elitist perspective, but it is difficult not to grasp in it something much more than an unconscious prevision when he writes:

> ... and I hope history will not find its whole significance in general propositions, and regard them as its blossom and fruit. On the contrary, its real value lies in inventing ingenious variations on a probably commonplace theme, in raising the popular melody to a universal symbol and showing what a world of depth, power and beauty exists in it.[3]

History from Below

"Social" history, "oral" history, "new history," "psychohistory," history "from below," and life history demonstrate broad, interesting areas of convergence but *should not be confused.* They have in common the fact that they do not feel themselves to be obsessed and thus paralyzed by the question of what history really is and what it is not. This question has weighed heavily for decades on the historiographic tradition, which betrayed all too clearly the anxiety of preserving in all its purity a conception and practice of history limited to elites, political and at the outside intellectual. This, however, excluded on principle everything linked to the material needs and daily survival of vast human masses.

French historiography, which has pioneered history from below, is clearly not impeded or slowed by late-idealist or ideal-Marxist vetoes. It is capable of tackling subjects which are apparently peripheral but really basic for a synchronic model and for the multidimensional reconstruction of sociohistorical fragments – such as the history of madness, of climate, of attitudes to death, of public festivities, of rural society, and so forth. In other words, history from below is the history of the everyday, the clarification and interpretation of life practices, not relived sentimentally as mere popular folklore but critically rethought as psychologically reassuring visions of the world, and at the same time as constellations of cognitive values, linked to and verified by the experience of life each day.

Life History as Method. The conscious critical adoption of life history as the basic method of sociological analysis is not simple, nor can it hastily be considered a convenient short-cut, as it has sometimes been interpreted by students of "community," socially as generous as they are culturally ingenuous. Only by way of a long series of intellectual experiences and practical tests in the field have I arrived, in my current phase of development, at the point of confronting the problem of the *autonomy of the biographical method* and its decisive character in the future of research in the social sciences. Interested as I was, in the 1950s, in the human consequences of technical and economic–industrial development, I then began to collect life histories and autobiographical documents in some Italian communities which seemed to be profoundly affected by the process of industrialization.[4]

At first, this research concerned Northern Italy for the most part, and the effects on the agricultural community around a "mass production" plant, rapidly expanding as was Olivetti in those years. Later, I sponsored and carried out similar research in the South. It was my intention – or rather, I nurtured the hope – that by means of the research I might find a positive solution to the deficiencies of sociological studies carried out only on the basis of rigidly structured questionnaires. For some time I had the impression that research of that kind, although very rigorous from the formal methodological point of view, generally ended up by regarding as resolved problems which in reality had not even been touched upon. From the time of my visits to Chicago, and long, impassioned discussions with Leo Strauss, the immortal author of *Natural Right and History* and *Thoughts on Machiavelli*, it seemed clear to me that the world of values not only should not escape the attention of the social sciences in the name of a raw, fragmentary "factuality" of a paleopositivist kind, but that shared experiences and values were their living thread and privileged object.

However, I did not manage to see with the necessary conceptual clarity how this implied a reversal of the prevailing methodological positions, which unconsciously quantified the qualitative, and I failed also to see how this reversal would not take place and would be destined to remain an ambiguous prologue if a break in the method of conceptual expression and the practice of the social sciences did not come about. I could understand that life history was an often valuable contribution to directing research, but I did not realize that the ancillary function to which it was relegated did not simply conform to the canons of an objectivity still conceived of in grossly naturalistic terms. In addition it corresponded precisely to the wish of the researchers not to take up a position, and their logical refusal to situate themselves politically and socially, so as not to destroy their chances in the market. In this sense, I must acknowledge that the way in which life history was presented as a method of "field-work" in my *Trattato di sociologia*[5] is not in itself erroneous but, from the position my reflections on these themes attained, is basically incomplete and insufficient.

I was especially struck by the *synthetic character* of the autobiographical account as a *practice of life*. However, at the same time I felt the danger of *literariness*. That is, I was held back and tormented by the incontestable fact that the individual biography was, after all, an account of a unique and irreducible destiny. I could not see the nomothetic elements present in the descriptive. This had a reductive effect on my manner of viewing life history. At most, I recognized in it an integrative function which was in the strict sense unverifiable. I regarded it as useful as an instrument of *background research* – a usefulness to which today too I attribute a fundamental importance – but I could not grasp the basic elements of what I now call the *dialectic of the social* and which lies essentially in the complex, non-*a priori* determinable relation between *givenness* and the *lived*. Certainly, the structural frame, givenness, was primary in my concerns, but I could not understand that by itself givenness understood as *reified factualness*, a fact closed on itself and distanced from the living, is nothing. It cannot even be analyzed by the social sciences as their real object, without lapsing into the fetishism of elementary empirical data held to be theoretically autonomous and self-explanatory, as if truly the *facts spoke for themselves*. Like a clumsy pathologist, by error going into the operating theater, I conscientiously dismembered the living with the same meticulous care with which he would set about the autopsy of a corpse.

Biography and Context. For this reason, I attempted very carefully to connect the individual biography with the global, structural characteristics of the given, lived, historical situation. My problem was always that of the human and social consequences of the process of industrialization. This is the same problem that I was later to identify as the problematic relation between technicoformal rationality and substantial rationality: what Weber, from the depths of his age-old pessimism, called "material rationality," as befitted an orphan of Bismarck, an elitist *malgré lui*, concerning the practical possibility of formulating in a politically valid manner – that is, intersubjectively binding – common, collective ends.

In this perspective, biographies had the goal – heuristically speaking – of illuminating the transition between the peasant world and technically oriented industrial society. I held that through biographies "transition" was no longer a mere abstract category, a purely analytical term. It was personified and so to speak fleshed out by specific types whose biographical elements provided sociological material in its particular nature. However, the material provided by biographies was always only material I considered to be illustrative. In the *Trattato di sociologia*, I did not go beyond the notion of life history as endowed with a primarily integrating function as regards quantitative data. The examples I quoted then did not depart from the traditional type of monograph, moving between the rigorous inventory of anthropological authority and what is called today in the United States "investigative journalism." I was well aware of the ecological studies of the Chicago School of the 1930s,[6] but I did not omit the basic research of Frédéric Le Play on family budgets, and I also spent a little time on the Italian contributions, though these were still very undecided between an ingenuous populist protest, social documentation, and evocative history.

Despite the limitations which appear today in certain formulations in the *Trattato* – limitations connected primarily with the schematic, dichotomous opposition between the descriptive moment and nomothetic standardization – I think that from then on the importance of life history was indisputable. As I argued, this was because "it allows us to move to analysis in depth," just as in its whole scope there appeared to me to be its characteristic difficulty "because it demands an immediate contact, one of reciprocal confidence between the object of research and the researcher." The discovery of the interactionist relation implied by this "confidence" as basic and specific in life history must consequently be seen to be extraordinarily productive in shaping a critical sociology.

Autonomy of the Biographical Method. I maintain that the discussion of the biographical method and its autonomy should be reopened. The use of biography in the social sciences, despite the particular favor shown to it for some time, has not exhausted all its possibilities and indeed has even retarded the advance of the conceptual, and practical, awareness that life history as a method in the full sense necessarily implies a break as regards current methods, and that in addition this break rests and is manifested on the basis of a systematic uncertainty in its present use. This involves a rigorous accounting as regards:

(1) The *Erlebnis*, especially in Wilhelm Dilthey's theorization, as the possibility of "reliving" existential and historical experience in terms of "interior interconnection," not assured by reference to a psychologizing subjectivism and voluntarist idealism.

BIOGRAPHY AND THE SOCIAL SCIENCES 63

(2) *Verstehende Soziologie*, Weber's "understanding sociology," whose attempt, so widely misunderstood by interpreters of a more-or-less-strict historicist persuasion, to construct a synchronic or "ideal-typical" model – only with diachronic historical materials – can be appreciated. This however does not escape the well-known deficiencies of formalism and methodological individualism.
(3) Intuitionist currents, formerly harshly criticized by Max Weber: whoever wants a sermon should go to a monastery; whoever wants visions should go to the cinema.
(4) The minimalist use, ancillary and illustrative, pioneered by Thomas and Znaniecki in their classic work *The Polish Peasant in Europe and America*, confined by them however in the framework of a function broadly illustrative of socio-anthropological considerations *separately* gathered and analyzed.
(5) The *dépassement* suggested by Daniel Bertaux,[7] which falls under the attack of Robert K. Merton as "empathic participationism," essentially acritical.

Individual and Group

Traditional biographical method prefers secondary materials ("more *objective*") to primary ones, or those collected directly by the researcher in contact with the subjects of the study, systematically bringing the secondary to the primary. Despite this epistemological abdication, this method retains the value of breaking with traditional methodologies: it is a new world, and fragments of society long crushed by a kind of formal, sociological encirclement and suffocation break the barrier and force themselves on our knowledge. However, the biographical method does not realize and indeed betrays the greater part of its heuristic potential when it accepts being a marginal methodology of social history and a sociology in search of a "concrete shell." The elementary condition for a renewal of biographical method runs by way of a reversal of this tendency. *We must abandon the privilege accorded to secondary biographical materials.* We must bring back to the very heart of the biographical method primary materials and their *explosive subjectivity*. We are not only interested in the objective richness of primary biographical material; we are chiefly concerned with its *subjective fullness of meaning* in the context of complex interpersonal communication – reciprocal between the narrator and the observer.

Here we are approaching the central problem. *How can the subjectivity inherent in autobiography become scientific knowledge?* If the biographical method decides no longer to dodge and renounce the subjectivity and the absolute historicity of its material, in what manner can it ground its heuristic value?

Let us be satisfied with tracing the general, hypothetical lines of a reply.

Every autobiographical narrative recounts, according to a horizontal or vertical section, a human practice. Now if, as Marx put it in the sixth thesis on

Feuerbach, "the human essence ... in its reality is the ensemble of the social relations," any individual human practice is a synthetic activity, an active totalization of a whole social context. *Life is a practice which appropriates social relations (social structures), internalizes and retransforms them into psychological structures for its de- and restructuring activity.* Every human life reveals itself through its less generalizable aspects as a vertical synthesis of a social history. All behavior, every individual act, appears in its most individual forms as a horizontal synthesis of a social structure. How many biographies are needed to arrive at a sociological "truth," and what biographical material will be most representative and give us first some general truths? Perhaps these questions have no meaning, because — and in full consciousness we emphasize this point — our social system is completely within each of our actions, our dreams, fantasies, accomplishments, and behavior, and the history of this system is completely within the history of our individual life.

In the strict meaning of the term, we "imply" the social through a synthetic interpolation which de- and restructures it, endowing it at the same time with psychological forms. However, because it is the product of a synthetic practice, the relation which links an action to a social structure is not linear, and the close relationship which runs from a social history and a life is certainly not a mechanical determinism. We must abandon the determinist model which directed the attempts to interpret the individual through sociological frameworks, borrowed from bad textbooks of a naturalistic science which the most alert scientists themselves had already abandoned. The individual is not an epiphenomenon of society. In relation to the structures and history of a society, he is an active pole, and he impresses himself on it as a synthetic practice. Far from reflecting the social, the individual appropriates it, mediates it, filters and retranslates it by projecting it in another dimension which then becomes that of his subjectivity. He cannot break away from it, but he does not suffer it passively, and indeed he reinvents it every second.

Here Sartre's formulation seems to me the only possible one, at least in the sense of a suggestive literary example. Man — and I would add, man invented by the bourgeois revolution — is the singular universe. Through his synthetic practice he singularizes in his actions the universality of a social structure. By means of his de- and retotalizing activity, he individualizes collective social history. Here we are, therefore, at the heart of the epistemological paradox with which the biographical method presents us. What an action or the history of a life has in common with the actions and the histories of other individuals — the general perspective which alone could be scientific knowledge — cannot be compared with everything this action or this history contains which is absolutely specific. Uniqueness will never be the grounds for science but an unexplained, prescientific residuum, chance. A social anthropology which considers each person as the individualized and active synthesis of a society eliminates the distinction between the general and the particular in an individual. If we are, if every individual represents, a *singular* reappropriation of the social and historical universal which surrounds him, we *can know* the social by departing from the point of the irreducible specificity of individual practice.

From the restoration of subjectivity to science: what makes an action unique or a history individual presents itself as a means of access – often the only possible one – to the scientific knowledge of a social system. This is not a linear path, and it is often cryptic, requiring the invention of keys and new methods in order for it to be pursued.

Biography and Society. The anthropology which we have just sketched legitimizes our attempt to *read a society through a biography*. It subsequently legitimates the heuristic value of a biography all of whose epistemological specificity should be preserved. However, sociological biography is not only an account of lived experiences but also a social *microrelation*. The most solitary autobiographical monologue represents no less than an attempt at communication and implies all the same the ghost of an interlocutor. Now the sociologist who stimulates, who collects, an oral account is a real interlocutor who *impersonates* a neutral, absent ghost. We distrust this wizardry and restore to the biographical interview all its consistency as *social interaction*. The biographical accounts we use are not monologues delivered before an observer reduced to the condition of the human support of a tape recorder. Every biographical interview is a complex, social interaction, a role system, a system of expectations, orders, norms and implicit values, often also of sanctions. Every biographical interview hides tensions, conflicts, and power hierarchies. It appeals to charisma and to the social power of scientific institutions as regards the subaltern classes, and evokes their spontaneous defensive reaction. They do not recount their own lives and their own *Erlebnisse* to a tape: they tell them to an individual. The form and the *content* of a biographical account change according to the interviewer. They depend on the *interaction which represents the social terrain of communication*. They are situated within a relational interaction. The interviewer is never absent even if he simulates absence. He is always reciprocal even if apparently he rejects every reciprocity. The illusion of objectivity negates the interactional quality of the biographical account: if at times it acknowledges this, it does so in order to exorcise its operative role and to relegate it to the margins, among the subjective residues before which the objectivity of the human sciences shows itself always to be sullied. This concerns, then, the restoration of the biographical account to the fullness of its relational nature and its communicative intentionality. We shall then define another of its basic characteristics, possibly the most unrecognized, that *every individual act is the totalization of a social system.*

Every account of an action or a life is at the same time an act, the totalizing synthesis of lived experiences and a social interaction. A biographical account is not at all a news report; it is a social action by means of which an individual synthetically retotalizes his life (biography) and social interaction in progress (the interview) in the midst of an account-interaction. Does the biographical account retell a life? We shall rather argue that it recounts a present interaction by way of the course of a life. There is no greater biographical truth in an oral, spontaneous account than in a newspaper, an autobiography, or in certain memories. We cannot acquire this biographical truth simply by loading ourselves with the interaction truth which fills out the account. The sociological reading of a biography moves by way of the hermeneutics of the social action which reinvents the biography by telling it in the framework of an interaction – an interaction which the observer must not evade and must live in an active manner right to the end.

The sociological analysis of a biography takes us to the hermeneutics of an interaction. Here we are, therefore, at the *clinical pole* which appears to characterize knowledge of the individual in the human sciences. "It is the transposition of the clinical situation to different disciplines which deal with man which cause explicitly to reappear the problem of knowledge of individual *contents*."[8]

> The clinical situation places patient and therapist in an immediate relationship, the observer and the observed. By "immediate relationship" we must understand a relationship not wholly conceptualized which develops at the outset confusedly the relationships between the one and the other, in such a way that the situation which becomes stabilized cannot correctly be described as a totally asymmetrical encounter between an active subject and a passive object, but rather as a couple whose partners play alternating roles.... Spontaneously, the clinical situation is experienced through the magical, mythical means of communication. The central epistemological problem is how to explain the development of this situation within a range of authentic knowledge, without degenerating either into an irrational technique of mechanical objectification or into a practice of enchantment.[9]

These are articulations between the observer and the observed within a reciprocal interaction. Scientific knowledge demands a hermeneutics of this interaction. The biographical account is perceived as social action. The biographical interview seems to me a perfect example of the clinical pole of the human sciences.

Every biographical account sends us back to the de- and restructuring of an act or individual history viewed as the horizontal or vertical section of a social system. This consequently gives us: (a) a totalizing image of a social system, from the social space wherein is sketched out sociality, and where social action is analyzed (history of a life, description of an action), and (b) a totalization under way (a biographical account) as the active synthesis of the totalizing image and the interaction present where it is situated. In biography, society, perpetually being born, coexists with structured society. Social action in being coexists with reified social action. *The biographical account owes its immense, unexplored, theoretical importance to this basic sociological ambiguity, and also its largely ignored or betrayed heuristic fertility.*

Human Practice as Totalizing Practice. The act as the active synthesis of a social system, and individual history as social history totalized from a practice: these two propositions imply a heuristic passage which sees the universal through the singular, which seeks the objective by hinging on the subjective, and which discovers the general through the particular In my view, the biographical method invalidates the universal validity of the Aristotelian proposition "There is no science which is not science of the general." No. There can be science of the particular and the subjective, and this science arrives by other paths – paths which often seem paradoxical – at a knowledge of the general. But Aristotle's argument goes further. Indeed it rejoins the formal-discursive logic which is the model of Western scientific thought. The critique of the hegemony of the general in scientific axioms conceals a critique of the hegemony of the "concept," of the process of abstraction which creates it, the deductive threads which make it plain, and the inductive fabric which together test them. It involves the "tree" of logical, linear propagation.

Let us go still further. The notion of totalizing human practice (which I take from Sartre, but which we find still more rigorously formulated in Tarde and Simmel, to speak only of sociologists) refuses to consider human behavior (actions, biographies) as the passive reflexes of a conditioning which comes from the general – that is, from society. On the contrary, this behavior expresses a synthetic practice which de- and restructures social determinisms. It is not the mechanical result of external influences, though these are appropriated through a synthetic activity which retranslates them into individual actions which are not reducible to their determining factors. Certainly we cannot linger over these analyses (we refer to the whole tradition at their root). However, we do emphasize their main characteristic. Man is not the passive object which mechanistic determinism claims. The terrain of each action or human behavior witnesses the *active copresence* of external conditioning and human practice, which filters and internalizes them while it totalizes them. In this area, nothing is passive, a simple reflection, or an epiphenomenon. The mechanistic and determinist model cannot account for the doubly dialectical role (negation and negation of the negation) intrinsic to human practice. The rejection of the dichotomy between the active subject and the passive object in the field of human behavior extends to that manner of behavior peculiar to scientific intentionality and to its object, individualized human behavior. Here, too, there are not an object which knows and one which is known. The observer is strangely, ridiculously, involved in the area of his object. The latter, far from being passive, continually modifies his own behavior as a function of the behavior of the observer. This circular feedback process makes any presumption of objective knowledge absurd. Knowledge does not have the "other" as its object; its object is the unforeseeable (in its specific forms, *a priori*) interaction, reciprocal between observer and observed. Thus it becomes a dual knowledge through the *intersubjectivity of an interaction.* The deeper and more objective the knowledge, the greater will be the integral and intimate objectivity. The observer will not know his object through and through – and we emphasize *scientifically* – save at the expense of being known by it in an equally profound manner. Knowledge then becomes what sociological methodology has always wished to avoid becoming: a *risk*. Even, it is the "reflectiveness" of the pupil in the friendly pupil of whom Plato spoke in the *Phaedrus*.

The specific nature of the biographical method implies the transcendence of the logico-formal framework and the mechanistic model characteristic of established scientific epistemology. If we wish to use the heuristic potential of biography sociologically, without betraying its essential characteristics (subjectivity and historicity), we must project ourselves *d'emblée* out of the classical epistemological framework. We must seek elsewhere the epistemological foundations of the biographical method, in a *dialectical reason* capable of understanding the reciprocal synthetic praxis which governs the interaction between an individual and a social system. We must seek them through the construction of nonmechanistic, nondeterminist heuristic models – models characterized by a permanent feedback of all the elements in them, "anthropomorphic" models which only a nonanalytical, nonformal logic can grasp. This, then, is a dialectical reason, historical and extraneous to any "occasionalism"; it is capable of an approach toward specificity – "the specific logic of the specific object" (Marx) – of not reducing the concept to a conceptual construct and of rising "from the abstract to the concrete" (Marx).

This dialectical reason does not claim hegemony. It has nothing to do with *Diamat* or with the Engels of the *Dialectics of Nature*. It willingly acknowledges for formal logic and deterministic models an axiomatic role in the sciences of nature. It acknowledges for them a role in the sciences of man where these see themselves as sciences of the general. However, when it is a matter of not sending the individual back into the sphere of the unknown and of chance, and when we are dealing with the consideration of human practice, only dialectical reason allows us scientifically to understand an action, to reconstruct the processes which make behavior the active synthesis of a social system, and to interpret the objectivity in a fragment of social history by starting from the nonevaded subjectivity of an individual history. Only dialectical reason allows us to attain the universal and the general (society) by emphasizing the individual and the singular (man)

The specific character of biographies reaches to the discussion of the assimilation of all sciences to the science of nature. If, epistemologically, we wish to respect biography, we are forced to admit a radical gap between nomothetic intentionality and descriptive intentionality, a break which implies having recourse to two different reasonings. Biography revives the *Methodenstreit*. It thus becomes the single occasion for reopening a more profound discussion on the logical, epistemological, and materiological foundations of sociology. It is also the occasion for a new reflection on the foundations of the social.

The Social Nature of the Individual. A man is never an individual. It would be better to call him a *singular universe*. He is "totalized" and at the same time universalized by his epoch: he retotalizes it by reproducing himself in it as singularity. Universal by way of the singular universality of human history, singular by way of the universalizing singularity of his projects, he demands to be studied simultaneously in the two senses.

We must find an appropriate method. The general lines of Sartre's regressive–progressive method for a social science of biography are well known: the horizontal and vertical reading of the biography and the social system, a heuristic movement of coming and going from biography to the social system, and vice versa. The fusion of this double movement means the exhaustive reconstruction of the reciprocal "totalizations" which express the dialectical relation between society and a specific individual. The integral knowledge of one man thus becomes the integral knowledge of another. Social collective and singular universal mutually illustrate each other. The attempt to understand biography in its total uniqueness on the basis of the sixth thesis on Feuerbach becomes that of the interpretation of a social system.

As a difficult synthesis of a structural and an historical approach, this methodology does not turn down the contribution of nomothetic knowledge. Indeed, it even requires it, though in order to integrate it in a heuristic movement into hermeneutic, nonlinear models which appeal to dialectical, not formal, reason. In the biographical method we shall find the classical methodologies of sociology. However, they serve us as a backdrop, indispensable but analytical instruments, and thus relatively marginal to a central synthesis which attempts to restore the synthetic unity of a social system from the reciprocal, *active* articulation between a society and individual practice.

This nonanalytical method poses additional important problems. First, how is this double movement between the individual and the collective poles of any social terrain structured? What are the phases and stages which mediate between the two poles? By way of what *mediations* does a specific individual totalize a society, and a social system project itself toward an individual? The second problem: with its constant reference to individual practice, is not the epistemological perspective of the biographic method not perhaps implying a nominalist, atomized conception of the social as it establishes some *series* of interactions (the "social" of Tarde, Simmel, Von Wiese, Moreno, and even Sartre)? Third problem: does not our approach to biographic method not perhaps negate any practical possibility of its use? If the model of good sociological utilization of biography is the 2500 or so pages of *L'Idiot de la famille*, is there not perhaps a risk of provoking the sociologists into silence, or rather causing their anxious return to classical methodologies?

These are logically heterogeneous problems, but they go back to what Sartre called the "problem of mediations."

> Valéry is a petit bourgeois intellectual – of that there is no doubt. But any petit bourgeois intellectual is not Valéry. The heuristic insufficiency of Marxism (and I should add of the traditional biographic method) is contained in these two phrases. To grasp the process which

produces the person and his product within a given class and society in a given historical moment lacks in Marxism (and in sociology!) a *hierarchy of mediations.*[10]

It is necessary to "*find the mediations* which would allow us to generate the singular concrete, the life, the real, dated struggle by setting out from the *general* contradictions of the productive forces and relations of production."[11] Each individual does not totalize a global society directly. He does so through the mediation of his immediate social context, and the limited groups of which he is part, since these groups in turn are *active* social agents which totalize *their* context, etc. In the same way, society totalizes each specific individual by means of the mediating institutions which totalize it ever more precisely as regards the individual in question.

The Field of Social Mediations. The simultaneous heuristic passage from biography to society and vice versa implies consequently a *theory* and a typology of the *social mediations* which make up the active fields of reciprocal totalization. As Sartre said, we must establish a hierarchy of these spaces for mediation. We must define their functions, and their methods of incidence on individuals of whom they are part. We must also read them from "the other side," that is, by setting out from the perspective of the individual who in turn synthesizes them horizontally (his immediate social context, the context of his context, etc.) and vertically (the chronological sequence of his impact on the different spaces of mediation – the family, infant peer groups, and those of school age, etc.). Above all, we must identify the most important spaces, those which serve as pivots between structures and individuals, the social fields where the singularizing practice of man and the universalizing effort of a social system confront each other most directly. What are these spaces?

> At the level of relations of production and of sociopolitical structures, the singular individual is conditioned by his *human relations.* There is no doubt that this conditioning, in its first, general truth, does not take one back to the "conflict of the productive forces with relations of production." However, all of this is not lived so simply.... The individual lives, and knows more or less clearly what his condition is, through his membership of groups. The greater part of these groups is local, defined, and immediately given.[12]

We may therefore reply: these are restricted or primary groups. Families, peer groups at work, in the neighborhood, in school classes, in barracks, etc. – all these groups participate at the same time in the psychological dimension of their members and in the structural dimension of a social system. By means of the de- and restructuring of the context which it carries out, group practice mediates and actively reproduces the social totality in its formal and informal microdocuments, its lines of power and communication, its norms and sanctions, and its methods and networks of affective interaction, etc. The group itself becomes itself in turn, and simultaneously the object of the synthetic practice of its members. *Each of them reads the group from his individual perspective.* Each of them builds himself psychologically as an "I," starting from *his* reading of the group of which he is part. The primary group is shown also to be the basic moment of mediation between the social and the individual. It defines itself as the social terrain where the totalization of his social context, and the totalization which all group members employ individually within the group totalization, coexist indissolubly. The field offers itself as a space for articulation where the public and the private are reciprocally joined together and disappear into one another, along with the structures and the "I," the social and the psychological, the universal and the singular. It is the privileged place of the *singular universal* which seems to be the protagonist of the biographical method as we understand it.

Within the system of mediation which enunciates the interrelation between a biography and a social structure, the primary group occupies a crucial pivotal space. However, if these are the role, the meaning, and the heuristic expectancy of the primary group, why do we not make that the chief, direct protagonist of the biographical method? *Why not substitute for natural biography the biography of a primary group as a basic heuristic unit for a renewed biographic method?*

The Biography of the Primary Group. This idea is less far-fetched than it may seem. For example, it gives an answer to two other problems we indicated above. Every theory of the bases of the social or of sociological method which starts from any social atom (the individual, elementary interaction) falls into nominalism, into an atomist logic and social psychology. The majority of theories of social action have stalled at this very point. Now, I believe that an approach which stands resolutely beside dialectical reason can avoid these dangers, even if it is based on individual practice. Sociological nominalism is no longer conceivable where a concept no longer possesses the form of abstraction typical of formal logic. Besides, how could nonlinear models of interpretation of the social conform to the linear series of atomistic sociology? There remains the real danger of psychologistic reduction, but in any case the choice of the primary group as basic heuristic unit takes us at once beyond any risk of nominalism, atomism, and psychologism. This is because, if we use a correct interpretative model, a primary group cannot be reduced to the network of its elementary interactions. At every second it overcomes these, and emerges as a *social totality*, defined not by its "internal system" of psychosocial relations, but by the system of strictly social functions which root it in its context. As for the problem of the operational potential of the biographical approach we propose here, the abandonment of the individual in favor of the group does not eliminate all the difficulties but nonetheless considerably diminishes them. Taken as the due point of departure, the heuristic coming and going, the group allows us to eliminate the most complex stage of the whole biographical method – the understanding of the infinitely rich totalization which an individual uses in his context and which he expresses through the cryptic forms of a biographical account. Recourse to biographies of primary groups lets us avoid this initial step. It allows us to situate ourselves at the start not at the level of the individual in a situation – the level dominated by the psychological dimension – but at that of the immediately social aspect of the primary group. We know hardly anything about the individual as the "ensemble of social relations," of which Marx spoke. The inattentiveness of scientific psychology, and its indifference in the face of the social, offer us no intrapsychic or relational model of the social individual. We know much more about groups. Certainly, the rejection of deterministic models and the idea of the group as active totalization of its context make useless and misguided most of our knowledge about groups. However, we possess models which can be rethought, and hypotheses which can be reintegrated into the framework of a different logic and heuristic intention. With groups, we are immediately in the social (a social which does not exclude the individual), and we are not working in the void of a field which has still to be cultivated (the singular universal). We know where to go and how to search.

The Individual Is Not a Social Atom. The biographic method has almost always turned to the individual. This choice of the banality of the evident hides a gross misunderstanding. This is because the individual is not, as has too often been believed, a social atom and thus the most elementary heuristic unit of sociology. Simmel saw this clearly at the beginning of his *Soziologie.* Far from being the simplest element of the social, its irreducible atom, the individual is a complex synthesis of social elements. He does not ground the social but is its sophisticated product. Paradoxically, the authentic element of the social in my view is the primary group, the apparently complex system which in reality is the most simple object for the sphere of sociology. We measure and identify, by relation to this relatively stable *Grundkörper*, all the mobile, rich, fluctuating complexity between multiple, contradictory totalizations which characterize the so-called elementary interactions and the growth of sociality in relation to this *Grundkörper*. We measure the giddy, dense and complex synthesis which an individual represents from the point of view of sociology. If we accept the individual as "register" of sociological knowledge, why should the primary group not also constitute the register of the biographic method? If our working hypotheses are valid, the renewal of the biographic method requires a new theory of social action. This theory would no longer be based on the action of one or more individual agents but on that of a *social totality*, the restricted group read by means of "anthropomorphic" models, nonmechanistic ones.

The biography of the primary group poses new problems in its turn. How can we obtain the biography of a group? Does it involve juxtaposing or crosstabulating the individual perspectives which its members have of the group and its history? Will it not be necessary to establish a continuous interaction with the group in its totality? Again, how will the dialectic, taken between the totalization the group makes of its context and the totalization each member of the group makes of this totalization, be identified? By what mediations can we integrate into our sociological perspective the basic models and techniques of observation set out by psychology, psychoanalysis, and family and group therapy? A whole body of theoretical reflection awaits us, in order that we can one day make the journey from the most simple to the most complex: the discovery and identification of the *specific (historical) terms of the individual's sociality*.

Notes

1. Friedrich Nietzsche, "The Use and Abuse of History," in *Thoughts out of Season, Part III*, translated by Adrian Collins (Edinburgh: Foulis, 1910).
2. *Ibid.*, p. 24.
3. *Ibid.*, pp. 53–54.
4. I have written extensively on industrialization as a global social process; see my *Sindacato, industria, società* (Turin: UTET, 1970).
5. Cf. my *Trattato di sociologia* (Turin: UTET, 1968).
6. For example, Clifford R. Shaw, *The Jack-Roller: A Delinquent Boy's Own Story* (Chicago: University of Chicago Press, 1930) and Paul C. Cressey, *The Taxi-Dance Hall* (Chicago: University of Chicago Press, 1932).
7. Cf. Daniel Bertaux, *Destins personnels et structure de classe* (Paris: Presses Universitaires de France, 1977), but especially the report presented at the 1978 world sociological congress at Uppsala.
8. Gilles Gaston Granger, *Pensée formelle et sciences de l'homme* (Paris: Aubier-Montaigne, 1968), p. 189.
9. *Ibid.*, p. 188.
10. Jean-Paul Sartre, *Critique de la raison dialectique* (Paris: Gallimard, 1960), p. 44.
11. *Ibid.*, p. 45.
12. *Ibid.*, p. 49. Sociology, therefore, as a science not of the reified social but of "social action," or the social in action, as Weber intuited (*soziales Handeln*), widely misunderstood by his commentators, old and new.

PART TWO
VARIETIES OF RESEARCH INTERVIEWS: TYPES AND MODES

PART TWO

Varieties of Research Interviews: Types and Modes

Nigel Fielding

Interviews divide into types (eg., standardized) and modes (e.g., telephone interviews). Bogardus [6]† discusses interaction in non-research interviews, revealing communicative effects of participants' purposes. Advocates of standardized interviews, primarily used in surveys, have long-debated proponents of non-standardized interviews, chiefly used in qualitative research. Lazarsfeld [7] suggests common ground, and discusses when to use open-ended and closed questions. Fifty years later, Beatty [8] maintains researchers remain divided. Interviewers' 'humanizing' role was curtailed following evidence questioning rapport (Weiss (1968) found confiding respondents' answers least valid, and Goudy and Potter (1975) that rapport did not improve data).

Schober and Conrad's research [9] supports Lazarsfeld's 'tools for the job' perspective. Both standardised and non-standardised types produce high accuracy when respondents are clear how questions relate to them. When they are not, non-standardised methods are more accurate, but take longer. Pawson [10] criticises polarisation into structured *versus* unstructured types, incorporating a realist theory of explanation into interview design. But Hamilton-Smith and Hopkins (1998) encountered problems in Pawson's method.

Comparing modes, Woltman, Turner and Bushery (1980) found personal interviews collected fuller response than telephone interviewing. Jordan *et al* (1980) found telephone interviewing produced less data, and more evasion and extremeness (but see Marin and Oss-Marin 1989). Goyder (1985) shows declining interview response relative to questionnaires, but when Campanelli and Thomas (1994) compared these methods to recover work histories, questionnaires missed 25% of labour force events; Schober and Conrad's trade-off between completeness and time investment reappears.

Self-administration can help. Aquilino (1994) found admitting drugtaking most likely in personal interviews including self-administered questions, less so without. Tourangeau and Smith (1996) and Tourangeau, Rasinski and Jobe (1997) found computer-assisted modes with and without self-administration had similar response rates on sex topics but self-administration reduced gender disparity in partner numbers.

We now profile each mode. On individual interviews, Gorden [11] highlights social psychological dimensions. Schuman [12] uses the tale of a qualitative interviewer to present survey interview fundamentals. Suchman and Jordan [13] argue survey interviews suppress interactional resources mediating interpretational uncertainties. Johnson and Delamater (1976) confirm these resources' value, finding interviewers deviate from schedules to get sensitive information.

Merton and Kendall's seminal article [14] presents 'focussed interviews'. Featuring non-direction, specificity, range and depth, the method seeks subjective experience to test and derive hypotheses. Written after focus groups blossomed, Merton [15] confesses surprise at their success. Oriented to hypotheses, focussed interviews cannot be conclusive on distributions but focus groups are often treated as if they are. Bogardus [16] establishes enduring issues in group discussions: disclosure, dynamics and procedural problems. For Alderfer and Smith [17] group discussions reveal dominance patterns and differing cognitions. Thompson and Demerath (1952) note that groups encourage disclosure and precision. Chandler (1954) and Banks (1957) found consistency in individual and group responses but a tendency to toe the group line. On group composition, Lovin-Smith and Brody (1989) confirm that males interrupt females more than vice versa. Supportive interruptions occur most in single-sex groups.

Morgan [18] introduces 'focus groups', the commonest group format. Careful design and combination with other methods maximise advantages (see also Morgan 1995). Kitzinger [19] illustrates focus groups' complementary and argumentative benefits. Agar and MacDonald [20] found focus groups uncovered new information but it could only be understood with interview data. Other literature includes Sweeney, Soutar and Hausknecht (1997), introducing online focus group technology. Dreachslin (1998) considers group composition in conditions of increasing diversity. Desvouges and Frey (1989) found group discussions useful in pre-testing surveys.

Developed for crime investigations, cognitive interviewing is introduced by Geiselman *et al* ([21]; see also Gieselman *et al* 1984). Gerber and Wellens (1997) used it to test survey questions, and Kohnken *et al* (1999) found it increased correctly-recalled details and, somewhat less so, incorrect details.

Cavan [22] discusses tracing how attitudes develop using life history interviews. Faraday and Plummer [23] stress the method's role in generating concepts. Bertaux [24] profiles procedure and draws contrasts with statistical research. Subsidiary literature includes Bertaux and Kohli (1984) on the method's uses. Blackman (1992) considers implications of life histories being read by their subjects, who speak through them to their community (also see Chambon, 1995; Bowes, Dar and Sim, 1997). Freedman, Thornton and Camburn (1988) offer a 'life history calendar' to collect life-course data. Biographical Interpretive Method is exemplified by Hollway and Jefferson [25]. Developed in interviews with Holocaust survivors, BIM elicits narratives non-directively (see also Rosenthal 1993).

Comparing telephone interviews, personal interviews and questionnaires, Ibsen and Ballweg [26] review sampling and validity issues. Smit and Dijkstra (1991) found refusal depended on how much information telephone interviewers provided. Aquilino and Lo Sciuto (1990) report similar drugtaking admissions from telephone and personal interviewing. Keeter (1995) estimates non-coverage error. De Leeuw, Hox and Snijkers [27] assess data quality in computer-assisted interviews. Freeman (1983) maintains Computer Assisted Telephone Interviewing increases control over data collection (see also Shanks, Nicholls and Freeman, 1981). Doreian, Woodard and Kuo (1995) profile Computer-Assisted Personal Interviewing (see also Martin, O'Muircheartaigh and Curtice, 1993). Murray and Sixsmith [28] note advantages of online interviewing, including data quality, but also sampling and deception problems. Gaiser (1997) presents an online focus group method.

For Lather [29] feminist interview methods relate to a wider feminist project empowering the researched. Kasper's [30] example of feminist interviewing emphasises 'subjects' as experts and setting stereotypes aside. Elsewhere Cook and Fonow (1986) see feminist interviewing as challenging concepts of objectivity.

Note

†. Refers to the article number in this collection.

References

Aquilino, W.S. (1994) 'Interview Mode Effects in Surveys of Drug and Alcohol Use', *Public Opinion Quarterly*, 58(2), 210–240.

Aquilino, W.S. and L. Lo Sciuto (1990) 'Effects of Interview Mode on Self-Reported Drug Use', *Public Opinion Quarterly*, 54(3), 362–395.

Banks, J. (1957) 'The Group Discussion as an Interview Technique', *Sociological Review*, 5(1), 75–84.

Bertaux, D. and M. Kohli (1984) 'The Life Story Approach: A Continental View', *Annual Review of Sociology*, 10, 215–237.

Blackman, M.B. (1992) 'The Afterlife of Life History', *Journal of Narrative and Life History*, 2(1), 1–9.

Bogardus, E. (1926) 'The Group Interview', *Journal of Applied Sociology*, 10, 372–82.

Bowes, A., N. Dar and D. Sim (1997) 'Life Histories in Housing Research', *Quality & Quantity*, 31(2), 109–125.

Campanelli, P. and R. Thomas (1994) 'Practical Issues in Collecting Lifetime Work Histories in Surveys', *Bulletin de Méthodologie Sociologique*, 42, 114–136.

Cavan, R. (1929) 'Topical Summaries of Current Literature: Interviewing for Life History Material', *American Journal of Sociology*, 15, 100–115.

Chambon, A.S. (1995) 'Life History as Dialogical Activity', *Current Sociology*, 43(2–3), 125–135.

Chandler, M. (1954) 'An Evaluation of the Group Interview', *Human Organization*, 13(2), 26–28.

Cook, J. and M. Fonow (1986) 'Knowledge and Women's Interests', *Sociological Inquiry*, 56, 22–29.

Desvouges, W. and J. Frey (1989) 'Integrating Focus Groups and Surveys', *Journal of Official Statistics*, 5, 349–363.

Doreian, P., K. Woodard, and W. Kuo (1995) 'Using a Highly Portable Computer to Gather Qualitative Social Network Data', *Quality & Quantity*, 29(2), 125–139.

Dreachslin, J.L. (1998) 'Conducting Effective Focus Groups in the Context of Diversity', *Qualitative Health Research*, 8(6), 813–820.

Freedman, D., A. Thornton and D. Camburn (1988) 'The Life History Calendar', *Sociological Methodology*, 18, 37–68.

Freeman, H.E. (1983) 'Research Opportunities Related to CATI', *Sociological Methods & Research*, 12(2), 143–152.

Gaiser, T.J. (1997) 'Conducting On-Line Focus Groups', *Social Science Computer Review*, 15(2), 135–144.

Gieselman, R.E., R.P. Fisher, I. Firstenberg, L. Hutton, S. Sullivan, I. Avetissian, and A. Prosk (1984) 'Enhancement of Eyewitness Memory: An Empirical Evaluation of the Cognitive Interview', *Journal of Police Science and Administration*, 12, 74–80.

Gerber, E.R. and T.R. Wellens (1997) 'Perspectives on Pretesting: "Cognition" in the Cognitive Interview?', *Bulletin de Méthodologie Sociologique*, 55, 18–39.

Goudy, W. and H. Potter (1975) 'Interview Rapport: Demise of a Concept', *Public Opinion Quarterly*, 39, 530–543 .

Goyder, J. (1985) 'Face-to-Face Interviews and Mailed Questionnaire', *Public Opinion Quarterly*, 49(2), 234–252.

Hamilton-Smith, N. and M. Hopkins (1998) 'Theory-Driven Interviewing', *Bulletin de Méthodologie Sociologique*, 60, 80–105.

Johnson, W. and J. Delamater (1976) 'Response Effects in Sex Surveys', *Public Opinion Quarterly*, 40, 165–181.

Jordan, L.A., A.C. Marcus, and L.G. Reeder (1980) 'Response Styles in Telephone and Household Interviewing', *Public Opinion Quarterly*, 44(2), 210–222.

Keeter, S. (1995) 'Estimating Telephone Noncoverage Bias with a Telephone Survey', *Public Opinion Quarterly*, 59(2), 196–217.

Kohnken, G., R. Milne, A. Memon and R. Bull (1999) 'The Cognitive Interview: A Meta-Analysis', *Psychology, Crime and Law*, 5(1–2), 3–27.

Lovin-Smith, L. and C. Brody (1989) 'Interruptions in Group Discussions', *American Sociological Review*, 54, 424–435.

Marin, G. and B. van Oss-Marin (1989) 'A Comparison of Three Interviewing Approaches for Studying Sensitive Topics with Hispanics', *Hispanic Journal of Behavioral Sciences*, 11(4), 330–340.

Martin, J., C. O'Muircheartaigh and J. Curtice (1993) 'The Use of CAPI for Attitude Surveys', *Journal of Official Statistics*, 9(3), 641–661.

Morgan, D.L. (1995) 'Why Things (Sometimes) Go Wrong in Focus Groups', *Qualitative Health Research*, 5(4), 516–522.

Rosenthal, G. (1993) 'Reconstruction of Life Stories', *The Narrative Study of Lives*, 1, 59–91.

Shanks, J.M., W. Nicholls and H. Freeman (1981) 'The California Disability Survey', *Sociological Methods & Research*, 10(2), 123–140.

Smit, J.H. and W. Dijkstra (1991) 'Persuasion Strategies for Reducing Refusal Rates in Telephone Surveys', *Bulletin de Méthodologie Sociologique*, 33, 3–19.

Sweeney, J.C., G.N. Soutar and D.R. Hausknecht (1997) 'Collecting Information from Groups' *Journal of the Market Research Society*, 39(2), 397–411.

Thompson, J. and M. Demerath (1952) 'Some Experiences with the Group Interview', *Social Forces*, 31, 148–154.

Tourangeau, R., K. Rasinski and J.B. Jobe (1997) 'Sources of Error in a Survey on Sexual Behavior', *Journal of Official Statistics*, 13(4), 341–365.

Tourangeau, R. and T.W. Smith (1996) 'Asking Sensitive Questions', *Public Opinion Quarterly*, 60(2), 275–304.

Weiss, C. (1968) 'Validity of Welfare Mothers Interview Responses', *Public Opinion Quarterly*, 32, 622–633.

Woltman, H.F., A.G. Turner and J.M. Bushery (1980) 'A Comparison of Three Mixed-Mode Interviewing Procedures', *Journal of the American Statistical Association*, 75(371), 534–543.

6

Methods of Interviewing

E. S. Bogardus

Interviewing, one of the important methods now being used in social research, is as old as the human race. Moreover, it is as extensive as the leading professions of the day. The physician, the lawyer, the priest, the journalist, the detective, the social worker, the psychiatrist and psychoanalyst make regular use of it. Their experience with the personal interview method may be of value to the student of social research, but space here permits only an introductory reference to the employment of the interview in these fields.

1. The physician's interview with his patient is more or less "confidential." His well-known professional ethics, namely, that he will not betray any "secrets" that the patient may tell him, are highly significant. The patient may talk freely to the physician, because he knows that the latter will not gossip about him. Hence, he talks about himself with more freedom than he would to his close friends.

The patient, suffering from severe pain, is forced by the desire for relief to talk about himself with complete detail, with abandon, without regard to his own misdoings, without giving much consideration to personal status. Further, the physical examination is no respecter of personal status. Its revelations cannot be argued against, and thus, the patient is motivated to tell "the whole story" about himself.

The physician usually begins by asking the patient to describe his pains, their location, when they were felt first, how the patient's appetite is, and so on, gradually getting as complete a picture of the patient's experiences in connection with his difficulty as possible. He rarely takes notes, but by asking "leading" questions keeps the patient talking about himself until important clues are disclosed.

If the patient be too ill to speak concerning himself, then the patient's nurse or caretaker is asked to describe how the patient acts. The physician rarely asks the patient or his caretaker to state an opinion regarding the nature of the disease; he primarily seeks descriptions of experiences and conditions. When there is a trained nurse, the physician looks at the patient's daily record sheet, and asks the nurse for a description of conditions but only infrequently for an opinion.

2. The lawyer also has a professional ethics of secrecy regarding what his clients tell him about themselves. The client is in trouble, is in danger of losing social status or personal property. He may be lured on by greatly aroused emotions of injustice. Moreover, he knows, if he thinks at all broadly, that the lawyer's chances of winning the case are much better if he gives him all the data, even that which is damaging to himself.

Whereas the doctor visits the patient, that is, is sent for, the client visits the lawyer; he comes not physically and mentally, but socially and mentally in trouble. His problem and his need for aid start him out freely upon his story; there is no necessity to seek an adequate *entree* to the experience of the client. As in the case of the physician, the lawyer conducts his interview in private, even in greater privacy – behind locked doors. In both cases the interview may easily assume a confessional nature.

Important principles have been developed for securing accurate and complete testimony in court. What actually happened, the relation of what a witness remembers to what happened, and the relation of what he tells to what he remembers are three main problems, and are discussed by John H. Wigmore under the form of three principles, the principles of Perception, of Recollection, and of Narration.

> (1) Assuming that the witness' Recollection fairly represents and corresponds to his Perception; then if his Narration or Communication fairly represents and corresponds to his Recollection, and is intelligible by the Tribunal, the elements of testimonial value are complete; but not otherwise …
>
> The simplest form of testimonial statement (from which others may be conceived as deviations) is an (1) uninterrupted narrative (2) expressed in words (3) uttered orally (4) and intelligible directly by the tribunal.[1]

When the witness tells his story in private the facts are likely to be told with some circumlocution but freely, but when he goes into court he is aware that he is to be examined, which arouses defense mechanisms.

> (2) He is to have it (the story) dragged out of him piecemeal, disjointedly, by a series of questions … In the first place then he is in the worst possible frame of mind to be examined – he is agitated, confused, and bewildered.[2]

Experience indicates that a witness does best when (1) allowed to use a narrative form, (2) when least interrupted, (3) when encouraged to follow a time order, and (4) when answers are not suggested by questions, but when questions are used simply to release narratives. Persons display a variety of ways in "witnessing," and hence the examiner must change his methods accordingly. (1) The rambling witness requires a close and catechetical examination. (2) The dull and stupid witness calls for an inexhaustible patience on the part of the advocate. (3) The timid and self-conscious witness needs to have his attention taken off the effects regarding himself or others that he imagines is going to be produced. (4) The bold and zealous witness is easily led astray by his own exaggerate egoism and is usually a dangerous witness from the standpoint of truth. (5) The hostile witness is of value to truth only in indirect ways, by studying his negative reaction – otherwise he is to be avoided. (6) The lying witness may be (a) an innocent liar, (b) a careless liar, or (c) a wilful liar. The classification suggests in itself the attitude to take toward him. (7) The flippant witness is to be circumvented, to be treated as a "wild animal ready to tear you if she should get near enough." Her "frenzied exuberance" is to be encouraged, for thereby she will "give herself away." (8) The dogged witness is to be approached by "getting little answers for little questions," and to get him loosened up, and accustomed to talking. (9) The hesitating witness is to be allowed to take his time. His weighing and balancing of answers needs to be studied. Sometimes, he may hesitate simply in order to be "scrupulously accurate." (10) The nervous witness is to be dealt with gently and to be encouraged. (11) the humorous witness may have his good humor appealed to, and may be as he is, a jolly good fellow. (12) The cunning witness is not cunning so much as he thinks he is. He is to be met with cunning and needs to have his real character "shown up." (13) The canting hypocrite is likely to believe in "religion and his own goodness," and to approach a downright lie by shirking it and by using phrases that disclose his weaknesses. (14) The positive witness can be led into contradiction of what she or he has already said.[3]

3. Through the personal confession of the worshipper, the priest becomes the interviewer. Again, trouble, in this case, "sin," is worrying the confessee. He seeks the father confessor and feels that the freer and fuller he makes his confession the more thoroughly his sins will be forgiven. Hence, he is likely "to blurt it all out," to make his confession sudden and complete. He believes in the priest as a worthy confidant, more trustworthy in "keeping a secret" than closest friends. In order to view the confession of sin more freely the priest may even receive the confession through a curtain. Sometimes a ritual is built up whereby individuals as a group may confess their manifold and grievous sins in a general way, but not as particular offenses.

The sinner possesses a stronger urge to tell the whole truth even than the patient or the client; the former must face a physical examination, and the latter, a court trial. The sinner is stirred to tell all, for he cannot escape the Eye which seeth in secret and knoweth the innermost thoughts.

It may not be inappropriate to refer here to the "impersonal confession," providing the term is understood to mean not a complete degree of impersonal relations but rather a short-cut intimacy and a confidential relation largely assumed. It sometimes occurs when a person is away from home and is feeling homesick, or isolated, and craves to have some one to talk to, or "to pour out his troubles to." He has broken relationships with some intimate friend or relative, and is seeking emotional relief.

Perhaps he feels guilty and is seeking an impartial and disinterested court before which to justify himself.

A person "falls in" with some one on a train, or at some lounging place, and before he is aware of what he is doing, he is relating his personal troubles to some one who only a few moments before was "a perfect stranger." This stranger has shown a sympathetic interest, and yet enough anonymity exists so that the talker's defense mechanisms are not aroused. The talker does not expect that the stranger will contact the former's circle of personal friends. Hence, the conversation may take on "impersonal confession" traits. In this way the talker secures "relief of mind" without losing status within his groups "at home." In fact, he may even picture himself as a martyr and see a martyr's halo round his head as he proceeds to unravel his experiences to the casual acquaintance or stranger.

> (3) I remember the case of a "successful" business man who told me the story of his marital differences one night on the rear platform of an observation car. We had met the night before and talked of fishing. He made a very "complete statement," although I could scarcely be termed an "intimate." The next afternoon his wife and I were sitting together in almost the same place. She said: "Jim *never* talked to anyone; she couldn't *imagine* what we found to talk about till one-thirty." I said 'fishing and politics,' and added that 'your husband seemed to be a great fisherman.' She replied that 'he was; he'd go off on long trips two or three times a year; but she wouldn't go, – she hated fishing; he just couldn't seem to *understand* her.' And in a little while she made her confession. I felt somewhat as I imagine a priest feels – but I had learned a good deal of sociology.[4]

4. The journalist is an interesting type of interviewer. He is handicapped because he is not sent for, as is the doctor or lawyer.

> (4) The interview, proper, however, is a difficult thing. It is the most subtle and most fascinating of all kinds of news gathering – and the most difficult.[5]

He must make his own entree into the interviewee's personal life. He often must overtake persons who are shunning him, and secure a "story" from them against their wishes. As the symbol of publicity he is evaded by many different types of people, as different as the timid and the guilty.

Both his difficulties and his desires for news are urgent and so often he goes to extreme lengths in forcing an interview, even using threats. Competition with the reporters of other newspapers stimulates him to make new and ingenuous attempts in securing a successful interview. He may even try to make the interviewee angry, and thus "give away" important secrets unintentionally and impulsively in self-defence. He may assume the role of a host, thus placing the interviewee under obligations to him. At any rate his time is short and the urge for news is great. In consequence, he capitalizes both time and acquaintance to the limit. "He frames the questions and keeps the whole matter in his own hands." Moreover, he has "a nose for news," and manifests "a quick perception of news values in even chance remarks."[6]

5. The detective is the chief expert in interviewing people who do not want to be interviewed. He resorts to all types of deception in order to attain his ends. In the most unexpected ways he appears on the scene – as a lucky fisherman in the mountains, in the guise of "a prominent citizen" at a banquet, or even a kindly stranger doing a friendly deed. He trails the "subject" for miles, hundreds of miles, and when the latter feels that he is safe from pursuit and all his defense mechanisms are relaxed the detective, disguised, appears as an old farmer, a dancing partner, or a helpless cripple, and innocently obtains the long sought-for interview.[7]

Commissioner G. S. Dougherty in describing what he calls "the humane third degree" states that he does not rely on threats, piling up charges against the subject, or on "rough methods" and thus antagonizing the subject and making him stubborn, but that he tries to create an atmosphere of confidence on the part of the suspect in him, the detective. He does this by being thoroughly human, by giving the suspect status, and even getting him to experience a sense of pride in confessing.[8]

6. Of all interviewers the social worker has much in common with the student of social research. Both are dealing with social problems, with conflict situations, with individuals as persons, with the nature of social stimuli and responses. The social worker has emphasized "the first interview."[9] It is suggested by Miss Richmond that the client's home is the best place to hold the first interview. Here the client feels most at ease and here are opportunities to consider the client in relation to his natural surroundings. This conclusion, however, overlooks the fact that the home surroundings are full of objects that act as inhibiting stimuli and prevent a "free and full confession." Children or elders may be going in and out, or standing outside listening, and thus causing the client to make guarded statements.

> (5) One of the most important results of a successful first interview is the substitution of a personal relation and sense of loyalty for the client's standard of behavior toward impersonal institutions. In so far as note-taking emphasizes the impersonal side, it is wiser to take no notes in the presence of the client that would not appear to him at once as the obvious and courteous thing to do. No rule can be laid down, however. The nature of the task and the conditions under which the interview is held must modify our method. The worker who can forget his pencil,

visit a family for the first time, conduct a First Interview full of names, addresses, ages, and family details, and then come back to his office and dictate a clear and accurate statement, has at his command better technique than one who is the slave of a schedule or blank form ... When the history becomes more personal in its nature, she (a certain medical-social worker) has the habit of dropping pen and pencil and all that would tend to interfere with spontaneity of intercourse.[10]

The social worker is beginning to distinguish between methods of interviewing and interviewing as a process, and to become aware of the need for understanding the nature of the process of interviewing as a necessary qualification for conducting an interview; he is focussing attention on studying the physical setting of the interview, on the kinds of persons the interviewer and the interviewee are, and on what each knows about the other.[11]

7. The psychiatrist also has much to offer by way of technique of interviewing. It is his business to examine the hidden springs of action. Moreover, he brings to bear upon his problems a modern psychological training.

In an "unpublished document" Dr. Adolf Meyer speaks of the necessity for "perfect privacy," the choosing of "a quiet, confidential hour," the avoidance of "self-humiliation" by the patient, and of "unnecessary argument."

(6) For any examination the *mode of approach* is absolutely decisive of the result. The reserve of the patient is usually a factor to be reckoned with, or, if not the reserve, at least the unwillingness to show a clear picture of decidedly peculiar experiences. It is, therefore, necessary to gain the confidence by treating the patient "as a sensible man or woman," and, whenever the patient does not speak freely, to begin with questions about whether they have all they need for their comfort, to pass some of the least irritating topics, such as will most likely elicit a pleasant answer and create a congenial starting point.[12]

The psychiatrist suggests letting a patient talk "on and on." The getting off of the point, the garrulity and so forth, throw light on the psychology of the patient's mind and help the interviewer to evaluate and interpret the testimony.

A successful opening for an interview is suggested by Dr. William Healy from his experiences in meeting parents of delinquent boys:

(7) The opening of the interview with some such friendly and reasonable statement as the following has been found in itself to have a rationalizing effect. One may say: 'Well, you people do seem to have a difficult affair on your hands with this boy. Let's sit down and talk it all over, and study it out together – how it all began and what's going to happen. I'm at your service. Did you ever think it all out carefully? ...' The response is nearly always gratifying.[13]

The psychoanalyst specializes in getting at data concealed beneath the threshold of the subconscious. He is dealing with the patient's mental ills and trying to find out things about the patient which he does not know about himself. He is an expert in one of the subtle phases of interviewing whose procedure may at times approximate that of the hypnotist.

Since the patient is often in a very subnormal mental state, it is easy for a psychoanalyst to "dominate" the patient and make the latter a sort of mental slave, extracting from him almost any type of confession that the sensitive patient feels is expected.

The psychoanalyst specializes in drawing out from the patient his "forgotten" childhood experiences by subtle forms of suggestion. In getting an individual to tell about his emotional strains, dreams involving sex factors, and his inmost thoughts, the specialist first gets the patient's complete confidence, and then by suggesting or even imagining happenings, often succeeds in getting a complete story. By unravelling a patient's experiences and feelings the specialist in this field becomes an expert in making objective what goes on in what to most individuals is the most inner sanctum of their personality. Sometimes the specialist is aided by the terrifying fears which haunt the patient's mental life. At any rate psychiatrists and psychoanalysts secure from their patients what a doctor or lawyer ordinarily does not get, and what a priest may only approximate, a picture of innermost feelings and thoughts.

Notes

1. John H. Wigmore, *Principles of Judicial Proof* (Little, Brown & Co., 1913), p. 484.
2. Quoted by Wigmore from *Hints on Advocacy*, By Richard Harris, Am. Edit., 1892, p. 29.
3. Based on discussion by W.C. Robinson in *Forensic Oratory; a Manual for Advocates*, 1893, p. 126, and Richard Harris, *op. cit.*, pp. 65, 107. John H. Wigmore's *Principles of Judicial Proof* (*op. cit.*), pp. 526–537.
4. Read Bain "The Impersonal Confession and Social Research," *Journal of Applied Sociology*, May–June, 1925, p. 359.
5. Harrington and Frankenberg, *Essentials in Journalism* (Ginn, 1912), p. 119.
6. *Ibid.*, p. 129.
7. Cf. G.S. Dougherty, *The Criminal as a Human Being* (Appleton, 1924), ch. II.
8. *Ibid.*, Ch. IV.
9. Cf. Mary E. Richmond, *Social Diagnosis* (Russell Sage Foundations, 1918), Ch. VI.
10. *Ibid.*, pp. 127–8.
11. Bradley Buell, "Interviews, Interviewers, and Interviewing," *The Family*, May, 1925, pp. 86–90.
12. Quoted by Mary E. Richmond, *ibid.*, p. 115
13. *The Individual Delinquent* (Little, Brown & Co., 1914), p. 35.

7

The Controversy Over Detailed Interviews: An Offer for Negotiation

Paul F. Lazarsfeld

If two people vigorously disagree on whether something is blue or green, the chances are that the object is composed of both colors and that for some reason the two contestants are either unable or unwilling to see more than the one. If in methodological discussions, competent workers assume vehemently opposite positions, it is generally a good time for someone to enter the scene and suggest that the parties are both right and wrong.

A recent issue of *Public Opinion Quarterly* (Summer, 1943) provides one of the many indications that such a situation has come about in the public opinion field. A representative of the Division of Program Surveys in the Department of Agriculture reports on large-scale research work, the core of which is an interviewing technique "intended to draw full intensive discussions" and using "various non-directive means of stimulating full discussion in the interviewing situation."[1] Preceding this report is an article by a well-known psychologist who dubs this technique "depth interview" and describes it in rather uncomplimentary terms. One of his conclusions is that "there is little or no evidence to support the tacit assumption that the so-called depth interview yields more valid responses from people than do other types."[2] For him, simple "yes–no" questions, used judiciously, are sufficient.

The matter is important from more than a scientific point of view. Applied social research is a new venture. Only yesterday did the government begin large-scale studies in public opinion. The market and consumer studies which are now finding acceptance in many industries are likewise all of recent date. Managers in business as well as in public administration are faced with sharply contending factions among research professionals. Should they succumb to skepticism or discouragement and fail to give this new branch of the

Source: *Public Opinion Quarterly*, vol. 8, 1944, pp. 38–60.

social sciences the opportunity to prove itself, then development might be seriously retarded. It therefore seems justified to present the problem to a larger public with an earnest effort toward impartiality.

Employing a neutral terminology, we shall allude to our subject as the "open-ended interview." The term serves to describe a crucial aspect of this type of interviewing – the fact that "open-ended interviews" do not set fixed answers in terms of which a respondent must reply. Eventually a more animated expression may be desirable. (To save space we shall abbreviate the term and refer to it hereafter as OI.) Rather than asking for a definition it would be better if the reader visualizes the situation in which an OI occurs. In the interview situation the interviewer by an appropriate introduction attempts to establish the best possible rapport between himself and the respondent because he is aware that he may have to interview the respondent an hour or longer. He then proceeds to ask one of the ten or fifteen questions which have been assigned to him by the central office. Sometimes the respondent himself immediately plunges into great detail, and the interviewer simply permits him to continue. If the first answer is brief, however, the interviewer is instructed to "probe." There are quite a number of devices for eliciting detailed, free response. Mere silence will sometimes induce the respondent to elaborate. Or, the interviewer may just repeat the respondent's own words with an appropriate inflection. Asking for examples will often prove helpful. Then again questions such as the following are used: "How did you happen to notice it? What makes you think so? How did you feel about it before? Do most of your friends have the same opinion?" The trained OI field worker has the goal of his inquiry clearly imprinted in his mind, but he adapts his inquiry to the concrete situation between the interviewee and himself.

If properly conducted, such an OI will result in a detailed document which covers the whole area under investigation, including the interviewer's observations of the respondent's reactions and background.

The OI is suggested by its proponents in opposition to what one might term the "straight poll question." The latter gives the respondent the occasion to answer only "Yes," "No," "Don't know," or to make a choice among a small number of listed possible answers. Between these two extremes there are, of course, several steps. Actually there is hardly a poll where there is not some freedom left for the respondent to express himself in his own way. It is not necessary here to discuss where the straight poll question ends and the OI begins. For all practical purposes the distinction is clear enough.

A rather thorough survey of published and unpublished studies based on the OI technique was made for the purpose of this paper. It is necessary to describe and classify these in some detail because many current misunderstandings come from an insufficient distinction among the different functions of the OI; if people disagree on its usefulness, they very often do not have the same functions in mind. It is the plan of this paper to present the main uses of the OI at their very best and to stress the advantages which are generally singled out by the advocates of this technique. Then we shall select a specific criterion for evaluation and summarize pertinent criticism. It is hoped that as a result we shall end up with a balanced view on the subject.

The Six Main Functions of the OI Technique

1. Clarifying the meaning of a respondent's answer. Before asking him whether war profits should be limited, we have to find out what the respondent thinks the word "profit" means. Some people talk of the total income of a company as profit, others believe it is the difference between wholesale and retail prices, still others are of the opinion that war profits are the difference between pre-war and war earnings. By discussing the general subject matter with him we are very likely to obtain a fairly clear picture of what would be equivalent to his private definition of these terms. One frequently underestimates the number of terms which seem obvious to the interviewer but which are ambiguous or even unknown to the lower educated section of the population.

In other cases it is not so much the meaning of words as the *implication of an opinion* which has to be clarified. If a respondent is in favor of reducing taxes, does he know that as a result many government services will have to be reduced? If he is in favor of free speech, does he realize that such freedom must also pertain to people who may express opinions that are very distasteful to him?

If respondents are asked to voice their thoughts on a course of action, it is important to know against what *alternative possibilities* they had weighed their choice. A respondent is for the continuation of the Dies Committee: has he weighed that against the possibility that the Department of Justice can adequately handle the problem of subversive activities, or did he feel that if the Dies Committee does not do so, no one else will? Another respondent is for government regulation of business: does he prefer this to completely free enterprise, or has he considered the different ways by which an individual business man can be regulated through his own trade organizations?

Finally, the OI permits a respondent to clarify his opinion by introducing *qualifications.* He is in favor of rationing if it is administered fairly for everyone. He is in favor of married women getting defense jobs if it has been made sure that there are no unemployed men left. The respondent might not volunteer such qualifications if the interview is a too hurried one.

2. Singling out the decisive aspects of an opinion. If we deal with attitudes toward rather complex objects, we often want to know the *decisive aspects* by which a respondent is guided. Take the opinion on *candidates* for public office. At this moment, for example, the Republicans in some mid-western states prefer Dewey to Willkie as Presidential nominee. What does Dewey stand for in the eyes of these people? Party Loyalty? Isolationism? Administrative ability? Gang-busting? Here again the OI would proceed in characteristic fashion. What has the respondent heard about the two candidates? What does he think would happen if Dewey were to become President? And so on. In the end we should be able to distinguish groups for which Dewey means quite different things, and fruitful statistical comparisons on a number of social characteristics could be carried through.

Similar possibilities can come up when people are called upon to judge *concrete situations*. They do or do not like the working conditions in their plants. If the answer is in the negative, what features do they especially dislike? In order to get a reasonable idea of people's complaints a rather detailed discussion is necessary; the OI is a good device for this purpose. Other examples of such procedure can easily be found: to what does the respondent attribute rising prices? Or the increase in juvenile delinquency?

Here belong also some recent efforts in the field of communications research. People like or dislike a film or a radio program. Through detailed discussions it is possible to bring out quite clearly which elements in the production make for the audience's reaction.[3]

The singling out of decisive aspects also pertains to issues. If respondents are against sending lend-lease supplies to Russia, it is important to know what about such a policy they dislike. Do they disapprove of Russian communism, or do they think that the Russians do not need the supplies, or do they feel that other parts of the world war panorama are more important? Here, again, the OI would not only ask for an opinion on the basic issues but would probe the respondents for further details.

Very often the decisive aspects of a candidate, a situation, a document or an issue will be elicited by starting a discussion with the words: "Why do you think so?" Or, "Why do you prefer ...?" But hardly ever will one such question give all the necessary information. If people prefer Dewey as the Republican nominee and are asked why they do so, they will very often say, "Because he is the better man," or, "Because a friend feels the same way." Then the interviewer must keep in mind the fact that he is looking for decisive features and must keep on asking questions. For instance: "What makes him a better man?" Or, "Why do you think your friend favors him?"[4]

3. What has influenced an opinion. If people approve of an issue or vote for a candidate (or buy a product), it is useful to divide the determining factors of such action into three main groups: the *decisive features* of the object in question, which account for its being chosen; the *predispositions* of the respondents, which make them act one way or another; and the *influences which are brought to bear upon them*, especially those which mediate between them and the object of their choice.[5] The use of the OI to investigate the first group has just been discussed. The quest for predispositions (attitude, motives) will be dealt with under points four and five. We now consider the use of the OI in the search for *influences*.

The typical research situation here is one wherein we try to assess the importance of a certain event. Let us turn, for example, to people who bought bonds after listening to Kate Smith or who started storing potatoes after a government campaign to this effect had been started or who improved their production records after a system of music-while-you-work had been introduced in a plant. A well-conducted OI should provide enough information so that the causal role of the exposure can be appraised. The rules for such interviews have been rather well worked out.[6]

If the respondent claims that the specific speech had an effect on him, a sort of cross-examination is necessary along the following lines: Wasn't he ready to perform the final act before he heard the speech? Didn't something else happen after the speech which is a more likely explanation for his action? If the respondent denies being affected by the speech, then the whole interview has to be conducted as if the purpose were to break down this contention: Why didn't the respondent act before he heard the speech? Did he have any other sources of information? In other words, the technique consists of checking up on whether, according to logical and psychological commonsense, the respondent would have acted otherwise than he did if he had not heard the speech or read the pamphlet. Obviously it is not possible to anticipate all the questions which have to be asked in order to bring to light the elements preceding the final act and surrounding the influence under investigation. The task of the OI is to draw out those factors so sharply that the reader of the interview can form a judgment as to whether any causal role of the influence should be assumed or not.

This technique of unearthing influences by OIs is especially pertinent to advertising problems because of the insistent use of the same "stimuli" in radio programs or magazine campaigns. With the Government turning to "campaigns" to influence the consumption or saving habits of the citizenry, however, it would deserve more attention from students of public opinion. During election campaigns similar problems come up, particularly if an effort is made to study those people who at the beginning of the campaign had not yet formulated opinions.

4. Determining complex attitude patterns. A fourth group of applications comes into play when we turn to the classification of rather complex attitude patterns. If we want to ascertain how active people are in their war participation or how disturbed they are by current food shortages, the OI actually discusses such subject matters with the respondents, getting their recent experiences and reactions. The purpose is to make an adequate classification of the material so obtained. Further assumptions come easily to mind. People can be classified according to how satisfied they are with local handling of the draft situation, according to the ways they adjust to the lack of gasoline, according to their satisfaction or dissatisfaction with the amount of information they get on the war, etc. This procedure is singularly characteristic of Rensis Likert's work in the Department of Agriculture.[7]

If it is used to assess the extent to which respondents are concerned with a certain problem and how intensely they feel about it this approach assumes special importance. Two respondents might give the same answer to a simple opinion poll question. For the one, however, it is an important issue on which he has spent much thought, whereas the other may have formed his opinion spontaneously as the poll investigator asked him about it. The possible perfunctory nature of replies to public opinion polls has been the object of much criticism. Those who feel strongly in favor of the OI emphasize that right at this point such a danger is obviated – the danger that poll results will be misleading because they do not take into account intensity of feeling or amount of concern.

This role of the OI does not necessarily terminate with a one-dimensional rating scale of, say, intensity of feeling. The OI is suitable for more complex ratings as well. In a study of people's reactions to changes in food habits, sponsored by the National Research Council, the interviewers were instructed to "watch carefully for all offhand comments to one of the following frames of reference: Money, Health, Taste, Status."[8] The procedure was to talk with people about current food shortages, the adjustments they had made, and the points at which they experienced difficulties. From their discussion it was possible to classify them into four groups according to which of the four contexts they spontaneously stressed. The study found, for example, that high-income groups refer to health twice as often as money, whereas in low-income groups money is the frame of reference three times more frequently than is health.

Finally we have what is known as the "gratification study." In an analysis of the gratification people get from the Professor Quiz programs, for example, a variety of appeals could be distinguished. Some listeners are very much intrigued by the competitive element of the contest; others like to test their own knowledge; still others hope to learn something from the questions posed on the program.[9] We could not expect the untrained respondent to explain clearly the psychological complexities of his interest or his reaction. It is not even likely that he would classify himself accurately if we let him choose among different possibilities. Again the OI is needed to provide the necessary information for the trained analyst. Its practical use lies in the following direction: If we know what attitudes are statistically dominant we can either strengthen the "appeal" elements in the program which are likely to get an enlarged audience; or we can try to change these attitudes if, for some ulterior reason, we consider the prevailing distribution unsatisfactory.

Such studies have also been made in the public opinion field; for example, in analyzing the gratification people get out of writing letters to senators.[10]

5. *Motivational interpretations.* Ratings, attitude types, and gratification lists are only, the beginning of a conceptual line which ends in studies based on broad motivational interpretations. We cannot hope here to present systematically the ways in which psychologists distinguish between the different kinds of "drives" according to their range, depth, or the specificity of their relations to the world of objects.[11] The picture would not be complete, nevertheless, if we were to omit a mention of the use of the OI technique for the purpose of understanding people's reactions in such broad conceptual contexts.

The OI collects a variety of impressions, experiences, and sidelines which the respondent offers when he is asked to discuss a given topic. The man who does the study then makes a kind of psychological construction. He creates a picture of some basic motivation of which all these details are, so to speak, manifestations.

Consider an example. In studying certain groups of unemployed one makes a variety of observations: they walk slowly, they lose interest in public affairs, do not keep track of their time, express opinions only with hesitation, stop looking for jobs – in short, they can best be understood as discouraged, resigned beings whose psychological living space has been severely contracted. On the basis of this conceptualization we would not expect them, e.g., to join revolutionary movements which require initiative. If, on the other hand, we are interested in retaining whatever morale they do have left, we would reject the idea of a straight dole in favor of work relief which would keep them psychologically "on the go."

There is only a rather short step from this example to the kind of OI studies which we want to discuss. For a number of reasons most of them have been done in the field of advertising.

People who talk about their shoe purchases often mention how embarrassing it is to expose one's feet in stockings, how one is virtually a prisoner in the hands of the salesman, etc. They are also likely to point out that such-and-such a salesman was friendly, or that they do like stores where the customers are not seated too near each other. The study director finally forms the hypothesis that the shoe-buying situation is one likely to evoke a feeling of inferiority. To alleviate this feeling and thus lead to a larger and more satisfied patronage, a number of obvious suggestions can be made for the training of salesmen and the arrangement of the store.

Finally, take series of OI's where women say that they like fruits in glass jars because then they can see the product and also because they feel there is greater danger of food spoiling in tin cans. The conclusion is not that lots of fruits in glass jars should be shown. A motivational interpretation which takes all the pertinent remarks in the OI's into consideration will rather proceed as follows. Glass jars have something reassuring about them, whereas tin cans have a slight connotation of a dungeon in which the food and even oneself is jailed. The appropriate advertising for glass jars, therefore, would show them among flowers, in rays of sunshine, to stress the exhilarating elements in the whole complex. Visibility would then be only one of these elements.

To discuss this use of OI's in a short space is impossible, especially since its logic has not yet been thought through very well. The social scientist who tries to clarify such analysis faces a conflict between two goals to which he is equally devoted. On the one hand, these interpretations serve to integrate a host of details as well as make us aware of new ones which we might otherwise overlook; often they are very brilliant. On the other hand, they violate our need for verification because by their very nature they can never be proved but only made plausible. It is no coincidence that in the two examples given above we have added to each interpretation some practical advice derived from it. What such motivational analysis does is to see past experiences as parts of some psychological drive which can be reactivated by related material, be it propaganda or institutional devices.[12]

6. *Clarifying statistical relationships.* In the five areas outlined so far the OI was the point of departure for all subsequent analysis. Now finally we have to deal with studies where statistical results are available and where the OI serves to *interpret and refine statistical inter-relationships.* The procedure could be called the analysis of deviate cases.

When, for instance, the panic was studied which followed the famous broadcast on the "Invasion From Mars," it was found that people on a lower educational level were most likely to believe in the occurrence of the great catastrophe.[13] Yet some lower-educated people were not frightened at all. When these deviate cases were subject to an OI, many turned out to be mechanics or people who had mechanical hobbies; they were accustomed to checking up on things, a habit the "regular" people had acquired by a successful formal education. On the other hand, quite a number of well-educated people were frightened. When an OI was made with them, the following was sometimes found: During the broadcast they had been in special social situations where it was not clear who should take the initiative of checking up; the lack of social structure impeded purposeful action, and everyone got panicky.

Another example can be taken from unemployment studies. In general it is found that the more amicable the relations in a family prior to the depression, the more firmly would the family stand the impact of unemployment. Again we can inspect deviate cases. A couple fights constantly before the depression, but after the husband becomes unemployed, they get along better. A detailed interview reveals the probability that here the husband wanted to be submissive and the wife dominant, but folkways prevented them from accepting this inverse role. Unemployment, then, enforces a social situation here which is psychologically adequate. Or, a good marriage breaks down surprisingly quickly as a result of the husband's unemployment. A specification of the case shows that the man's sexual habits are rather vulnerable and become disorganized under the blow of the loss of his job.[14]

The general pattern of these studies proceeds from an empirical correlation which is usually not very high. We take cases which do not follow the majority pattern and try to gain an impression or to account for their irregularity. The political scientist is used to such procedure.[15] He knows, for instance, that the more poor people and Catholics live in a given precinct of a big city, the more Democratic votes he can expect. But here is a precinct which qualifies on both scores, and still it went Republican. What accounts for this deviation? Is the Democratic machine inefficient? Has a special local grievance developed? Was there a recent influx of people with different political tradition? This is quite analogous to what we are trying to do when we are faced with individual cases which went statistically out of line. With the help of the OI we try to discover new factors which, if properly introduced, would improve our multiple correlation.

Usually the matter is put by saying that detailed case studies help us to understand an empirical correlation. This is quite all right as far as the psychology of the investigator goes. It would be more correct, however, to say that the OI helps to develop hypotheses as to the conditions under which you would expect our first correlation to become higher. If it were our task to formulate in general terms why the OI is so helpful to the better understanding of an attitude, our starting point would actually be here. We would have to make quite clear that the insight gained by a qualitative approach is nothing else than a hypothetical relation between a number of factors. But that would go beyond the purpose of this section, in which we intended to give no more than a vivid picture of the actual research experiences out of which the OI technique has grown. It is to the controversial aspect of the problem that we now turn.

The Issue Becomes a Problem

The six areas just outlined could be looked at in two ways. For one, they represent desirable goals for public opinion research. We need more detailed knowledge as to what the answers of our respondents mean, on what specific points their opinions are based, in what larger motivational contexts they belong, etc. At the same time, the different applications of the OI also imply criticism to the effect that one straight poll question will hardly ever reach any of these goals successfully.

One can agree with this criticism without concluding that the OI technique is the only remedy. If this paper were written for a psychological journal, for instance, the course of our discussion from here on would be prescribed. We should have to compare results obtained by straight poll questions with those collected by OI's and decide which are preferable according to some adequate criteria. The present analysis, however, falls under the heading of "Research Policy." The research administrator has to make decisions as to the most desirable procedures long before we have provided all the necessary data on the comparative merits of different research methods.

What line of argument would one take in such a situation? No one can close his eyes to the shortcomings of many of the current opinion-poll practices. Having begun with the simple problem of predicting elections, they use, very often, a greatly oversimplified approach for the gauging of attitudes toward complex issues. We shall also agree that a well-conducted OI gives us a fascinating wealth of information on the attitude of a single respondent. When it comes to the statistical analysis of many OI's, the matter is already not so simple. It is in the nature of this technique that just the most valuable details of one OI become difficult to compare with the answers obtained in another interview. It can safely be said that the proponents of the OI technique have made much more progress in the conduct of the interviews than in their statistical analysis.

But even if the OI technique were not to have methodological troubles of its own, it would still be open to one very serious objection. It is necessarily an expensive and slow procedure and, as a result, studies which are made for practical purposes will always be based on a small number of cases. It is inconceivable at this moment that an agency would have the resources or the time to make many thousands of OI's on one subject. This is a decisive drawback. True, a surprisingly small number of cases is needed for a fairly correct estimate of how many Republicans there are in a community or how many people save their fat and grease. But do we want to stop here? Don't we want to know in which social groups some of those activities are more frequent than in others? Aren't we trying to account for the reasons why some people do a thing and others do not? And how can this be done except by careful cross-tabulation of one part of our data against other parts? And for this, a much larger number of cases is needed.

In other words, the OI technique, even if it were perfect in itself, places us in a dilemma. By laying all the stress on the detailed description of the single respondent's attitude, it forces us into relatively small numbers of interviews. This in turn handicaps another important progress in public opinion research: the progress which consists of comparing carefully the distribution of opinions in different sub-groups of the population and relating a given opinion to the personal characteristics and to other attitudes of the respondent.

From the standpoint of research policy, therefore, which is the standpoint taken in this paper, the whole problem comes to this. Is there not some way to use all the good ideas which the proponents of the OI technique have and still to develop methods which are more objective, more manageable on a mass basis – which, in short, give us sufficient material to do a thorough analysis of the factors which make for a given distribution of public opinion?

Under these aspects we shall go once more through the six areas discussed above. In each case we shall look for procedures which combine the administrative advantages of the straight poll question with the psychological advantages of the OI. Quite frankly we want to "eat our cake and have it, too." All folklore notwithstanding, research progress consists in the art of doing things which at first seem incompatible. As we proceed, it will turn out that these compromise techniques do not make the OI superfluous but give it a new and, as we feel, more valuable place in the whole scheme of public opinion research.

To bring out more clearly our trend of thought, we begin with a little scheme. To the left we have our six areas; to the right we have short names for the procedures which would overcome some of the shortcomings of the straight poll question and still be more formalized and manageable on a mass basis than the OI. It is to the short description and evaluation of the right side of the scheme that we now turn.

1. Clarifying meaning by the use of interlocking poll questions. In the first area we dealt with the clarification of the respondent's opinion. Did he know the significance of what he was talking about? In the course of an OI, by making

Current Applications of the OI Techniques	Possible Objective Alternatives for the OI
1. Clarifying the meaning of a respondent's answer	1. Interlocking system of poll questions
2. Singling out the decisive aspects of an opinion	2. Checklists
3. Discerning influences	3. None
4. Determining complex attitude patterns	4. Scales and typologies
5. Interpreting motivation	5. Projective tests
6. Clarifying statistical relationships	6. None

the respondent elaborate in more detail, we will find out. But after all, the number of possible variations is not so great; it is often possible to get by explicit questions all the material we can use for comparative analysis of many interview returns.

Consider the following two cases. Studenski has pointed out that when people are asked whether they want lower taxes, most of them will say "yes."[16] After having asked this general question, however, he then asked a series of specific questions on whether the government should discontinue relief, work projects, expenses for national defense, expenses for schools, police, etc. Respondents who wanted taxes reduced but services maintained had obviously, to say the least, an inconsistent attitude toward the problem.[17] In a different context, Kornhauser has pointed out the shortcomings of the question: Should Congress pass a law forbidding strikes in war industries or should war workers have the right to go on strike? Obviously there are other devices, such as an improved arbitration system or the endowment of union leaders with some semi-public power to keep their members from striking. By offering a whole set of such alternatives it is undoubtedly possible to get a much clearer picture of the respondent's real attitude.

In this and many similar examples the technique used consists of an interlocking system of poll questions, each of which is very simple but which through proper cross-tabulation permits the separation of respondents according to the extent to which they see the implications of their opinion.

Although we cannot go into details here, we have studied dozens of pertinent cases and are satisfied that for any given topic it is always possible to find an appropriate system of interlocking questions. The right procedure consists of beginning the study with a considerable number of very detailed OI's. These should come from different parts of the country and should serve to develop the structure of the problem. Experience shows that after one to three hundred such reports have been studied, very few new factors come up. At this point we can begin to develop a set of specific questions centering around the main attitude and bringing out its implications and qualifications. There is no reason why we should not ask specifically (by the use of ordinary poll questions) what knowledge and experience the respondent has in this field; what his opinions are in related fields; whether he does or does not expect certain things to happen; whether he has ever thought of the problem, or whether he cannot make up his mind about it, and so on.

Here we come across a very characteristic relationship between the OI and more formalized methods in opinion research. The OI serves as a source of observation and of ideas from which sets of precise poll questions can be derived which will be more manageable in the field and more susceptible to statistical analysis. On one occasion the useful suggestion was made that the special job of converter should be developed: that people should specialize in studying OI's and seeing how they could be converted into systems of interlocking questions.

So far not enough thought has been spent on making this conversion procedure an explicit research operation for which standard examples and rules should be developed. Once this is done, it will probably turn out that in the area under discussion here the OI, although much preferable to isolated straight poll questions, is not so good as a well-structured set of straight poll questions. The proponents of the OI technique at this point usually see only the justified goal and the shortcomings of current public opinion polls. They have seldom the occasion to see in their own studies the hundreds of OI's which either do not yield really useful information or are so unique that if they are submitted to a comparative analysis, all the details which make them invaluable as a first phase of an investigation are lost when the final report is reached.

Sometimes when we want to clarify the meaning of an answer, especially. in regard to qualifications, check lists can be considered an appropriate procedure. Since, however, check lists are more frequently indicated when it comes to the assessment of decisive features, they will be discussed under the next heading.

2. *Using check lists to get at the decisive aspects of an opinion.* If we want to know what people like about a candidate or what bothers them about the present rationing system, we can make a list of the probable answers and ask the respondents which answer fits their case.

The advantages and disadvantages of check lists have been repeatedly discussed. The minimum requirement is that they contain an exhaustive list of all the possibilities, for it is known that items not mentioned in a check list are less likely to be mentioned by the respondents. But even a good check list has certain dangers. If people are asked what wish they would make if they had a magic ring, they seldom mention "being very bright," because they do not think of intelligence as something that can be wished for. If, however, they get a check list of possible wishes which includes "intelligence," they are more likely to pick it. The less concrete the topic is, the more will the check list influence the answers.

As long as all this is not better explored by comparing the results from large-scale check lists and from the classifications of free answers, it is not possible to make a valid decision. Yet with the help of a careful analysis of

OI's it seems logical to assume that exhaustive check lists can be safely constructed – ones which would be as safe as the results of open-ended interviewing. For complex topics the cautious research student will, of course, be hesitant to rely too easily on check lists. When in doubt he will prefer to rely on OI's recorded by conscientious interviewers and classified by sensitive analysts for the study of decisive features.

In studying the decisive aspects of opinion there are cases where the more formalized alternative for the OI would not be a check list, but a system of interlocking questions. This is especially true in dealing with opinions on policy issues. Suppose people have expressed themselves on the idea of married women working in war industry and are opposed to it. The open-ended question, "Why do you feel this way?" brings out a variety of comments which show that people look at the matter from a number of aspects: some feel that it is bad for the home if women stay out too much; others feel that women are not equipped for factory work or that working conditions are not adequate for them; still others do not want women to compete with men for jobs. Here are four features of the whole problem on which respondents could be asked their opinions explicitly. Do you feel that women are equipped for war jobs? Do you feel that they are a competitive danger for men? Etc. By cross-tabulating the answers to the sub-issues against the main issue of women in war work, one probably would get a better idea of the general attitude pattern than if the "reasons" were directly tabulated.

Again the OI is indispensable in preliminary studies to give one an idea as to what aspects should be considered. If, however, a large number of interviews is to be collected, the interlocking system of questions might be preferable, especially if great effort is made to get an appropriate conversion of preliminary OI's into a system of more precise questions.

3. Are there other ways of studying what has influenced opinion? Whether it is possible to discern influences which are exercised upon people is a controversial question. In more extreme cases such decisions are obviously possible or impossible. If a child goes down to the grocer's "because my mother sent me down," we should consider such a statement as equivalent to a controlled experiment. Putting it rather exaggeratedly: if we set up two groups of well-matched children and had the mothers of the children in one group tell them to go to the grocer's, we should certainly expect to find more children from the "experimental" than from the control group at the grocer's. On the other hand, if a person has committed a crime and we ask him whether that is due to the fact that his parents immigrated to this country, we shall consider whatever he says not very reliable. The command of the mother is much more "discernible" as an influence than the whole background of family life.[18]

Fortunately, in public opinion research we are mostly interested in rather "discernible" influences. Whether people began to salvage paper under the influence of a government campaign or whether a specific pamphlet made them contribute blood to the Red Cross can be discovered fairly well by direct interviewing. For such studies the OI appears to be an important research tool. Thus, it becomes even more urgent to make its use as expert as possible. Sometimes it is not used wisely. Studies of the following kind have been circulated. People who began to can fruit were asked why they did so. Sixty per cent said "because of the campaign," 15% "because it is necessary for the war effort." Here is obviously a meaningless result – for OI or otherwise. Many of the 15% may have learned from the campaign that private canning was a patriotic duty. However, the interviewer was too easily satisfied with the first answer which came to the mind of the respondent instead of asking "Where did you learn that canning is important for the war effort?"[19]

We do not wish to discuss here under what conditions controlled experiments are possible and justified. Just for the record, we might add that the result of a controlled experiment does not necessarily indicate correctly the effectiveness of a real campaign. In a controlled experiment we expose some of the people artificially and may then find that they are strongly influenced by the campaign material. In real life people select themselves for exposure. It might well be that mainly those who are not affected by a radio speech are willing to listen to it. This is, for instance, one of the problems in educational broadcasting, where there is a wide difference between experimental and actual success of programs.

4. Scales and typologies for the analysis of attitude patterns. When it comes to the objective correlates for the use of the OI in the classification of complex attitude patterns, we find ourselves in a peculiar situation. The topic has been a favorite one for social-research students; we have discussed "case studies" versus quantitative methods for a decade.[20] An appropriate instance comes from the study which this writer made during the presidential election of 1940. The task was to appraise how interested people were in the election. Had we used the OI technique, the interviewer would have talked with the respondent and by taking down what he said, by observing his participation in the discussion, he would have formed an opinion on his interest and then noted it in the form of a rating. Instead we asked the respondent three questions: whether he had tried to convince someone of his political ideas; whether he had done anything for the success of his candidate; and whether he was very anxious to see his candidate elected. Each respondent got a definite score according to how he answered the three questions.[21]

But how does such an objective scale compare with the impressionistic ratings obtained from an OI? The problems involved can best be explained by an example.

If in everyday life we call another person timid, we do so because of the way he walks or because of his hesitant speech and sometimes because of cues of which we are not precisely aware ourselves. In each case we use whatever cues the situation offers; they might be quite different from one case to the next. A "timidity rating," on the other hand, would provide us with a list of items on which an interviewer would have to get an observation for every case, if necessary by asking a direct question. The more timidity characteristics on this list applied to the respondents, the higher would be his timidity score. Using such a scale, the interviewer could not make use of incidental observations if they were not included in the list, even if in a special case he had a strong conviction that the respondent was much more timid than his scale value indicated.

All this can be directly applied to our problem. A good OI reproduces the full vividness of an actual observation; but if nothing characteristic happens in the interview situation or if the interviewer misses cues, then we have little on which to base our final classification. With the scale we can count on a definite amount of data, but some of them might be rather artificial and often we must forego valuable observations within our reach. *Thus, a scale because of its rigidity will hardly be as good as an OI under its best conditions but can hardly let us down as much as an OI sometimes does.*

Sometimes we classify material not in a one-dimensional order but according to types of attitude, types of interest, or types of gratification. The objective tools for this purpose do not present problems which go beyond what we have said about the use of scales. Suppose, for instance, we want to classify people into three groups, according to whether they look at postwar problems mainly from a domestic–economic, a foreign affairs–peace, or a civil liberties–justice point of view We would set up a number of questions and classify people according to the pattern of the answers they give. The standard example for such procedures can be found in Allport and Vernon's Study of Values Test.[22] These psychologists took as a starting point Spranger's well-known personality types. People are characterized according to the values they are most concerned with: power, money, religion, beauty, wisdom, or personal contacts. In order to get to a formalized classification, the test asks people, for instance, what they look for first when they enter a living-room, what historical person they would be most interested in meeting, and so on. A respondent who looks at the books in the room first and who would like most to meet Einstein, etc., would be classified as an intellectual type.

In deciding whether such objective tests or an impressionistic classification based on an OI is preferable, one should keep in mind the fact that it is difficult to develop good test questions of this kind. Impressionistic classifications, even if they have methodological disadvantages, are more easily made in a new situation. One practical solution, therefore, might be to use OI's whenever a problem comes up only once. If we deal with recurring problems such as, for instance, people's eagerness to help in the war effort or their attitude toward our allies or toward government regulation of business, more explicit and standardized criteria for classification might be desirable.

There is also the possibility of trying a combination of both approaches. Taking once more the example of interest in the election, the interviewer might first ask standard questions of the type mentioned above; then he might continue the discussion and note any additional observations which might suggest a correction of the rigid score. Such procedures are often used when it comes to classifying people according to socio-economic status. It seems useful to classify people first according to the rental area of the city in which they live. Then, after the interviewer has talked with the respondent, seen how he dresses and how his living-room looks, he might make an impressionistic correction of the original score.

5. *Is there an easy way to get at motivation?* When we discussed broad motivational interpretations, we stressed all the hazards involved in this method. Correspondingly, it is very difficult to find an objective or formalized method for such an approach. Projective tests come nearest to it. The general idea of these tests is that people are presented with unstructured material. Here is a crying girl; other children are asked to guess why she is crying. Or, an inkblot is shown to some people, as in the Rohrshach test, and they are asked to state what form it signifies to them. It is then assumed that the way people interpret such material, which has no definite meaning of its own, is indicative of what the people themselves are concerned with.[23]

Applications to a public-opinion problem can only be invented because, to our knowledge, such studies have never been tried. If one wants to test people's attitudes toward public administration, one might, for instance, tell a short story of a successful public official who was suddenly dismissed. What was the reason? Was he found to be corrupt? Or was he the victim of a political intrigue? Or didn't he agree with the government's policy?

After Pearl Harbor, when so many people were concerned about the weakness of the American Navy, it would not have been easy to ask direct questions on this subject; few people would have cared to give an unpatriotic answer. One might, however, have shown them a series of pictures of battleships varying in degree of technical perfection. Which, in the opinion of the respondent, is an American and which a Japanese battleship? The proportion of people picking out the poor ship as an American model might have been a good index of the extent of concern about American armaments.

The psychological assumptions involved in a projective test have yet to be studied exhaustively. The answers are usually quite difficult to classify, and much depends upon the interpretation of the analyst. In the future such techniques may provide a very important tool for public opinion research. For the moment it can hardly be claimed that they are much better formalized than a good OI. If, therefore, one is interested in broad motivational interpretations, a well-conducted OI is probably still the best source for material.

6. *The meaning of statistical relationships.* Nothing has to be added to our discussion of the analysis of deviate cases in the preceding section. Here the OI is in its most legitimate place.

Some Conclusions

If we now summarize briefly this critical survey of the OI technique, we can make a number of points as to its position in the general scheme of public opinion research.

We saw that the problem is not new. Since the beginning of social research, students have tried to combine the value of detailed qualitative applications with the advantages of more formalized techniques which could be managed on a mass basis.

We saw, furthermore, that a line along which such an integration could come about emerges. The OI is indispensable at the beginning of any study where it classifies the structure of a problem in all its details. It is also invaluable at the end of a study for anyone who is not satisfied with the mere recording of the low correlations we usually obtain. Good research consists in weaving back and forth between OI's and the more cut-and-dried procedures.

The conversion of OI's into sets of specific poll questions has shown up a new skill in our field and one which has found much too little attention.

The stress on this problem of conversion has revealed a weakness on both sides of the controversy. The proponents of the OI have successfully denounced the shortcomings of single straight poll questions, but by stressing so strongly the informality of the OI they have driven the poll managers to a defensive position, which is delaying the whole progress of opinion research. Field staffs are not equipped to make difficult decisions in the course of the interview. However, the idea of interconnected question sets converted from preceding OI's shifts the weight of the problem from the field staffs to the central office. The attack should be directed against the directors of polls, who do not take the time and the effort to structuralize the problem and to devise the interlocking question structure which any well-trained field staff should be able to handle.

Concerning the classification of complex attitude patterns, another point can be made. Public opinion research has grown so quickly that much of the work is handled by people who do not know the history of social research in the last thirty years. Much valuable thinking and experimenting done in universities long before election results were predicted is immediately applicable to this new field. The construction of scales and the whole tradition of attitude measurement has developed its own logic, which can be profitably applied to the present controversy.

The same efforts have also opened up a considerable number of problems which have not yet been solved at all. The value of check lists, the use of projective tests, and the question of whether simple propaganda influences can be discerned by direct interview are characteristic examples. At all these points patient and painstaking work is needed. The solution of these problems will only be retarded if we let research administrators believe that they face different schools of research, whereas they deal only with different guesses as to what the final answers to these problems will be.

The hope might be expressed that this paper will not be regarded as an attempted judgment in the OI controversy. It tries to show that the problem consists of many different parts. For some problems the OI is indispensable; for others it is definitely wasteful. Often we do not really know the right answer. In these last cases the prudent administrator will do best to look for the combination of methods best adapted to the specific research task on hand.

Notes

1. Hans E. Skott, "Attitude Research in the Department of Agriculture," *Public Opinion Quaterly*, 1943, 7, 280–292.
2. Henry C. Link, "An Experiment in Depth Interviewing," *Public Opinion Quarterly*, 1943, 7, 267–279.
3. P. F. Lazarsfeld and R. K. Merton, "Studies in Radio and Film Propaganda," *Transactions of the New York Academy of Sciences*, Series II, 1943, 6, No. 2, 58–79.
4. It should be emphasized that the question "why" is useful also for the other purposes which will be discussed in the remaining four points. This is easily understood if one considers that the word has hardly any meaning in itself. It is about equivalent to saying that the respondent should talk some more. "Why" is a good start, but it seldom leads to a constructive end if it is not followed by specific questions directed toward what the interviewer really wants to know.
5. Paul Lazarsfeld, "The Art of Asking Why," *National Marketing Review*, I, 1935, 32–43.
6. Paul Lazarsfeld, "Evaluating the Effectiveness of Advertising by Direct Interviews," *Journal of Consulting Psychology*, July–August, 1941.
7. Lickert's work is mainly done for Government agencies and therefore cannot be quoted at the present time. The present paper owes much to discussions with him and some of his associates, especially Bill Gold.
8. Kurt Lewin, "Forces Behind Food Habits and Methods of Change," The Problem of Changing Food Habits, *Bulletin of the National Research Council*, Number 108, October 1943.
9. Herta Herzog, "On Borrowed Experience," *Studies in Philosophy and Social Science*, 1941.
10. R. Wyant and H. Herzog, "Voting Via the Senate Mailbag," *Public Opinion Quarterly*, 1941, 5, 590–624.
11. Gordon W. Allport, "Attitudes," *Handbook of Social Psychology* (ed. C. Murchison), Worcester: Clark University Press, 5935, 798–844.
12. Rhoda Metraux, "Qualitative Attitude Analysis – A Technique for the Study of Verbal Behavior," The Problem of Changing Food Habits, *Bulletin of the National Research Council*, No. 108, October 1943.
13. Hadley Cantril, Herta Herzog, and Hazel Gaudet, *Invasion from Mars*. Princeton: Princeton University Press, 1939.
14. Mirra Komarovsky, *The Unemployed Man and His Family*. New York: Institute of Social Research, 1940.
15. Harold F. Gosnell, *Getting out the Vote*. Chicago: Chicago University Press, 1927.
16. Paul Studenski, "How Polls Can Mislead," *Harpers Magazine*, December 1939.
17. This is the technique which Henry Link used in a more recent study ("An Experiment in Depth Interviewing," *Public Opinion Quarterly*, 1943, 7, 267–279). He first obtained a broad commitment on world participation for the post-war period from his respondents; then he asked a series of definite questions: for the sake of America's participation in world affairs, what would people be willing to accept? A

standing army? Higher taxes? A lower standard of living? Etc. As a device to clarify the implications of people's opinions this is an appropriate procedure, but it is very confusing if it is suggested as a substitute for or even an improvement on the OI in all areas. It is precisely the purpose of the present paper to provide a general scheme, so that in discussing "depth interviews" each participant can point to the specific sector of the entire field he has in mind.

18. E. Smith and E. Suchman, 'Do People Know Why They Buy?" *Journal of Applied Psychology*, 1940, 24, 673–684.

19. We find here a mistake which corresponds to the objection we voiced above against Henry Link's paper. Because he used interlocking questions in one area, he thought that be had shown the uselessness of the OI technique in all other areas. Many of the proponents of the OI, on the other hand, do careful interviewing for the description of attitudes; but when it comes to the discerning of influences, they do bad interviewing and subject their returns to poor classification.

20. Paul Wallin, *Case Study Methods in the Prediction of Personal Adjustment* (ed., Paul Horst). New York: Social Science Research Council, 1941.

21. If such an interest score was used, it was found that for men the correlation between interest and voting was .20, whereas for women it was .50. Women, if they are not interested, do not vote. Men vote even if they are not interested, probably because they are more subject to social pressure. For a general theory of this score procedure see P. Lazarsfeld and W. Robinson, "Quantification of Case Studies," *Journal of Applied Psychology*, 1940, 24, 831–837.

22. Forms of the Allport-Vernon Value Test are distributed by the Psychological Corporation of New York.

23. P. Symonds and W. Samuel, "Projective Methods in the Study of Personality" (Chap. VI of Psychological Tests and Their Uses), *Review of Educational Research*, 1941, II, 80–93.

8

Understanding the Standardized/Non-Standardized Interviewing Controversy

Paul Beatty

1. Introduction

About fifty years ago, a controversy between two seemingly irreconcilable schools of thought in the survey field reached full force. Some researchers believed that obtaining useful survey information required loosely structured "in depth" interviews; others countered that more structured surveys were highly preferable to this cumbersome method. Lazarsfeld's (1944) "Negotiation" between the two viewpoints is widely regarded as a classic, suggesting common ground that future researchers could work together on. Ironically, today we are witnessing a controversy that is strikingly similar in some important ways. Some researchers argue that standardized interviewing is inherently riddled with interviewer–respondent communication problems; consequently, social scientists should rely on more conversational interviews to obtain valid information (Suchman and Jordan 1990; Mishler 1986; Briggs 1986). Supporters of standardized interviewing defend the validity of the methodology in spite of some common pitfalls, arguing that standardization is an essential characteristic of modern survey research (Fowler and Mangione 1990). Recent criticisms of standardized interviewing have been the focus of increasing debate (Schaeffer 1991), and a clear-cut compromise between advocates of standardization and non-standardization is not apparent. These interviewing styles differ in many substantial ways.

If one understands the conflict between the two viewpoints, however, there are logical compromises. But understanding how this conflict evolved is

---

Source: *Journal of Official Statistics*, vol. 11, no. 2, 1995, pp. 147–160.

a tricky matter. Looking at methodological pieces from the past on interviewing is insufficient, as they provide little insight into how interviewing was actually conducted; likewise, interviewer training manuals from the past explain little of the basis for the strategies they employed. To completely understand the forces that have moved surveys toward standardization, as well as those that have resisted, it is necessary to look at both works together. When this is done, new insights emerge regarding what issues have been left unresolved in the debate, and what common ground exists between the two schools of thought. Though no one can predict the future with certainty, the most logical directions that researchers should follow seem surprisingly clear.

2. The Early Development of Standardized Interviewing

Standardization as it exists today was developed to gain tighter control of the errors produced by interviewers. Researchers maintain this control through the precise scripting of questions and development of standardized behavior appropriate for interviewers to follow in all situations. The goal, as noted by Groves (1989, p. 358), is "nothing less than the elimination of the interviewer as a source of measurement error." This has not, however, always been a priority in survey research; in fact, this goal developed quite gradually.

A fundamental debate motivated changes in the degree of question scripting and interviewer standardization: should interviewers be "knowledgeable experts" who "conversationalized" respondents through interviews, using questionnaires as guidelines; or should interviewers be non-experts who obtained information on a mass-scale using standardized techniques? This debate goes back to the 1930s when interviewers were first used for academic research. Most researchers viewed interviewers as an escape from the restrictions of closed, self-administered questionnaires and were anxious to use this potential freedom (Converse 1987). The U.S. Department of Agriculture's Division of Program Surveys, headed by Rensis Likert, pioneered the methodology. This method was a scientific extension of an earlier program within the Department, in which mobile observers discussed an informal set of topics with arbitrarily selected farmers. With the new method, the questions were standardized, probing was neutral, and probability sampling was used. However, the interviews retained a conversational tone, consisting entirely of open-ended questions, and interviewers necessarily had wide latitude in determining when respondents had adequately answered the questions. To compensate for that, interviewers were highly trained, generally holding graduate degrees. Following the field period, the open-ended data demanded meticulous attention for complex coding. The process had high validity, but was expensive and time consuming. There were reliability concerns as well (Hyman 1991; C.F. Cannell, personal communication, May 1993).

This method was initially viewed as being more sound than traditional "polling" methods, which relied on unskilled interviewers asking easily-coded "yes/no" type questions. While the polling method generated faster answers at significantly lower cost, more academically-minded researchers viewed poll questions as "incomplete, artificial, and rigid, almost bound to distort people's attitudes" (Converse 1984, p. 272). Then Lazarsfeld (1944), in a widely known article, forcefully argued that a compromise position was viable – relying on "interlocking poll questions" with some open questions providing elaboration. With that, a move toward greater standardization was begun (Hyman 1991).

Still, while questions became more closed and interviewers became part time and less-skilled (C.F. Cannell, personal communication, May 1993; Hyman 1991), standardization did not develop to anywhere near the extent we see today. By 1945, the National Opinion Research Center (NORC) had made major strides toward standardizing interviews and reducing the amount of interpretation required by interviewers, but some open questions were still used. At the Bureau for Applied Social Research, Lazarsfeld had encouraged compromise, but always believed that the meanings of questions should be more fixed than actual wordings. Consequently, they still used looser forms of interviewing. The University of Michigan's Survey Research Center (SRC) also compromised. They moved toward standardization, but continued a considerable commitment to asking open questions, even though they had no experimental evidence supporting the utility of the method (Converse 1987).

Standardization continued to grow because it was cheaper, faster, and seemingly effective. Furthermore, Hyman (1954) began to rigorously explore the effect of interviewer variation resulting from non-standardized behavior, which paved the way for further methodological work. It is logical, then, to wonder why resistance to standardization continued. SRC's *Manual for Interviewers* (1954, pp. 29–31, 33) provides some insight into the continuing compromise position there. The manual balances such statements as "the questionnaire helps to standardize the interview," with instructions such as "use the questionnaire, but use it informally;" another set of instructions reads "ask the questions exactly as worded on the questionnaire," while a few pages later, the interviewer is empowered to "reword the question slightly ... as a last resort" to clear up misinterpretations. The manual instructs interviewers to work in a dual role, as a "technician who applies standard techniques to each interview," while maintaining the role of "human being who builds up a permissive and warm relationship with each respondent." On the one hand, we see a genuine desire to embrace standardization – even though interviewers are given some leeway, they are instructed to use it with great caution. There are many mentions throughout the manual that standardization is a key component of surveys' usefulness. "Obviously," states the manual, "if a question is differently worded for different respondents, it will not yield comparable results." Given a statement such as that, it is surprising that interviewers maintained as much discretion as they did.

3. The Importance of Rapport

It is also clear, however, that another issue is considered of great importance for the success of survey interviewing: rapport between the interviewer and respondent. Likert's (1947, pp. 199–200) interest in open interviewing can be partially explained by its perceived importance in generating rapport:

> Most attitude scale research was based on work with students. They, at times ... insisted that none of the alternatives gave them an opportunity to express their attitudes correctly. These objections were usually ignored ... When it was tried on the adult population ... respondents, in their homes, were told that the fine points in their thinking did not matter, that they had to restrict their thinking on the problem to the dimensions seen by the experimenter ... [and then] rapport went out the door and often the interviewer was close behind ... The importance of respondent co-operation throughout the interview and the necessity of limiting the procedures used in polls and surveys to those which build and develop this rapport does not yet seem to be recognized generally.

Likert adds, in an otherwise diplomatic piece, "No wonder most polls restrict the interview to not more than ten minutes." For Likert, rapport and open-ended questions were closely linked – if the interview was too structured, rapport would necessarily suffer.

Clearly, Likert's definition of rapport involved a spirit of cooperation and respect between the interviewer and respondent. This type of task-directed "rapport" is still a goal of survey researchers today (C.F. Cannell, personal communication, May 1993). Nevertheless, the concept was never well-defined. Hyman (1954) was one of the first to recognize the difference between "total" involvement with the interviewer and more fundamental "task" involvement. Task involvement could help respondents assume their roles and increase response validity – but total involvement could lead to response bias, with respondents agreeing with perceived interviewer opinions. Later studies conceptualized rapport as involving both professional interest and personal warmth (Weiss 1968; Henson, Cannell, and Lawson 1976).

While researchers failed to clarify the ambiguity of the term, they simultaneously regarded rapport as essential – and rapport was often seen as contradictory to standardization. SRC's Manual for Interviewers (1954, pp. 25 and 34) makes this quite clear. The word "rapport" appears dozens of times, most prominently in this statement of purpose: "Your goal is 'rapport' with the respondent ... [This] designates the *personal relationship of confidence and understanding* between the interviewer and respondent which provides the foundation for good interviewing" (italics mine). Elsewhere, whole sections are designed to help maintain rapport ("the interviewer recognizes that good rapport must be maintained throughout the interview to insure [*sic*] full and valid information") that explain its many benefits (such as "good rapport stimulates discussion"). In short, the 1954 manual stresses the importance of rapport above virtually anything else. The manual also indicates that too much standardization was at odds with rapport building. Consider this excerpt:

> You should keep the questionnaire in sight during the interview, glancing at it before asking each question. Put each question to the respondent in a natural and conversational tone of voice, not obviously reading it. Try to avoid drawing too much attention to the questionnaire since your goal is to set up a friendly relationship between yourself and the respondent; too much obvious attention to the questionnaire makes for an atmosphere of interrogation, which is something you want to avoid. Each question should be asked in a manner implying that it presents an interesting topic, and that you are extremely interested in having the respondent's ideas on it (p. 31).

Although standardization seemed more desirable over time, the higher importance of rapport stood as a barrier to its development. However, the original "task-oriented" conceptualization of rapport no longer fit, with several references to personal relationships and personal interest in respondents' answers. A clean definition of the concept remained elusive in spite of its deemed importance.

Weiss's (1968) study of response validity delivered the first serious blow to rapport. Interviewers in this study rated respondents on a scale from "confiding" to "hostile," taken as a measure of "total involvement." Respondents' answers were verified through record checks. Surprisingly, the most "confiding" respondents provided the least valid information, indicating that this type of rapport could actually be harmful.

Further attacks on rapport developed from the fact that it had no consistently applied definition. Goudy and Potter (1975, p. 541), citing various definitions used over the years, noted that no matter how rapport was defined, there was no evidence that it improved interviewing productiveness; in fact, citing an observation by Gordon (1969), they questioned whether rapport might actually be destructive: "Often the neophyte thinks he has conducted an excellent interview because 'rapport was perfect' and the respondent was 'completely at ease, talked spontaneously, and documented that she had enjoyed the interview.' Yet when the interview is analyzed it is found to be incomplete, superficial, and ambiguous." Goudy and Potter (1975, p. 543) therefore concluded:

> When we realize that problems exist in reading questions correctly, recording information, and coding that information [they cite multiple sources here] then studying rapport seems less important. Unless agreement on a conceptual and operational definition can be reached and unless elements in the interviewing situation purporting to constitute

rapport can be isolated and tested, further empirical studies of rapport may be useless ... [Researchers should] abandon the concept [of rapport], admit that interviewing is an art that may contain certain scientifically controllable elements, and work to attain reliability and validity in interview data through interview effects currently measurable.

Thus, by the mid-1970s, survey researchers were questioning the wisdom of the rapport-building approach, turning their attention to "interview effects currently measurable." Research on controlling interviewer variation through standardization, previously hindered by concerns for rapport, had new opportunities to flourish.

4. Reduction of Interviewer Effects

The demise of rapport has made a major impression on interviewing methodology as practiced today. Until this point, relatively flexible interviewing could be defended on several grounds: first, it facilitated rapport-building, providing a basis for the interviewer–respondent relationship. This was regarded as essential for validity and generating discussion. Also, but less noticeably, it provided a diagnostic capability for communication problems. Of the two justifications, rapport arguably attracted more attention; with that gone, there was little standing in the way of more standardized interviews. Meanwhile, researchers had become increasingly curious about the errors introduced by interviewers. Kahn and Cannell (1957) developed theoretical frameworks to describe interviewer/respondent interactions in psychological terms, while Hyman led a series of NORC projects on interviewer effects, culminating in his 1954 book. These works, however, were primarily descriptive. For example, Hyman explored whether interviewers' own opinions and ideologies influenced respondents. His goal, though, was *understanding* where these biases were, not formulating a plan: to reduce them. *Reducing* interviewer error was a different matter altogether, as this would require exercising a great deal of control over interviewers – not an option considering the importance of rapport. The interest in controlling interviewer effects had clearly grown as rapport's importance faded. Cannell, Marquis, and Laurent (1977, pp. 1 and 77) noted that in spite of increasingly complex demands from survey research, "little has been done toward perfecting the interview procedure as a method of data collection." Their summary of interviewing research led to specific recommendations for interviewer controls, which would "improve communication between the participants in the interview but will not direct the responses." As more time passed, methodological work was created with the goal of stamping out interviewing error altogether. Such efforts focused on the development of training techniques an precise prescriptions for what interviewers are told to do (Groves 1989).

Fowler and Mangione (1990) provide a thorough overview of the philosophy and practice of standardized interviewing as it has become. They recommend reading questions exactly as worded, using only nondirective probing, and maintaining a neutral interviewing stance with no interviewer discretion in recording answers. They also call for practice-oriented training, systematic interview monitoring, and close-super-vision, in further attempts to control interviewer variation. But perhaps the result of this movement may be examined most clearly in its practical application: the interviewing manual from SRC (1983), *General Interviewing Techniques* (GIT). The GIT manual differs from the 1954 manual chiefly in its emphasis on examples designed to develop precise, standardized behavior from interviewers. Gone is the 1954 manual's friendly prose describing the ideal relationship between the respondent and interviewer, motivated by explanations about how the interviewer fits into the big picture. GIT is an ambitious technical document, three times the size of its 1954 counterpart, filled with expanded sections on question asking, clarification techniques, probing, feedback, and so on. Its purpose is not general description; it is intensely specific, containing dozens of examples and seven lengthier exercises for trainees.

Consider the case of probing: the 1954 manual devotes eight pages to the topic, offering a list of possible probes to use when rapport alone was insufficient to elicit complete answers. The 1983 GIT devotes 30 pages to the topic, providing a complete list of acceptable probes, with practice exercises to illustrate proper applications. Training materials such as this clearly document the attempted suppression of any interviewer variation.

The increase in survey standardization clearly brought many advantages. First, the survey process became much faster. This is particularly important in an age when surveys are the basis of forecasting elections and economic outcomes, developing business strategies, and making other time-sensitive decisions. Without standardization, it is difficult to conceive the amount of processing that would be necessary before data would be available for large academic research programs. Statistical precision is another benefit; increasingly elaborate statistical methods may be applied to data collected through standardized methods. Stouffer *et al.*'s (1949) landmark analyses relied on simple tabulations; analyses today draw upon such techniques as multiple regression and log-linear models, which require much stronger assumptions about the data. Also, as we have seen, standardization gave survey researchers new power to study and attack the most easily measurable sources of survey error, including interviewer error.

There are, however, important sources of survey errors that are more difficult to measure. Less structured interviewing, as mentioned previously, had two advantages. The most noticeable of them, rapport, had been discredited. Yet the other, diagnosing communication problems, had not been addressed directly as interviewer style changed. This shortcoming, I argue, is the root of the current standardized/non-standardized interviewing controversy.

5. The Current Controversy

The basis of current attacks on the usefulness of standardized interviewing is that it strangles communication with respondents. Interviewers have very little discretion – to exercise in resolving communication problems. A possible alternate type of interviewing, as described by Groves (1989, p. 404), dictates that "interviewers should be trained in the concepts inherent in the questions and be allowed to probe, rephrase, and adapt the questionnaire to individual respondent needs." Mishler (1986) and Briggs (1986) provide detailed justifications for non-standardized interviewing and suggestions for alternate strategies. Mishler calls for interviewers and respondents to work together to "jointly construct" meanings of questions and answers, while Briggs lays out a plan for "acquiring metacommunicative competence" to interpret interview data.

More recently, Suchman and Jordan (1990, pp. 232 and 241) claim that the conflict between interviews as conversations and interviews as data-collection interactions has never been adequately resolved. According to their argument, surveys rely on conversational norms to succeed (i.e., asking and answering questions) while suppressing "interactional resources that routinely mediate uncertainties of relevance and interpretation [in conversations]". They conclude that "the standardized interview has become such a fragile, technical object that it is no longer viable in the real world of interaction" a strong indictment. However, the entire debate, based on a resurgent interest in diagnosing communication problems, is quite understandable when one considers the evolution of interviewing in theory and practice. These problems have been set aside in the ambitious effort to wipe out interviewer error, and Suchman and Jordan are simply bringing them back to the forefront.

Critics of Suchman and Jordan might counter that though survey interviews do have certain problems, their representations are highly overstated. They surely present worst-case scenarios: rambling, undirected interactions between interviewers and respondents in which the interviewer follows no observable conventions for clarification of misunderstandings (such as repeat of question, providing definitions or guidelines, and neutral probes) and keeping the respondent focused (through feedback to emphasize the proper role of the respondent). Training interviewers to perform these tasks is essential for successful standardized interviewing (Fowler and Mangione 1990); furthermore, Billiet and Loosveldt (1988) have shown that better trained interviewers were more likely to obtain adequate answers to questions demanding more respondent instructions, probing, and feedback. Suchman and Jordan have not provided examples of the failure of proper interviewing to yield useable survey data; they have merely provided examples that interviewing, when performed poorly, can yield unusable data, which is not the same thing.

Yet, though their specific examples are easily criticized, their general notions cannot be easily dismissed. The strict rules of GIT de-emphasize any intelligent contribution from interviewers; thus, it is possible that meaning may not be standardized even though the literal wording of the question has been properly conveyed. For example, Suchman and Jordan document one case of a respondent's confusion about what constitutes an "alcoholic beverage" (the respondent failed to treat wine as an alcoholic beverage, which seemingly contradicted previous answers). The interviewer clearly exacerbates the situation by following procedures that most survey researchers would consider inadequate. Nevertheless, it is not clear that an interviewer could have eradicated the problem using GIT techniques – at least given the questionnaire as written. Standardized interviewing did not address the problem of communicating correct meanings to the respondent. Furthermore, one could argue that even if interviewers did have adequate discretion to address ambiguities and misunderstandings, they are unable to pay attention to such matters because these tasks have lower priority than following highly detailed rules.

Theoretically, if interviewers were allowed more leeway to diagnose communication problems and clarify the meanings of questions, the goals of current survey research would be more successfully met: to standardize the meanings of questions so that we may infer something about the population in question. Yet, we have seen that standardization of interviews addresses important concerns that Mishler, Briggs, and Suchman and Jordan ignore, and as Schaeffer (1991, p. 368) notes, "reforms that ignore the justification for standardization run the risk of repeating old mistakes." The question then becomes: what level of standardization maximizes the usefulness of survey research? Arguments have been raised on extreme positions for and against standardization, which may seem incompatible. Is there a compromise that addresses the concerns of both sides?

6. Moving Toward Sensible Compromise

Before we can move forward, it is important to remember the needs that standardization fulfills. The benefits of practical simplicity, timeliness, and greater statistical power have cemented standardization into the core of modern surveying. To deny this is to ignore the most practical facts of the matter.

This does not mean, however, that compromise is impossible and will not occur. We are, after all, interested in reducing *total* error in surveys. If attacking the slightest interviewer deviation brings about modest reduction of interviewer error – but simultaneously causes a *greater increase* in error from the respondent, who is unable to draw on the communicative resources of an informed, intelligent interviewer – then the strategy is self-defeating. Technologically, we could eliminate interviewer error altogether by using computers to conduct interviews, either by phone or through computerized self-administered methods (U.S. Office of Management and Budget 1990). Arguably, one reason that researchers do not widely do this is because human interaction still has powerful advantages. In fact, survey researchers first used interviewers to capitalize on these advantages. The benefits necessarily go hand-in-hand with some drawbacks. It is essential for researchers desiring the "total elimination" of interviewer error to accept that this is impossible. Following precise interviewing rules remains critical to collecting the rewards standardization brings, but standardization advocates must recognize that tightly prescribed interviewer behavior does have an ultimate point of diminishing returns.

On the other hand, "interviewer liberation" offers little hope for the future of survey research. Liberating interviewers merely trades one set of problems for another – and "may .mask an unwillingness to face similar problems posed by other styles of research" (Schaeffer 1991, p. 370). Briggs's (1986), for example, criticizes standardized interviews because interviewers may misunderstand norms of conversation and respondent frames of reference indifferent respondent groups. While researchers should be concerned about these issues, Briggs' proposed solutions return to previous problems of low reliability, high interviewer variance, inefficiency with large samples, and high cost. In addition, the fact that even slight wording changes can dramatically alter response distributions has been well documented (Schuman and Presser 1981). Given these drawbacks, the difficulties of measurement without standardization are apparent. The real question that remains is: how can researchers solve communication problems while harnessing the full benefits of standardization?

Survey questions themselves are of central importance. Successful standardized interviewing depends upon questions that can be clearly and consistently understood by respondents (Fowler and Mangione 1990). This is a crucial point, because detractors of standardization such as Suchman and Jordan use poor questions as examples of standardization's failure (Schaeffer 1991). Yet, standardization advocates open themselves to attack because "many questions ... in major surveys with large samples carried out by very professional organizations, could be readily identified as not meeting [basic] standards." This "creates [problems] difficult to solve ... in a standardized way" (Fowler and Mangione 1990, p. 137).

The importance of pretesting, which allows one to assess questionnaire communication difficulties through dozens of fresh perspectives, must therefore continue to grow. Too often, researchers regard pretests as a convenience for "when time allows" (Converse and Presser 1986). Casual attitudes toward pretesting must be continually discouraged if standardized surveys are to be successful. In addition, Fowler (1992) has explored systematic pretest methods, using them in one case to identify and correct unclear terms that were likely biasing survey estimates. Another more systematic method is cognitive interviewing, designed to help researchers understand how respondents interpret questions. The volume of research recently published in this area (Willis, Royston, and Bercini 1991; Jobe and Mingay 1991; Tanur 1992) indicates that enthusiasm for the collaboration between cognitive psychology and survey methodology continues to rise. Interestingly, the use of cognitive interviewing to improve the viability of standardized interviewing is similar to what Lazarsfeld suggested in 1944 – the use of closed questions with more open-ended techniques used for development and elaboration. More quantitative procedures such as behavior coding may also grow (at least to the extent that such labor-intense activities can be carried out in a timely manner). Some researchers who design and analyze large-scale surveys have only cursory knowledge of these procedures, so there is hope that their effect on survey quality will continue to expand.

Also, researchers need to reevaluate the sort of behavior they identify as "good interviewing" and reward interviewers for accordingly. They should keep in mind that the goal of standardized survey interviewing is to obtain complete answers to questions uniformly administered and clearly understood. Often, however, interviewer success is measured by how well the interviewer conforms to specifically prescribed behaviors (Was that an acceptable probe? Was that acceptable feedback given to the respondent?) While these are important – directive probes and inappropriate feedback can damage data quality – this approach is incomplete. It is possible that communication problems arise because interviewers spend too much time making sure that they conform to highly specific criteria (which they are rewarded for), and not enough time evaluating whether respondents understand and answer questions correctly (which they *should* be rewarded for). This weakness can be overcome *within* the constraints of standardized methodology – not by allowing much "interviewer leeway," but by avoiding overzealous enforcement of the smallest letter of the law when clear answers are obtained through generally acceptable means.

Researchers also need to spend more time teaching interviewers the concepts inherent in the questions they ask – not so that interviewers can create conversations, but so interviewers can judge the completeness of respondents' answers. Recent studies have shown that non-scripted interviewer behavior – perhaps one-sixth of interviewer activity – usually centers on clarifying inadequate answers, such as through probing (Sykes and Collins 1992). Also, questions requiring the most probing are most likely to create interviewer: effects (Mangione, Fowler, and Louis 1992). These studies confirm that greater emphasis on questionnaire development, which will reduce the amount of probing necessary during interviews, is time well spent. Yet, some probing is inevitable in interactions of this sort. Researchers can do much more to ensure that non-directive probing is based on a sound understanding of survey objectives, rather than interviewers' own speculation of what constitutes a complete answer. Question-by-question specifications (Q–×–Q's) should be written consistently, and more time should be spent to ensure that interviewers understand them. Interviewers often read the Q–×–Q's for the first time when a respondent indicates that he or she does not understand a question. Standardized practice essentially teaches interviewers to follow algorithms in order to elicit responses; this practice may have led to unwarranted optimism that interviewers can do their job successfully with very little understanding of the questions they ask.

Another issue – interviewer style – has received comparatively little attention recently, but the appropriateness of personal (as opposed to formal) styles of interviewing may not be a closed issue. A study by van der Zouwen, Dijkstra, and Smit (1991) suggests that personal interviewing styles – such as allowing interviewers to act in an "understanding manner" – may generate more complete or accurate answers from respondents under some circumstances. Unfortunately, interviewers employing this style tend to use more suggestive probes and accept incomplete answers from respondents. Thus, respondent performance may improve through a more personal relationship, but extra steps must be taken to guard against interviewer error. Traditionally, maximizing the interviewer-respondent relationship and ensuring standardized-measurement have been viewed as contradictory goals – as we saw in the debate surrounding the term "rapport." Yet, researchers may find choices other than "conversation," with all the unstructuredness it implies, and a completely scripted, austere interaction. Exploring the consequences of various interviewer styles, while maintaining the general rules of standardization, is an important topic for research.

These are the areas where the most energy should be spent in reducing survey communication error. Many of them take place during questionnaire design, before interviewers are involved; others involve adapting the role of the interviewer. Advocates of both standardization and non-standardization raise important points – issues that have been debated since the earliest beginnings of survey research. But it is important to note that while the issues raised by non-standardization advocates can be addressed within the context of standardization, the reverse is not true. That is, precision of measurement, timeliness, and other issues previously discussed are extremely difficult to achieve without reasonable control of variation introduced by interviewers. Thus, the most logical course of action is to address communication difficulties within the context of standardized interviewing, and to empirically investigate the point where standardization starts to substantially interfere with communication.

Perhaps reaching a consensus has been difficult because researchers with very different aims have been involved in the debate. Most criticisms of current survey practice noted here come from anthropologists or sociolinguists, interested in exploring "the interview as a communicative event" (Briggs 1986, p. 2). Briggs's (1986) discussion of "acquiring metacommunicative competence," focuses on a variety of anthropological and sociolinguistic studies in a Spanish-speaking community. Most of these are non-quantitative. Mishler's (1986) chapter on the "joint construction of meaning" between interviewers and respondents uses a physician/patient interview as an example. In both cases, the emphasis is on understanding details of individual behavior, mostly in a non-quantitative manner. However, as Fowler and Mangione (1990, p. 12) point out, the purpose of standardized survey research is to measure, or produce "quantitative or mathematical descriptions of the population ... [There is] no intrinsic interest in the answers of these individuals per se." It is not surprising that researchers of the former type, looking to standardized survey researchers for a systematic interviewing framework, may find standardized, measurement-oriented interviewing to be inadequate. This is especially true since the success of surveys has been traditionally judged by sampling designs and response rates – measures of statistical accuracy rather than communicative accuracy. And, even though standardized survey researchers have become more interested in communication issues in the last decade, this interest has emerged primarily from psychology, not anthropology or sociolinguistics. Thus, the two schools of thought may have had little basis for communication themselves.

The lack of mutual understanding of advocates of standardization and non-standardization remains considerable and troubling. Literature advocating either side is common, but there is little acknowledgment of specific points of the others' arguments. That is one reason it is valuable to examine old interviewing manuals and old methodological pieces. It is easy for both sides of the current debate to write off the other as short-sighted, or ignorant of larger issues. When we look into the past, however, we see that elements of this debate have been present for a long time; we can also see what concerns have motivated changes in research methods. These are not new problems, but the debate over them continues. We have much to learn about tangible issues, such as where standardization breaks down (Schaeffer 1991), but these are clouded by fundamental misunderstandings such as this.

7. Conclusion

While arguments of the need for conversational interviews are overstated, they are also understandable. Over the last fifty years, survey researchers' views of the ideal interaction between interviewers and respondents have changed considerably. Interviewers were initially valued for the freedom they brought, though researchers increasingly realized that freedom went hand-in-hand with interviewer-introduced error. Paralyzed by rapport for some years, researchers finally confronted interviewer error head-on as rapport faded into the background. New awareness of the benefits of standardization continued this process. The resulting attempt to eliminate interviewer error also sharply reduced the ability of interviewers to resolve communication difficulties, due to the extremeness with which these changes were attempted. Only in the last few years have researchers started to understand this deficiency and compensate for it with increased attention to questionnaire design and evaluation prior to interviewing. The proper conclusion is not that standardized interviewing is unworkable, but that it is time for a greater understanding between its advocates and opponents. The elements of this debate have been present for over 50 years – whether "various non-directive means of stimulating full discussion in the interviewing situation" (Skott 1943) are preferable to "more objective methods of research" (Lazarsfeld 1944). Once again, it is time for negotiation. Rather than standing on opposite sides of the rift, all social researchers need to appreciate the legitimate concerns addressed by those on the other side, and work together toward fashioning strategies that will maximize the usefulness of survey research into the next century.

References

Billiet, J. and Loosveldt, G. (1988). Improvement of the Quality of Responses to Factual Survey Questions by Interviewer Training. *Public Opinion Quarterly*, 52, 190–211.

Briggs, C.L. (1986). *Learning How to Ask: A Sociolinguistic Appraisal of the Role of the Interviewer in Social Science Research.* Cambridge, MA: Cambridge University.

Cannell, C.F., Marquis, K.H., and Laurent, A. (1977). A Summary of Studies of Interviewing Methodology. Vital and Health Statistics, DHEW Publication no. (HRA) 77–1343, ser. 2, no. 69. Washington, D.C.: U.S. Government Printing Office.

Converse, J.M. (1984). Strong Arguments and Weak Evidence: The Open/Closed Questioning Controversy of the 1940s. *Public Opinion Quarterly*, 48, 267–282.

——. (1987). *Survey Research in the United States: Roots and Emergence 1890–1960.* Berkeley, CA: University of California.

Converse, J.M. and Presser, S. (1986). *Survey Questions: Handcrafting the Standardized Questionnaire.* Newbury Park, CA: Sage.

Fowler, F.J. and Mangione, T.W. (1990). *Standardized Survey Interviewing: Minimizing Interviewer-Related Error.* Newbury Park, CA: Sage.

Fowler, F.J. (1992). How Unclear Terms Affect Survey Data. *Public Opinion Quarterly*, 56, 218–231.

Gordon, B.L. (1969). *Interviewing: Strategy, Techniques, and Tactics.* Homewood, IL: Dorsey. Cited in Goudy, W.J. and Potter, H.R. (1975). Interviewer Rapport: Demise of a Concept. *Public Opinion Quarterly*, 39, 530–543.

Goudy, W.J. and Potter, H.R. (1975). Interviewer Rapport: Demise of a Concept. *Public Opinion Quarterly*, 39, 530–543.

Groves, R.M. (1989). *Survey Errors and Survey Costs.* New York: John Wiley.

Guenzel, P.J., Berckmans, T.R., and Cannell, C.F. (1983). *General Interviewing Techniques.* Ann Arbor, MI: The University of Michigan.

Henson, R., Cannell, C.F., and Lawson, S. (1976). Effects of Interviewer Style on Quality of Reporting in a Survey Interview. *The Journal of Psychology*, 93, 221–227.

Hyman, H.H. (1954). *Interviewing in Social Research.* Chicago: University of Chicago Press.

——. (1991). *Taking Society's Measure: A Personal History of Survey Research.* New York: Russell Sage.

Jobe, J.B. and Mingay, D.J. (1991). Cognition and Survey Measurement: History and Overview. *Applied Cognitive Psychology*, 5, 175–192.

Kahn, R. and Cannell, C.F. (1957). *The Dynamics of Interviewing.* New York: John Wiley.

Lazarsfeld, P.F. (1944). The Controversy Over Detailed Interviews – An Offer for Negotiation. *Public Opinion Quarterly*, 8, 38–60.

Likert, R. (1947). The Sample Interview Survey: A Fundamental Research Tool of the Social Sciences. In *Current Trends in Psychology*, ed. W. Dennis, Pittsburgh, PA: University of Pittsburgh.

Mangione, T.W., Fowler, F.J., and Louis, T.A. (1992). Question Characteristics and Interviewer Effects. *Journal of Official Statistics*, 8, 293–307.

Mishler, E.G. (1986). *Research Interviewing*. Cambridge, MA: Harvard University Press.

Schaeffer, N.C. (1991). Conversation with a Purpose – or Conversation? Interaction in the Standardized Interview. In *Measurement Errors in Surveys*, eds. P. Biemer, R. Groves, L. Lyberg, N. Mathiowetz, S. Sudman, New York: John Wiley.

Schuman, H. and Presser, S. (1981). Questions and Answers in Attitude Surveys. San Diego: Academic Press.

Skott, H.E. (1943). Attitude Research in the Department of Agriculture. *Public Opinion Quarterly*, 7, 280–292. Cited In Lazarsfeld, P.F. (1944). The Controversy Over Detailed Interviews – An Offer for Negotiation. *Public Opinion Quarterly*, 8, 38–60.

Stouffer, S.A., Suchman, E.A., DeVinney, L.C., Star, S.A., and Williams, R.M. (1949). *The American Soldier, Volume I: Adjustment During Army Life*. Princeton, NJ: Princeton University.

Suchman, L. and Jordan, B. (1990). Interactional Troubles in Face-to-Face Survey Interviews. *Journal of the American Statistical Association*, 85, 232–241.

Survey Research Center, The University of Michigan (1954). *Manual for Interviewers*. Ann Arbor, MI: University of Michigan.

Sykes, W. and Collins, M. (1992). Anatomy of the Survey Interview. *Journal of Official Statistics*, 8, 277–291.

Tanur, J.T., ed. (1992). *Questions About Questions: Inquiries into the Cognitive Bases of Surveys*. New York: Russell Sage.

U.S. Office of Management and Budget (1990). Computer-Assisted Survey Information Collection. *Statistical Policy Working Paper* 19. Springfield, VA: National Technical Information Service.

van der Zouwen, J., Dijkstra, W., and Smit, J. (1991). Studying Respondent-Interviewer Interaction: The Relationship Between Interviewing Style, Interviewer Behavior, and Response Behavior. In *Measurement Errors in Surveys*, ed. P. Biemer, R. Groves, L. Lyberg, N. Mathiowetz, S. Sudman, New York: John Wiley.

Weiss, C.H. (1968). Validity of Welfare Mothers' Interview Responses. *Public Opinion Quarterly*, 32, 622–633.

Willis, G. B., Royston, P., and Bercini, D. (1991). The Use of Verbal Report Methods in the Development and Testing of Survey Questionnaires. *Applied Cognitive Psychology*, 5, 1–17.

9

Does Conversational Interviewing Reduce Survey Measurement Error?

Michael F. Schober & Frederick G. Conrad

Introduction

In the typical survey interview, interchanges like this one sometimes occur:

Interviewer (I): Last week, did you do any work for pay?
Respondent (R): Well, that depends. What exactly do you mean by work?

The interviewer is now faced with a choice. Should she use her knowledge to answer the respondent's question, or should she leave the interpretation of "work" up to the respondent?

According to the prevailing philosophy of survey interviewing, *standardization*, the interviewer must leave the interpretation of the question up to the respondent. Interviewers must present exactly the same stimulus to all respondents, always reading exactly the same question and never interpreting the question in any way (Fowler 1991; Fowler and Mangione 1990). When a respondent solicits help, the interviewer should use "neutral probing" techniques: repeat the question, ask for the respondent's interpretation (e.g., saying "whatever it means to you" or "we need *your* interpretation of the question"), or present the response alternatives (Would that be a yes or a no?). The idea is that respondents can only be guaranteed to be answering the same question if the stimulus – the words uttered by the interviewer – is uniform from one interview to the next. This stimulus uniformity should reduce measurement error resulting from the interviewer.

Source: *Public Opinion Quarterly*, vol. 61, 1997, pp. 576–602.

In contrast, critics in the survey world (Suchman and Jordan 1990, 1991) and in other disciplines (e.g., Briggs 1986; Holstein and Gubrium 1995; Kvale 1994) would argue that the interviewer in our example should help the respondent and define "work for pay." The argument is that response validity is undermined if respondents interpret questions idiosyncratically. Indeed, substantial evidence in the survey world supports this contention (see, e.g., Belson's [1981, 1986] findings that even ordinary words like "weekend," "children," "you," and "generally" in surveys are interpreted in many different ways). As a remedy, these critics have proposed or indirectly endorsed *conversationally flexible* interviewing techniques. Interviewers should engage in something more like ordinary conversation, deviating from the standardized script to assure that respondents interpret questions consistently and correctly.

Proponents of flexible interviewing claim that it should lead to more accurate responses than standardized interviewing does (Suchman and Jordan 1990,1991), but proponents of standardization argue just the opposite (Fowler 1991; Fowler and Mangione 1990). Who is correct? As Schaeffer (1991) puts it, "It is an open question whether systematically giving participants more access to "normal" conversational resources would improve the quality of the interaction or the resulting data" (p.371). This study is a first attempt at just such a systematic comparison.

The Debate

Proponents of standardization argue that the assumptions of flexibility ignore the history of what led to standardization in the first place. Standardized techniques were developed because of evidence that interviewers were influencing responses and because researchers needed greater statistical precision and more affordable ways to test large populations (see Beatty 1995). Proponents of standardization point out that the arguments for flexibility are based on a few extreme examples of flawed interactions (Kovar and Royston 1990). They suggest that it is poor question wording rather than standardized interaction that leads to problems, and these problems might be remedied with better question pretesting. In addition, problems due to respondents' misunderstanding may be rare enough to be unimportant in large-sample surveys.

In contrast, proponents of flexibility argue that rigid adherence to survey scripts jeopardizes validity (Suchman and Jordan 1990, p. 233) because there is no guarantee that all respondents will interpret questions the same way. Standardization, the argument goes, does not allow the "full resources of conversational interaction" that are necessary to assure consistent interpretations. This claim is consistent with a long tradition of empirical research, both in the laboratory and based on naturalistic observation, that shows how conversational interaction can be essential for understanding (see, e.g., Brennan 1990; Cicourel 1973; Clark 1992, 1996; Clark and Wilkes-Gibbs 1986; Goffman

1981; Goodwin 1981 Gumperz 1982; Krauss and Fussell 1996; Rogoff 1990; Sacks, Schegloff and Jefferson 1974; Schegloff 1984; Schiffrin 1994, Schober and Clark 1989; Tannen 1989, among many others).

We agree with Schaeffer (1991) and Beatty (1995) that both positions have merit. But we propose that they are correct under different circumstances. Consider this question: "How many hours per week do you usually work?" A respondent who has a nine-to-five job with no overtime probably will not need any clarification to interpret this question as intended. In this case standardized interviewing should promote accurate responses.[1] But a respondent who works as a freelance writer, and whose lunches with editors and ruminations while jogging might legitimately be considered work, may be unsure what "work" means in this question. In this case flexible interviewers might help the respondent interpret "work" as the question author intended, thus promoting more accurate responses.

Note that the question itself is not ordinarily ambiguous – "How many hours per week do you usually work?" is, in fact, a commonly used, well pretested survey question, and the words in the question should be familiar to native speakers of the language. What is ambiguous is the way "work" and the respondent's circumstances correspond. This depends on how the survey organization defines what counts as work and what does not – and this definition may differ from how most respondents ordinarily understand "work."[2] We call these ambiguous correspondences between questions and situations "complicated mappings."

Given this line of reasoning, we predict that standardized interviewing should lead to accurate responding when the concepts in a question map onto a respondent's life circumstances in a straightforward way. In contrast, when the mapping is complicated, more respondents should be able to answer the question as intended if interviewers can clarify official definitions, thus improving overall response accuracy.

Measuring Accuracy

Gathering empirical evidence on how standardized and flexible interviewing affect accuracy is particularly important since "both positions are held more on theoretical than empirical grounds" (Fowler 1991, p. 269). But gathering such evidence is also particularly difficult to do (van der Zouwen, Dijkstra, and Smit 1991; Wentland 1993). Comparing responses with official records or personal diaries is expensive, and there is no way to ensure that official records or diaries are correct, if they are even available.

Instead, researchers have relied on surrogate measures. For example, Hyman (1954) counted interviewers' probes under different interviewing techniques, under the assumption that interviewers probe less when respondents understand questions better. Fowler's (1991) approach is to quantify how much responses vary for different interviewers, on the assumption that less "interviewer-related error" reflects greater response accuracy. But there is no guarantee that either of these surrogate measures truly captures respondents' understanding or accuracy.

The purpose of our study was to directly compare response accuracy under standardized and flexible interviewing techniques. So that we could assess accuracy of the data with confidence, we had respondents answer questions on the basis of fictional scenarios we designed, rather than asking them about their own lives. We used real questions from major government surveys. In all cases, the sponsoring organizations had published explicit definitions for the concepts in the questions. Thus we knew the correct (with respect to these definitions) answer for all question-scenario combinations and we could easily determine respondents' accuracy.

We implemented standardization following Fowler and Mangione's (1990) prescriptions. These require interviewers to use neutral probes to help responses match the question's objectives, which must be inferred from the official definitions. Interviewers must avoid influencing responses in any way, including presenting definitions to respondents. Interviewers should nonetheless be taught the definitions so that they can judge the completeness of the respondents' answers (see Beatty 1995).

We recognize that this version of standardization is not practised universally. Some organizations that subscribe to the theory of standardization allow interviewers to provide scripted definitions on request. According to Fowler and Mangione (1990, p. 21), such practices are not standardized: not every respondent is presented with the same stimulus, and interviewers are not guaranteed to present definitions consistently. The more stringent version we tested was clearly standardized.

We saw several alternatives for implementing flexible interviewing. In order of increasing departure from standardization, the possibilities are as follows. (1a) Interviewers could read scripted definitions for concepts in the questions, but only when respondents explicitly request them. (1b) Interviewers could provide customized (unscripted) definitions only at the respondent's request. (2) In addition to providing definitions on demand in (1), interviewers could resolve confusions and clarify concepts whenever they judge it necessary, even if the respondent does not request help. Interviewers could do this either with scripted definitions and probes (2a) or by improvising (2b). (3) In addition to providing clarifications on demand (1) and voluntarily (2), interviewers could initially present the question in their own words, based on their own understanding of the survey designers' intentions. In this study, we used (2b), because it involves the greatest degree of flexibility while preserving initial question wording.

These variations of flexible interviewing techniques differ from more radical proposals, for example, that interviewers should engage in unscripted interactions in which respondents help set the research agenda itself (see, e.g., Mishler 1986). The conversationally flexible alternatives (1)–(3) are designed to promote consistent interpretations of the questions in the surveys, and in this respect they share the goals of standardized interviewing. Where they differ is in what leads to consistent interpretations.

We are aware that in practice many survey interviewers probably use some combination of standardized and flexible interviewing. Here we used a pure version of each technique so that we could directly evaluate the competing theories.

Method

Design

Different respondents participated in either standardized or flexible interviews. In each interview, the interviewer asked 12 questions about fictional scenarios; respondents were not answering about their own lives but about these fictional circumstances. All respondents were asked the same questions; what differed was the type of interaction in the interview.

Participants

The 43 "respondents" were experimental subjects, all fluent speakers of English. Forty subjects were recruited from advertisements in the *Washington Post* and paid $25 each, and three were volunteers from the Bureau of Labor Statistics (BLS) staff (not survey professionals). In selecting respondents for standardized or flexible interviews, we roughly balanced gender and education level. All respondents had at least a high school diploma. Of the 21 respondents in the standardized interviews, 11 were women and 10 were men; 3 had completed high school only, 6 were current college students, and 12 had completed college. Of the 22 respondents in the flexible interviews, 11 were women and 11 were men; 6 had completed high school only, 4 were current college students, and 12 had completed college.

In all other respects, respondents were assigned to interviewing conditions arbitrarily. Of the 21 respondents in the standardized interviews, 5 were black and 16 were white; their average age was 32.2 years, ranging from 18 to 70 years. Of the 22 respondents in the flexible interviews, 9 were black, 10 were white, and 3 were Asian; their average age was 35.5 years, ranging from 18 to 59 years.

The 22 interviewers (21 white and 1 black) were professional Census Bureau interviewers; all but one had at least 30 months of experience at the Hagerstown, Maryland, Census Bureau telephone facility. The 11 standardized interviewers (10 women, 1 man) averaged 43 months of experience, ranging from 5 to 81 months. The 11 flexible interviewers (7 women, 4 men) averaged 69 months of experience, ranging from 36 to 100 months.

Each inteviewer, calling from the Hagerstown telephone facility, called two respondents who had come into the BLS laboratory (except for one interviewer who only called one respondent), for a total of 43 interviews.

Questions

Four of the 12 questions were about employment, selected from the Current Population Survey (CPS); four were about housing, selected from the Consumer Price Index Housing survey (CPI Housing); and four were about retail purchases, selected from the Current Point of Purchase Survey (CPOPS), which is part of the Consumer Price Index program. All questions had been pretested, most extensively those from the CPS. Some of the questions were familiar to the interviewers, who averaged 53 months of experience administering the CPS (40 and 66 months for standardized and flexible interviewers, respectively). The CPOPS questions were familiar to only five of the 22 interviewers (one standardized and four flexible); no interviewers had administered the CPI Housing survey.

We modified some questions slightly to include the proper names of people described in the scenarios, so that the questions would be about "Carla" or "Harry" rather than about the actual respondent. For example, one employment question was, "Last week, did Pat have more than one job, including part-time, evening or weekend work?" One housing question was, "How many other rooms are there, other than bedrooms and bathrooms?" One purchasing question was, "Has Kelly purchased or had expenses for household furniture?" (appendix A includes all 12 questions.)

The key concepts in all questions were officially defined by the sponsoring survey programs. These published definitions are among the training materials provided to interviewers in the actual government surveys. For example, "household furniture" is defined as "tables, chairs, footstools, sofas, china cabinets, utility carts, bars, room dividers, bookcases, desks, beds, mattresses, box springs, chests of drawers, night tables, wardrobes, and unfinished furniture. Do not include TV, radio, and other sound equipment, lamps and lighting fixtures, outdoor furniture, infants' furniture, or appliances." For the complete set of definitions used in this study, see appendix A.

The questions were always asked in the same relative order as in the actual survey instruments from which they were drawn. For example, in the actual CPOPS instrument our fourth purchasing question appears after our third purchasing question, even though the CPOPS instrument contains intervening questions that we did not ask. Some actual CPS respondents might not be asked all four of our employment questions, depending on their answers to previous questions.

We counterbalanced the order in which questions from a particular domain (housing, work, or purchases) were asked. There were six possible sequences for the three domains; for every interviewer (each of whom interviewed two respondents), two of the six orderings were chosen at random, without replacement. This was done to minimize any effects of domain order and to assure that the orders were used equally often.

Scenarios

The fictional scenarios on which respondents based their answers included floor plans, purchase receipts, and descriptive texts. The scenarios were designed so that the content of one had nothing to do with the content of the others. Each floor plan was from a different imaginary house or apartment; each purchase was made by a different person from a different establishment; each work situation was about a different person.

These scenarios were available to the respondents both before and during the interviews. However, they were never available to interviewers and so the interviewers never knew the correct answer. Interviewers could also never predict correct answers from any interview they had previously conducted because respondents interviewed by a given interviewer were always presented with different versions of the scenarios (see the next section). The way the knowledge was allocated to the participants was therefore analogous to its division in an actual survey. Respondents knew the "facts," and interviewers knew the questions and concepts.

Mappings

There were two versions of each scenario, one that corresponded to the concepts in the question in a straightforward way (a straightforward mapping) and one that corresponded to the concepts in the question less clearly (a complicated mapping). In the "household furniture" example, the scenario that led to a straightforward mapping was a purchase receipt for an end table. In contrast, the scenario that led to a complicated mapping was a purchase receipt for a floor lamp, which the official definition excludes as a piece of furniture (the complete set of scenarios is available from the authors).

For each respondent, two of the four scenarios in each domain (housing, work, purchases) had a straightforward mapping to their respective questions and two had a complicated mapping. Each respondent had a different sequence of mappings for each of the three domains, so that respondents could not predict complexity of the mappings. Also, interviewers could not predict the complexity of the mappings, because the two respondents assigned to each interviewer had complementary mappings. For example, the mappings for one respondent in the housing domain might have been complicated, straightforward, straightforward, and complicated; the second respondent for the same interviewer would have had mappings for the same questions of straightforward, complicated, complicated, and straightforward.

So in this experiment respondents had complicated mappings 50 percent of the time. This was so that we could directly compare accuracy for both kinds of mappings. In ordinary surveys respondents probably experience complicated mappings less than 50 percent of the time, but the actual proportion no doubt varies from respondent to respondent, from question to question, and survey to survey.

Interviewer Training

The interviewers were trained in group settings for a total of approximately 90 minutes.[3] We wanted to ensure that standardized and flexible interviewers had the same knowledge about the key concepts in the survey questions, so that any differences in respondent accuracy could not be attributed to one group's greater familiarity with the definitions. So all interviewers first studied the key survey concepts, were quizzed, and discussed the concepts as a group. The interviewers were quizzed on situations that were different from those they would later encounter in the interviews.

Then half the interviewers (11) were selected arbitrarily for separate 1-hour group training in standardized interviewing techniques, and the other half (11) were trained in flexible interviewing techniques. Training consisted of discussion of interviewing theory and role-playing exercises (details are available from the authors). but the interviewers were never informed of the experimental hypotheses.

The standardized interviewers read the relevant sections from the U.S. Department of Commerce's *CPS Interviewing Manual* (1994, pp. A2-6 to A2-8), which are consistent with Fowler and Mangione's (1990) prescriptions. They were trained to read questions exactly as worded and to provide only non-directive probes, but they were never to provide definitions for the survey concepts (we explained that the concepts training had been necessary so that interviewers would be able to judge when respondents had answered a question completely). The probing techniques included rereading the question, providing the response alternatives, and asking the respondents to interpret questions for themselves.

The flexible interviewers were trained to read the questions exactly as worded (just as standardized interviewers do), but then they could say whatever they wanted to assure that the respondent had understood the question as the survey designer had intended. This included reading or paraphrasing all or part of a question, reading or paraphrasing all or part of a definition, and asking questions of the respondent to elicit information so that the interviewer and respondent could jointly reach a correct response. Interviewers could intervene at the respondent's request or voluntarily; that is, interviewers were licensed to intervene whenever they thought the respondent might have misunderstood the question.

All interviewers were instructed to review the concepts before the experimental interviews, and to make sure they had the definitions available during the interviews.

Experimental Procedure

When respondents arrived, we obtained their consent to participate and to be audiotaped. An experimenter then read a set of instructions (see appendix B for exact wordings) and answered questions about the procedure. All respondents were told that getting the right answers to the survey questions depended on their paying close attention to details on each page of their scenario packet.

Respondents who would be participating in flexible interviews were given further instructions to encourage active participation. (In our pilot studies, we found that some respondents would only ask questions in the interview when they were explicitly instructed to do so.) They were told to work with the interviewer as a partner to make sure that they had understood the questions in the way the survey designers intended, and that the survey designers' definitions might differ from their own (see appendix B).

Respondents were then left alone to familiarize themselves with the scenarios, which would also be available to them during the telephone interview. When they felt ready, they were called on the telephone by an interviewer and asked the 12 questions. The interviews were unobtrusively audio-recorded.

Results

Implementation of Interview Techniques

In order to interpret our accuracy results, we need to be sure that interviewers correctly implemented both interviewing techniques. It appears they did. First, standardized interviews contained a high proportion (70 percent) of sequences in which the interviewer asked the question exactly as worded and the respondent immediately provided an answer, followed by no other "moves," as in this example:[4]

I: Has Dana purchased or had expenses for meats and poultry.
R: Yes.
   [Interviewer goes on to next question.]

This contrasts with a low proportion (10 percent) of such sequences in the flexible interviews.[5]

Second, far more of what the flexible interviewers said would be considered "illegal" in pure standardized interviewing. Flexible interviewers rephrased all or part of questions, provided all or part of a definition (either verbatim or paraphrased), classified the respondent's description of their circumstances, offered to provide clarification, confirmed or disconfirmed the respondent's interpretation of questions, and requested particular information about the respondent's circumstances.

For example, in the following exchange the flexible interviewer paraphrased the long definition of "household furniture" to answer the respondent's question:

I: Has Kelly purchased or had expenses for household furniture.
R: Um . is a lamp furniture?
I: No sir, we do not include lamps and lighting fixtures.
R: Okay, no.
[Interviewer goes on to next question.]

In pure standardized interviewing, the interviewer should not have answered the respondent's request for clarification, because by doing so she interpreted the survey question for the respondent. In the next example, the flexible interviewer would have violated the rules of standardized interviewing several times:

I: Last week did Pat have more than one job, including part-time, evening or weekend work?
R: Um . s- say that again, because *[laughter]*
I: *La-*
R: She has many clients which she . but it's the same kind of job.
I: Okay. U:h *that would-*
R: *In other* words she is um .
I: Well what kind of work *does she do.*
R: *She ba-* she babysits, and she *has*
I: *O-*
R: different clients.
I: Okay, that would be considered as all one job,
R: *All right*
I: *no matter* how many people she- she worked *for.*
R: *Yes* if it's the same type of job, yes, she has one job *and that's
I: *And is this-* this is the only thing that she does.
R: Yes, and this is it.
I: Okay, so we'll say no for this. She only has one job?
R: She only has one job.
I: And um . [goes on to next question]

This flexible interviewer explicitly tells the respondent how to answer the question given the respondent's description of the scenario. In contrast, a standardized interviewer might have dealt with the respondent's failure to provide a single answer to the question by saying something like, "Let me repeat the question. Last week, did Pat have more than one job, including part-time, evening, and weekend work?"

Such directive interventions occurred for 85 percent of the questions in flexible interviews, but for only 2 percent of the questions in standardized interviews. In fact, all of the 2 percent "illegal" interventions in standardized interviews were incomplete repetitions of the question, but the individual words all appeared in the same order in the full survey question; by some counts these would be legal. In any case, this was the only deviation from standardization that these interviewers ever engaged in. Clearly, the two types of interviews in this experiment were implemented in qualitatively different ways, and much as we had intended.

Response Accuracy

Overall Response Accuracy

Recall that a response in this experiment is accurate if it matches what the official definition dictates. We counted as responses what respondents said (as seen in the transcripts) rather than what the interviewers wrote down, although these almost always coincided. Only three out of the 504 responses were erroneously recorded by interviewers, one in a standardized interview and two in flexible interviews.[6] (For the one interview that was not audio-recorded, the interviewer's tallies could not be verified. In this case, we trusted the interviewer's tallies because they matched the experimenter's tallies during the course of the interview.)

Response accuracy was nearly perfect in both standardized and flexible interviews when the mapping between the question and the scenarios was straightforward, 97 percent and 98 percent, respectively. But the picture was very different when the mapping was complicated. In the standardized interviews, accuracy was very poor, 28 percent. In the flexible interviews, accuracy was nearly 60 percentage points higher, 87 percent. This interaction (mapping × interview technique) was highly reliable ($F(1, 41) = 130.01$, $p < .001$). This interaction was also reliable for all questions ($F(1, 11) = 100.74$, $p < .001$).[7] So flexible interviewing led to superior accuracy when it was not obvious to respondents how the questions corresponded to their circumstances, and this was true for all questions.

Respondent Characteristics and Accuracy

We found no reliable differences in the pattern of results for respondents of different educational levels or races.[8] Of course, our sample was small; this lack of respondent effects would have to be replicated with a larger sample before we can be sure flexible interviewing benefits respondents of various educational levels and races equally.

One characteristic we examined, gender, differentially affected response accuracy (interaction of interview type and gender, $F(1, 39) = 6.20$, $p < .02$). Women were reliably more accurate (97 percent) than men (88 percent) in flexible interviews ($F(1, 20) = 11.74$, $p < .005$), while women and men were equally accurate (61 percent and 64 percent) in standardized interviews ($F(1, 19) = 0.64$, n.s.). Focusing just on flexible interviews, women outperformed men when the mappings were complicated ($F(1, 20) = 6.34$, $p = .02$) and marginally outperformed men when mappings were straightforward ($F(1, 20) = 3.75$, $p < .07$).

There are a number of possible explanations for this gender effect, but our data do not allow us to evaluate any of them. Although this certainly warrants further attention, the gender difference is minor relative to the very large increase in accuracy resulting from the flexible interviewing technique.

Interviewers and Accuracy

One goal of standardizing interviews is to reduce interviewer-related variance (Fowler and Mangione 1990). Because flexible interviews involve extensive probing, one might expect greater interviewer effects for flexible interviews than for standardized interviews. One reason to expect this is because Mangione, Fowler, and Louis (1992) found that the questions in standardized interviews requiring the most probing were most likely to create interviewer effects.

This turned out not to be the case here. Interviewer variance was no greater in flexible interviews than in standardized interviews (interaction of interviewers and interview type, $F(20, 42) = 1.11$, n.s.). Of course, there were only two respondents per interviewer, and so we cannot compute a measure of interviewer-related variance like rho (Fowler and Mangione 1990), which requires that the respondents assigned to interviewers represent the sample as a whole. Our data do not rule out the possibility that in a larger sample flexible interviewing could lead to greater interviewer effects than standardized interviewing.

Accuracy of Flexible Interviewers' Interventions

One of the potential dangers of flexible interviewing is that interviewers can mislead respondents. That is, even if interviewers sometimes provide information that helps respondents to produce accurate answers, interviewers may also provide information that can lead respondents astray.

To test this, we identified those cases in which flexible interviewers provided explicit, directive information (49 percent of the cases where the mappings were straightforward, and 75 percent of the cases where the mappings were complicated). We used a stringent criterion for accuracy: we considered any information that did not appear in the definitions to be inaccurate. Take this example:

I: How many hours per week does Mindy usually work at her job.
R: She usually works fifty- a average of fifty hours a week.
I: Fifty hours a week?
R: Mm-hm?
I: That the average work week?
R: Yeah for the last six months thos- that's what's- that's . was her average work hour week. Fifty hours.
I: All right [continues]

In this case we counted the interviewer's comment "That the average work week?" as inaccurate, because it endorses the incorrect (for this survey) interpretation of "average" for "usually," rather than the correct interpretation of "most frequent" (see appendix A).

We also counted as inaccurate definitions that interviewers improvised when no official definition had been provided, as in this example, where the interviewer invents a definition for "farm":

R: . What do you mean by a farm?
I: A farm? It would be a . you know any . farm that would be producing . any- any, yeah anything uh could be cattle or uh . vegeta- vegetables, or orchard . uh that uh would be producing for . income . for the household it wouldn't be a . a farm just for the uh . household use only.

Under this stringent criterion, flexible interviewers provided only accurate help in 93 percent of the cases where they provided any help. When interviewers provided accurate information, respondents answered accurately 87 percent of the time and inaccurately the remaining 6 percent of the time. On the 7 percent of occasions when interviewers provided any inaccurate information, respondents still produced the correct answer 4 percent of the time and produced incorrect answers 3 percent of the time. So flexible interviewers generally provided highly accurate information, and providing inaccurate information did not necessarily lead respondents to produce incorrect answers.

All 11 flexible interviewers presented far more accurate than inaccurate information. Four provided perfectly accurate information. Four others presented inaccurate information on one question out of the 24 total questions they asked – a rate of 4.2 percent inaccuracy. Two interviewers presented inaccurate information on two questions (a rate of 8.3 percent), and the remaining interviewer on three questions (a rate of 12.5 percent).

When did Flexible Interviewers Intervene?

Interviewers sometimes intervened because respondents asked for help, and sometimes they intervened voluntarily. They intervened for both straightforward and complicated mappings, but more often for complicated (88 percent) than for straightforward mappings (51 percent). This partially reflects the fact that respondents almost never asked for help with straightforward mappings.

Recall that the interviewers had no evidence at the outset whether respondents were faced with complicated or straightforward mappings. So why did they intervene voluntarily? Sometimes it was because respondents had displayed uncertainty in their answers or failed to answer the questions definitively. The most common way that respondents showed they were uncertain was to describe their situation; they did this for 58 percent (37 of 64) of the complicated cases where interviewers intervened voluntarily. In this example, the interviewer begins to provide substantive help after the respondent describes the scenario at length:

I: How many hours per week does she u- does Mindy usually work at her job.
R: Well Mindy's job schedule varies.
I: *mm-hm*
R: *as far as* what she usually works
I: Mm-hm
R: in the average of how many hours she works there's a difference, um . in the past six months, three of the months she worked fifty hours, but then there are two that was you know one at forty and one at ten. So her average would be about forty hours a week, but I would say she usually works . between forty . forty and fifty, there's an odd week here and there, but USUALLY, between forty and fifty.
I: Okay you mentioned of the last six months for . half of them she worked fifty hours.
R: Yes.
I: And . fifty percent
R: Actually there are only five months here, *yes.*
I: *Five* months?
R: So yes, over- over three fifths of the time she works fifty hours a week.
I: Okay. So fifty percent of the time or more .
R: She's working fifty hours a week.
I: Okay and we would consider fifty percent of the time or more or the most frequent schedule during the por- past four or five month to be her usual number of hours and you said that was fifty hours for *most* of the time.
R: *Yes.* Yes.
I: Okay.

Interviewers also intervened voluntarily when respondents asked them to repeat the question (9 percent of cases, 6 of 64), when respondents explicitly said they were unsure about the answer (6 percent of cases, 4 of 64), and in a variety of less frequent circumstances for the remaining 27 percent (17 of 64) of the cases.

A closer inspection of the interaction shows that interviewers really did increase response accuracy by providing unsolicited help. Flexible respondents only requested help for 38 percent of the complicated mappings, but, as we have seen, they were accurate for 87 percent of them. They were virtually as accurate when the interviewers volunteered help (86 percent accuracy, 55 out of 64 cases) as when they explicitly requested help (94 percent accuracy, 46 out of 49 cases). In contrast, when interviewers failed to provide any help at all (11 complicated-mapping cases), respondents only produced 4 accurate answers, a rate of 34 percent. This is nearly as poor as the standardized respondents' 28 percent accuracy rate for complicated mappings.

While flexible respondents got help when they needed it, they also got help when, it would seem, they did not. Respondents almost never asked for help for straightforward mappings (1 percent of the time), but they nonetheless received unsolicited help for 51 percent of the straightforward cases. One cost of flexible interviewing may be that interviewers provide a substantial amount of unnecessary help in addition to the needed help.

Were respondents more accurate if they explicitly asked for help? We see no evidence that they were. Respondents who asked for help frequently were no more accurate than respondents who asked for help rarely ($r = .15$, n.s.). In a sense, it did not matter how much respondents explicitly asked for help, because interviewers provided help whether or not respondents asked for it. In other words, respondents in flexible interviews all benefited from flexibility, but only sometimes as a result of their own initiative.

Effectiveness of Standardized (Nondirective) Interventions

According to proponents of standardization, well-trained standardized interviewers should be able to get respondents to answer appropriately by using neutral probing techniques (Fowler and Mangione 1990). In the vast majority of our standardized cases (70 percent), interviewers did not probe at all; respondents answered the questions directly. Respondents almost never explicitly asked for help interpreting the questions (only on four questions out of all 252 asked), and when they did, they were told that the interpretation was up to them.

But respondents did provide less explicit evidence of uncertainty. In these cases, interviewers sometimes provided effective and legal standardized probes that clearly led to improved response accuracy, as in this next example from a question with a complicated mapping. The interviewer leaves the interpretation up to the respondent and repeats the question; the respondent then produces the correct answer:

I: How many people live in this house.
R: Currently? Or
I: Okay uh we need your interpretation.
R: *Um*
I: *How many* people . live in this house.
R: Three.
I: Three.
I: Okay, [continues]

One probing technique that some interviewers used was to elicit a correct response by repeating the question with different contrastive stress, as in these two examples from different inteviewers and respondents:

I: How many bedrooms are there in THIS house.

R: Uh, there are two bedrooms. And one den is being used as a bedroom.
I: How many BEDROOMS are there in this house.
R: Two.
I: [continues]

I: How many hours per week does Mindy usually work at her job.
R: Um: it varies, but she seems to average . m: . about thirty eight hours.
I: How many hours per week does she USUALLY . work at her job.
R: Um, fifty hours.
I: [continues]

But this strategy did not always lead to a correct response, as in this case:

I: *How* many- how many hours per week does Mindy usually work at her job?
R: Um during which month. In general?
I: Uh, this would be uh how many hours does she USUALLY work at her job.
R: Okay
I: *Cou-*
R: *U:*m
I: Could you tell me
R: Uh, thirty hours.
I: [continues]

So neutral probing was not always effective, as we also saw in the response accuracy data.

Although our standardized interviewers overwhelmingly used only legal probing techniques, it seems to us on closer examination that at least some of these probes are not, strictly speaking, neutral: they convey information about the official definitions. Consider this example:

I: Has Alexander purchased or had expenses for college tuition or fixed fees.
R: Um he's go:t . um tuition for secretarial school.
I: Pardon me, I- I didn't .
R: He has tuition for secretarial school.
I: Has Alexander purchased or had expenses for COLLEGE tuition..
R: No.
I: or fixed fees.
R: No.
I: [continues]

When the interviewer repeated the question with contrastive stress, might this not have signalled to the respondent that, for current purposes, secretarial schools should not be considered colleges? Contrastive stress is one technique speakers in ordinary conversation use to call attention to novel or unexpected features of their utterances (see Chafe 1976). In this example, the respondent produced the correct response, but we have no guarantee that the respondent would have made the same choice without the unscripted emphasis used by the interviewer in this probe.

In fact, virtually all the legal moves a standardized interviewer can make are, strictly speaking, not neutral, because they can convey information to the respondent about how he should interpret the question. When an interviewer repeats a question after a respondent has given a tentative answer, she may be signalling to the respondent that his answer was wrong. Even the choice not to probe implies the interviewer's willingness to accept the respondent's interpretation of the question; if the interviewer moves on without probing, she has implicitly signalled that the respondent's interpretation is indeed the appropriate one (for further discussion, see Clark and Schaefer 1989; Clark and Schober 1991; Schober 1998b; Schober and Conrad 1998; Schwarz 1994, 1996, among others).

Duration of Interviews

Although flexible interviewing led to massive improvements in accuracy, and although flexible interviewers rarely misled the respondents, the technique did have a significant cost: flexible interviews took much longer than standardized interviews did. The median time to complete flexible interviews was 11.47 minutes, compared to 3.41 minutes for standardized interviews; one flexible interview lasted over 35 minutes, and the shortest flexible interview took as long as the longest standardized interview (about 6 minutes). As shown by the total number of words per question uttered by respondents and interviewers, flexible interviews took longer than standardized interviews regardless of whether mappings were complicated (933 vs. 211 words) or straightforward (727 vs. 158 words) (interaction of interview type and mapping, $F(1, 40) = 2.56$, n.s.).

So there is a clear trade-off between improved accuracy and saving time. But this trade-off may be less extreme than it seems. First, our interviewers were new to the definitions and the technique. As a result, some flexible interviewers were not adept at focusing on just the relevant parts of definitions and read entire lengthy definitions verbatim, as in this inelegant example:

I: Last week, did Pat have more than one job, including part-time, evening or weekend work?
R: W:hat . is a job.
I: All right. Uh, a job exists when there is a definite arrangement for regular work every week, or every month, for pay or other compensation. By other compensation that would be profits, anticipated profits or pay in

kind, such as room and board. A formal, defin- definite arrangement with one or more employers to work on a continuing basis for a specified number of hours per week or days per month, but on an irregular schedule, during the week or month is also a job. It is possible for individuals to have more than one employer, but only one job. If an individual does the same type of work for more than one employer in an occupation where it is common to have more than one employer, do not consider the individual a multiple jobholder. Examples improve . in- include rather, private households or domestic workers . including babysitters, chauffeurs, gardeners, handypersons, cooks, and maids.

R: You said do NOT include? . babysitters?
I: Uh, let's see: .
R: The last sentence.
I: All right . let's see do not . If an individual does the same type of work for more than one employer, in an occupation where it is common to have more than one employer, do not consider the individual a multiple jobholder. Examples include private household or domestic workers . include- including babysitters, chauffeurs, gardeners, handypersons, cooks, and maids.
R: Okay. And the question again was .
I: Last *week*
R: *just*
I: did Pat have more than one job, including part-time, evening, or weekend work.
R: N:o, she had one job.
I: [goes on to next question]

In comparison, the interviewer in this example gets right to the point:

I: Last week, did Pat have more than one job, including part-time, evening or weekend work.
R: Last week?
I: Yes.
R: U:h more than one job?
I: Yes.
R: She had many jobs.
I: What does she do.
R: What does P- she babysits.
I: Okay, so she works for different employers.
R: Yes, different families.
I: Okay, she doesn't do this in her home.
R: No?
I: Okay. Did she do anything else besides her babysitting job.
R: No?
I: Okay. [goes on to next question]

Here the interviewer asks the respondent to describe Pat's circumstances as soon as the respondent says, "She had many jobs"; this might have signalled that the respondent was unsure about the interpretation of the question (see, e.g., Brennan and Clark [1996] and Schober [1998a] on the implications of using different wording than one's conversational partner – in this case, "many" vs. "more than one"). With one phrase, the interviewer elegantly classifies Pat's work as one job by calling it "her babysitting job." More experienced flexible interviewers might use strategies like these, which in turn might lead to shorter flexible interviews.

Second, our experiment implemented pure versions of the interviewing techniques. According to common wisdom, ordinary interviews deviate from standardization and thus take longer than pure standardized interviews. To evaluate the potential impact of moving to flexible interviewing, the appropriate comparison is between our flexible interviews and ordinary interviews, rather than our flexible and standardized interviews. The increase in duration for flexible interviews may therefore be smaller in practice than in our study.

Discussion

As Tourangeau (1990, p. 251) puts it, "it is not a foregone conclusion that the costs of standardization outweigh the gains or that the gains can be preserved while the costs are reduced." As a first attempt to address the issue, our study shows that there are circumstances under which the costs of standardization do outweigh the gains, if high response accuracy is the goal.

Flexible interviewing led to nearly 60 percent greater accuracy when the mapping between the question and the respondent's situation was complicated. This large accuracy increase was obtained without lengthy interviewer training, using typical telephone interviewers, and without increasing interviewer effects over what we found in the standardized interviews. Flexible interviewing led to greater response accuracy for respondents of different races, genders, and levels of educational attainment.

But this accuracy came at a real cost – a more than threefold increase in duration. As we have noted, however, our flexible interviews may be longer than they would be in actual practice, and our standardized interviews may be shorter than ordinary "standardized" interviews; this requires further investigation in real survey settings.

We believe flexible interviewing is a promising alternative to explore. But we agree with Schaeffer's (1991, p. 368) point: "Reforms that ignore the justification for standardization run the risk of repeating old mistakes." We do not advocate implementing flexible interviewing without further careful research with different samples and different kinds of surveys.

In particular, a number of questions need to be addressed. How far do our results extend beyond the laboratory, when the frequency of complicated mappings is not controlled? Can flexible interviewing work for all interviewers and all respondents? Do different versions of flexible interviewing affect response accuracy differently and have different costs? How would flexible interviewing affect response accuracy for attitude or opinion questions?

In any case, the results of our study suggest at least the following conclusions.

1. *Mappings are a potential source of measurement error for any question.* Every survey question contains terms that have the potential to be understood differently than the survey designers intended, even if the questions have been pretested. This is because respondents' circumstances may not map onto the official definitions in a straightforward way. Mapping problems differ from the question-meaning (word and sentence) problems that pretesting can effectively address, because they involve the *correspondence* between official question meaning and respondents' personal circumstances, and this is hard (if not impossible) to anticipate.

Our position is that while pretesting and wording changes are necessary to reduce predictable misunderstandings, they cannot accommodate all complicated mappings. Respondents' circumstances are too varied; official definitions for the words in a question can be too long and complex, and they will never match every respondent's intuitions about what words mean. Flexible interviewing may turn out to be a solution when complicated mappings are frequent (provided that official definitions have been developed); when complicated mappings are rare, flexible interviewing may not be worth the expense.

2. *Different interviewing techniques may be appropriate for different circumstances.* We have shown that standardized interviewing techniques can lead to measurable inaccuracy in responding, and that, under some circumstances, flexible interviewing can lead to measurably improved response accuracy. But flexible interviewing is no panacea – it has real costs. Our data begin to quantify the trade-offs that survey researchers face as they weigh their simultaneous needs for accurate responses, speedy interviews, reasonable interviewer training costs, and reasonable question development costs (including developing definitions of question concepts), among others. In some circumstances, cost constraints may require survey researchers to accept the reduced certainty of response accuracy inherent in standardized interviewing. In other circumstances, accurate responses may be worth any price.

Appendix A: Questions and Definitions of Key Concepts[9]

Housing Questions (From CPI Housing Survey)

1. How many *bedrooms* are there in this house?

A bedroom is a finished room specifically designed by the owner to be used for sleeping. A bedroom does NOT have to be used for sleeping in order to qualify as a bedroom. For example, a bedroom that is being used as an office should be counted as a bedroom.

Do NOT count as a bedroom any room that was designed for another purpose but is being used as a bedroom. For example, a den being used as a bedroom is still a den and should not be counted as a bedroom.

Do NOT count as a bedroom any dens, living rooms, or other rooms that can be converted at night for sleeping.

Do NOT count any bedroom that the renter is denied access to or use of by the owner.

A one-room efficiency apartment does not have a bedroom.

2. This question has two parts. How many *full bathrooms* are there in this house? How many *half bathrooms* are there?

A full bathroom has (1) a flush toilet, (2) a bathtub or shower, and (3) a sink or washbasin with running water. Bathrooms that contain all of the above items, whether separated by a partition or door, are to be considered a full bathroom.

A half bathroom has any two of these three items: (1) a flush toilet, (2) a bathtub or shower, and (3) a sink or washbasin with running water.

If the only bathroom facilities do not meet the definition of a full or half bath, code zero. (For example, if there is only a flush toilet in a room.)

If a bathroom is shared by the occupants of more than one housing unit, the bathroom is included with the unit from which it is most easily reached.

3. How many *other rooms* are there, other than bedrooms and bathrooms?

Include whole rooms such as living rooms, dining rooms, kitchens, lodger's rooms, finished basements or attic rooms, recreation rooms, and permanently enclosed sun porches. Rooms used for offices by a person living in the unit are also included in this survey. Rooms are counted even if they are not used.

Do NOT include bedrooms, bathrooms, unfinished attics or basements, halls, foyers or vestibules, balconies, closets, alcoves, pantries, strip or Pullman kitchens, laundry or furnace rooms, open porches, and unfinished spaces used for storage.

A partially divided room, such as a dinette next to a kitchen or living room, is a separate room ONLY if there is a PERMANENT PARTITION FROM FLOOR TO CEILING BETWEEN THE TWO AREAS. An L-shaped room, a "great" room, or a step-down is therefore counted as one room unless there is a permanent partition dividing the room into parts.

If a room is used by occupants of more than one unit, the room is included with the unit from which it is most easily reached.

Do NOT count any rooms that the renter is denied access to or use of by the owner. Do count rooms REGARDLESS of their year-round usability.

Bathrooms: exclude all bathrooms. While some rooms, such as a small room with only a wash basin, do not meet the definition of a bathroom, they are also to be excluded from the count of other rooms.

4. How many people *live in this house?*

A person is considered to be living in a housing unit even if the person is not present at the time of the survey. Live-in servants or other employees, lodgers and members of the household temporarily away from the unit on business or vacation are included in the count.

Do NOT count any people who would normally consider this their (legal) address but who are LIVING away on business, in the armed forces, or attending school (such as boarding school or college).

Do NOT count overnight lodgers, guests and visitors. Do NOT count day employees who live elsewhere.

Work Questions (From CPS Survey)

1. Does anyone in this household have a *business* or a farm?

A business exists when one or more of the following conditions is met: Machinery or equipment of substantial value is used in conducting the business, or an office, store, or other place of business is maintained, or the business is advertised by: listing in the classified section of the telephone book, or displaying a sign, or distributing cards or leaflets or otherwise publicizing that the work or service is offered to the general public.

2. Last week, did Chris do any work for *pay?*

Include piece rate income as earnings. Persons working in garment making or food packaging often receive this type of income. Also count college assistantships and fellowships and on the job training as earnings.

DO NOT INCLUDE PAY IN KIND, such as food or lodging for work, or expense accounts as earnings.

3. Last week, did Pat have *more than one job*, including part-time, evening or weekend work?

A job exists when there is a definite arrangement for regular work every week or every month, for pay or other compensation (e.g., profits, anticipated profits, or pay in kind, such as room and board). A formal, definite arrangement with one or more employers to work on a continuing basis for a specified number of hours per week or days per month, but on an irregular schedule during the week or month, is also a job.

It is possible for individuals to have more than one employer, but only one job. If an individual does the same type of work for more than one employer in an occupation where it is common to have more than one employer, do not consider the individual a multiple jobholder. Examples include private household or domestic workers including babysitters, chauffeurs, gardeners, handypersons, cooks, and maids.

4. How many hours per week does Mindy *usually* work at her job?

50 percent of the time or more, or the most frequent schedule during the past 4 or 5 months.

Purchase Questions (From CPOPS Survey)

1. Has Carla purchased or had expenses for *car tires?*

New, recapped, or retreaded tires for automobiles. Do not include tires for vans and trucks.

2. Has Alexander purchased or had expenses for *college tuition or fixed fees?*

Tuition and fixed fees paid to public or private institutions offering credit beyond the high school level. Do not include payments to vocationally oriented schools such as business, technical, trade, or secretarial; do not include payments for room and board, books, lab fees, etc.

3. Has Kelly purchased or had expenses for *household furniture?*

Tables, chairs, footstools, sofas, china cabinets, utility carts, bars, room dividers, bookcases, desks, beds, mattresses, box springs, chests of drawers, night tables, wardrobes, and unfinished furniture. Do not include TV, radio, and other sound equipment, lamps and lighting fixtures, outdoor furniture, infants' furniture, or appliances.

4. Has Dana purchased or had expenses for *meats and poultry?*

Beef, lamb, pork, game; organ meats, such as kidneys, sweetbreads, chitterlings, heart, tongue; sausages and luncheon meats; poultry, such as chicken, turkey, pheasant, goose, duck. Include canned ham. Do not include other canned meats and canned poultry, or any prepared meats and poultry.

Appendix B: Instructions to Respondents

Instructions

We'll be asking you to answer 12 survey questions, each about a different fictional situation. You'll be using a 12-page packet, where each page describes one of these situations. For the first question, you should use the information on the first page. For the second question, use the information on the second page, and so on. Sometimes a page contains a very short story about someone's living or working situation; sometimes you'll see a floor plan of a house or apartment; sometimes you'll see a receipt from a purchase.

You'll be talking on the phone with a professional survey interviewer. The interviewer will know that you are answering these questions based on what is in your packet, but they won't know what is on each page of your packet. That is, they will *not* be seeing a packet that looks like yours, but only a list of questions, and so they don't know what the right answer is. We would like you to answer using the information available on each page.

Before the interview starts, we would like you to get to know the situations by reading each page *very* carefully. You don't need to memorize the information on each page; during the interview you should use the packet to help you answer the questions.

According to the definitions of this agency (the Bureau of Labor Statistics) there is a correct answer for each question. Sometimes getting the right answer depends on your having paid attention to details on each page.

It is VERY important that you fully understand these instructions. If you have ANY questions, please ask them now.

Now, please turn to your packet and begin familiarizing yourself.

Additional Instructions for Flexible Interviews

Sometimes these survey questions use ordinary words with slightly different meanings than you may be used to. This is because surveys sometimes need to have technical definitions different from ordinary definitions. You shouldn't feel at all reluctant to ask if you aren't sure what we mean by a perfectly ordinary word. In fact, we WANT you to ask if you have ANY uncertainty about how to interpret the question – even if this feels silly to you. So, even if you know perfectly well what a "person" or a "house" is, if a question includes those words you may need to ask the interviewer for a definition. The interviewer will be more than happy to help you as much as possible.

It may be that if you don't ask about word meanings, you won't be able to get the right answer, because you may be thinking about the question differently than the people who wrote it. For example, imagine that you see a shopping receipt that shows that Gina bought butter. If the interviewer asked you, "Did Gina buy any fats or oils?" you might want to say yes, because butter seems to be a fat. But the official definition of "fats or oils" excludes butter, and so the correct answer would be no. If you didn't ask whether butter is a fat or not, you probably would get the wrong answer.

It is VERY important that you fully understand these instructions. If you have ANY questions, please ask them now.

Now, please turn to your packet and begin familiarizing yourself with the situations.

Notes

1. Of course, respondents can answer inaccurately for many other reasons: memory errors, estimation errors, etc. But understanding questions appropriately is a prerequisite for accurate responding.

2. Surveys do not always have official definitions for key concepts; this is especially likely for onetime ad hoc surveys. And when they do, the definitions are not always consistent. Definitions can even differ between surveys administered by the same organization. One major U.S. government agency, for example, conducts two surveys that ask about half bathrooms; one survey defines half bathrooms as having either one or two fixtures (toilet, sink, or shower/tub), and the other requires two fixtures.

3. Ninety minutes of training is far less than the 2–3 days of training that Fowler and Mangione (1990) report is optimal for standardized interviews. But these interviewers were all experienced professionals who had already undergone formal training; our training consisted of additional training in the particulars of an interviewing technique.

4. In the transcribed excerpts, the following conventions are used: a period between two spaces (.) represents a pause. A colon within a word indicates a lengthened sound. Overlapping speech is enclosed in asterisks. A hyphen at the end of a word (it) indicates that the word was cut off. Question marks indicate rising intonation, and utterance-final periods indicate falling or flat intonation, so utterances that have the grammatical form of questions may end with a period. Words or syllables in all capital letters received extra emphasis.

5. As a result of technical error, one flexible interview was not audio-recorded and so could not be transcribed, so this analysis, as well as all others involving transcribed interviews, is based on all 21 standardized interviews and 21 of the 22 flexible interviews. In addition, we omitted one response by one respondent from all analyses because he failed to understand the task and answered the question about his own home, rather than the experimental scenario.

6. In the two cases in flexible interviews, the respondent gave a numerical answer (e.g. "three bedrooms") and the interviewer recorded a different number ("one bedroom"). The one recording error in standardized interviews involved the question, "Did Dana have any purchases or expenses for meats and poultry?" In this case, the respondent said "poultry, no meat"; the interviewer coded this as a "no" response, but the respondent probably (correctly) meant "yes," and this is how we scored the response.

7. This was computed by treating questions (rather than respondents) as the random factor in an analysis of variance.

8. We excluded three respondents from the analysis of race effects because their racial grouping (Asian) was only represented in the flexible interviewing condition.

9. Key concepts are italicized.

References

Beatty, Paul. 1995. "Understanding the Standardized/Non-Standardized Interviewing Controversy." *Journal of Official Statistics* 11:147–60.

Belson, William A. 1981. *The Design and Understanding of Survey Questions.* Aldershot: Gower.

———. 1986. *Validity in Survey Research.* Aldershot: Gower.

Brennan, Susan E. 1990. "Seeking and Providing Evidence for Mutual Understanding." Doctoral dissertation, Stanford University.

Brennan, Susan E., and Herbert H. Clark. 1996. "Conceptual Pacts and Lexical Choice in Conversation." *Journal of Experimental Psychology: Learning, Memory and Cognition* 22(6):1482–93.

Briggs, Charles L. 1986. *Learning How to Ask: A Sociolinguistic Appraisal of the Role of the Interview in Social Science Research.* Cambridge: Cambridge University Press.

Chafe, Wallace L. 1976. "Givenness, Contrastiveness, Definiteness, Subjects, Topics and Point of View." In *Subject and Topic,* ed. Charles N. Li, pp. 25–56. New York: Academic Press.

Cicourel, Aaron V. 1973. *Cognitive Sociology: Language and Meaning in Social Interaction.* New York: Free Press.

Clark, Herbert H. 1992. *Arenas of Language Use.* Chicago: University of Chicago Press.
——. 1996. *Using Language.* Cambridge: Cambridge University Press.
Clark, Herbert H., and Edward F. Schaefer. 1989. "Contributing to Discourse." *Cognitive Science* 13:259–94.
Clark, Herbert H., and Michael F. Schober. 1991. "Asking Questions and Influencing Answers." In *Questions about Questions: Inquiries into the Cognitive Bases of Surveys*, ed. Judith M. Tanur, pp. 15–48. New York: Russell Sage Foundation.
Clark, Herbert H., and Deanna Wilkes-Gibbs. 1986. "Referring as a Collaborative Process." *Cognition* 22:1–39.
Fowler, Floyd J. 1991. "Reducing Interviewer-Related Error through Interviewer Training, Supervision, and Other Means." In *Measurement Errors in Surveys*, ed. Paul P. Biemer, Robert M. Groves, Lars E. Lyberg, Nancy A. Mathiowetz, and Seymour Sudman, pp. 259–78. New York: Wiley.
Fowler, Floyd J., and Thomas W. Mangione. 1990. *Standardized Survey Interviewing: Minimizing Interviewer-Related Error.* Newbury Park, CA: Sage.
Goffman, Erving. 1981. *Forms of Talk.* Philadelphia: University of Pennsylvania Press.
Goodwin, Charles. 1981. *Conversational Organization: Interaction between Speakers and Hearers.* New York: Academic Press.
Gumperz, John J. 1982. *Discourse Strategies.* Cambridge: Cambridge University Press.
Holstein, James A., and Jaber F. Gubrium. 1995. *The Active Interview.* Thousand Oaks, CA: Sage.
Hyman, Herbert H. 1954. *Interviewing in Social Research.* Chicago: University of Chicago Press.
Kovar, Mary G., and Patricia Royston. 1990. "Comment on Suchman and Jordan." *Journal of the American Statistical Association* 85(409):246–47.
Krauss, Robert M., and Susan R. Fussell. 1996. "Social Psychological Models of Interpersonal Communication." In *Social Psychology: Handbook of Basic Principles* ed. E. Tory Higgins and Arie Kruglanski, pp. 655–701. New York: Guilford.
Kvale, Steinar. 1994. "Ten Standard Objections to Qualitative Research Interviews." *Journal of Phenomenological Psychology* 25:147–73.
Mangione, Thomas W., Floyd J. Fowler, and T. A. Louis. 1992. "Question Characteristics and Interviewer Effects." *Journal of Official Statistics* 8:293–307.
Mishler, Elliot G. 1986. *Research Interviewing.* Cambridge, MA: Harvard University Press.
Rogoff, Barbara. 1990. *Apprenticeship in Thinking: Cognitive Development in Social Context.* New York: Oxford University Press.
Sacks, Harvey, Emanuel A. Schegloff, and Gail Jefferson. 1974. "A Simplest Systematics for the Organization of Turn-Taking in Conversation." *Language* 50: 696–735.
Schaeffer, Nora Cate. 1991. "Conversation with a Purpose – or Conversation? Interaction in the Standardized Interview." In *Measurement Errors in Surveys*, ed. Paul P. Biemer, Robert M. Groves, Lars E. Lyberg, Nancy A. Mathiowetz, and Seymour Sudman, pp. 367–91. New York: Wiley.
Schegloff, Emanuel A. 1984. "On Some Questions and Ambiguities in Conversation." In *Structures of Social Action*, ed. J. Maxwell Atkinson and John Heritage, pp. 28–52. Cambridge: Cambridge University Press.
Schiffrin, Deborah. 1994. *Approaches to Discourse.* Cambridge MA: Basil Blackwell.
Schober, Michael F. 1998a. "Different Kinds of Conversational Perspective-Taking." In *Social and Cognitive Psychological Approaches to Interpersonal Communication*, ed. Susan R. Fussell and Roger J. Kreuz. Mahwah, NJ: Erlbaum.

———. 1998b. "Making Sense of Questions: An Interactional Approach." In *Cognition and Survey Research*, ed. Monroe G. Sirken, Douglas J. Herrmann, Susan Schechter, Norbert Schwarz, Judith M. Tanur, and Roger Tourangeau. New York: Wiley.

Schober, Michael F., and Herbert H. Clark. 1989. "Understanding by Addressees and Overhearers." *Cognitive Psychology* 21:211–32.

Schober, Michael F., and Frederick G. Conrad. 1998. "A Collaborative View of Standardized Survey Interviews." To appear in *Interaction in the Standardized Survey Interview*, ed. Hanneke Houtkoop-Steenstra, Douglas Maynard, Nora Cate Schaeffer, and Johannes van der Zouwen.

Schwarz, Norbert. 1994. "Judgement in a Social Context: Biases, Shortcomings, and the Logic of Conversation." In *Advances in Experimental Social Psychology*, vol. 26 ed. M. Zanna, pp. 123–62. San Diego, CA: Academic Press.

———. 1996. *Cognition and Communication: Judgmental Biases, Research Methods, and the Logic of Conversation.* Mahwah, NJ: Erlbaum.

Suchman, Lucy, and Brigitte Jordan. 1990. "Interactional Troubles in Face-to-Face Survey Interviews." *Journal of the American Statistical Association* 85(409):232–53.

———. 1991. "Validity and the Collaborative Construction of Meaning in Face-to-Face Surveys." In *Questions about Questions: Inquiries into the Cognitive Bases of Surveys*, ed. Judith M. Tanur, pp. 241–67. New York: Russell Sage Foundation.

Tannen, Deborah. 1989. *Talking Voices: Repetition, Dialogue, and Imagery in Conversational Discourse.* Cambridge: Cambridge University Press.

Tourangeau, Roger. 1990. "Comment on Suchman and Jordan." *Journal of the American Statistical Association* 85(409):250–51.

U.S. Department of Commerce. 1994. *Current Population Survey Interviewing Manual* (CPS-250). Washington, DC: Bureau of the Census.

van der Zouwen, Johannes, Wil Dijkstra, and Johannes H. Smit. 1991. "Studying Respondent–Interviewer Interaction: The Relationship between Interviewing Style, Interviewer Behavior, and Response Behavior." In *Measurement Errors in Surveys*, ed. Paul P. Biemer, Robert M. Groves, Lars E. Lyberg, Nancy A. Mathiowetz, and Seymour Sudman, pp. 419–37. New York: Wiley.

Wentland, Ellen J. 1993. *Survey Responses: An Evaluation of Their Validity.* San Diego, CA: Academic Press.

10

Theorizing the Interview

Ray Pawson

Introduction

There is a timeless quality to methodological debate in sociology. Readers will recognize the mode instantly, if I give it the label of the '*polarity principle*'. It operates as follows. Whatever the issue, be it a matter of fundamental strategy or the application of practical skill, two camps of basically opposite persuasion will draw up and glare at each other, with the result that the development of the said method will be forever framed in a discourse of dualism. The reason for the methodological bifurcation is, of course, that most of the said polarities seem to be 'nested'. Thus, if we start with a broad epistemological opposition ('positivism' versus 'phenomenology'), this tends to have implications for explanatory scope ('nomothetic' versus 'idiographic'), for data collection strategy ('quantitative' versus 'qualitative'), for population studied ('sample' versus 'case study') and so on.

I must not exaggerate. There are other methodological voices, of course. These espouse a strategy which will be equally recognizable when I refer to it as the '*pluralist principle*'. This approach has always struck me as being most memorably characterized by Bell and Newby's (1977) adjective, namely *decent* methodological pluralism. What tends to be argued here is that proper, get-your-hands-dirty researchers have little truck with these supposed polarities, since in actual research practice it is often sensible, indeed advantageous, to operate with a combination of diverse methods. It goes without saying that there are studies which have pooled the survey with the ethnography, the formal and informal interview and so on, and thereby produced a more comprehensive understanding of the institution under study. Oddly enough, the same example is always quoted, I'm sure you know it – Barker's *Moonies* (1984).

My purpose here is not to express a preference for the polarity principle or the pluralist principle. Indeed, this somewhat tetchy introduction should be recognized for what it is, namely the construction of yet another methodological dualism. My task is thus to declare a plague on both the houses of the purists and the pragmatists. My reasoning is that despite the seeming gulf between them, their opposition in fact leaves methodological debate unchanged. The 'purist' approach to methodological rule-making is the 'rational reconstruction' which attempts to achieve the logical consistency of an entire methodological apparatus with some basic epistemological/ontological axiom. Disagreement on these basic axioms automatically leads to the nested oppositions described above. Yet pluralists, with their a-bit-of-this-and-a-bit-of-that approach, actually develop no new thinking, no methodological refinements beyond the fuzzy mid-way compromise. Their argument tends to go as follows. Quantitative method is good for structural/institutional features, qualitative approaches are best for the meaningful stuff; our investigation needs both, so let us do the decent thing and make the best of both worlds.

Sociological method has been shaken but not stirred by these antagonisms for many a year. Against such a framework, I want to promote a *'parley principle'*. In order to get out of the trenches, in order to promote general methodological development, there needs to be genuine synthesis between the ranks of opposites. The place to start is with the most stultifying bifurcation of all – that between 'theory' and 'method'. Even the metaphors used to describe these domains ('armchair theorists' as opposed to 'field workers',

Figure I: Structured Interviews

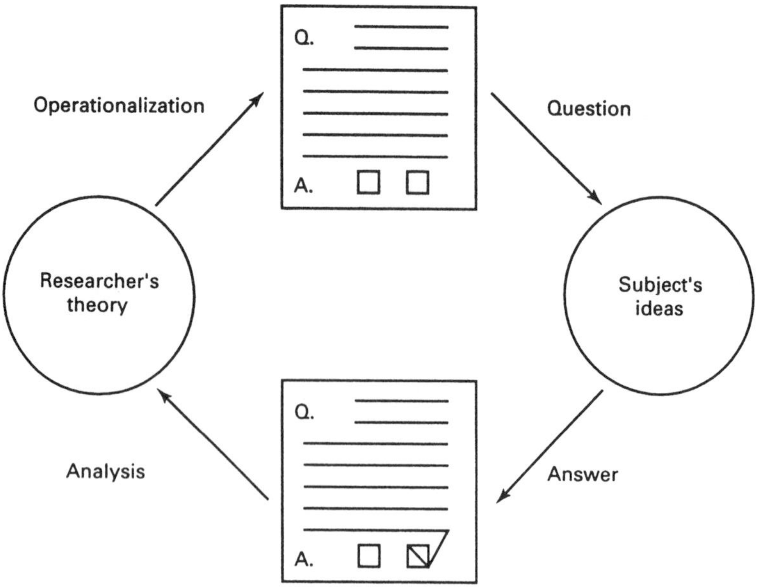

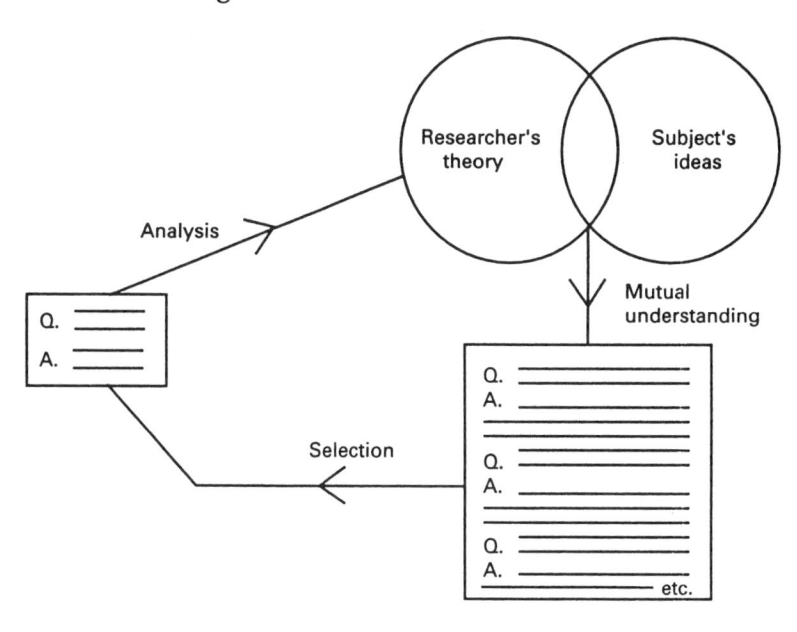

Figure II: Unstructured Interviews

'grand theorists' versus 'underlabourers') have the ring of intellectual apartheid. One has to go right back to Mills (1959) and Merton (1957) for real attempts at a dialogue. It is interesting to note that even the great synthesiser of modern sociology, Giddens, strikes a state of repose when it comes to discussing the implications of his structuration theory for empirical method.

> The concepts of structuration theory, as with any competing theoretical perspective should for many research perspectives be regarded as sensitising devices, nothing more. (1984: 362)

Although the scope of this paper is sounding ever more grandiose, I do not pretend to further the Mertonian or Millsean thesis here. I actually have a very modest ambition, in respect of but one example. Methodological writing on 'interviewing' typifies what I have been saying here (technically-driven, two main styles and a mid-way compromise). The paper suggests we begin to parley. What if we give theorists the responsibility to design an interview? What might they come up with?

Old Antagonisms

In one way or another, in order to get their data, sociologists end up in talking to people. Thus, despite possibly being *the* most inspected piece of social interaction, researchers remain at loggerheads on how to harness the flow of information that emerges from these dialogues. I refer, of course, to the battle lines between 'structured' and 'unstructured' interviewing and as a preface to attempting to transcend this distinction, I reduce a few decades of argumentation between the two to the following couple of paragraphs.

Figure I represents the flow of information in the more formal, structured approaches. The subject's ideas and the subject matter of investigation are one and the same thing. The rationale is to provide a simple, neutral stimulus in order to tap the true 'responses" or true 'values' of individual subjects. The usage of an identical stimulus with all respondents is said to allow for proper comparison to be made across the entire field of potential viewpoints. Critics of such an approach stress that the researcher's conceptual system is *imposed* entirely on the flow of information. The subject's response is limited entirely to a set of operational fragments. Set questions and predetermined response categories offer little opportunity to question, or even understand, the researcher's chosen theoretical framework.

Figure II represents the flow of information in the unstructured (qualitative) interview. The subject's ideas and the subject matter of investigation are one and the same thing. Data collection has the task of creating a conversational setting in which the information provided is faithful to the frame of reference of the respondent. The investigator offers minimal steerage of the research topic within broad areas of discussion as they seem appropriate to each respondent. Critics of such an approach stress that the information collected in such a situation is diverse and discursive and thus hard to compare from respondent to respondent. Researchers are accused of *selecting* from this massive flow of information and thus fitting together small fragments of the respondent's utterances into their own preferred explanatory framework. Whilst the data is supposed to emerge in 'mutual' understanding, the researcher's theory is never clearly on view to the subject.

This particular opposition has proven more dogged and less prone to a collapse into pluralism than any other domain in the technical repertoire of sociology. The reason for this, of course, is the enhanced celebration of the unstructured model as a feature of the development of certain fashionable research strategies which regard themselves not merely as 'qualitative' but as 'participatory' or 'emancipatory' (Oakley 1981; Barnes 1992). Pluralist thinking on the interview exists of course, but tends to play safe with a horses-for-courses approach – if you want factual information, go for the structured approach – if you want interpretative detail, go unstructured (Malseed 1987). Alongside this, perhaps, is the much used but little celebrated pluralist midway compromise, the semi-structured interview which recognizes that by offering respondents a chance to elaborate on their fixed-choice answers that both hard comparable and rich, meaningful data can ensue.

In advocating a 'theory-driver' position within this debate, I will in fact seek out a midway position (c.f. Foddy 1993:73) which combines a 'structured' and 'unstructured' approach. However, I wish to do so in a manner which transcends the fuzzy mid-ground compromise and promises more than the creation of a comprehensive, many-sided data set. The point of trying to synthesise these methods is to go beyond saying *what* they cover, and to show *why* both qualitative and quantitative information are needed in sociological explanation and, above all, to show *how* it is to be melded together.

Enter Theory

The starting point for this effort is to rethink the 'task' of the interview as well as the 'positioning' of the respondent. Perhaps the crucial difference in what I advocate is a change in thinking about the subject matter of the interview (c.f. Pawson 1989, Ch. 10). Both 'mainstream' models tend to suppose that the subject of the interview is its subject matter. The task is thus to ascertain (according to the favoured method) information which is faithful to the subject's thoughts and deeds. On the theory-driven model *the researcher's theory is the subject matter of the interview, and the subject is there to confirm or falsify and, above all, to refine that theory.*

To many, the (italicized) statement above will seem a curiosity, since theoretical considerations are seldom taken to have such an immediate 'reach' into the world of data and the concerns of the subject. Nothing could be further from the truth. I want to illustrate this inevitable and intimate interrelationship between theory and method with some of my own research on the rehabilitative potential of education in prisons. This is an ongoing project

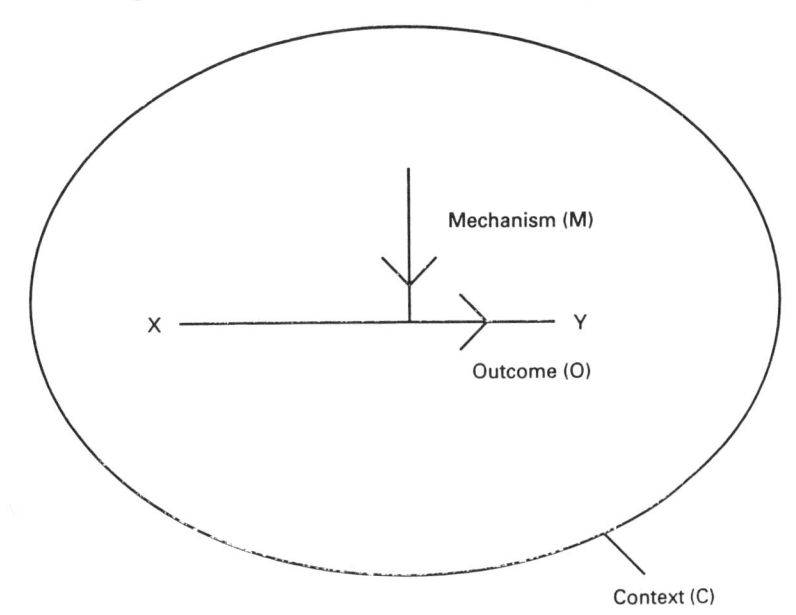

Figure III: Basic Elements of Realist Explanation

carried out collaboratively with 'corrections' researchers in the UK and Canada (Duguid 1981). It is an evaluation of some long-standing higher education courses carried out within prison walls, and seeks to discover whether attending such courses is associated with reduced reconviction rates. In order to answer such a question, we suppose it is necessary to learn what it is about 'education' which might change an inmate's reasoning about crime, and to discover what individual circumstances and institutional contexts might prove favourable to such a transformation. Now, as the reader will be able to imagine, we pursue a whole range of particular theories in exploring such questions. For the purposes of this paper, the detail of our meagre efforts in this direction are unimportant, since our hypotheses carry certain broad features which I believe to be common to the explanatory structure of most substantive theory in sociology. It is these general features of explanation which must be attended to if we are to advance methodological thinking on the interview.

In my view, the starting point of any attempt to understand the synthesis of the quantitative and qualitative is to celebrate the potential of the 'realist' approach to social investigation. Realism's head start over other attempts to codify the rules of sociological method is its commitment to 'ontological depth' in explanation, that is to say – the notion that since social events are interwoven between various layers of social reality, then so must be any account of them. There has been a plethora of attempts to portray the fine texture of this interlinkage, so much so that realism risks becoming an incoherent sack-of-potatoes of a method. I cut a very long story short here by asserting that in my book (Pawson 1989) realist explanation can be boiled down to three key features (see Figure III).

These three features can be woven together to form a fundamental explanatory strategy for social research and one that is particularly well suited to getting to grips with the way the social world is put together. Explanatory propositions are made as follows

> The basic task of sociological inquiry is to explain interesting, puzzling, socially significant outcome patterns (O) between events or happenings or social properties. Explanation takes the form of positing some underlying mechanism (M) which generates these outcomes and thus consists of propositions about how the interplay between agency and structure has consistuted these outcomes. Explanatory closure requires that, within the same investigation, there is also an examination of how the workings of such mechanisms is contingent and conditional, and thus are only fired in particular historical or institutional contexts (C).

As an example of realist theory-making in action, let me demonstrate this schema using the 'campus-in-a-prison' example. The starting point is the assumption that prison education courses do not 'work' towards rehabilitation in some undifferentiated way. Attending such a course involves a myriad of different events and experiences. Explanatory work begins by considering cases in which there is a positive outcome (O) – i.e. the cessation of criminal activity on release. The key theoretical activity is to speculate upon the mechanisms (M) involved in 'education' which might provoke a prisoner into reckoning that a way of life they once considered justified is justified no longer. In higher education our weapons are the rather gentile ones of reasoning, thought and reflection, and in a massively abbreviated way, I can give some examples (in theory) of how these might sediment into an underlying process of change. Education might be a spur to self-realization and self-confidence (M_1), to economic potential and career-building (M_2), to increased social skills and public acceptability (M_3); to moral change and civic responsibility (M_4), to cognitive change and deepening self-reflection (M_5).

These mechanisms are paraphrased here not because they are exhaustive and efficacious or even particularly wise and worthy. Indeed, as everyone knows, they can be woefully far-fetched in many prison contexts, where there are a whole range of contravening forces (M_6) in operation. This brings me to the next great explanatory imperative which is to consider the impact of different institutional and social contexts (C) on the process described above. Any educationist would concede that one needs the appropriate 'students' and 'climate' to sustain objectives. Theory thus has the job of speculating on 'for whom and in what circumstances' such mechanisms might be influential.

Prison organization itself, of course, is a response to the different characters and circumstances of the inmates. Thus we have young offenders institutes (C_1), open prisons (C_2), dispersal prisons (C_3), training prisons (C_4) and so forth as well as different security classifications for inmates within each establishment. Such managerial thinking impinges on the success of a prison education course at two different levels. Each of the potential mechanisms for reform through education above is going to have more (or less) scope according to the profile of the 'typical' inmate. Thus by dint of the age (C_5), offence (C_6), custodial record (C_7) etc. certain establishments will have an 'availability' of suitable types. Regime differences will also bite at the institutional level and since prisons are also about security, surveillance and control, the precise 'ethos' of the establishment (C_8) will limit the chances of success of any rehabilitation mechanism incorporated within an educational programme.

Of course, there is more to 'rehabilitation' then this. This little realist snapshot is intended primarily to list the kind of 'ingredients' which one would use in a full explanation (and evaluation). It thus acts as a prelude to my main question about how to track such ingredients through into the data. Before we reach that point, let me add one further and entirely typical explanatory assumption which I also take as a prerequisite for understanding the interview. This concerns what Giddens calls the 'knowledgeability' of the actor in processes of social transformation. People are always knowledgeable about the reasons for their conduct but in a way which can never carry total awareness of the entire set of structural conditions which prompt an action, nor the full set of potential consequences of that action (Giddens 1984). For

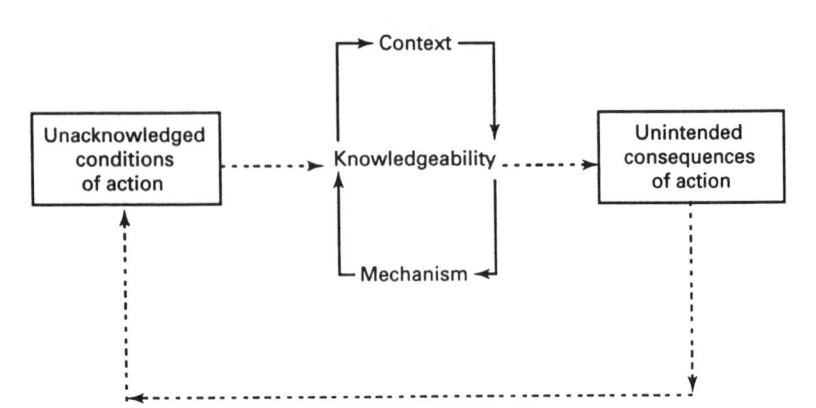

Figure IV: Structuration Theory and the (Partly) Knowledgeable Actor

instance, prisoners will enter an education with a clear understanding of why it is a reasonable choice from the (few) opportunities available, without necessarily appreciating that certain of their background features (age, criminal history, previous education, etc.) have made their candidature more likely. Nor will their reasons for trying education (sanctuary from the wings, choosing the lesser of several evils, a good doss, etc.) necessarily correspond to the outcomes that can ensue (developing interests, rehabilitation). In attempting to construct explanations for the patterning of social activity, the researcher is thus trying to develop an understanding which includes hypotheses about their subjects' reasoning *within* a wider model of their causes and consequences. This positioning of the actor within sociological explanation is summarized in figure four which borrows from Giddens (1984: 5).

At the risk of repetition, let me stress that Figures III and IV represent an entirely general picture of sociological explanation. For instance, exactly the same ingredients (ontological depth, the duality of agency and structure, contextually conditioned causal mechanisms, knowledgeable action with unacknowledged conditions and unintended consequences) can be found in explanations of everything from social mobility (Goldthorpe *et al.* 1980) to car park crime (Tilley 1993). The task now is to say – if this is the structure of 'theory' and 'theory' is the subject matter of the interview, what are the implications for the way we construct data?

The Theory-Driven Interview

Carried to the point of data collection, these explanatory imperatives prefigure a *division of labour* in the practice of interviewing, one based squarely in a *division of expertise* about different aspects of the topic under investigation. Between them the researcher and subject know a great deal about their

THEORIZING THE INTERVIEW 159

subject matters, the trick is to get both knowledge domains – 'scholarship' and 'savvy' – working in the same direction.

How does such a task break down? As a first approximation, we can say (using realist explanatory distinctions) that the understanding of *contexts* and *outcomes* should be led by the researcher's conceptualizations. In relation to my working example, on matters such as the calculation of 'reconviction rates', the categorization of 'offence' types, the measurement of 'educational background', the phrasing of questions on 'custodial record' and so forth, the conceptual distinctions involved should be derived from the researcher's theory and these meanings should be made clear to the respondent in the getting of information.

Exploring explanatory *mechanisms* is another matter. In the example, these speak of the reasoning, choices, motivations which develop during prison education programmes. Typically, it will be the case that the researcher will have a range of provisional expectations about what these may be. Equally typically, the 'hypotheses' will be 'theoretically over-determined' in that a whole range of potential mechanisms may be consistent with the outcomes postulated in the inquiry. Even in the 'mini-theory' of rehabilitation described above, I managed to speculate upon potential changes in personal, economic, social, moral and cognitive mechanisms within the prison classroom. In short, in the realm of 'generative mechanisms', the researcher will often

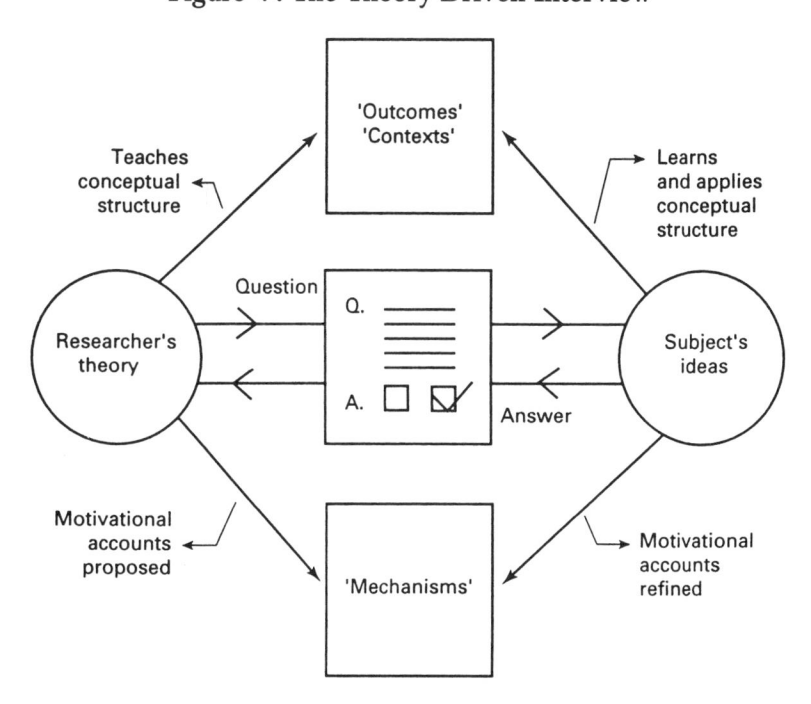

Figure V: The Theory-Driven Interview

assume that the balance of expertise lies with the informant in describing the detailed way in which reasoning contributes to social change.

Here we reach the crux of my argument. In my suggestion of such a division of labour, the reader may be experiencing a sense of *déjà vu* and a corresponding disappointment. Do not the convential (purist or pluralist) models of the interview acknowledge the difference between 'factual' and 'attitudinal' questions or between 'institutional' and 'affective' domains, and lay down a rather well-worn technical apparatus for tackling each – namely the 'structured' and 'unstructured' interview? Well, yes indeed they do, but the whole point I am making is that these distinctions actually misunderstand the division of labour between researcher and informant, and thus misspecify the requisite technical apparatus. By leading with theory, we can come to a better understanding of the division of expertise in the interview, which I try to capture in Figure V and which is distinctive in bringing to the fore two erstwhile hidden features of data collection namely: a) the teaching-learning function and b) the conceptual focusing function.

Fear not, dear reader. Although Figure V may look the demented scribbling of a city-centre traffic-flow planner, it does in fact depict an *information flow* which is common to *all interviews*. This flow needs to be understood clearly and then manipulated sensitively if we are to locate subject's knowledge into sociological explanations. The information highway on the model remains a good old-fashioned structured question and answer sequence running through the centre of the figure. Thankfully, the most common interviewing experience is that if one puts a straight question, most of the time one gets a straight answer. This little miracle happens routinely because researcher and subject share a taken-for-granted set of conceptual building blocks. Social interaction is premised on this realm of the *accepted-as-real* which allows us to know we are talking about the same thing. (Giddens 1984: 331).

This item-by-item, utterance-by-utterance, membership category-by-membership category understanding is, however, only the beginning of the story. Our everyday familiarity with conversational practices will always make interviews happen but not always allow for the apposite data to be constructed. This is where the 'teacher–learner' function comes in. We are interested here in concepts to do with 'outcome' end 'context' elements in the explanatory structure, and the issue is to consider how can we know that the subject is attending to the researcher's understanding of these items. The traditional (structured interview) answer to this problem is to rely on precision in question wording and clarity in operationalization. Whilst the precise turn of a phrase is, of course, important, my basic objection is that operational definitions alone are rarely sufficient to teach the subject the underlying research tack. In reducing the inquiry to variables and values on variables they, in fact, construct meaning in a manner contrary to the way theory will have been devised.

Theory has a complex and deep structure (recall Figure III) and basically the researcher will have come to learn the meaning of any individual concept therein, through its place in these elaborate propositional nets. Method-driven interviews traditionally pay little heed to this important source of conceptual clarity. So whilst researchers will know full well they are asking questions about a prisoners educational background (C_1) as part of a proposition about how further education (M_1) in providing cognitive change (M_2) might produce more potential for rehabilitation (O_1) in inmates who have been deprived of early opportunities (C_2), the inmate can remain blithely unaware of these purposes and meanings. Usually it is the case that this collateral information is smuggled in, rather implicitly across the pages of the questionnaire. What I am suggesting here is that the researcher/interviewer play a much more active and explicit role in teaching the overall conceptual structure of the investigation to the subject for this in turn will make more sense of each individual question to the respondent. In practice this means paying more attention to 'explanatory passages', to 'sectional' end 'linking' narratives, to 'flow paths' end 'answer sequences', to 'repeated' end 'checking' questions and so on. It also means being prepared to take infinite pains to describe the nature of the information sought and thus a sensitivity to the struggles the respondent may have in using what are ultimately the researchers' categories. This function is depicted in Figure V (on the north-western ring-road).

As every interviewer will know, respondents also travel these outer perimeters. So, as well as providing straight answers to straight questions, subjects ponder (mostly in silence) – 'who is this person?', 'what is she after?', 'why am I being asked?', 'what have others said?', 'what should I be saying?', and so on. The theory-driven model I am presenting here has a unique tack on such 'hypothesis-seeking' behaviour. The aim is not to *minimize* it (as in the structured approach), nor to *wallow* in it (as in the unstructured approach), but to *channel* it. That is to say, the battery of questions posed and explanatory cues offered should be understood as putting the subject in a position which allows them to think (still in silence, incidentally) – 'yes, I understand the general theoretical tack you are exploring, this makes your concepts clear to me, and applying them to me gives the following answer'. This partricular information flow is depicted in the 'north east' of Figure V. Elaborate as it may seem this in fact describes the thought process which underlies the typical question and answer sequences found in most detailed formal questionnaires and interviews. Elsewhere (Pawson 1989, Ch. 10) I have provided some working examples of how to facilitate the teacher–learner function.

However, a further step is needed in respect of those aspects of explanation to which interviewees have a privileged access, namely their own reasoning processes. This is where the 'conceptual focusing' function comes in. Such a process is intended to describe the collection of data on explanatory mechanisms (M), the coverage of which is conspicuously absent in Pawson (1989). Thus the 'southern' ring-road in Figure V depicts an extension of interviewing process which allows subjects to have their own say (decidedly out loud) about how their thinking has driven them to particular actions. The key point, however, is that they deliver these thoughts on their thoughts in the context of and, (perhaps) as a correction to, the researcher's own theory. To explain – the overall structure of the researcher's questions will, in general, contextualize the area in which the subject's make decision and highlight some potential decision making activity which goes on therein. The subject's task is to agree, disagree and to categorize themselves in relation to the attitudinal patterns as constructed in such questions *but also* to refine their conceptual basis. It is at this point that mutual knowledge is really achieved. The subject is saying in effect 'this is how you have depicted the potential structure of my thinking, but in my experience it happened like this …'

In short, I am postulating a formula for 'attitude' questions (more properly, items in the cognitive and affective domains generally) in which the respondent is offered a formal description of the parameters of their thinking *followed by* and opportunity to explain and clarify this thinking. To repeat, sociological explanations offer hypotheses about their subjects reasoning within a wider model of their causes and consequences and the attraction of the particular model is that it reflects a division of labour which is best able to put these pieces together.

An 'example' is overdue at this point (and shall be delivered!). First, I should point out that what I describe as the 'formula' in the previous paragraph does *not* imply the existence of some singular and unique technique which captures the idea. The 'I'll-show-you-my-theory-if-you'll-show-me-yours' strategy has echoes in a number of existing methods. Two that come instantly to mind are *vignettes* (in which the stimulus stories are constructed to smuggle in the key theoretical parameters under investigation, upon which the respondent is asked to reflect) and *pilot interviews* (which say – answer these questions and please also tell me what you think of 'em).

Dons and Cons

My detailed illustration comes (appropriately enough) from some pilot interviewing I did on a small scale UK version of the campus-in-a-prison project at HMP Full Sutton. Towards the end of the studies of the first cohort of men through the course, I made an attempt to draw an overall picture of the men's accounts about how (if at all) the course had changed their attitudes, reasoning, outlook, etc. There are, of course, no standard questionnaires or attitude scales ready-made for such a specific purpose so I had to invent one. What I ended up doing was modifying a 'discussion document' produced by the then Northern Regional Education Officer which took as its task to list and elaborate upon the potential 'aims and objectives" of the prison education service. The adaptation took the form of rewriting each statement of aspiration contained in the document, so that they became a sort of attitude rating questionnaire to which the men could agree/disagree and so forth.

As a research instrument, this could certainly be improved upon. It omits some entire categories of potential change and I'm pleased to report that we are working on a much more comprehensive attack on the problem in the Canadian version of the study. However, the example does have the basic methodological features alluded to here. It was written by an 'insider' with an eye on encouraging penal educators to look beyond getting their students through 'GCSE', 'City and Guilds' or whatever. It relates the classroom experience to broader concerns about prison and after. It contains (and this is the important bit) the accumulated wisdom (or as I would prefer to say- 'theories') of practitioners on personal change associated with educational programmes in prisons. A little sub-plot here is that given its origins, which I made known to my subjects, there was a 'whiff' of the Home Office about the construction of the items. This, I recall, added a little spice when I came to get the men to complete and comment upon the questionnaire.

The actual form of questionnaire was as follows. The students were presented with the list of statements representing possible goals of a prison education course and they were asked to respond according to each item in respect of how the statement applies to their experience of the Full Sutton course. They were required to place answers in one of four categories as follows

This applies to me ...
> to a considerable extent   1
> to a moderate extent   2
> to a slight extent   3
> not at all   4

There follows a list of the statements and for each I record the mean response score using the scale as above.

The course:

		Mean response
a)	helps inmates to accept themselves and their feelings more fully	3.4
b)	helps inmates to become more self-confident and self-directing	2.4
c)	helps inmates to become more acceptable persons to society	3.1
d)	helps inmates to accept more realistic goals for themselves	2.5
e)	helps to change the moral outlook of the inmates	3.1

f)	helps inmates to become more flexible in their opinions	2
g)	helps inmates to behave in a mature fashion	2.8
h)	helps inmates to change their maladjustive behaviours	2.8
i)	helps inmates to become more acceptant of others and of other points of view	2.2
j)	helps inmates to reject their criminal past	4
k)	helps inmates to assume responsibility for their own lives	3.4
l)	helps inmates improve their power of concentration and persistence	1.8
m)	helps inmates to discern previously undiscovered talents	2
n)	helps inmates to correct their personality characteristics in constructive ways	2.8
o)	helps inmates to experience success	2.2
p)	helps to provide a basis on which inmates can build new life	2.6
q)	helps inmates to achieve control over their actions and choices	2.6

Rather a lot can be learned by the simple device of *ordering* the responses from those features which the men found consistent with their own experience down to those which they considered inapplicable. As ever in data analysis, it is the patterns of response we are seeking to uncover and this can be aided by the device of superimposing some breaks and boundaries within this rank order. In the following I distinguish those objectives which collectively met with i) considerable to modest agreement, ii) moderate to slight agreement and iii) slight to no agreement. I also insert a mid point axis (score 2.5) which can help us see the general balance of sentiments.

1–2	*considerable to moderate agreement*
	'improve powers of concentration and persistence'
	'become more flexible in opinions'
	'discern previously undiscovered talents'

| 2–3 | *moderate to slight agreement*
'experience success'
'acceptant of others and other points of view'
'self-confident and self-directing'
'accept more realistic goals'...................(2.5)
'behave in a more mature fashion'
'correct personality characteristics in constructive ways'
'change their maladjustive behaviours'

| 3–4 | *slight to no agreement*
'more acceptable persons to society'
'change moral outlook'
'accept themselves and their feeling more fully'
'assume responsibility for their own lives'
'reject their criminal past'

It is possible to make some rough and ready sense of the above configuration by seeking to uncover the 'themes' which underlie the difference between those aspirations with which the men concur and those of which they are sceptical. It can be seen readily enough that the items with which the men concur concern the improvement in 'mental powers', 'learning skills', 'flexibility of viewpoints' end so on. In short, the connecting thread here is a recognition of personal change along a dimension that perhaps speaks for itself – namely *academic related change*. The roots of scepticism about the transformative capacity of education seem more diverse. There would seem to be (at least) two distinctive features which underlie doubt. The first is when the items refer to *public acceptability*. The thinking here, presumably is that all prisoners know they are no longer free agents, expect a tough reception on release and do not expect things will be dramatically different, with or without a diploma. The second dimension which the inmates declare untouched by their presence in the academy can be thought of as items pertaining to *personal character*, especially those statements getting at their inner self and most specifically, of course, the only item on which there was unanimity, namely item (j) and its insinuation that education allows them to reject their criminal past.

What we have to this point is an unremarkable, not to say undistinguished, piece of attitudinal scaling which produces, incidentally, some rather unwelcome results – there being only the faintest whiff of 'rehabilitation' in all this data. Orthodox methodological thinking divides habitually at this point. The quantitative instinct would be to get more formal – the pilot items could be beefed up, a proper factor analysis could be attempted, and a rather larger sample could be constructed (have I mentioned that the above data is culled from seven inmates?) The qualitative instinct would be to ditch the lot as arbitrary number-crunching and to go for personal involvement as the high road to understanding personal change.

It is possible to escape these weary old methodological straightjackets by considering more closely the men's reasoning in response to being presented with this battery of propositions. I can still recall vividly the Full Sutton students' outward reaction to this exercise two years on. They moaned, they groaned; a couple of them were on the point of refusing to complete the task at all (until I threatened them with more lectures on mobility tables). The roots of this discomfort were exactly the same as most people feel when they are asked to complete such exercises, but in this case MAGNIFIED several times. That is to say, attitudinal statements are normally regarded as irritating simplifications and only with some generosity can one reduce the richness of life's experiences down to the pre-set categories. In this particular instance, some of the simplifications were regarded as more than mere irritations but were seen as positively insulting (in certain respects which I will come to in a moment).

The methodological point that shines through this, however, is that the questions perform a much more significant function than as the specific *stimuli* to respective *responses*. Neither are they an *invitation* for respondents to muse on whatever aspects of their experience are central to them. Taken as a piece, these formal questions set a clear agenda which represents a body of theory, offering up the researcher's potential explanations for a closely circumscribed set of actions. Their key role, therefore, should be to involve the respondent in a closer articulation and clarification of these theories. This can be done (and was done in this instance) by the simple device of getting the respondents to explain *why* they have plumped for the particular responses to the particular items. This is a common place enough tactic in semi-structured interviewing, but one that is never understood in the way that I am presenting it here, namely – as a superb vehicle for the here's-my-theory-what's-yours strategy of data collection. What is induced by this process is a great deal of conceptual hair-splitting and this is precisely the kind of data which leads to better focused explanation.

Let us look more closely at a couple of examples of this process at work. Question (j) about inmates rejecting their criminal pasts because of contact with education got short shrift, yet the subsequent account of *why* the statement is disregarded, prompts the inmates into a much more subtle level of reflection on their own reasoning. The following extracts give the accounts of four men on why they registered 'not at all' in answer to this question. As always, transcripts fail to give the underlying 'mood' of the answer which might be summarized helpfully here as 'furious', 'imperious', 'cool', 'cooler', respectively.

- But to *reject* your criminal past, I'm not rejecting it. I'm not rejecting what I've done, but you don't reject it do you, you ... you take and you ... you step on from there and you try and learn from it. You don't go, well you don't know. Its a part of ... its a part of you.
- I know why overall I've scored so low its because its I ... I ... I do have thin thing umm ... about personal responsibility, you know I ... I ac-

knowledge that I'm in prison through my own fault, and umm ... if I'm going to stop coming into prison it will be down to my own motivation.
- I mean its (the question) assuming that its (the course) is gonna change somebody's whole outlook on life and behaviour and everything I don't relate to it, don't relate it at all. I mean I can see that the more educated you are the more you can get away I suppose. But I don't connect with it at all.
- In my case, when I commit a crime I know I'm doing wrong and I know if I'm going to get caught, I'll go to prison. So its not as though I'm *rejecting* it.

A similar theme emerges in relation to the question of whether education can help inmates to accept 'themselves and their feelings more fully'.

- I feel that I excepted myself and my feelings before I came onto the course, before I knew of the existence of the course.
- I fully accepted my feelings a long time before I came here.
- I agree that this course and education still could really help those people who don't really understand yourself (themselves). Firstly I understand myself and I don't really see that (the course) leading me in to that direction. Really (this) is one thing I have to discover myself.

What even these few clarifications reveal is a tension in most of these prisoner's beliefs about education. It is recognized as 'improving' and yet they want to take credit for the improvement. They 'learn' but not as empty buckets filled with knowledge against their better judgment. It is recognized that education can lead to self-understanding but only because prison conditions are already conducive to intense self-reflection, since they provide many hours, days and years of opportunity for the same.

This tension was perhaps best expressed by 'No7' who was most hostile to this particular phase of the research because he felt the questions were 'patronizing' and that they were full of 'civil service rhetoric'. He set out to swat down their 'preconceived ideas' with a series of 'not at alls' in his written responses. Under follow-up questioning, he relents a little and finds that he was 'making a nonsense of some of his own scoring.' Basically he back tracks because

- I will go down the road of agreeing, because, err ... I feel that education is a civilizing process ... it could well prove a contributing factor in the adjustment to acceptable behaviour. Change is something that comes within but you would be taking on board education.... it's a catalyst ... more than a catalyst, as I've said before its a civilizing process

Here is another man choosing his words carefully and, being an educated sort, he does indeed know his 'catalysts' from his 'contributing factors'. Actually, the most telling phrase he uses here is probably 'taking on board education' and this is an image which comes through most strongly in all of the men's discussion. *If we take as the starting point that many prisoners routinely engage in self-scrutiny and choice-making then what a rigorous period of education can perhaps provide, is a means of extending, deepening and affirming such processes.* Or to put this back into prison parlance.

- It's not the course that's changed you as such, it's you've developed an interest inside you, you know.
- By and large you've got your own ... you've got your own way of working ... and you can work in a number of directions ... you're sort of given advice on which way to go and that, but at the end of the day its your choice.

The sprinkling of metaphors in the above on 'interests inside you', 'taking on board of education', 'stepping on from there', contains important messages about the importance and nature of cognitive change as a potential mechanism for rehabilitation. The upshots of such reasoning will be explored in the research to come. Here I should return to the general methodological significance of this tale. I readily admit that the example came unfortunately *before* the rationale I am in the process of relating. To me it came as a (minor methodological) Eureka – after months of going round the houses, trading anecdotes about early educational experiences, the nature of crime, their likelihood of re-offence or rehabilitation, the influence of family, peers, teachers, Uncle Tom Cobbley and all – this simple formal schedule did the trick. All at once they talked about *their* world in *my* language.

Conclusion

This paper ought to have brought on a strong sense of recognition to researchers who will know that the processes described here are already part and parcel of the negotiation of meaning which goes on in any substantial interview. The paper will have worked if these same researchers believe that the conceptual framework elaborated here provides a better methodological foundation than hitherto for understanding, controlling and developing these negotiations. In particular I have tried to rethink the boundary line between the researcher's and subject's knowledge.

In advocating this approach as one with general utility in data construction, I should make it clear that I am not simply putting the 'trick' or the 'technique' up for inspection. All this is not simply a matter of piling up a set of attitudinal statements and getting them explained. What I am actually counselling is the *information flow* as depicted in the model in Figure V. Its key aspect is the creation of a situation in which the theoretical postulates/conceptual structures under investigation are open for inspection in a way that allows the respondent to make an informed and critical account of them. Much more could be said about when, why and for whom one would adopt the approach. Here I only need stress that it involves a highly specific and carefully planned route march which goes between the qualitative and quantitative traditions.

Bibliography

Barker, E. 1984 *The Making of a Moonie*, Oxford: Basil Blackwell.
Barnes, C. 1992 'Qualitative Research', *Disability, Handicap and Society* 7 (2): 115–24.
Bell, C. and Newby, H. (eds) 1977 *Doing Sociological Research*, London: George Allen & Unwin.
Duguid, S. 1981 'Prison Education and Criminal Choice', *Canadian Journal of Criminology* 23 (1): 15–24.
Foddy, W. 1993 *Constructing Questions for Interviews and Questionnaires*, Cambridge: Cambridge University Press.
Giddens, A. 1984 *The Constitution of Society*, Cambridge: Polity.
Goldthorpe, J. H. *et al.* 1980 *Social Mobility and Class Structure in Modern Britain*, Oxford: Clarendon.
Malseed, J. 1987 'Straw Men', *Sociology* 21 (4): 629–31.
Merton, R. K. 1957 *Social Theory and Social Structure*, Greencoe: Free Press.
Mills, C. Wright 1959 *The Sociological Imagination*, New York: Oxford University Press.
Oakley, A. 1981 'Interviewing women: a contradiction in terms' in H. Roberts (ed.) *Doing Feminist Research*, London: Routledge.
Pawson, R. 1989 *A Measure for Measures: A Manifesto for Empirical Sociology*, London: Routledge.
Tilley, N. 1993 'Understanding Car Parks, Crime and CCTV', *Police Research Group Paper No 42*, London: Home Office.

11

Dimensions of the Depth Interview[1]

Raymond L. Gorden

What is the "depth interview"? The term is put in quotes because it is more often used with mysterious overtones than as a scientific word with a clearly delineated referent. The term has grown in popularity in motivation research, market research, and studies of human relations in industry and of other areas of pure and applied social science. The principal aim of the social scientist in interviewing is valid and reliable information, not therapy or motivation; however, this is not to deny that many interviews are conducted with more than one aim.

The success of depth interviewing will, in the long run, depend upon having (*a*) a frame of reference which provides a theoretical bridge between the type of information needed and the techniques to be used in obtaining it; (*b*) interviewers trained in the skills and sensitivities needed to detect which dimension they are dealing with at a given moment as the interview progresses; and (*c*) interviewers trained in the skills and techniques applicable to each dimension. Toward this end, a theoretical frame of reference is presented for distinguishing significantly different dimensions of depth.

Definitions

The definition of any type of interview might be in terms of the techniques or the observable operations. Thus the interviewer in the depth interview could be said to be "permissive," "reflective," "non-directive," or to be following the principle of "minimal activity."

A second and basically different definition of the depth interview is in terms of the types of information needed. The latter must be translated into social-psychological categories sufficiently abstract to be widely applicable. This has

Source: *American Journal of Sociology*, vol. 62, 1956, pp. 158–164.

advantages over the first type of definition: first, it avoids the assumption that the specific techniques to be used have already been discovered and developed; second, it defines the goal as clearly as possible before the issues of apparently contradictory techniques and tactics must be faced. These two reasons are logically related to a third: that the effectiveness of various interviewing techniques cannot be tested until a criterion of success is developed.

Not every failure to obtain valid and reliable information is due to the fact that the information is too deep. It may be due to the interviewer's failure to communicate his wishes clearly to the respondent. However, here we are primarily concerned with barriers to communication and are assuming that the interviewer has been successful in communicating the question.

The "depth" of any item of information depends upon its meaning for the respondent, which, in turn, depends upon how he perceives the relationship between the information and the total social context in which it is given. What is in one social situation a mere "objective fact," as, for example, the respondent's age, may be a devastating threat in another.

How, then, is any kind of information deeper than another if it depends upon the situation? This is a particularly important question in view of the fact that the "deep" information is presumed to be accessible to the interviewer under certain conditions, and his hope for success depends upon his manipulating the respondent's definition of the situation in such a way as to make what would ordinarily be deep information come to the surface. The word "ordinarily" is important as recognizing the norms regarding what should be communicated to whom under what conditions, as well as how the communication is to be carried out. The further the interviewer varies his techniques and tactics from the prevailing norms of social conversation, the deeper the information he obtains.

Degree of Ego-Threat

The respondent tends to withhold any information which he fears may threaten his self-esteem. There may be merely very mild hesitancy or complete repression. Three broad categories may be defined on the basis of the degree or kind of secrecy.

The strongest tendency to withhold information is often referred to as "repression." The respondent not only refuses to admit the information to the interviewer but also hides it from himself, to preserve his self-esteem and escape a guilty conscience. He is perfectly honest when he says that he does not know or that he has forgotten. This dimension has primarily occupied the psychiatrist, psychoanalyst, and clinical psychologist.

A less intense threat to self-esteem is found when the respondent, though he consciously possesses the information, hesitates to admit it to the interviewer because he anticipates that the latter will disapprove. Often the respondent is torn between the temptation to withhold the information and the yearning for catharsis. If he is made to feel confident that the interviewer will not condemn him, he may welcome the opportunity to "tell all."

Quite commonly, a victim of a community disaster suffers strong feelings of guilt over his "cowardly" behavior in the panic. His need for catharsis is evident in his expression; he may freely admit that he has not told his family or any of his friends about his behavior. Also it is common for the respondent to say at the end of the interview that he feels much better "since having a chance to talk."

Sometimes the respondent indulges in some shrewd interviewing of the interviewer to discover the latter's attitudes. For example, the respondent who would like to confess socially disapproved forms of sex behavior may first try to discover the interviewer's probable reaction by mentioning a case similar to his own and may even try to provoke the interviewer into condemning it. If the interviewer condemns the hypothetical case, the respondent will not tell about himself. Confession is easiest if the interviewer is a stranger whom the respondent never expects to see again,[2] but in any case a generally accepting and sympathetic attitude toward the respondent as a person goes far to elicit candid responses.

A less intense threat to the respondent's self-esteem exists if the respondent is willing to give information to the interviewer but fears losing status if the information goes any further. This respondent must be assured that his anonymity will be respected. This is not always easy to do. The respondent may fear that the interviewer will be unable to conceal the source of the information, even with the best of intentions. Indeed, the higher the respondent's status, the more difficult to give information describing his role in the community without revealing his identity.

This was clearly demonstrated in the contrast between the attitude of the officials in a disaster-struck town and that of the average citizen toward having interviews tape-recorded. It was extremely rare to have an ordinary citizen object to the tape-recorder, hut objections from officials were quite common. It appears that the higher the social status, the greater the possible discrepancy between the person's actual behavior and that expected of him. If the leaders had sufficient opportunity to rehearse the role expected of them under crisis conditions, it would be no crisis for them. Also, as the group becomes smaller, assuming that the group itself will not be anonymous, the less chance there is of keeping any particular individual anonymous.

Not only must the interviewer assure the respondent of anonymity at the beginning of the interview, but he also must be sensitive to any need for further reassurance as the interview progresses.

Degrees of Forgetting

Almost as frequent a barrier to candor is the respondent's inability to recall certain types of information. Simple facts which are not ego-involved, such as the date of first going to work at a factory, cannot be accurately determined in a superficial interview. This was discovered when respondents' replies were checked against company records.[3]

It is difficult for an interviewer to predict which items of information will be difficult for a given respondent to recall. Only after a great deal of experience in interviewing a particular type of respondent for a specific type of information, will he acquire moderate skill in predicting degrees of difficulty. Not infrequently the respondent gives a spontaneous and sincere reply, only to contradict himself later when recall was somehow stimulated.

Several specific techniques have been developed to stimulate the recall of forgotten material, one of the best of which is given by Merton.[4] He points out that it is possible to create a mood of "retrospective introspection" in which the respondent imaginatively transports himself backward in time to an actual experience. Then, by certain types of probing to encourage a network of associations, the interviewer can help the respondent to recall specific details and experiences.

The memory dimension of the depth interview is a much more frequent obstacle to obtaining the needed information than is suspected by the inexperienced interviewer, and the techniques which are used to penetrate it are quite different in principle from those needed to penetrate ego-involvement. To complicate the interviewer's task further, the respondent does not say "I have forgotten" but usually continues talking, filling in the gaps in his memory with whatever his imagination suggests.

Degrees of Generalization

Specification may be conceived to be at one pole of a continuum and *generalization* at the opposite pole. In this scheme the term "generalization" designates information relatively free of time, place, or specific events and situations. In certain types of interviewing problems it is relatively simple to elicit a generalized statement but difficult to obtain concrete details of the events leading to the generalization.

There are at least four basic reasons why it is necessary to encourage the respondent to be specific. First, he may make errors in generalizing. Even though generalized information is what is needed for a particular study, the generalizations which the respondent has on the top of his mind may not fit the concrete experiences from which they have supposedly been drawn. This is an especially acute problem in interviewing victims of community disasters. It was not unusual for a local norm to be expressed as a myth which crystallized soon after the crisis was over. These generalized statements might have been about the behavior of women as contrasted to that of men or about the "miraculous" way in which the rescue and first-aid work was carried out, for which the factual basis could not be found. In some cases the generalizations were merely projections of the norms as individuals tried to assess the buzzing confusion.

Second, a respondent is frequently unable to generalize. This may be because the concepts or categories relevant to the interviewer's problem have no direct clear meaning for him, a situation familiar to the anthropologists, who have learned, for example, that a direct generalized question about the kinship structure or the value system of a primitive tribe will not elicit meaningful answers. Unfortunately, this problem is not peculiar to studies of primitive societies but is found very frequently in any study of contemporary communities which attempts to reach an analytical level. For example, if an interviewer were to ask a twelve-year-old boy in a slum area of Chicago, "What is the most common way that conflicts between you and your parents are resolved?" there would be little chance of his being able to give a general answer.

Third, it is often found that a respondent uses evasive generalizations to conceal the real situation. In this case the respondent's inability or unwillingness to give concrete examples throws doubt upon the accuracy of the generalization.

Fourth, it is sometimes necessary for the interviewer to obtain generalized information indirectly by means of specific examples where the general category has a negative value. For example, if the question "Is there discrimination against Negroes in this restaurant?" is put to a white waitress who has recently arrived from the South, she might report that there is none, since nothing "bad" goes on in the restaurant, or she may realize that, since the interviewer is interested in discrimination, he would probably consider the existing relationships as "discrimination." Also, since she considers this to be only a Yankee's point of view, she is not going to give any facts which can be used by the interviewer to draw his own "biased conclusions."

There are certain similarities between the evasive generalization and the value-laden generalization, but in the former the respondent's use of the generalized form is a symptom of his resistance, while in the latter it is caused by the interviewer's use of the generalized rather than the specific form of the question.

It should also be noted that no statement has been made as to whether the general or the specific information is the more difficult to secure. This varies from one situation to another. Thus (*a*) the generalized information is more difficult to obtain when it calls for more abstract intellectual categories rather than for information on attitudes (this is also true if the respondent is expected to classify concrete events into categories not already in his mind); (*b*) on the other hand, the specific information is more difficult to obtain when the concrete event was either so ambiguous, confusing, or emotion-provoking that the respondent never had a clear perception of the event or so complex that he had only a general picture of it, or when the process of abstraction by the respondent was so automatic that he could not report the specific perceptions leading to the generalization.

Degree of Subjectivity of Experience

Both subjective and objective materials constitute social facts. By our definition, a fact is "objective" if it can be readily observed and agreed upon by independent observers. From the standpoint of interviewing, the most significant difference between subjective and objective material is that the latter is less likely to be distorted or inhibited by highly active interviewing methods. For example, it is possible that the "third degree" could be used to learn whether the respondent had buried the body in the swamp or had thrown it into the river. On the other hand, it is highly unlikely that the same degree of activity could be used to obtain the sequence of definitions of the situation in a crisis. This is not to imply that subjective information can never be obtained by vigorous methods. Some conditions under which activity is appropriate in the interview have been demonstrated by Richardson.[5]

The subjective dimension constitutes a commoner problem for the clinical psychologist and psychiatrist, who are more interested in unique experiences, than it does for the sociologist, who is primarily concerned with more widely shared experiences.

It should be noted that experiences cannot be dichotomized into the purely unique and the shared but that, in actuality, they fall along a continuum and are a matter of degree. For example, the schizophrenic may use many words esoterically; yet, if they were completely unique, never being shared by other schizophrenics or used consistently by one, the therapist could never understand them.

Conscious Versus Unconscious Experience

Here the term "unconscious experience" refers to behavior which the respondent cannot report because he was not conscious of it at the time and not because of a fading memory, ego-threat, or the uniqueness of the experience. For this reason the answers to the following would be difficult to obtain: "What is the difference between the way you speak to a Negro and the way you speak to a Caucasian?" "When do you use the prepositions 'of' and 'at' after a verb in the English language?" "Which sock do you usually put on first in the morning?"

There are at least three types of unconscious behavior. The most common is simply custom. The degree to which it is unconscious is indicated by Sapir.[6] Next there is the unconscious behavior which Blumer calls "circular reaction," which is the immediate, unwitting response of one person to the subliminal cues furnished by another.[7] Finally, there is the unconscious behavior found under conditions of acute emotional stress in crises. This differs from circular reaction, in that no interaction with other people is needed.

Disasters provoke many examples of unconscious behavior. For example, persons fleeing from their homes to escape an explosion frequently take the longest route in order to leave by the rear door which they habitually use. Perhaps more to the point: a man rescued several people from a burning building but had no recollection of the acts which were clearly observed by several others; a crowd at an air show obeyed the master of ceremonies' suggestion to extinguish all cigarettes and refrain from starting automobiles when an airplane crashed into the grandstand and parking area, yet many who obeyed the order could not report what made them do so.

Details of these types of behavior are very difficult to obtain from the respondent. However, it was not uncommon for respondents to say that they had never been aware of certain aspects of their behavior during the crisis until after the interview had been under way for some time.

Degree of Trauma

Here "trauma" is used to denote an acute unpleasantness associated with an experience. The unpleasant feeling is often brought to consciousness when the respondent is reporting the experience. It is not due to his embarrassment or his fear of losing status or of embarrassing the interviewer; it is because reporting the experience forces him to relive the original emotions.

Here there is no chance of the respondent's obtaining release from a guilty conscience by "confessing his sins," because he has no sins. A comparison of the length of the interviews with disaster victims having traumatic experiences, such as having members of the family killed, with the length of interviews with people who suffered no loss shows that the former tended to give either extremely long or extremely short interviews. In the prolonged interviews there was a tendency to talk repeatedly of the most traumatic portion of the experience. For example, a woman whose daughter, who was standing beside her at the air show, was killed when an airplane crashed into the crowd, repeatedly referred to the horrors of seeing her daughter mutilated. However, a respondent who had had a similar experience would not mention that a member of his family had been killed; this information had to be obtained from other sources.

We make no pretence of explaining why one respondent dilates on the "gory details" while another adroitly avoids the subject. It is possible that the respondent has a need for catharsis after a traumatic experience just as he does when he has feelings of guilt. A permissive attitude in the interviewer might encourage the respondent to talk, particularly if he cannot forget or repress the ordeal. The respondent's repressing a traumatic experience may have some relationship to the length of time after the event. However, it is not sidereal time which is relevant but social-psychological time calibrated by certain local events. Most significant of the latter seemed to be the funerals.

Contrary to expectations, in a community disaster it was easy to induce the respondent to talk before the funerals about the death of friends and members of the immediate family. However, after the funerals his attitude changed markedly. The funeral as a community event seemed to symbolize the establishment of a new social equilibrium: it marked the end of the past horror and the opening of a new chapter in the history of the individual and the community. The individual respondent's attitude seemed to be "Let's not discuss the dead." Somehow the disaster victims seemed to be more dead after the funerals than before.

Degree of Etiquette

Here we refer to the respondent's perception of the etiquette between himself and the interviewer with respect to particular types of information. Communication is given its form by taboos, secrets, avoidances, "white lies," what Simmel referred to as "vital lies," and etiquette; and certain symbols and attitudes circulate only in restricted channels or between people in certain social relationships. The respondent must perceive his relationship with the interviewer as one permitting the communication desired. The respondent may have the information clearly in mind but feel that it would be impolite to divulge it, a state of affairs corroborated by the fact that many of the most clear-cut examples are unprintable.

The etiquette barrier can be broken down by using an interviewer in a more appropriate role. Sometimes it is not enough to select the correct interviewer, but, in addition, special techniques must be used to define the situation as one permitting a breach of the usual etiquette.

Chronological Aspect

"Chronological aspect" refers to the relationship between the time an experience occurred and the time from which the respondent is actually or imaginatively viewing it. Of the many logically possible aspects which might occur in the interview, we will mention the two most frequently encountered.

First is the "introspective past," which refers to information about an event which the respondent is reporting from the same point in time as the event. In effect, he speaks about the past in the present tense, trying thus to relive the original experience in every detail. Merton refers to this as "retrospective introspection." Here we are seeking the person's original subjective experience without distortions due to hindsight.

In a disaster people have great difficulty in correctly defining a crisis, and their definitions often progress through several stages. The individual tries to make sense out of what happened by seeing the original experience in the light of information obtained after the event. This general tendency constitutes an interviewing problem because if we wish to understand why the respondent acted as he did, we must discover how he defined the situation immediately before and during his action.

Second is the "retrospective past," which refers to information about a past event which the respondent is reporting from the vantage point of the present. Here the perspective is quite different because the respondent has the advantage of having had time to rearrange his own personal experiences in relation to one another and he also has the advantage of much new information from other people involved in the same situation. One of the most difficult tasks of the interviewer is to separate the data in the retrospective past from those in the introspective past. In general, it is easier to obtain information in the retrospective past.

Conclusions

The foregoing scheme should be useful in three ways. First, it should help the interviewer by sensitizing him to some of the complexities of the depth interview and allowing him to apply his techniques and skills more critically. It might also make him more alert for new insights, techniques, or tactics.

Second, the scheme should help the student of the interview as a process by furnishing what Merton would call a "theory of the middle range" which has been derived inductively and is at a high enough level of abstraction to be applicable to many instances of a certain class. It should not only help locate some of the basic problems but also give some hint of the possible limitations of generalizations based upon the study of one type of interview. It presents the interview as a dynamic process in which there is a constantly shifting relationship between the type of information sought and its meaning.

Finally, the scheme may be useful in developing a realistic design of research by calling attention to some of the problems of collecting valid and reliable data. Although the scheme was developed in the course of the writer's experience in interviewing, it may throw light upon the over-all strategy and the relative desirability of using questionnaires, observation, projective techniques, or interviewing in gathering the data.

Notes

1. Many of the ideas presented in this paper were gained while the writer was acting as assistant field supervisor of the Disaster Study Project at the National Opinion Research Center, University of Chicago.

2. The writer agrees with Stephen A. Richardson that if the interviewer remains in a community, and it is evident that he is talking to many people, he may be suspected of passing on highly confidential information and lose public confidence.

3. B. V. Moore, "The Interview in Industrial Research," *Social Forces*, VII (1929), 445–52.

4. Robert K. Merton, "The Focused Interview," *American Journal of Sociology*, LI (May, 1946), 541.

5. Stephen A. Richardson "The Rise of Leading Questions in Non-schedule Interviews" (unpublished paper).

6. Edward Sapir, "The Unconscious Patterning of Behavior in Society," in E. S. Dummer (ed.), *The Unconscious: A Symposium* (New York: A. A. Knopf, 1927), pp. 114–42.

7. Herbert Blumer, "Collective Behavior," in Robert E. Park (ed.), *An Outline of the Principles of Sociology*, (New York: Barnes & Noble, 1946), p. 224.

12

Artifacts are in the Mind of the Beholder*

Howard Schuman

You may have heard of the symbolic interactionist at a small liberal arts college who several years ago received a questionnaire from the ASA asking about his attitudes toward certain professional issues. He was deeply offended that his own organization would engage in such a foolish exercise. In the first place, why assume that he carried around bundles of attitudes at all, let alone that he would display them on request to an impersonal piece of paper? On the contrary, he knew that he acted on the basis of meaning derived from concrete social interaction with others, mediated by interpreting the indications of these others and developing lines of action toward them. How could he conceivably pretend to respond to the insignificant other represented by a questionnaire when it violated the very nature of the social act? Moreover, he knew that many other sociologists would feel the same way and they also would throw the questionnaire into the nearest wastebasket, so that even in its own terms this so-called survey would fail to represent the profession, let alone tap the true channels of communication and organized nature of influence within the ASA.

So indignant was this symbolic interactionist, whom I will call Sy for short, that he decided to circulate a petition and send it as a protest to ASA headquarters, lest they fail to see what blasphemy was being perpetuated, no doubt unthinkingly, on the spirit of the profession. To allow others also to speak their minds, he drafted the following petition to his colleagues:

Do you agree that the Association should not waste our money and our time by sending attitude questionnaires, as they are called, to ASA members across the country?

Please indicate your view below.

The petition was mailed to sociologists in many departments. In fact, to be perfectly fair Sy employed the ASA directory and selected a name from each

---

Source: *American Sociologist*, vol. 17, 1982, pp. 21–28.

page, using a dusty random number table that he had accidentally retained from a required course in statistics years past.

Just before mailing the petition, it occurred to Sy that sociologists might differ in their stance toward the petition depending upon where they had attended graduate school, some departments being even more stultifying than others. So he asked for the name of the school and the date of graduation; and as an afterthought, since it was so simple, he also asked recipients of the petition to jot down their age and sex. Finally, in a generous note he volunteered to receive the replies, tally them, and communicate the word to those in Washington whose mischief had required this remedial action on his part. Drawing on his own personal finances – for he was no captive of the federal grant and contract system – he posted the letters himself, and with a heavy sense of responsibility waited for the replies.

The results did not flood back quite as rapidly and fully as he had expected, but a few weeks later Sy had received some 100 petitions out of the nearly 500 he had mailed out. He was pleased to see that most of the senders agreed with his own position, but there were enough dissenters to pique his curiosity as to the identity of these benighted souls. As he studied the petitions he noted that they differed, as he had suspected, in the graduate schools attended, and what is more they also differed in unexpected ways in age and sex. He even found, through ingenious use of the postmarks on the returned envelopes, a surprising difference by region of the country in the proportion of those who agreed with the sociologically correct position. Since present region of the country and region of graduate training appeared to be related, it seemed wise to consider both simultaneously, lest one be confused with the other, and at the suggestion of a colleague from the remote methodological wing of his department, he finally put all this information onto punch cards. Working late at night so as not to be seen by his best friend, a phenomenologist, he even began to learn the local computer system.

I will not carry further this story, which you may regard as apocryphal or not depending upon your temperament and capacity for belief. Let me only report that Sy eventually quit his job in the college sociology department and joined a large survey organization, where he now juggles 3, 4, and even 5 variable tables, has substituted Goodman for Blumer as his favorite University of Chicago faculty member, and is involved at the moment in designing two surveys, analyzing a third, and taking a crash course in LISREL.

You wonder about his state of mind, his having made such a sea change at a late stage of life. I can only answer in the slightly adapted words of W. H. Auden (1975: 147):

> Is he free? Is he happy? The question is absurd: Had anything gone wrong, we should certainly have heard.

This little narrative points up, I think, both the strengths and weaknesses of survey research as a major force in 20th century social science. On the one hand, surveys start from two of our most natural intelléctual inclinations. One is to ask questions of other people and treat their answers with some seriousness. That no doubt happens at our yearly conventions. Someone says to someone else:

How have you been?
Did you get tenure?
What did you think of the session on – ?
Do you know of a good restaurant nearby?

The second inclination is to draw samples to represent a much larger universe. Important aspects of sampling are not intuitively obvious – are in fact strongly counter-intuitive – but the simple idea of inferring from part to whole occurs all the time, from sampling food to sampling ASA sessions. Surveys are useful because they put together these two basic ways of gathering information, and add to them analytic techniques that guard against mistaking chance happenings for real patterns, help unconfound variables, test some causal assumptions (even if indirectly), locate interesting interactions, and more generally go below and beyond the surface of individual answers. This combination of questions, samples, and analysis accounts for much of the drawing power of surveys, seducing many a sociologist like Sy away from other pursuits. The psychologist Edward Tolman once reflected on why he had spent so much of his life studying rats. After noting their many virtues and few vices, he concluded enthusiastically that rats are "marvelous, pure, and delightful" (Tolman, 1945). So also the r x c table.

But this blend of the natural and the sophisticated, which gives surveys their strengths, also contains weaknesses, as Sy's inadvertent investigation indicated. Too much can be inferred from answers taken at face value to questions of dubious merit. Whether one considers Sy's own question wording biased or not is *not* the main point: all answers depend upon the way a question is formulated. Language is not a clean logical tool like mathematics that we can use with precision. Instead, as Fleming wrote, we are immersed in a sea of words, our own distinctive medium, and language shapes us as much as we shape it (Fleming, 1967). As if this complexity were not enough, our answers also are influenced by who asks the question. Your expressed views about this particular session or even about a good restaurant may vary depending upon who asks you the question. All this raises the possibility that survey data, at least attitude survey data, may be transient, bound only to the immediate situation, and thus not have the underlying continuity and causal force that often is sought when surveys are carried out. Moreover, quite apart from the problems of questions and questioners, the response rate of 20 percent for Sy's investigation left enough room for bias as big as an elephant to get through. Most surveys do better than Sy's, but response rates have been dropping of late, and many surveys today lose roughly a third of their sample to non-response, thus compromising the essential character of probability sampling. In sum, the major strengths of surveys also contain the possibility of artifacts that undermine these very strengths.

Beyond such artifacts there is the larger issue of whether surveys should be done at all in many situations that sociologists feel called upon to study. Wouldn't we be better off in many instances going out into the field to observe social interaction at first hand? Or studying the functioning of organizations and larger collectivities through tracing their history, drawing upon documents, looking directly at products and processes and people? Or if we feel a need for more control and quantification, there is the Bales-type indoor group and the neat hypothesis-testing laboratory experiment. To this large issue I must say: yes. My own experience has been that often the first advice a person contemplating a survey should hear is that her or his problem is one that might better – and certainly more cheaply – be studied in other ways. Surveys are expensive, time-consuming, and often not the most fruitful way to investigate a subject, and it is too bad when they are done merely because they are fashionable, sound scientific, or simply are available and take little thought. But having said this, it still is true that surveys often are the best, if not the only, way to study large populations, and I want to concentrate on the problems, already mentioned, of language, interviewing, and sampling that arise even when surveys seem appropriate – the artifacts referred to in the title to this session.

The basic position I will take is simple: artifacts are in the mind of the beholder. Barring one or two exceptions, the problems that occur in surveys are opportunities for understanding once we take them seriously as facts of life. Let us distinguish here between the simple survey and the scientific survey. (I avoid employing the opposition of polls and surveys, because that distinction probably is more etymological and status-related than conceptual.) The simple approach to survey research takes responses literally, ignores interviewers as sources of influence, and treats sampling as unproblematic. A person who proceeds in this way is quite likely to trip and fall right on his artifact. The scientific survey, on the other hand, treats survey research as a search for meaning, and ambiguities of language and of interviewing, discrepancies between attitude and behavior, even problems of non-response, provide an important part of the data, rather than being ignored or simply regarded as obstacles to efficient research.

Let me give some examples, chosen to represent different types of artifacts or opportunities, as the case may be. First consider the issue of interviewer influence. We know from research going back to *The American Soldier* that many black respondents give different answers on certain racial questions to white interviewers than to black interviewers (Stouffer *et al.*, 1949), and more recent research has shown, not surprisingly, that the same is true for white respondents (Hatchett and Schuman, 1975–1976). Thus it would be artifactual if one inferred attitudes simply from a cross-racial interviewing situation, or perhaps even from same-race interviewing. But when these findings are treated as data, rather than as difficulties, they tell us something important about racial interaction in America, for there certainly is good reason to think that the same differences occur for same race and cross-race communication more generally. Moreover, these results based on race of interviewer can be elaborated in many different directions. For example, do you believe that younger black Americans are less concerned about white feelings than their parents? Then you might want to test the hypothesis that race of interviewer will be a less potent variable when younger blacks are interviewed. Or you might be interested in discovering whether cross-sex interviewing involves the same forces as cross-race interviewing, and again this can be tested. Thus one makes *use* of the fact that the survey interview is a social situation, rather than simply stating this over and over as though it were some sort of criticism of surveys.

Of course, it must be admitted that if every response were so dependent on the immediate characteristics and behavior of the interviewer the survey would not be a useful means of gathering more standard information. But there is no evidence that this is the case, and a fair amount of evidence shows that it is not. Even though race of interviewer is one of the most visible and powerful variables we know of, once we move away from questions dealing with black and white views of one another, the data appear not to be influenced by who does the interviewing. Even black reports of discrimination experience do not differ by race of interviewer (Schuman and Converse, 1971). In general, systematic influence due to interviewer characteristics is both limited and delimitable, providing an opportunity to learn, but not a serious obstacle to general use of surveys.

Next consider the wording of questions. Some years ago John Mueller observed that questions on American involvement in Vietnam seemed to yield different amounts of support depending on whether Communist involvement in the war was stressed (Mueller, 1973). Recently Stanley Presser and I (1981) tested this supposition in a split-ballot experiment in national surveys, asking the following question of half the sample:

If a situation like Vietnam were to develop in another part of the world, do you think the United States should or should not send troops?

For the other half, the phrase "to stop a Communist take-over" was added after "send or not send troops." As Mueller's non-experimental comparisons had suggested, sending troops is endorsed by about 15 percent more of the American public when the rationale about a Communist take-over is added (Schuman and Presser, 1981). Is this an artifact? I suppose so, if one generalizes answers to either form of the question beyond that wording. But in juxtaposition the two sets of results tell us something important about potential public response to another crisis like Vietnam and to Presidential speeches attempting to justify military action. At a theoretical level, the results also provide an opportunity to study symbols and their meaning and effects in public life. Again, what is an artifact if treated naively reflects a fact of life if taken seriously.

Beyond specific wording changes as in the Vietnam example, there is a larger principle at work in all survey questioning. It can be called simply "question constraint." People take survey questions very seriously and try hard to answer within the terms of the wording provided. As James Davis (1976) once noted, this points to the validity of the survey approach. If you ask people whether they favor a Constitutional amendment to prohibit abortion, many people will give a very different answer than if you ask them whether they favor government financing of abortions. This may seem inconsistent to those who believe that abortion is a single all-or-nothing issue, but in fact it is quite reasonable to see abortion and many other rubrics as covering clusters of issues, and for the exact nature of the issue as framed in the question to influence responses – just as the exact phrasing of a proposed law influences votes for or against its passage in a legislature, or judicial decisions once it is passed.

One other even more subtle example of question constraint is worth noting, for it shows that open interviewing is not always freer than the more common closed survey question. In an experimental comparison in 1976, we asked people to name the most important problem facing the country at present. In the open version of the question we stopped there, allowing people to answer (we thought) in any way they chose, without further suggestion from us. In the closed version, we asked them to choose from eight alternative responses, such as inflation, unemployment, crime, etc. To our surprise, crime was mentioned significantly more often to the open question rather than the closed, with only slight differences in other responses. After much thought, our best interpretation is that the phrase "facing this country" discourages a response like crime, which is apt to seem a more local matter to many respondents. The closed question, by including crime as a listed alternative, legitimizes it and allows an increase in its choice (Schuman and Presser, 1981). The importance of the example lies in showing that question constraint can occur without our realizing it, and that a more phenomenological approach is not always as liberating as is intended. This is not meant to discourage such a phenomenological approach to survey research, which I think is much needed, but simply to emphasize that there is a second general truth beyond the one about bias being in the mind of the beholder – namely, no method offers a panacea, and self-criticism is always essential if we are to find meaning rather than artifacts in data.

Next, consider a striking example involving the effect of question context on responses. Some 30 years ago Hyman and Sheatsley asked a question about whether Russian reporters should be allowed to report freely from the United States, and also a parallel question about American reporters doing the same in the Soviet Union. The investigators were wise enough to recognize that one question might influence the other, and therefore asked the questions in reverse order on half their questionnaires. What they found was quite interesting. [The results were never published in detail, but are mentioned in Hyman and Sheatsley (1950). For the detailed 1948 results, plus our 1980 replication findings, see Schuman and Presser (1981).] When the Russian reporter question came first in 1948, only 36 percent of the public agreed to such open reporting. But most of the public did favor allowing American reporters to report from the Soviet Union, and when this question came first and the Russian reporter question followed it, approval for Russians to report from the United States doubled, going up to 73 percent. What is going on here is pretty clear: the Russian reporter item taken alone is responded to largely in terms of degrees of anti-Communism or perhaps fear of Communism. But when it follows a parallel item on American reporters it takes on quite a different meaning: a norm of reciprocity is evoked in somewhat the same terms that have been discussed by sociologists from Marcel Mauss to Alvin Gouldner. If we expect the Russians to allow reporting from their country, we must do the same in return.

The results became even more striking when we repeated the experiment in 1980: resistance to allowing Russian reporters into the United States had diminished appreciably over the 32 years since the item was asked first, probably due to a decreased fear of Communist espionage. But there was no change at all in the same question when it came second, no doubt because the norm of reciprocity itself had not changed. Thus answers to the question not only varied by context, but this variation in turn interacted with time. Furthermore, the change in the meaning of the question itself is not due to defects in wording or a lack of pretesting, as indeed often is the case, but results from the intrinsic ambiguity of language – what John Searle (1979) refers to as contextual dependence, though this seems an even richer example than the made-up ones usually produced by philosophers of language.

Is this reporter example an instance of artifact? I suppose from one standpoint it is, for a survey investigator having a time series from only one of the contexts would draw different conclusions than an investigator relying on the context only. But in another sense, the ambiguity of meaning here almost certainly reflects the ambiguity of social reality, and having survey data on both contexts allows us to grasp this ambiguity and obtain an understanding from these two simple items of an important change and an important constant in American life, as well as of the difference between an attitude toward an object and an attitude toward a norm. In the end, whether a finding like this one is to be treated as a survey artifact or a survey discovery depends, paradoxically, on the context in which investigators themselves operate: if data are interpreted too literally, then artifacts abound, but if data are seen as a field in which we search for meaning, then this example is a sign of the richness of survey research.

You may rightly reply that the example is all well and good, but that in most cases surveys do not include experimental variations that allow us to investigate the multiple meanings of questions. In practice then, artifacts, not opportunities, are what are common in survey research. But in addition to the fact that surveys can and should include more experimental variations in context, wording, and mode of interviewing, there is a simple practical solution to the problem of question ambiguity that has long been known: don't rely too much on a single item. By approaching an issue from several directions in an interview one normally can bring into focus the idea one is interested in, separating it from other meanings that are conjoined with it in any one item. The theoretical distinction provided by the reporters experiment may not be perceived in that case, but at least the danger of serious misinterpretation can be avoided.

Let me turn to still another concern about surveys, which often is treated as a sign of artifact: the low relation generally found between answers to attitude survey questions and supposedly relevant behavior that occurs outside the survey. Without going into detail, there are several reasons to believe that the wrong inference has been drawn from these low correlations. First, too often in days past, and even today, it has been assumed that a particular survey response should predict behavior when the briefest reflection will indicate that no such prediction was warranted. The fact that I may have thought John Anderson the ablest of the candidates for President in 1980 did not mean that I would vote for him, since in a three-candidate election one's choice between the two more likely winners can carry more weight than one's preference for a third. Such attitude-behavior discrepancies do not in the least invalidate inquiries about attitude. Second, recent research has shown that much of the problem in predicting behavior has to do not with the invalidity of attitudes but with the unreliability of single behavioral acts. Further, this unreliability can be diminished greatly by obtaining multiple indicators from a class of behaviors: for example, religious activity is measured not only by a single behavior such as church attendance, but by a whole series of behaviors including church attendance, donating money to the church, taking part in church activities, etc. When a behavioral index of this type is constructed, then the correlation with an index of attitudes rises from the levels of .15 to .30 to levels of .50 and .60, about as high as validity coeffcients ever go. Such substantial increases now have been obtained in at least three independent investigations, and there is reason to think that the old attitude-behavior problem, so often used as a sign of survey failures, may become a sign of the efficacy of attitude measurement in surveys. (See Fishbein and Ajzen, 1974; Weigel and Newman, 1976; and Epstein, 1979.)

I don't wish to turn away completely from the individual act and the individual attitude item, for even here the survey may prove more useful than is often recognized. Consider the most famous attitude–behavior failure in the sociological literature: La Piere's 1934 report of a complete disjunction between behavioral intention toward Chinese and actual behavior toward a Chinese couple. Leaving aside all the methodological criticisms that have been made for and against that study, there is the larger issue of why the disjunction occurred. Did the proprietors, in answering the questionnaire, picture Chinese only as laborers in pigtails and coolie hats, and not even recognize the real couple as Chinese? Or did the proprietors act, as often suggested, in terms of an overriding belief that the less disturbance the better? How can we learn more about these and other possibilities? One good way, not perfect by any means but among the best available, is to ask and then to listen as well as we can for each proprietor's personal definition of the situation. If we attempt to do this with a concern not merely clinical, but with the goals of representing a meaningful population of proprietors; of proceeding systematically so as to avoid bias in our inquiry; and of gathering information in a form that can be analyzed internally and connected to such social categories as age and sex, then we have reinvented the attitude survey in its richest form. Thus La Piere might have used his finding not as a stopping point, but as a reason for doing a more probing survey. (This paragraph is adapted from Schuman and Johnson, 1976.)

I now need to mention one other type of artifact that is in many ways more troublesome than those already considered, for it goes to the heart of the probability sampling method that is basic to large-scale surveys. In early years, surveys regularly succeeded in interviewing 80 to 85 percent of the persons identified as potential respondents. In the last 20 years, this figure has declined until even 75 percent is considered relatively good, and 65 percent is by no means uncommon. It can hardly be assumed that the loss is conveniently random, and particularly with the fast growing practice of telephone surveys, there is evidence that low SES persons are especially likely to be omitted (Groves and Kahn, 1979). Here again artifact occasionally becomes opportunity, as House and Wolfe suggested in using survey response rates as an indicator of urban–rural differences in helping behavior and as a reflection of crime rates (House and Wolf, 1978). But in this case the usage does not solve the survey problem, and we are still stuck with inadequate survey data. Unless we can learn more about non-respondents directly, and use this information to adjust survey data as needed, we run the risk of serious artifact entering our tables, all the more dangerously because it is so easy to forget. I regard this problem as the most serious one facing users of the method today, just because it does not allow for experimental investigation within the survey itself.

Let me sum up now my answer to the question posed in the title to this thematic session: "Fact or Artifact? Are Surveys Worth Anything?" The distinction between fact and artifact has to do for the most part not with the survey method itself, but with our use of it. Used simplistically, we all will be tripping on our own artifacts, and of course there are times when all of us do use it simplistically. But if the survey method is treated as one way in which we search for the meaning of human action, then even its artifactual aspects – perhaps especially its artifactual aspects – help in that search.

No matter what method we use as sociologists, we are always dealing with *data about* social reality, not with social reality itself. We are always drawing inferences, making interpretations, testing ideas. The survey researcher, but also other researchers as well, may be likened to the men living in the cave in Plato's allegory (Cornford, 1945:227–235). Chained to one spot deep within the cave, they could only stare at the wall in front of them. Behind them figures of men and animals and other objects moved along a track, and light from a fire still further back cast the shadows of these objects on the wall in front of the men. For the men, then, the shadows were the only reality they knew – their data it might be said – and from these shadows they had to infer as the best they could, the true nature of the world.

Plato believed that there was a method that would allow such men to rise, figuratively speaking, and see the true objects, the fire, and in fact the whole world outside the cave, even the sun and the moon and the stars. Some sociologists also believe that there is a method that will do the same – the one most often cited being field observation or participant observation, because it involves observing natural interaction in a natural setting with our own senses. But without doubting the very real advantages of such field studies, we should be wary of assuming that what we perceive most easily with our own eyes and ears is somehow more valid than what we learn through instruments. Else we should insist that the world is flat because it so clearly looks to be flat at the level of ordinary human perception. Nor is viewing the stars with our own eyes somehow truer than looking at them through a telescope, or in fact abandoning sight altogether and studying the sky by means of radio waves. The survey method is also an artificial way of bringing the human scene into focus – where artificial simply means a way created by people. It certainly should be treated with care and skepticism, and as only one of several different methods by which we search for meaning. But I am convinced that the survey will continue to be of great value to sociologists – not because it is free of artifacts, but because it has the capacity to illuminate even its own artifacts.

Note

* Paper read at the thematic session on "Fact or Artifact? Are Surveys Worth Anything?" Annual Meeting of the American Sociological Association, New York City, August 27, 1980. The main research cited here is based upon work supported by the National Science Foundation under Grant No. Soc7615040. [Address correspondence to: Howard Schuman, Institute for Social Research, University of Michigan, Ann Arbor MI 48106.]

References

Auden, W. H. 1975 *Collected Shorter Poems, 1927–1957.* New York: Vintage Books.
Cornford, Francis M. 1945 *The Republic of Plato.* New York: Oxford University Press.
Davis, James A. 1976 "Are surveys any good, and if so, for what." Pp. 32–38 in H. Wallace Sinaiko and Laurie A. Broedling (eds.), *Perspectives on Attitude Assessment: Surveys and Their Alternatives.* Champaign, IL: Pendleton Publications.
Epstein, Seymour 1979 "The stability of behavior: 1. On predicting most of the people much of the time." *Journal of Personality and Social Psychology* 37: 1097–1126.
Fishbein, Martin and Icek Ajzen 1974 "Attitudes toward objects as predictors of single and multiple behavioral criteria." *Psychological Review* 81:59–74.

Fleming, Donald 1967 "Attitude: The history of a concept." Pp. 287–365 in Donald Fleming and Bernard Bailyn (eds.), *Perspectives in American History*, V. I. Cambridge, MA: Charles Warren Center in American History, Harvard University.

Groves, Robert M. and Robert L. Kahn 1979 *Surveys by Telephone: A National Comparison with Personal Interviews.* New York: Academic Press, Inc.

Hatchett, Shirley and Howard Schuman 1975–1976 "The effects of race-of-interviewer on white respondents." *Public Opinion Quarterly* 39:523–528.

House, James S. and Sharon Wolf 1978 "Effects of urban residence on interpersonal trust and helping behavior." *Journal of Personality and Social Psychology* 36: 1029–1043.

Hyman, Herbert and Paul Sheatsley 1950 "The current status of American public opinion." Pp. 11–34 in J. C. Payne (ed.), *The Teaching of Contemporary Affairs. Twenty-first Yearbook of the National Council for the Social Studies.* Arlington, VA: National Council for the Social Studies.

Mueller, John E. 1973 *War, Presidents and Public Opinion.* New York: John Wiley and Sons.

Schuman, Howard and Jean Converse 1971 "The effect of black and white interviewers on black responses." *Public Opinion Quarterly* 35:44–68.

Schuman, Howard and Michael P. Johnson 1976 "Attitudes and behavior." Pp. 161–207 in Alex Inkeles, James Coleman, and Neil Smelser (eds.), *Annual Review of Sociology*, Vol. 2. Palo Alto, CA: Annual Reviews Inc.

Schuman, Howard and Stanley Presser 1981 *Questions and Answers in Attitude Surveys: Experiments on Question Form, Wording, and Context.* New York: Academic Press.

Searle, John R. 1979 *Expression and Meaning.* New York: Cambridge University Press.

Stouffer, Samuel A., E. A. Suchman, Leland C. DeVinney, S. A. Star, and Robin M. Williams, Jr. 1949 *The American Soldier: Adjustment during Army Life.* Princeton, NJ: Princeton University Press.

Tolman, Edward C. 1945 "A stimulus–expectancy need-cathexis psychology." *Science* 101:616–666.

Wiegel, Russel H. and Lee S. Newman 1976 "Attitude–behavior correspondence by broadening the scope of the behavioral measure." *Journal of Personality and Social Psychology* 33:793–802.

13

Interactional Troubles in Face-to-Face Survey Interviews

Lucy Suchman & Brigitte Jordan

1. Interviews as Interaction

For statistically based social science, survey research is the principal means of obtaining data about the social world. The interview from this point of view is a standardized data-collection procedure that uses a questionnaire as its instrument of measurement; however, the interview is an essentially interactional event as well. From the moment that the interviewer sits down across from the respondent and begins to talk, the survey interview assumes and relies on a wealth of conventions and resources from ordinary conversation. At the same time, the concern with standardized procedures and the statistical notion of error that standardization is intended to address impose constraints on the survey interview that make it significantly different from ordinary conversation. Those constraints have consequences for both the way the interview proceeds and the data that it produces.

In this article we look at the survey interview as a standardized procedure that relies on, but also suppresses, crucial elements of ordinary conversation. Our analysis is based on videotapes of five special interviews, three using the General Social Survey (GSS) and two using the National Health Interview Survey (NHIS). The videotapes were made for research purposes in conjunction with the Seminar on Cognitive Aspects of Survey Methodology sponsored by the Committee on National Statistics of the Commission on Behavioral and Social Sciences and Education of the National Research Council. [For a report on that seminar see Jabine, Straf, Tanur, and Tourangeau (1984).] They show interviews with volunteer respondents. Trained U.S. Census Bureau interviewers were hired by the committee to administer the NHIS questionnaire as they

---

Source: *Journal of the American Statistical Association*, vol. 85, no. 409, 1990, pp. 232–253.

would for the survey; similarly, trained interviewers administered the GSS questionnaires. These particular interviews, however, were not part of the respective surveys. Our analysis of the videotapes was carried out during the summer of 1986, funded by the Committee on Cognition and Survey Research of the Social Science Research Council and by Xerox Palo Alto Research Center. We take the five interviews as case studies that reveal classes of trouble of a potentially more widespread nature. Although we cannot know the precise distribution of such troubles across survey interviews, their presence in these five at least raises the possibility of a more general problem. Our discussions of the data with veteran survey researchers lead us to believe that the troubles identified are not totally idiosyncratic.

Our argument is the following.

1. There is an unresolved tension between the survey interview as an interactional event and as a neutral measurement instrument. On the one hand, the interview is commonly acknowledged to be fundamentally an interaction. On the other hand, in the interest of turning the interview into an instrument, many of the interactional resources of ordinary conversation are disallowed.

2. The success of the interview as an instrument turns on the premise that (a) relevant questions can be decided in advance of the interaction and (b) questions can be phrased in such a way that, as long as they are read without variation, they will be heard in the intended way and will stimulate a valid response.

3. The premises of 2 fail insofar as (a) topics that come from outside a conversation run the risk of irrelevance, and (b) as an ordinary language procedure, the survey interview is inherently available for multiple interpretations of the meaning of both questions and answers.

4. Compared with ordinary conversation, the survey interview suppresses those interactional resources that routinely mediate uncertainties of relevance and interpretation.

We find that the validity of survey data is potentially undermined by the same prohibition against interaction that is intended to ensure reliability. As a remedy, we recommend a collaborative approach that would allow the kinds of interactional exchanges between interviewer and respondent necessary to ensure standardized interpretations, without introducing interviewer bias. This idea was advanced by Briggs (1986) and Mishler (1986), but it has yet to receive the exploration that it deserves and the development that would enable its serious incorporation into survey research practice.

The analysis is organized as follows. In Section 2 we look at the differences between the survey interview and ordinary conversation, focusing on the survey instrument's external control over who speaks and on what topic, prohibitions against any redesign of questions by the interviewer and special requirements placed on the form of answers, problems of question relevance and meaning, and failures in the detection and repair of misunderstanding. Section 3 makes recommendations for a research program to explore a more collaborative, interactional approach to achieving survey reliability and validity.

2. Differences Between the Interview and Conversation

> The interviewer is charged with the responsibility of conducting *inquiry* in something of the manner of a *conversation*. The product of the encounter is supposed to be good "hard" data – the stuff of codes and numbers and computer analysis. The process is supposed to be at least somewhat "soft" – the stuff of pleasant acquaintance. (Converse and Schuman 1974, p. 22)

In what follows we look closely at just how the survey interview is "in the manner of a conversation" and, more important, how it is not. The constraints on the interview we observe that distinguish it from ordinary conversation are all imposed in the interest of *standardization*. Standardization is what identifies the interview process as a scientific procedure. To ensure the standardization of the procedure, the interactivity of ordinary conversational processes is suppressed. Nevertheless we argue that this strategy mistakes sameness of words for stability of meanings. Stability of meaning, the real basis for standardization and ultimately for validity, requires the full resources of conversational interaction.

Local Versus External Control

Researchers interested in face-to-face communication have taken ordinary, naturally occurring conversation as the primary form of interaction, and as the baseline for their analyses. [See Sacks, Schegloff, and Jefferson (1974). For useful surveys of recent work in conversation analysis, see Levinson (1983) and Heritage (1985).] The organizational properties of ordinary conversation represent the minimal constraints required for orderly, mutually intelligible talk. The central organizational feature of ordinary conversation is that who talks, and about what, is controlled from within the conversation by the participants.

In an important sense, local control over the conversation is what sustains participants' interest in talking to each other. The basic assumption in ordinary conversation is that the participants will find a topic that is of mutual interest and explore it to whatever depth they choose. In contrast to this local control from within the conversation, the survey instrument is constructed ahead of time and is imposed on the participants from the outside. The interviewer is the administrator of the survey researcher's agenda, and the respondent is a data point in the sample. Turns at talk are preallocated such that invariably the interviewer asks the questions and the respondent answers them. The choice and order of topics – what is talked about and when – is established by an absent third party, and is not subject to alteration according to any local interests of either interviewer or respondent.

The questionnaire designer attempts to control not only *what* gets talked about in the interview, but precisely *how* topics get talked about as well. In particular, the standardized procedural model of the interview is enforced through the mandate that the interviewer effectively *not* be available for interaction. Interviewers are enjoined (though perhaps with only limited success) against any variation from the question as written. This injunction against interaction reflects the idea that the survey interview has been successfully standardized only to the extent that there is no variation in the words that the interviewer speaks. We return to the problems in this notion of standardization in the following, and suggest an alternative. For the moment, we observe simply that one result of the invariance approach to standardization is that although the interview has the superficial appearance of interaction (two or more people sit down facing one another to talk), that appearance is misleading. As respondents realize that their expectations for ordinary conversation are violated (and violated without recourse), they may react with boredom (with consequent intellectual if not physical withdrawal) and impatience (resulting in answers designed to "get it over with"). More fundamentally, the injunction against interaction means that certain basic resources for establishing shared understanding, essential to successful communication, are effectively prohibited.

Recipient Design of Questions

To the extent that ordinary conversation is locally controlled, speakers can be sensitive to the history of the current talk and can accommodate specific hearers. In contrast, interviewers are trained not to redesign questions based on either information acquired in previous responses or the observable circumstances of a particular respondent. Questions cannot be modified on the spot as they would be in ordinary conversation, but rather must be designed for anyone and must exhaust the range of possible circumstances. The use of an exhaustive specification of conditions, in advance of a response, is intended to obviate the need for negotiation between interviewer and respondent. This strategy, however, results in questions that are awkward and whose construction is difficult to parse. Typically, we get a string of "or's" or modifying clauses incorporated into the question itself. [The examples in this article are meant to illustrate a class of interactional troubles. The following transcript notation is used: * denotes an item of analytic interest, :: denotes a prolongation of the preceding word, // is the point of onset of overlapping talk, · indicates falling intonation, ? represents rising intonation, and – denotes an abrupt shift or break in an ongoing utterance. Speakers are designated as I (interviewer), R (single respondent), Mrs. (wife in family interviews), Mr. (husband in family interviews), or the first initial of an additional family member.]

> *I: During those two weeks, did anyone in the family receive health care at home or go to a doctor's office, clinic, hospital or some other place. Include care from a nurse or anyone working with or for a

medical doctor. Do not count times while an overnight patient in a hospital.
Mrs.: (pause) No:: (NHIS, E family)

In the case of a negative answer to an initial inquiry, the concern that some condition might be missed that falls within the criteria of the question is legitimate; for example, respondents might say they had not received care in response to the first sentence in the aforementioned question if they had only spoken to a nurse. But in the case of an affirmative to the initial clause, the continuation of the question becomes not only awkward, but inappropriate:

I: Was the total combined family income during the past twelve months, that is, yours, your wife's, Judith's and Jerry's more or less than twenty thousand dollars.
Mrs.: More.
*I: Include money from jobs, social security, retirement income, unemployment payments, public assistance, and so forth. Also include income from interest, dividends, net income from business, farm, or rent, and any other money income received.
Mrs.: More. It was more income. (NHIS, E family)

Ordinarily, the completion of a question effects a turn transition to the addressee, who is obligated to respond. In this case, Mrs. E provides a response at the first appropriate place, rendering the additional instructions irrelevant. The continuation by the interviewer effectively ignores that response and requires that Mrs. E reiterate an answer she has already provided.

A second aspect of the prohibition against redesign is that the interviewer is not allowed to make inferences based on information that has been heard before. Questions designed in anticipation of a particular answer cannot be redesigned in light of some other kind, with the result that potentially inappropriate or nonsensical questions must get asked:

I: When did you last see or talk to a doctor or assistant about the dermatitis under the neck.
Mrs.: I didn't.
I: The doctor was never seen?
Mrs.: No.
I: What was the cause of the dermatitis // under the neck.
Mrs.: //My violin. (laughs) The chin rest of my violin.
I: The chin rest of your violin. (long pause while interviewer writes) Did, uhm, the dermatitis under your neck result from an accident or an injury.
Mrs.: No, it wasn't an injury. It was a contact dermatitis.
So::
(portion omitted)

> I: About how many days since (pause) May twenty-ninth a year ago has this condition kept you in bed more than half of the day.
> Mrs.: Never. (smiles)
> *I: Were you ever hospitalized // for
> Mrs.: //No.
> I: Do you still have this condition.
> Mrs.: If:: I forget to put a handkerchief or something over my, the chin rest of my violin it comes back. So I'm very careful to use:: a covering. Over my chin rest. (NHIS, E family)

Converse and Schuman (1974) pointed to the "cross pressures between the social demands for conversations and the scientific demands for inquiry," and recommended the following:

> When questions prove peculiarly inappropriate to a given respondent's situation, there is probably no remedy better than bearing the incongruity with humor – with the respondent if need be. (p. 60)

Despite this recommendation, however, the proscription against redesigning questions is likely to extend to a prohibition against breaking the frame of the interview script at all. (The objection may be raised that although the interviewers behave here as they do under the scrutiny of a video camera, they should be expected to act quite differently in the field, in particular taking on much more of the interactive role that we recommend. The point is that precisely because they were under scrutiny, we can assume that these interviewers behaved according to what they took to be the normative prescriptions of their training. Our recommendation, then, should be taken as relevant to what we want those normative prescripts to be.) One consequence in this case is to inhibit whatever natural inclination the interviewer might have to shift her perspective to that of the respondent in advance of asking a question and to modify the question accordingly, or even to commiserate with the respondent about the troubles that the question as written poses for the respondent's particular situation. As well as setting up an interactional strangeness through inappropriate questions, or more important through the interviewer's failure to acknowledge inappropriate questions, this stand effectively denies the respondent's experience of the interview.

In addition to the redesign that speakers routinely provide based on their ability to take the role of the hearer and to recognize an inappropriate question before they ask it, the organization of conversation provides that instead of responding, the recipient of a question may decline to answer or may ask for some modification of the question's underlying premises. Addressees in ordinary conversation have the option of telling speakers that they are asking the wrong question, or that in asking the question they are assuming something about the addressee that is not the case. In contrast, the interview does not provide an opportunity for the respondent to make a correction to the question's premises. An answer to the question as written, and in the terms prescribed, is a nonnegotiable requirement for what constitutes an acceptable response.

This violation of the norms of ordinary conversation is exemplified in the following respondent's protest regarding a question on "the problems of the big cities":

> I: Solving the problems of the big cities.
> *R: Ahm:: (long pause) Some questions seem to be (little laugh) hard to answer because it's not a matter of how much money, it's –
> I: All right, you can just say whether you think it's too much, too little, or about the right amount, or if you feel that you don't know you can:: say that of course.
> R: Ah, from the various talk shows and programs on TV and in the newspapers, ah, it could be viewed that they're spending maybe the right amount of money, but it isn't so much the *money* that they're spending, it's other things that –
> I: Well, do you think we're spending too much, too little, or about the right amount.
> R: Ahm, I'll answer I don't know on that one. [GSS female black (FB) 30]

The respondent here expresses her trouble with the question, namely that solving the problems of the big cities is not for her a question of money. In response, she's asked to say whether she thinks "we're spending too much, too little, and so forth." The problem with this response is that the respondent is not being allowed to say what she thinks (the interviewer's apparent invitation notwithstanding); nor are the real constraints on what she can say, imposed by the interview schedule, acknowledged to be potentially troublesome. The solution the respondent adopts, to defer to a "don't know" answer, is interactionally graceful and expedites the business of getting on with the interview (which the interviewer's interruptions clearly demonstrate to be the business at hand), but loses for the record the respondent's opinion on this issue.

Finally, the prohibition against redesign leads to a depersonalization of the interview in ways that we believe detract from respondents' sense of involvement with or responsibility for the interview responses. In ordinary conversation, speakers demonstrate their involvement through the ways that their utterances are fit to the hearer's particular situation. In the interview, in contrast, variation occurs only as the substitution of items within a standardized format. In the cases analyzed here the interview, rigidly constrained by an externally imposed, often repetitious script, becomes observably boring to respondents. So, for example, a series of questions in the NHIS is repeated with different names in the names slot, or different conditions in the health-problem slot. Respondents are quick to discern this pattern, with the result that the interaction becomes pro forma and predictable:

> I: During those two weeks, did you work at any time at a job or business, not counting work around the house.
> Mr.: Yes.
> I: During those two weeks, did you miss any time from a job or business because of illness or injury.
> Mr.: No.
> I: During those two weeks, did you stay in bed because of illness or injury.
> Mr.: No.
> I: Was there any time during those two weeks that you cut down on the things you usually do because of illness or injury.
> Mr.: No.
> I: Okay, now we might show the calendar to *Mrs.* U.
> *Mrs.: I had a feeling that was coming.
> I: (little laugh) During those two weeks did you work at any time at a job or business, not counting work around the house.
> Mrs.: Yes. (NHIS, U family)

With a single respondent, a deliberate act of noncooperation would be required to terminate an interview before its official end. In the family interviews, however, members of the U family quietly leave the room until only Mrs. U remains to carry through the interview. In another case, Mr. E remains present throughout but turns to a magazine on his lap, leaving Mrs. E as the default respondent for questions about both herself and the children. In ordinary conversation, it is in part participants' local control over who will speak next and what will be said that maintains the unpredictability of the interaction, which in turn sustains its interest.

Requirements on the Answer

In addition to displacing control of questions from the participants to a third party, the interview schedule imposes external constraints on what form answers should take. These constraints result in two somewhat contradictory problems: In some cases, responses that require elaboration are disallowed; in other cases, responses that in ordinary conversation are good enough in survey interviews require unreasonable elaboration.

Elaboration Is Disallowed. The interviewer completing a schedule of precoded questions is required to elicit a response that corresponds to one of the available response options. This often requires pursuing an answer until it reduces to an acceptable response:

> I: First I would like to talk to you, Mrs. T, about some things people think about today. We are faced with many problems in this country, none of which can be solved easily or inexpensively. I'm going to name some of these problems, and for each one I'd like you to tell me

whether you think we're spending too much money on it, too little money, or about the right amount. First, the space exploration program. Are we spending too much, too little, or about the right amount.
R: We live in a society of persons and they feel that progress has to be made. And due to the, ah, the values of, you know, going into other territories, ah, those who are in authority feel that they're doing fine but the average person no doubt probably has some thought about it because they know that people are still starving to death.
I: Well first do, do you think we're spending too much, too little, or about the right amount on the space exploration program.
R: Based upon general conversations from persons, ah, it's ah, the common view is that they're spending maybe too much money.
I: Is that what you think?
R: Well, yes, they're spending too much.
I: Too much.
R: Yes. (GSS FB30)

Though we can assume that there is something in the common culture that we might call "interview mode" and that people have some idea of what it means to operate in that mode, it is not clear how widespread this notion is and what exactly respondents' expectations are about the survey interview. In this regard, the previous respondent is instructive in that we can see the process of her socialization over the course of the interview. Our hunch is that she initially takes the interview to have a kind of talk-show format, wherein she is to provide her opinions in the form of a commentary on topics raised by the interviewer. The extensive and elaborate opening remarks by the interviewer contribute to this expectation, and appear to be heard as an invitation to produce a response in kind. But what this respondent hears in the first question as an invitation to talk, to give her opinion, she discovers to be a fixed choice between items, where the possible terms of her answer are already decided and nonnegotiable. The interview is transformed from an interactive talk with someone to the solitary production of acceptable answers to questions; answers whose adequacy for the interview purposes respondents become able to evaluate, but in which they may have little personal investment.

Failure to allow stories and elaborations can create not only interactionally awkward situations but problems of validity as well, in that the story or elaboration may contradict the initial response. As long as interviewers stop at the first acceptable response, the validity problem will never become apparent. Coincidentally, we came across an example of this complication in an interview from an other research project:

(from an interview with Dr. P, 7124185)
I: When you think about other doctors in general, how would you compare yourself to them. Are you very similar or different?

R: I think I'm pretty similar to most doctors. *Except that a lot of doctors try to stay right in the mainstream of medicine. They don't like to be out, away from the drug-oriented type of medical treatment. In other words, you have a problem, you have a drug for it, and that'll take care of it. Or surgery or something. Cut it off, and you'll be fine (laughs). And most doctors have that attitude. Then there's a small group that believe in the reason that you have doctors in the first place. And that is that we're more holistic. So we can use a more natural approach. The hippocratic approach. So I think I'm more like that group.
I: You think that's a smaller group.
R: Yes, that's a smaller group now.

In this case, a response that starts out asserting R's likeness to the mainstream is transformed by the elaboration into an identification with a minority group. The more common form of this "yes, but" phenomenon results from a general bias of participants in conversation toward agreement, where the initial yes is subsequently modified to anything but yes (see Pomerantz 1984). If not pursued, such a misleading first response will be coded at face value and the qualifications or contradiction it masks may never be detected.

Elaboration is Pursued. Ordinary conversation is replete with statements that are offered as adequate for the participants' practical purposes at hand, but with the implicit understanding that no claims are made as to their certainty or accuracy. Offered as casual talk, such statements are taken in a survey like the NHIS as facts that can be subjected to detailed examination:

I: During those two weeks did she [daughter] miss any time from a job or business because of illness or injury.
*Mrs.: (pause, looking at Mr. E) I don't know, I don't know if she did have one day when she didn't go to work, when she didn't feel too well, I think one day, she didn't.
I: One day.
Mrs.: Mm hm.
(portion omitted)
*I: What condition caused her to miss work, and stay, or stay in bed during those two weeks.
Mrs.: (smiles, looks to Mr. E)
Mr.: I think she had a cold, didn't she?
Mrs.: Yes, she had:: She had a sore throat.
I: Sore::
Mrs.: Sore throat or cold.
Mr.: Sore throat or cold, yes.
(portion omitted)
I: When did [your daughter] last see or talk to a doctor or assistant about her sore throat.

Mrs.: Well, she didn't talk to one, to a doctor about the sore throat this time, but in the fall, I believe it was in October (looks to Mr. E), she had a flu. She was run down. And she was, I believe she was ill for about a week. She had a flu, and she had a fever. And she went to Dr. C, twice she went to Dr. C.
I: This was, uh, you stated in the fall::
Mrs.: In the fall of the year.
I: Has she seen a doctor about, uh, her sore throat::
Mrs.: No, not this week, no. Not this last time.
*I: What was the cause of, uh, her sore throat.
Mrs.: (shrugs) She had a cold. I don't know::
*I: Did the sore throat result from an accident or an injury?
Mrs.: No. (NHIS, E family)

Although Mrs. E at first expresses some uncertainty about whether her daughter even stayed home from work, and is clearly uncertain about her daughter's activities or condition on that day, she does her best to cooperate with the interviewer in providing facts about the case. The sore throat, offered as an acceptable reason to miss a day of work, is subsequently treated as a medical condition and pursued as such. Mrs. E's attempt to make sense of the question "When did [your daughter] last see or talk to a doctor about her sore throat," which of course presupposes that she did have a sore throat, and that it was severe enough to warrant talking to a doctor, leads to a diversion into another incident where her daughter did talk to a doctor, but which is unrelated to this condition.

Establishing Relevance

In any interaction, questions are heard and responses are produced against a background of unspecified assumptions about the world. Ordinary conversational interaction affords sufficient occasion to discover differences in worldview and sufficient leeway to accommodate differences, so explicit discussion of assumptions rarely takes place. In ethnographic field interviews, which are specifically concerned with such differences, background assumptions are frequently discussed and compared explicitly. In survey interviews, however, apparent mismatches in worldview are neither negotiated through interaction nor acknowledged, and are masked in precoded responses.

For example, questions about family health in the NHIS produce accounts of incidents that family members judge relevant to the topic. In follow-up questions, however, it becomes evident that the issues with which the NHIS is concerned are not health problems in whatever way the family would define them, but only insofar as a given trouble limits activities, particularly work and school activities, during a specific period of time. By the same token, interest in how the family deals with their health problems is confined to the extent to which they seek professional medical care of specified kinds. Over the course of the questions it becomes apparent that the questionnaire defines health and illness as having to do with loss of work time and use of medical facilities and staff. What family health and illness might be for the family is unclear, and not relevant.

One result of the effort to fit a family's problems into the criteria that the questionnaire provides is an escalation of routine troubles into medical conditions. Mrs. E, as we saw before, has a contact dermatitis where the skin under her chin breaks out when she plays her violin. She knows how to take care of it (by placing a handkerchief over the chin rest) and in no way treats it as a medical problem. Nevertheless, she is asked to recast her experience in medical terms. This insistence on calling mundane troubles medical problems is the direct outcome of differences in the ways in which the question's designer sees the world and the respondent experiences it. With respect to the intent of the question, mundane troubles have been successfully transformed into data about medical conditions. From the point of view of the respondents, this may or may not constitute a valid characterization.

A set of different but comparably stringent preconceptions inform the GSS. For example, the questions assume that people view themselves in terms of their relationship to a series of independent institutions, such as religion, politics, education, and the like. This assumption runs into trouble when one respondent is asked the following:

> I: Generally speaking, do you usually think of yourself as a Republican, Democrat, Independent, or what.
> R: As a person.
> I: As a Republican::
> R: No.
> I: Democrat::
> R: No.
> I: Independent or what.
> R: Uhm:: I think of myself as a (pause) Christian.
> I: Okay. (writing) But politically, would you have any particular:: (inaudible)
> R: I am one of Jehovah's Witnesses so, you know, when it comes to::
> I: I see.
> R: So I'm, I am acclimated toward government, but it is that of Jehovah God's kingdom.
> I: Yes. (GSS FB30)

What we see here are two different views of the world, where the respondent's category system does not separate the religious from the political (or, if one takes the intended narrow meaning of the question, does not include a political domain at all). In the face of such evidence for discrepant worldviews between researchers and respondents, it falls to researchers to establish that such different relevancies do not undermine the validity of survey responses.

Clarification of Meaning

In the survey interview, neither the respondent nor the interviewer has access to what is perhaps the most basic resource for shared understanding in conversation; namely, interactional procedures for identifying and repairing routine uncertainties of meaning, or troubles in understanding. The most ubiquitous of these procedures in normal conversation is a side sequence to the main line of talk, initiated by the recipient of a troublesome utterance, requesting clarification or elaboration. Because standardization is identified with not varying the wording of questions, however, the interviewer is not generally available for such clarifications.

The meaning of an utterance is not inherent to the language, but is a product of interaction between speakers and hearers. In ordinary conversation, utterances can be elaborated to whatever level of detail participants require. So if the response to a question is cursory, vague, or ambiguous, or if the questioner simply wants to hear more, he or she can ask the respondent to say more. The producer of a question is taken to have the license and authority to clarify what it is that the question is designed to discover. In the interview, however, the person who asks the question is simply its administrator, trained to resist the respondent's appeals to elaborate on its intent:

> I: All right, let me just ask the question again so I'm sure I have it correct. We have one day that he missed from school. Uh, not counting that day missed from school, during that period how many *other* days did he cut down for *more* than half the day, because of illness or injury. You would say no then, is that correct.
> Mrs.: To the best of my knowledge, it's no.
> son: (protests visibly but inaudibly)
> I: Okay, yeah. Now::
> son: (protesting more loudly)
> Mrs.: (puts hand on son's head, laughing) But he obviously was at school, so I cou – I couldn't know::
> I: Right. Well this would be cutting down on all, on the things that he *usually* does during the day.
> son: Yeah.
> I: For more than half the day.
> Mr.: For more than half the day.
> son: Yes.
> Mrs.: Well that's true, you usually write. Because he hurt his thumb he couldn't write.
> *I: Oh, all right. Now whatever you think is most correct then. Uh, we would go back to, we have one day, we're attempting to discover the days that he cut down or, during that period. And we know that he missed one day from school. Now in addition to that one day missed

from school, how many other days did he cut down more than half the day, because of illness or injury.
*Mrs.: Uh huh. I guess the problem I'm having with the question is, when you say cut down his activities, does that mean that, that he really, you know, wasn't:: doing things actively or that he wasn't doing what he would normally do::
*I: Well we, uh, we take the thing that the person would normally do. And this would mean that he would cut down on those activities that he would normally do during the day. He would cut down for, whatever activity he might be doing, for that portion of the day. That he would cut down more than half the day on his usual activities.
Mrs.: Mm hm, well I'm inclined to say yes I guess that, for about five days.
I: Five days in addition to the one::
Mrs.: Yes, in addition to the one day.
Mr.: That's stretching it.
Mrs.: You think so? We don't know, (laughing) there's a difference of opinion, so::
Mr.: But, okay that's, I guess that's as valid as (inaudible)
I: Uh huh. We take your best:: information. (NHIS, U family)

This sequence is most immediately striking for the preference accorded Mrs. U's responses over her son's, in spite of Mrs. U's own disclaimers that her knowledge of what he does during the day at school is limited. We cite the sequence here not for the trouble this creates between family members, however, but for the extent to which the interviewer manages to engage in the appearance of an interaction over the meaning of the question without ever really offering an alternative, clarifying version or an elaboration. She thereby adheres to the injunction against deviating in any way from the interview schedule. Our concern is that rather than preserving the question's intended meaning, this practice leaves interpretation to the respondent, in an entirely uncontrolled way.

Detection and Repair of Misunderstanding

Through the careful use of language, questionnaire designers attempt to craft survey questions that will be subject to a single, intended hearing. (In fact, some innovative research on the design of survey questions has emerged over the past few years. For example, the movement to study cognitive aspects of survey methodology has led to a change in the conception of pilot testing of surveys in several agencies of the federal government. The National Center for Health Statistics, the U.S. Bureau of Labor Statistics, and the Census Bureau have established laboratories in which techniques of cognitive psychology are routinely applied to the design of survey questionnaires. Using analyses of "think aloud" and retrospective protocols and other cognitive interviewing techniques, investigators iteratively refine questions so that their meaning to respondents matches those intended by the survey designer and required by the underlying concept for which the data are being gathered. Such laboratory pretesting does not by any means obviate the need for field testing to be sure that a questionnaire works under production conditions, but it does permit much more careful and flexible crafting of questions than a system that follows minimal pretesting directly with full-scale field testing.) Ordinary talk, however, is replete with alternate interpretations of meaning that, to the extent that they affect the adequacy of the communication in consequential ways, must be identified and remedied by the participants. Moreover, the occurrence of these alternate interpretations is not a product of sloppiness in the use of the language, but is inherent to the language in ways that only situated interaction can resolve. Successful communication is not so much a product of the avoidance of misunderstandings as of their successful detection and repair. [For example, see Jordan and Fuller (1975) and Schegloff, Jefferson, and Sacks (1977) for the importance of repair to conversation.]

Although the survey interviewer here is trained to read questions without variation, she seems less prepared to listen for misunderstanding and effect its repair. The consequence of undetected misunderstanding is a hidden source of invalid data. A particularly striking example of failure in this regard occurs in the supplementary interview with Mrs. U about her drinking practices. Mrs. U reports that during the two-week reference period prior to the interview she has had one to two glasses of wine every night with dinner, and that this amount of drinking is typical of her drinking not only for the past 12 months, but for the past six years. The interviewer then asks the following:

> I: During the past year, in how many *months* did you have at least one drink of any alcoholic beverage. In other words, out of the twelve months of the year, in how many months did you have at least one drink.
> Mrs.: One drink. Uhm, and alcohol. I'd guess, uh, I would say four months? Five months? Five months. (NHIS, U family)

Hearing this question in light of the previous response, one is struck by the apparent inconsistency in Mrs. U's answers. If she had a drink every day during the two-week reference period, and she reports this as typical of her drinking during the past six years, the implication that there were seven of those months in which she had no drink at all is surprising. One infers a possible miscalculation, or a misunderstanding. Further evidence of the latter comes in the next series:

> I: Was there ever a period in your life when you considered yourself to be a light drinker.
> Mrs.: (smiles) I guess yes.

I: For how many years were you a light drinker.
Mrs.: You know, do you define – How would you define light drinker?
I: Well this is ho – we would have you define it –
Mrs.: Right.
I: Uh huh.
Mrs.: You know, well if having one or two glasses of wine every night with dinner is (laugh) a light drinker, then I guess I would be characterized a light drinker.
(portion omitted)
I: Now, when you were a light drinker, how many drinks of alcoholic beverages did you have in a week.
*Mrs.: Oh, of alcoholic beverages in a week?
I: Uh huh.
*Mrs.: Very ra – you know.
I: That would be the total.
*Mrs.: Out of five months, five months out of the year:: I said that I may have alcoholic beverages. But to say in a week?
I: Uh huh.
*Mrs.: That's – during those five months? Maybe I'd have two::
I: Now uh, mm hm, now uh::
Mrs.: See I::
I: Now there, uh, if it, there's also the possibility that you might not consider yourself to be a light drinker, in which case you might say that you were never a light drinker as such, uh, was there ever a period in your life when you considered yourself to be a very light, occasional or infrequent drinker.
I: Well, you know, once again, you know, that category sounds right, if you, however you want to define::
I: You think that would be more accurate than, than the light drinker then.
*Mrs.: Especially since it *seems* that drinker refers to alcoholic beverages::
I: That's right.
Mrs.: Then in that case I would be an infrequent (pause) drinker.
I: All right, let's, let's change that then, and uh, move down here to this one.
Mrs.: Someone might consider me a wino, but I (laughs). (NHIS, U family)

In her response Mrs. U reminds us that she drinks one or two glasses of wine with dinner, and by that definition she characterizes herself as a light drinker. What follows is confounded by several problems, however. First and most serious, it becomes apparent that Mrs. U is making a distinction that the question writer did not intend, between alcohol – or hard liquor – and wine. (In retrospect, this explains the apparent contradiction between her report that she drank alcohol during only 5 of the previous 12 months and her earlier report that her daily drinking during the two-week reference period was typical of her drinking during those same 12 months.) The confusion is compounded when the interviewer repeats the question "When you were a light drinker, how many drinks of alcoholic beverages did you have in a week." Taking the "alcoholic beverages" to refer to hard liquor, Mrs. U has trouble answering. In response to this trouble, the interviewer offers her the next question, which provides the option of characterizing herself as a *very* light drinker, to which Mrs. U concedes (again with the understanding that "drinker" now refers to hard liquor). The interviewer does not seem to hear this misunderstanding, and unwittingly confirms the misinterpretation by answering "That's right" in response to Mrs. U's clarification that "it seems that drinker refers to *alcoholic* beverages." Finally, the confusion is exacerbated by the past tense of the questions, which presupposes that she no longer considers herself to be a light or very light drinker.

The completed questionnaire shows Mrs. U to consider herself an occasional rather than light drinker, a response based on the misunderstanding of the type of drink involved. This discrepancy, obvious from the interaction, is not visible in the interview schedule. What is visible is an apparent inconsistency in her answers; namely, that she now reports 2 drinks in a typical week, whereas earlier she reported 25 in two weeks. The credibility of both responses is thereby cast into doubt, yet the questionnaire provides no means for their reconciliation.

3. Validity and the Collaborative Construction of Meaning in Survey Interviews

We have framed the contrast between the survey interview and ordinary conversation as a matter of distant externally imposed versus local internally produced determinations of what gets talked about, in what way, and by whom. Even more than the lecture or debate (where speakership and topic are determined ahead of time but by at least one of the participants), the survey interview presents two parties with an agenda conceived by a third, the question writer, who is not present at the event. Validity in survey research therefore involves the extent to which a question is heard in the way that this third party intends.

Validity is not assured simply by having interviewers repeat the same words across different respondents. In contrast to a thermometer or other instrument of measurement, an interview, no matter how standardized, remains fundamentally a linguistic and interactional event. However successful the effort to improve the wording of survey questions may be, word choice will never eliminate the need for interviewers and respondents to negotiate the meaning of both questions and answers. To the extent that in the survey interview negotiation of meaning is suppressed, channels are lost through which the intent of the question writer could be communicated or the interpretations of the respondents assessed. And insofar as the meanings of questions and answers remain uncertain, so does the validity of the measures produced.

The problem of assessing the meaning of questions and responses extends beyond the interview situation. Even if questions and answers are interpreted in the way that their authors intended, it is by no means assured that other users of the data will share this understanding. Every researcher who employs survey data for descriptive or inferential statistics needs to know the sense in which the question was heard and answered to use the data legitimately. It follows that validity requires a mechanism to assure that all parties involved in the enterprise (including the author of the question, the interviewer, the respondent, the coder, and the analyst of the data) have a common understanding of what the question means and how the answer is to be taken. The only hope for such stable interpretations, and therefore for validity, is active collaboration between all of these parties.

To take this view seriously would mean rethinking the relations between participants in survey work to focus on the achievement of a joint sense of the meaning of questions. The questionnaire itself is the record of the question writer's agenda. Though the business of filling it out is in some sense the joint accomplishment of interviewer and respondent, it is the interviewer who directly controls the work. The interview schedule determines the course of the interaction and is physically as well as cognitively the focus of the interviewer's attention. At the same time, the form is unavailable to the respondent, who at best is able to watch the interviewer read and write. The respondent is thus required to focus attention on something to which there is no direct access, and to hold the floor for the interviewer across major gaps in the interaction. The consequence is an awkward if not untenable position for the respondent; namely, to be participating in an event that is organized by the task of filling out the form, and at the same time not to have a role in its management.

A material aspect of a more collaborative interview, therefore, might be a questionnaire that is at least visually available to both parties. One could imagine a technological improvement in the form of an interactive computer screen, where the interviewer acts as a kind of navigation guide for the respondent. But the same principle can be incorporated in interviews that use manual recording techniques. As well as increasing the respondent's participation and engagement, access to the record might afford a check on its accuracy as well as a greater commitment to producing a codable answer. For example, rather than concealing the option of "Don't know," the interviewer might enlist the respondent in producing a response, with something like "What we want to do if we can is to avoid 'Don't know' answers, because they are not counted, and your voice won't be heard."

Most important, as an alternative to the present injunction against interviewer-respondent interaction we would recommend allowing the interviewer to talk about the questions, to offer clarifications and elaborations, and to engage in a limited form of recipient design and common-sense inference. This change emphasizes the interviewer's role as the principal mediator between the intended meaning of the question and the interpretations of the respondent. By bringing the resources of everyday conversation to bear and engaging in interaction with the respondent, the interviewer might be better able to see how it is that the respondent is hearing a given question. Insofar as the interviewer is briefed on the intent of a question, he or she can then act as a kind of stand-in or representative of the question writer, thereby contributing to effective standardization.

It might be reasonable to expect that when participants are given the opportunity to discuss the meaning of questions and answers, interviews will be longer or fewer questions will be manageable within a single interview. But this is by no means a foregone conclusion. It may be that sufficient time is already expended on trying to make sense of questions that more effective interaction might make the interview more efficient. Clearly, recognizing the interviewers' role as the representative of the researcher to the respondent and as the adjudicator of meaning does assign them greater responsibility. That assignment may be less a change than an acknowledgment of what is already the case, however. To acknowledge the interviewers' role and to equip them with the means to fill that role more effectively might have a sufficient value with respect to the validity of the data to offset the costs of additional compensation and training. In the final analysis, if data are invalid it matters little how cheaply we can obtain them.

This analysis raises questions that are open to empirical investigation. Rather than speculate further on the answers, we propose that research be conducted on such issues as the following.

1. What are the effects of joint access to the survey instrument?
2. How can interviewer bias be avoided while admitting the negotiation of question meanings?
3. How difficult is it to train interviewers to discriminate between the two?
4. How might data quality be more rigorously assessed?
5. How much improvement in data quality might be obtained for what additional cost?

Our recommendation is that survey researchers acknowledge that the survey interview is fundamentally an interactional event. At present, the standardized interview question has become such a fragile, technical object that it is no longer viable in the real world of interaction. We believe that it can be made more robust through a finer discrimination between clarification and bias. The validity of data obtained through survey questionnaires hinges on the extent to which researchers who write the questions communicate their intended meaning to interviewers, who in turn convey the questions' meaning to respondents. Taking this fact seriously recasts participants' interactional expertise as a resource for survey research rather than a problem. In particular, interviewers, rather than administering a set of questions designed by a third party whose intentions are not known and for which they are not prepared to take responsibility, might then see the work of data collection as an enterprise for which they have some appreciation and about which they have something to say.

References

Briggs, C. L. (1986), *Learning How to Ask: A Sociolinguistic Appraisal of the Role of the Interview in Social Science Research*, Cambridge, U.K.: Cambridge University Press.

Converse, J. M., and Schuman, H. (1974), *Conversations at Random: Survey Research as Interviewers See It*, New York: John Wiley.

Heritage, J. (1985), "Recent Developments in Conversation Analysis," *Sociolinguistics*, 15, 1–16.

Jabine, T., Straf, M., Tanur, J., and Tourangeau, R. (eds.) (1984), *Cognitive Aspects of Survey Methodology: Building a Bridge Between Disciplines* (report, Advanced Seminar on Cognitive Aspects of Survey Methodology), Washington, DC: National Academy Press.

Jordan, B., and Fuller, N. (1975), "On the Non-Fatal Nature of Trouble: Sense-Making and Trouble-Managing in *Lingua Franca* Talk," *Semiotica*, 13, 1–31.

Levinson, S. C. (1983), *Pragmatics*, Cambridge, U.K.: Cambridge University Press.

Mishler, E. G. (1986), *Research Interviewing: Context and Narrative*, Cambridge, MA: Harvard University Press.

Pomerantz, A. (1984), "Agreeing and Disagreeing With Assessments: Some Features of Preferred/Dispreferred Turn Shapes," in *Structures of Social Action: Studies in Conversation Analysis*, eds. J. M. Atkinson and J. Heritage, Cambridge, U.K.: Cambridge University Press, pp. 57–101.

Sacks, H., Schegloff, E. A., and Jefferson, G. (1974), "A Simplest Systematics for the Organization of Turn-Taking for Conversation," *Language*, 50, 696–735.

Schegloff, E. A., Jefferson, G., and Sacks, H. (1977), "The Preference for Self-Correction in the Organization of Repair in Conversation," *Language*, 53, 361–382.

* * *

Comment

Stephen E. Fienberg

1. Introduction

Let me begin by noting that I found the article by Suchman and Jordan stimulating and exciting. The authors are to be congratulated for introducing new ideas to a statistical audience that has only recently begun to explore the underpinnings of the survey process.

The publication of this article marks a departure for the *Journal of the American Statistical Association* (JASA) in various ways. First, the authors are neither statisticians nor social scientists engaged in quantitative, statistical pursuits. Rather, they are anthropologists who are addressing from an ethnographic perspective a structure that underlies much of modern-day survey research, especially as it is practiced by the large U.S. government statistical agencies. Second, the article draws inferences from the content of a small number of survey interviews and not from the analysis of survey data in the usual statistical sense. Third, there are no formulas in the article, or any references to articles in statistical journals or any other standard statistical source. Although this article contains no major methodological or theoretical results, from a traditional statistical perspective, I would argue that it raises major methodological questions whose answers potentially might change the practice of the traditional survey interview. Finally, the article can be read by virtually every member of ASA and every subscriber of JASA, regardless of his or her formal statistical training.

Despite all its novel features, the Suchman and Jordan article can still be put into a more formal statistical perspective. The preparation of the article was at least in part stimulated by a set of statistical activities extending back to at least 1980, called "Cognitive Aspects of Survey Methodology." In Section 2, I give a brief history of these activities and several references to supplement those provided by the authors. Part of the importance of the history is the context of the preparation of the videotapes analyzed by Suchman and Jordan in their article, but this history gives a sense of alternative reactions to their suggestion that we rethink the interview as a fundamentally interactional event. Finally, in Section 3 I attempt to examine a few of the ideas raised in this article from a more formal statistical point of view, but in keeping with the spirit of the launching of the new general section of JASA, I will do so without formulas.

2. Some History of the Cognitive Aspects of Survey Methodology Movement

Survey researchers have evolved a highly developed art of questionnaire design and interview procedures, which is embodied in the interview structure of the two surveys discussed by Suchman and Jordan (e.g., see Payne 1951). There have also been many studies that attempted to test aspects of the art (e.g., see Bradburn and Sudman 1979; Schuman and Presser 1981; Sudman and Bradburn 1974). But until recent years research on the understanding of the survey interview situation has been relatively unsystematic, an experiment to answer a specific question here or a series of studies to answer a set of interrelated questions there.

In 1980, under the auspices of the Bureau of Social Science Research, Albert Biderman organized a workshop to study the possible uses of recent research in cognitive psychology in understanding how to redesign the questionnaire used by the National Crime Survey (NCS). Although this workshop did not solve the questionnaire problems of the NCS, it did alert traditional survey researchers who participated in it to the perspective that many forms of nonsampling error are occasioned by the cognitive processes that respondents are required to exercise in the interview process. A second workshop, sponsored by the Committee on National Statistics (CNSTAT) of the National Research Council in 1983, attempted to carry forward this agenda of encouraging survey researchers to draw on the concepts and methods of cognitive psychology and the expertise of cognitive researchers to investigate issues of nonsampling error more systematically (Jabine *et al.* 1984). This workshop used as its focus the questionnaire and interview structure of the National Health Interview Survey (NHIS) and the General Social Survey, conducted by the National Opinion Research Center. The videotapes analyzed by Suchman and Jordan were prepared for this workshop and they vividly illustrate aspects of the cognitive concepts memory, comprehension, and judgment or estimation.

As a participant in the CNSTAT workshop, I recall a discussion of a segment in one of these tapes in which a woman respondent was not able to tell the interviewer about an event – a minor automobile accident – that explained her difficulty in answering a series of questions that are part of the NHIS questionnaire. One of the other participants – a psychologist – finally said:

> Look, the trouble is the whole interview situation. The statisticians simply don't understand the dynamics. What we need to do is have the interviewer talk with the respondent about events and issues relevant to completing the questionnaire and then say: "Now let's fill out the questionnaire together so that the people in Washington can get the answers to questions important for national health policy."

This idea of rethinking the structure of the interview to take better advantage of the interactional dynamics of everyday conversation is explored in the more systematic critique of Suchman and Jordan. Their ultimate suggestion, to view the survey interview as a collaborative process, is much like that offered by the psychologist.

Lest we think that this is the first time investigators and methodologically oriented statisticians have suggested that the standardized questionnaire and interview may not be the optimal way to collect survey information, it is useful to recall the words of Cochran, Mosteller, and Tukey (1954) in their discussion of the Kinsey Report (p. 693):

> For what our opinion is worth, we agree with [Kinsey, Pomeroy, and Martin] that a written questionnaire could not have replaced the interview for the broad population contemplated in this study. The questionnaire would not allow flexibility which seems to us necessary in the

use of language, in varying the order of questions, in assisting the respondent, in following up particular topics and in dealing with persons of varying degrees of literacy. This is not to imply that the anonymous questionnaire is inherently less accurate than the interview, or that it could not be used fruitfully with certain groups of respondents and certain topics. So far as we are aware, not enough information is available to reach a verdict on these points.

Since the CNSAT workshop, several authors have explored the role of cognitive concepts in survey work in a variety of contexts (e.g., see Bradburn, Ripps, and Shevell 1987; Fienberg, Loftus, and Tanur 1985a,b,c; Fienberg and Tanur 1989; Hippler, Schwarz, and Sudman, 1987; Lessler and Sirken 1985). Three major U.S. government statistical agencies [the Bureau of the Census, the Bureau of Labor Statistics, and the National Center for Health Statistics (NCHS)] have established cognitive laboratories in which questionnaires are pretested and interview problems are explored. For example, NCHS, under the leadership of Monroe Sirken, is pretesting in its Questionnaire Design Research Laboratory changes to the NHIS and other major health surveys (e.g., see Lessler, Tourangeau, and Salter 1989). At the same time, NCHS is taking findings from the cognitive laboratory into the field to test their generalizability. For example, White and Berk (1987) investigated the finding of Fathi, Schooler, and Loftus (1984), that visits to health care providers are more easily and accurately recalled beginning with the earliest, in the context of a pretest for the NHIS.

To test the generalizability of laboratory-cognitive psychology results in the field, carefully planned experiments must be embedded within surveys. The design of such embedded experiments and the modes of inference for their analysis are considered in Fienberg and Tanur (1988, 1989).

3. Some Formal Methodological Observations

3.1 Validity and Errors of the Third Kind

It is typical for statisticians to divide the inaccuracies in sample surveys into two broad sources, sampling error and nonsampling error. But it is especially useful to distinguish a third source of error that is often included within nonsampling error: the error that arises from the discrepancy between the concept of interest and the quantity measured in the survey. This third source of error relates to the validity of the measuring instrument. Suchman and Jordan note that in a given survey interview situation, the current approach to standardization of procedure suppresses ordinary conversational processes. They argue that stability of meaning is what the interviewer should be striving for, and that such stability requires the full resources of conversational interaction. They claim that this is the ultimate basis for validity.

3.2 The Role of Local Control

In explaining the differences between the survey interview and ordinary conversation, Suchman and Jordan link these two forms of communication to external and local control, respectively. The term local control has a technical meaning introduced by Fisher (1935) in the context of designed experiments, and it may be useful to examine the links between the two meanings in some detail.

In designing an experiment, the experimenter gains local control through the grouping of the observational unit in blocks; in the survey setting, the interview is the locus of control. In experiments, we attempt to make the units within blocks as homogeneous as possible and thus introduce substantial differences or heterogeneity among blocks; in surveys, allowing the interviewer and respondent to interact as in an ordinary conversation leads to lack of standardization among interviews, that is, heterogeneity. In a designed experiment, the assumption of unit-treatment additivity and constancy of effects across blocks leads to a valid estimate of treatment effects; in surveys, if the use of ordinary conversation produces stability of meaning across interviews, then this should lead to valid estimates of the quantities of interest. In experiments with local control we still have residual heterogeneity, and this an experimental error; in surveys, even if we gain stability of meaning, we still expect to have residual forms of nonsampling errors.

Thus I would argue that we need to consider how to strike a balance between standardization (which eliminates certain sources of nonsampling error) and the level of interaction in the interview between the interviewer and the respondent (which controls other forms of nonsampling errors), especially those associated with cognitive processes, as well as aspects of errors of the third kind. This balance is akin to that which survey researchers currently strike between sampling error and nonsampling errors.

3.3 Implications for Statistical Models

Traditional forms of survey analysis have focused on individual survey questions, or perhaps a few questions at a time, perhaps through a two-way table. Only within the last two decades has there been an effort to bring the standard statistical arsenal of multivariate methods to bear on survey analysis. These methods treat the respondents as generating independent and identically distributed random quantities, once we control for certain background variables. But if we take seriously the view that standardization of the interview induces systematic biases into responses of individuals, then these methods are not really appropriate analytical tools. Rather, we need something like the Rasch model approach to survey analysis advocated by Dudley Duncan (see Duncan 1984, 1985, 1986; Turner and Martin 1984, part IV). The Rasch model allows for unique respondent effects as well as item or questionnaire effects in a simple additive form in the logistic scale.

3.4 Translating Results From a Collaborative Interview Into Standardized Form

Suppose that we follow the prescription provided by Suchman and Jordan, and we allow the survey interview to be turned into a collaborative enterprise between interviewer and respondent. Then how can we recapture the standardized and qualitatively formatted information that we originally set out to collect? This question has long been the focus of discussions between ethnographic researchers and their quantitatively inclined social-science colleagues (e.g., see Erickson 1977; Fienberg 1977), and there are no easy answers. Perhaps the suggestion at the CNSTAT workshop, of the interviewer and respondent completing the standardized questionnaire following a lengthy conversation, is not so outlandish after all. At any rate, I note that there is an even greater challenge here for survey statisticians once we begin to rethink the structure and role of the survey interview.

Additional References

Bradburn, N. M., Ripps, L. J., and Shevell, S. K. (1987), 'Answering Autobiographical Questions: The Impact of Memory and Inference on Surveys," *Science*, 236, 157–161.

Bradburn, N. M., Sudman, S., and associates (1979), *Improving Interview Method and Questionnaire Design*, San Francisco: Jossey-Bass.

Cochran, W. G., Mosteller, F., and Tukey, J. W. (1953), "Statistical Problems of the Kinsey Report," *Journal of the American Statistical Association*, 48, 673–716.

Duncan, O. D. (1984), "Rasch Measurement in Survey Research: Further Examples and Discussion," in *Surveying Subjective Phenomena* (Vol. 2), eds. C. F. Turner and E. Martin, New York: Russell Sage, pp. 367–404.

——. (1985), "Some Models of Response Uncertainty for Panel Analysis," *Social Science Research*, 14, 126–141.

——. (1986), "Probability, Disposition, and the Inconsistency of Attitudes and Behavior," *Syntheses*, 68, 65–98.

Erickson, F. (1977), "Some Approaches to Inquiry in School-Community Ethnography," *Anthropology and Education Quarterly*, 8, 58–69.

Fathi, D. C., Schooler, J., and Loftus, E. F. (1984), "Moving Survey Problems Into the Cognitive Survey Laboratory," in *Proceedings of the Section on Survey Research Methods, American Statistical Association*, pp. 19–21.

Fienberg, S. E. (1977), "The Collection and Analysis of Ethnographic Data in Educational Research," *Anthropology and Education Quarterly*, 8, 50–57.

Fienberg, S. E., Loftus, E. F., and Tanur, J. M. (1985a), "Cognitive Aspects of Health Survey Methodology: An Overview," *Milbank Memorial Fund Quarterly*, 63, 547–564.

——. (1985b), "Recalling Pain and Other Symptoms," *Milbank Memorial Fund Quarterly*, 63, 582–597.

——. (1985c), "Cognitive Aspects of Health Surveys for Public Information and Policy," *Milbank Memorial Fund Quarterly*, 63, 598–614.

Fienberg, S. E., and Tanur, J. M. (1988), "From the Inside Out and the Outside In: Combining Experimental and Sampling Structures," *The Canadian Journal of Statistics*, 19, 135–151.

——. (1989), "Combining Cognitive and Statistical Approaches to Survey Design," *Science,* 243, 1017–1022.
Fisher, R. A. (1935), *The Design of Experiments,* Edinburgh, U. K.: Oliver & Boyd.
Hippler, H. J., Schwarz, N., and Sudman, S. (eds.) (1987), *Social Information Processing and Survey Methodology,* New York: Springer-Verlag.
Lessler, J. T., and Sirken, M. G. (1985), "Laboratory-Based Research on the Cognitive Aspects of Survey Methodology," *Milbank Memorial Fund Quarterly,* 63, 565–581.
Lessler, J. T., Tourangeau, R., and Salter, W. (1989), "Questionnaire Design in the Cognitive Laboratory," Report 1 (Vital and Health Statistics Ser. 6: Cognition and Survey Research), National Center for Health Statistics, Hyattsville, MD.
Payne, S. L. (1951), *The Art of Asking Questions,* Princeton, NJ: Princeton University Press.
Schuman, H., and Presser, 5. (1981), *Questions and Answers in Attitude Surveys,* New York: Academic Press.
Sudman, S., and Bradburn, N. M. (1974), *Response Effects in Surveys: A Review and Synthesis,* Chicago: Aldine.
Turner, C. F., and Martin, E. (eds.) (1984), *Surveying Subjective Phenomena* (Vol. 1), New York: Russell Sage.
White, A. A., and Berk, M. L. (1987), "Recall Strategies in Personal Interviewing: Moving Results From the Laboratory to the Field," in Proceedings of the Social Statistics Section, American Statistical As*sociation,* pp. 66–71.

* * *

Comment

Robert A. Hahn

As all conscientious researchers know, you will never make a silk purse from a sow's ear – garbage in, garbage out. Yet too often researchers may accept with little examination "the data" analyzed to understand a phenomenon of interest. The term *data,* from the Latin plural "things given," suggests discrete chunks of reality that we collect, clean, analyze, and write up with confidence.

Suchman and Jordan closely observe videotaped interviews similar to those used in the General Social Survey (GSS, conducted by the National Opinion Research Center) and the National Health Interview Survey [NHIS, conducted by the Centers for Disease Control's National Center for Health Statistics (NCHS)]. By analyzing the interaction and communication between interviewer and respondent in facsimile GSS and NHIS interviews, they demonstrate that the researcher's confidence in the data may be misplaced. At least occasional misunderstanding of either the interview process or its contents apparently cannot be avoided or predicted. The standardized interview does not allow the respondent to ask or the interviewer to answer questions that might resolve misunderstandings about interview questions. Suchman and Jordan propose that the rules of ordinary conversation replace the standardization of survey interviews, to allow clarification of the interview procedures and questions.

NHIS and other NCHS surveys provide the most representative and comprehensive information available on the health status and health behavior of the U.S. population. It is thus important to scrutinize the sources of this information. Moreover, if there are basic problems in NHIS methodology, there are likely to be problems in most other health-survey research as well.

NCHS conducts and publishes extensive studies on the validity and reliability of its own methods and findings (NCHS Vital and Health Statistics Ser. 2). NCHS studies generally involve the statistical comparison of two independent sources of information to assess the shortcomings of one (or both) and the situations in which the collection of information may fall short. NCHS has explored cognitive science as well, a discipline that assesses the processing of human information (NCHS Report 1, Vital and Health Statistics Ser. 6, "Questionnaire Design in the Cognition Research Laboratory"). In one technique of cognitive science, protocol analysis, questionnaire respondents in a cognition research laboratory are asked to "think aloud" as they figure out their answers. Difficulties in the phrasing of interview questions or optional answers thus may be recognized and corrected.

Suchman and Jordan's method differs greatly from both NCHS methods of statistical comparison and cognitive science. By observing and interpreting what interview participants say and do, Suchman and Jordan attempt to understand the intentions of interview participants and the rules that guide (and misguide) communication (and miscommunication). Their subject and method are close to what anthropologists have referred to as "the ethnography of communication" (Gumperz and Hymes 1972).

Ethnographers of communication suggest that there is much more to human interaction and communication than the exchange and processing of information. To begin, there are very different kinds of verbal communication, such as stories, political talks, sermons and prayers, gossip, theater, scientific lectures, legal arguments, and conversation. For some cultural groups, there may be no such thing as a questionnaire interview. In addition to the kinds of communication recognized in a society, ethnographers of communication examine rules about who should and who should not participate in certain forms of communication, how topics are chosen, and how turns are taken. If a respondent is unfamiliar with a form of communication or its rules, he or she may not know how to participate appropriately, even if motivated. More than simple etiquette, the validity of information is at stake here. The ethnography of communication analyzes the societal context of information considered by cognitive science; it indicates what kinds of information are likely to be exchanged in different circumstances, as well as what sort of validity and other characteristics given information may convey.

Regarding survey interviews, Suchman and Jordan are not clear on several methodologic issues, namely reliability, validity, and the goals of interview standardization. Reliability is the constancy of response, regardless of validity, with repeated administration of a given question or other instrument. Validity applies at two levels in survey research. One is inferences drawn about individuals; in this context, validity concerns the truth of conclusions drawn about survey respondents. Suchman and Jordan address issues of validity at the level of inferences drawn about individuals.

Some claims about the individual are matters of fact and may be externally validated, for example, the number of times the respondent visited a physician's office in the preceding six months. Other claims about the individual may be validated only by what the respondent says, such as his or her reason or motive for visiting a physician; although a given reason may be true or false, there is no external validating standard. An internal standard is one from the same source as the original information, for example something else the respondent thinks, says, or does.

The second level of validity in survey research concerns inferences about a population; in this context, issues of validity focus on whether the sample population is representative and large enough to allow precise and valid conclusions about the distribution of characteristics in the population from which the survey sample is drawn. Valid inferences about individuals are a necessary but not sufficient condition for drawing valid population inferences. In survey research, the standardization of questions and procedures is not directed toward the validity of individual inferences. Rather, on the assumption that "the same" responses to "the same" stimulus questions are equivalent, standardization is supposed to enhance the reliability of answers among respondents, and thus the validity of inferences about the population. Standardization is intended to assure comparability.

Logical prerequisites to the valid assessment of individual characteristics are (a) the existence of variables on which individual members of the population can be compared, and (b) corresponding instruments by which person-to-person variations on each variable can be assessed. Variables may range from age, weight, and cholesterol level to ethnicity and marital status to attitudes about medical care or the quality of one's relationships, and from those with external validating standards to those with internal validating standards.

Survey interview instruments are successful in eliciting valid findings about individuals in the following situations: (a) Respondents understand and accept sincere participation in the interview mode of communication; (b) they understand the interview questions and response options, and in the manner the researcher intends; and (c) the questions assign each member of the population to one and only one value of each appropriate variable, and all reasonable options are included.

By ethnographic observation of NHIS and GSS facsimile interviews, Suchman and Jordan find evidence that each or all of these conditions for successful survey instruments may be precluded by inflexible, standardized survey procedures. Basic understanding of the interview may not be common to all respondents. Moreover, motives for participation may vary, and, as Suchman and Jordan suggest, motivation may be undermined by rigid, impersonal interview procedures. Then, although the interview question-and-answer options may be thought by the researcher and the interviewer to remain constant from interview to interview, questions and answers may be differently interpreted from respondent to respondent. The combination of possibly misunderstood interview objectives and processes with possibly misunderstood interview questions and answer options produces results whose validity is always in doubt. And, most crucial, the standardized interview does not allow the means available in ordinary conversation (and in other forms of interview; e.g., "open-ended" and "semi-structured" interviews) to clarify misunderstanding about the survey and its contents.

Survey researchers assume that all speakers of a language will give the "same meaning" to a given question and specified answer choices. Yet the concepts of *meaning* and *same meaning* are problematic. How do we identify the meaning of an utterance, and by what criteria do we say the meaning of utterance A differs from (or is the same as) the meaning of utterance B? In some sense, the meanings of a question and answer are embedded in the respondent's personal history – the way in which he or she may have heard and experienced these questions and answers before, along with everything associated with them. A respondent may give one answer on first hearing the question, another on brief reflection, a third on further querying of the interrogator, and still others (or perhaps the same ones, but in a new way) after deeper reflection, years of psychoanalysis, and the like. (In this case, though validity may increase, reliability is diminished.) Deeper inquiry may not greatly affect answers to questions about the number of times one has been to a physician in the last month, but may affect answers to questions about the motives for such visits. Which of these is the valid answer, and which, if any, responds to the researcher's question?

Survey research may effectively describe the distribution of certain more or less objective characteristics of the population; it may produce more questionable evidence on more subjective issues. In either case, survey instruments may produce results with greater validity if they allow respondents to query and interviewers to elucidate the procedure and its contents. The changes proposed by Suchman and Jordan should enhance the validity of inferences made on individuals. Their proposals merit further exploration and specification to assure that researchers do not abandon comparability in the pursuit of validity.

Additional Reference

Gumperz, J. J., and Hymes, D. (eds.) (1972), *Directions in Socio-linguistics: The Ethnography of Communication*, New York: Holt, Rinehart & Winston.

***

Comment

Mary Grace Kovar & Patricia Royston

The article by Suchman and Jordan is a welcome addition to the survey research literature. Their analysis of interviews as conversations highlights problems with questions and the mode of asking them that should lead to more research and better questionnaire design. Their way of looking at questions reveals the flaws, and sometimes – we regret to say – the silliness. All too often people who work with surveys are so accustomed to the words and procedures that they fail to look at them objectively. Suchman and Jordan's conceptual framework and skills provide a viewpoint not usually considered by survey researchers.

We agree without any reservation with the authors' statement that "validity is not assured simply by having interviewers repeat the same words across different respondents" (p. 207). Nevertheless, we would like to make three points: We think that the issues of questionnaire design and the role of the interviewer are much more complex than the authors indicate; that the National Health Interview Survey (NHIS) questionnaire and interviewer instructions are much less rigid than suggested in the article; and that in some cases the authors have failed to identify the true cause of the problems they observed. Therefore, the solutions they suggest do not necessarily solve the problems.

First, the complexity of the design issues associated with conducting a large-scale national survey must be considered. In the NHIS and some other national surveys thousands of people are interviewed each year. The hundreds of interviewers involved must distill individual stories into computer codes. Without standardized questionnaires and procedures, these surveys would not be feasible.

Along with standardized procedures, interviewers need some flexibility. Suchman and Jordan state that the interviewer must go through the questionnaire without change or clarification, and that "interviewers are trained not to redesign questions based on either information acquired in previous responses or the observable circumstances ..." (p. 194). For the NHIS, at least, that is not true. The U.S. Bureau of the Census interviewers who administer the NHIS are allowed considerable flexibility. For example, they are allowed to confirm information that the respondent has already provided; they do not have to ask a seemingly redundant question. Alternative wording is frequently provided, sometimes on the questionnaire and sometimes in the NHIS field representative's manual (Kovar and Poe 1985; Schoenborn and Marano 1988; U.S. Bureau of the Census 1987). The first pages of the manual are devoted to instructions on how to change wording to take into account families of one, two, and more than two individuals, and how the dashes, underlined words, and words in parentheses, brackets, and braces that are printed on the questionnaire indicate alternative phrasing. The manual also contains objectives, definitions, and clarifications for the interviewer's information and use in answering respondents' questions. Exchange *is* allowed in the NHIS.

A review of the manual for the questions that Suchman and Jordan use as examples suggests that some of the problems identified in the taped NHIS interviews occurred because the interviewers did not follow instructions and use the resources available to them. It would be useful to know why these things occurred so that the information could be used to improve training, the manual, or the questionnaire. One possible explanation is based on our own observations and conversations with interviewers. NHIS interviewers who are being observed by a supervisor tend to work to the rules. They ask every question, including all of the caveats; they make certain that they cannot be faulted for sins of omission. It appears that the interviewers whose videotaped interviews were the subject of this article worked to the rules when they were videotaped. Another possible explanation is that interviewers try to conclude lengthy interviews as quickly as possible, which is not conducive to careful listening and probing for the most accurate answers. They are aware of the concern about survey costs and respondent burden, and try to maintain a rapid pace for the interview.

The problem of interviewer performance is exacerbated by poorly worded questions. For example, some of the NHIS questions highlighted in this article have excessively long qualifying sentences or phrases. The intent is to remind respondents of all of the possible sources of medical care or income so that they will include everything when they answer. The impact is that some respondents are confused and cannot hear or remember the basic question. Other GSS and NHIS questions used as examples in the article are based on vague or ambiguous concepts. "Other doctors in general," "similar or different," and "cutting down on usual activities" are all ambiguous. Definitions are left to the respondent, which leads to a variety of response errors. The problem of badly worded and conceptually vague questions will be solved only by improving the questions, not by a less structured interview format.

In fact, a less structured format might introduce new problems. Making interviewers responsible for rewording questions would add to the substantial pressure already placed on them. In addition, it could increase the errors if the interviewers themselves misinterpret questions. Consistent misinterpretation by interviewers could result in a substantial bias.

Some of the solutions suggested by Suchman and Jordan, such as making the questionnaire visually available to both parties, sound intriguing, but at least for the paper-and-pencil version of the NHIS they would be difficult to implement. The NHIS questionnaire is enormously complicated, with networks of skips and check items. Trying to follow the skip patterns would confuse the respondent and distract attention from the questions; however, interviewers are now using laptop computers for a large part of the NHIS interview. The skip patterns are built into the programmed interview. It is feasible to find out whether problems that the authors identify would go away if respondents could also look at the computer screen. In addition, laptop computers offer opportunities to ask questions in different ways, depending on the characteristics of the respondent or the household.

Our suggested solutions differ somewhat from those proposed by the authors. Techniques are currently available for identifying the kinds of problems illustrated here, including wordiness (the inclusions for the income question), repetitiveness (restricted activity and alcohol questions), vagueness (doctor's comparison of himself with other doctors), and many others. Rather than compensating for poor design by allowing the interviewer to vary the way the question is asked, more effort should be devoted to eliminating these problems before they reach the field. The Questionnaire Design Research Laboratory at the National Center for Health Statistics has been conducting laboratory-based testing and evaluation for several years on precisely these kinds of problems (Lessler and Sirken 1985; Royston and Bercini 1987). Vague and ambiguous questions, excessive wordiness, redundancy, and many other problems are quickly identified in the laboratory. Interviews are conducted by questionnaire designers who know the objectives of each question and are alert to both verbal and nonverbal clues that the respondent has misinterpreted the question or is having difficulty answering. Discussing question interpretations and responses often provides insights into how to improve the question. These techniques, combined with the field pretests, should result in clear, direct, and efficient questionnaires.

Thus the problems due to poorly designed questions could be identified and corrected using the current laboratory pretesting techniques. Other problems, due to interviewer inattention or poor interviewing practice, could be solved by interviewer training that emphasizes listening to the respondent rather than simply recording a response, by restricting questionnaires to reasonable length so that the interviewer can be more relaxed and attentive, and by making maximum use of the capabilities of the laptop computer. If question wording is improved, the interview schedule is less complicated, and technology is used effectively, many of the problems noted by Suchman and Jordan should be alleviated.

Additional References

Kovar, M. G., and Poe, G. S. (1985), "The National Health Interview Survey Design, 1973–84, and Procedures, 1975–83," Report 18 (Vital and Health Statistics Ser. 1), National Center for Health Statistics, Hyattsville, MD.

Lessler, J. T., and Sirken, M. G. (1985), "Laboratory-Based Research on the Cognitive Aspects of Survey Methodology," *Milbank Memorial Fund Quarterly*, 63, 565–581.

Royston, P., and Bercini, D. (1987), "Questionnaire Design Research in a Laboratory Setting: Results of Testing Cancer Risk Factors Questions," in *Proceedings of the Section on Survey Research Methods, American Statistical Association*, pp. 829–833.

Schoenborn, C. A., and Marano, M. (1988), "Current Estimates, 1987," Report 166 (Vital and Health Statistics Ser. 10), National Center for Health Statistics, Hyattsville, MD.

U.S. Bureau of the Census (1987), *National Health Interview Survey: Field Representative's Manual* (No. 100), Washington, DC: U.S. Department of Commerce.

* * *

Comment

Emanuel A. Schegloff

In introducing the import of the conversational turntaking system before explicating a version of our understanding of it, in Sacks, Schegloff, and Jefferson (1974, pp. 701–702) we noted that a turn-taking system operates, as an economy does, to distribute a resource – turns at talk – among participants, and that the shape of that distribution should be supposed to affect what is being distributed, that is, the talk. We observed that

> Until we unravel its organization, we shall not know what those effects consist of, and where they will turn up. *But, since all sorts of scientific and applied research use conversation now, they all employ an instrument whose effects are not known. This is perhaps unnecessary.* (emphasis added)

The article by Suchman and Jordan cogently brings several lines of inquiry in recent studies of conversation and other talk-in-interaction to bear on the survey interview as a research instrument. In what follows, for the more general reference I use the term *talk-in-interaction* rather than *conversation* so as to include a range of "speech exchange systems" (Sacks *et al.* 1974, pp. 729–731), as well as variations of genre and setting within particular speech-exchange systems. I reserve the term "conversation" for that underlying, ordinary, unmarked speech-exchange system of which meetings, ceremonies, debates, talk-show formats, and interviews of diverse sorts appear to be systematic structural or procedural transformations.

Let us leave aside for the moment the ways in which talk-in-interaction is used by inquiry in the physical, biological, and medical sciences – for example, in the conduct of laboratory work or clinical research, and the effects that it has there. In the social sciences, the three most widely employed forms of talk-in-interaction are the psychological experiment, ethnographic participant observation, and the interview. In each of these, interaction between the investigator (or the investigator's agent) and the "subject(s)" is the instrument for data collection. It is high time indeed that we began to examine the actual, detailed course of these events *as interactions*, for it is only by arbitrary stipulation that what happens in the course of these interactions has been ruled irrelevant for the inquiries being conducted through them, and for the assessment of their results. One direction in which such an examination may be pressed with respect to behavioral science experiments is explored in Schegloff (in press).

Of course, interviews are but one of several forms for organizing talk-in-interaction that contrast with ordinary conversation. And *survey* interviews are but one of a range of forms of talk to which the term "interview" is applied. So there are at least two lines of inquiry relevant here: One is the examination of survey interviews as one distinctive modality among the range of forms of talk-in-interaction; the other is the bearing of this "interview" way of organizing talk on what is to be made of its products. Here I can offer only brief remarks on each of these lines of inquiry.

Note, then, that several of the features that Suchman and Jordan introduce that distinguish survey interviews from ordinary conversation distinguish other forms of talk as well, and something may be gained for the understanding of survey interviews from studies of these other forms. For example, the fact that talk is being done "on behalf of" an absent third party was treated by Heritage (1985) as critical in understanding certain features of the conduct of news interviews, and is relevant as well in understanding aspects of the turn-taking organization prevalent in official courtroom proceedings (Atkinson and Drew 1979). The conduct of interaction with a focus on filling out a form – a project that is mutually oriented to supplying the relevancies and directing the course of the interaction – is common to a wide variety of bureaucratic encounters and professional interviews, for example medical history-taking. Button (1987) described the consequences of a withholding of repair practices in interviews of a very different sort – employment interviews. And so forth.

The conduct of survey interviews, then, represents one configuration of organizational features, and shares some of these features with other forms of talk-in-interaction. Note that this is inescapable. The upshot of Suchman and Jordan's article *cannot* be efforts to remove or neutralize the interactional features of interviews. All talk-in-interaction faces certain generic organizational problems, and will perforce adopt some organized solution to them. Thus we have the following.

1. If (as is virtually always the case) the talk is to be organized to have one participant speaking at a time, there will be some organized procedure for allocating opportunities to talk, and usually for restricting their size; that is, there will be some form of turn-taking organization, and it will have

consequences that go well beyond simple "traffic management."
2. If there are to be coherence constraints, that is, if there are to be constraints on what can go in some turn at talk given what occurred in a preceding one or preceding ones, then there will be an organization of sequences (if actions are the relevant units), topics (if discursive contributions are the relevant unit), or both. In any case, interactional considerations are likely to be involved concerning both agreement and disagreement, and alignment and opposition, and aspects of the talk will be formed by reference primarily to these.
3. If there are to be ways of coping with transient or persistent troubles in speaking, hearing, understanding, or remembering, and so on, then some organization of repair will be in operation.
4. Almost certainly an overall structural organization will be in operation to shape the events composing the occasion, and to set the boundaries between it and surrounding events in time and space [see Suchman and Jordan's reference to "expedit[ing] the business of getting on with the interview" (p. 235)].
5. There will be relevant other sets of practices – regarding the telling of stories and the shaping of accounts, regarding the ways in which persons and places and events should be referred to or formulated, and so forth – that will of necessity enter into the constitution of the event called the interview.

And, almost inescapably, these will all be drawn from (or designed to contrast with) organized solutions to these problems in ordinary conversation, where they are designed to supply the interactional infrastructure for social organization – to allow the society to work in whatever way it works – and not to produce reliable and valid grist for social scientists' computational and analytic mills.

The last observation is especially important. The aspects of talk-in-interaction on which Suchman and Jordan focus are central properties of that medium through which the major institutions of society are embodied and enacted by its members. These properties thus inform ordinary persons' conduct of their affairs, and are not merely social-scientifically motivated analyses of them. This can be seen in various features of the excerpts with which Suchman and Jordan exemplify their points.

For example, Suchman and Jordan note that when a respondent's prompt response to a question about the family's combined income exceeding twenty thousand dollars is followed by a further expansion of the question that could only be redundant with the answer already given, that continuation requires that Mrs. E "reiterate an answer she has already provided" (p. 234). Note that Mrs. E does more than simply reiterate her earlier answer. She has already answered "More." Now she responds, "More. It was more income."

That addition by the respondent displays that *she* (and not just Suchman and Jordan) took that continuation of the question to be problematic in the following respects (among others): (a) it implicated whether the interviewer had understood her answer before; (b) it raises the issue for her whether her second response would be understood as directed to the question as initially asked [note that her addition to the answer ("more income") echoes elements of the *first* question, and ties her answer to it]; and (c) she displays an understanding that the reply "more" by itself might not be recognizable as an adequate/sensible answer to the question as expanded. All of this is built into her response, and displays her uptake of the interviewer's conduct and a stance toward it. What response that stance elicits in turn from the interviewer I cannot tell from the excerpt.

The same point must be appreciated for each of the elements in Suchman and Jordan's telling account in Section 2. They are describing orientations that inform the conduct of participants to talk-in-ordinary-interaction, and that are not automatically held in abeyance in interviews; indeed, whose relevance to answering interview questions can be seen in the details of the answers produced. I can cite but a single additional example.

The striking case of the interview with a doctor in which an answer is totally reversed after elaboration illustrates a point made by Sacks (1987, pp. 62–63), that there is a systematic place for "exceptions" in conversation, namely, at ends of turns. Indeed, I would guess that in this interview there was a moment's silence following the initial response ["I think I'm pretty similar to most doctors" (p. 236)], a silence that is regularly treated in conversation as prefiguring disagreement, to which the "exception" or backing off is a response. In light of the operation of such a mechanism, one wonders what systematic effects are introduced into surveys by what used to be called "the silent probe" following a respondent's initial response.

An impossible conundrum may seem to be posed here. On the one hand Suchman and Jordan appear to object to disallowing elaboration, and on the other they appear to object to its pursuit. The interviewer's silence, which might be the vehicle for allowing elaboration, can appear to prefigure rejection or disagreement with a response and prompt backdowns by a respondent in some contexts. Indeed! "All of the above!" It *does*, of course, depend on context – on what the question is, what type of response has been offered, and so forth. And this is what underlies Suchman and Jordan's recommendation that global or formulaic devices will not work as solutions to the management of interactional contingencies in interviews, that interviews be designed to exploit the properties of the interactions that they are in any case destined to inhabit, and that interviewers be better armed to do so in informed consonance with the goals of the inquiry.

Although an interview cannot in any case be like a thermometer (see Sec. 3 of the article), reliable exploitation even of a thermometer requires knowing the properties of mercury, the glass in which it is encased, and so on, and incorporating these properties in the extraction of the desired information from the measurement device. It is by no means clear that we have such elementary understanding of the constitutive components of the survey interview. In addition to the research that Suchman and Jordan recommend into the possibilities of a more overtly collaborative design for the interaction between interviewer and respondent, a more general inquiry into the features of the survey interview as an organized occasion of talk-in-interaction may help us think through in a thoroughly informed way how exactly to understand the methodological, epistemological, and theoretical features and status of the interview as a tool of inquiry.

We can then turn to the other settings in which talk-in-interaction is used as an instrument of research, and explore the effects of the forms that it takes there, and their effects on the goals of those lines of inquiry.

Additional References

Atkinson, J. M., and Drew, P. (1979), *Order in Court: The Organisation of Verbal Interaction in Judicial Settings*, London: Macmillan.

Button, G. (1987), "Answers as Interactional Products: Two Sequential Practices Used in Interviews," *Social Psychology Quarterly*, 50, 160–171.

Heritage, J. (1985), "Analyzing News Interviews: Aspects of the Production of Talk for an 'Overhearing' Audience," in *Handbook of Discourse Analysis, Vol. 3: Discourse and Dialogue*, ed. T. van Dijk, London: Academic Press, pp. 95–117.

Sacks, H. (1987), "On the Preferences for Agreement and Contiguity in Sequences in Conversation," in *Talk and Social Organization*, eds. G. Button and J. R. E. Lee, Clevedon, U.K.: Multilingual Matters, pp. 54–69.

Schegloff, E. A. (in press), "Reflections on Talk and Social Structure," in *Talk and Social Structure*, eds. D. Boden and D. H. Zimmerman, Cambridge, U.K.: Cambridge Polity Press.

* * *

Rejoinder

Lucy Suchman & Brigitte Jordan

As Fienberg points out in his commentary, the appearance of our article in the *Journal of the American Statistical Association* is evidence for a new, critical reassessment of received methods on the part of many statisticians and survey researchers. We commend the journal's editors for that openness, and thank them for the opportunity to engage in intellectual exchange with colleagues whom we otherwise would have little chance to meet, and whose perspectives have challenged and deepened our own. Judith Tanur and Robert Pearson, in particular, deserve our thanks for the support they have provided this project.

As anthropologists interested in talk-in-activity, we see the face-to-face survey interview as a deeply consequential form of interaction, for both social science and the public that makes up its object of inquiry. Our intent was not a critique of the survey enterprise; neither did we set out to propose detailed solutions to the troubles we unearthed. Rather, we saw ourselves engaged in learning something more about the structure of a particular kind of talk, the kind that occurs in the interaction between survey interviewers and respondents. We are convinced that whatever lessons might be drawn from our work, they will need to be drawn not by us but by practitioners in the survey field.

Our particular goal in this study was to engage in the kind of analysis of talk-in-interaction recommended by Schegloff in his commentary, when he suggests that the face-to-face survey, like many other forms of specialized talk-in-interaction, comprises systemic structural and procedural transformations of "ordinary" conversation. The intent of our analysis was to contribute something to the growing body of such analyses of talk-in-interaction. That we found particular forms of trouble, and that our findings might be relevant to current reconsiderations of the field of survey research, were unexpected outcomes of the work. We did not attempt, as several of our commentators point out, to consider the competing goals (e.g., large sample size) and requirements (e.g., budgetary constraints) of the survey research enterprise. We simply tried to say something about what we saw in the materials available to us that might be structural rather than thoroughly idiosyncratic aspects of the face-to-face survey as a form of talk-in-interaction.

As practitioners of survey research in the field, Kovar and Royston can appreciate the complexity of the problem of questionnaire design and use. They assert that interviewer practice in the field is in fact more open to interaction between interviewer and respondent than our limited view of it in simulated interview situations made evident. We find this not implausible, given that life "outdoors," to use Lave's (1988) phrase, is always more contingent, more subtly fitted to its circumstances than any form of simulated activity would suggest. If survey researchers know that the troubles we identify do not occur in the field, then all is well. But though we acknowledge the limits of our access to interviewer practice, we wonder to what extent anyone really does know what happens when interviewer meets respondent not in simulated or laboratory settings but in her or his natural habitat.

More seriously, we are concerned with a response to the troubles that we identify that locates the problem with the interviewer. In that regard, we find a certain double bind for the interviewer in Kovar and Royston's commentary. They seem to propose first that the interviewers we studied failed to follow the instructions in the NHIS interviewer handbook. At the same time, they fault the interviewers for having worked too much "to the rules" when videotaped. We believe that this point is not a failing on the part of these interviewers, but rather contradiction in the system of rules with which they are asked to comply.

The point that we hoped to make is precisely that the rigid form of interviewer behavior we saw is what interviewers do when they follow instructions to the letter; that is, when they act the way they believe they are supposed to act. If the reality of their everyday practice is otherwise, this could be taken to mean either that their real practice is a flawed version of the ideal, or (and this is the implication that we would hope our readers draw) that the ideal model of interviewing practice fails to acknowledge the reality of what actual practice necessarily requires. Accordingly, our call is for some investigation into possible revisions to the current ideal – revisions that would make the model of good practice for interviewers more conforming to actual practice and thereby more genuinely useful to those who are trying to upgrade the craft.

Our commentators offer several definitions of validity. Put simply, our own view is that valid data are those that measure what the researcher intends to measure. Invalid data, then, are data that suffer from what Fienberg calls "errors of the third kind," that is, errors that arise from the discrepancy between the concept of interest to the researcher and the quantity actually measured in the survey. One obvious way to reduce such errors is to make sure that not only the question is worded to maximize the intended reading, but that the interviewer be in a position to facilitate negotiations effectively about the meaning of the question whenever that necessity arises.

We believe that the critical requirement for competent interviewing is not (only) knowledge of the correct stance to take toward the various systems of rules involved, but fully informed participation in the survey research process. To maximize validity of the data obtained we propose a mechanism assuring that all parties involved, including the author of the question, the interviewer, the respondent, the coder, and the analyst of the data, have a common understanding of what the question means and how the answer is to be taken. The interviewer plays a particularly crucial role in this collaboration because he or she is the agent who imports the meaning intended by the researcher into the interviewing situation.

It is true that allowing more local determination of the interaction between interviewer and respondent would lead to greater heterogeneity in the questions asked and answered. In our view, this does not present a problem, since what we are looking for is not standardization of the interaction but stability of meaning across situations and respondents. And as Fienberg puts it, "in surveys, if the use of ordinary conversation produces stability of meaning across interviews, then this should lead to valid estimates of the quantities of interest" (p. 214).

Hahn worries that our proposals stand in danger of jeopardizing the comparability of data in survey research. As anthropologists, we share with Hahn a concern for comparison. But validity of inferences about individuals or groups is taken by anthropology as a prerequisite to comparison across people or cultures. As Hahn himself points out, we assume that "the meanings of a question and answer are embedded in the respondent's personal history – the way in which he or she may have heard and experienced these questions and answers before, along with everything associated with them" (p. 219). For that reason, comparison in anthropology has never turned on standardization.

We agree with Hahn when he says "Valid inferences about individuals are a necessary but not sufficient condition for drawing valid population inferences" (p. 218). We continue to believe that validity must come first: Only after we have ensured that validity of inferences made about individuals can we move to a concern with large numbers of people.

We do not mean to argue against research aimed to improve the design of survey questions. Nevertheless, we do believe first that the relevance of laboratory results to results in the field is still open to question and second that no amount of optimization on question wording will ever alleviate the need for interaction between interviewer and respondent. At the same time, we agree with Kovar and Royston that "Consistent misinterpretation by interviewers could result in a substantial bias" (p. 221). It is for this reason that we emphasize so strongly the importance of an informed interviewer who understands the question writer's intent.

Several of the commentators refer to our perspective as "ethnographic." Although it is true that such a perspective informs all of our work as anthropologists, we would like to make clear that the specific analysis that forms this article does not by any means constitute an ethnography of survey research. That would have required us to engage in investigations of the history, forms of participation, and underlying projects of survey research that would extend beyond what we *did* carry out – namely, a form of interaction analysis (Jordan, Henderson, and Tatar 1989). Hahn identifies our work with the ethnography of communication, which he says "indicates what kinds of information are likely to be exchanged in different circumstances, as well as what sort of validity and other characteristics given information may convey" (p. 217). Our understanding of the ethnography of communication, in contrast, is that it questions the very idea of "information" independent of specific occasions of interaction, with specific participants and purposes at hand.

That brings us to a point: that we tried hard to make clear in the article, but which the commentaries suggest remains obscure. We are not proposing that survey researchers abandon the structured interview in favor of something called "having a conversation." The question we raise is not whether the quantity of structure involved in the survey interview should somehow be less (analyses of conversation show there to be no such thing as an unstructured conversation, in any case), but rather where the structure should come from. The structure of conversation is not missing; it comes from inside the interaction. That is to say, it is generated by the participants in and through the course of their talk together, rather than being imposed from outside. At the same time, to say that the structure of the interaction must be endogenously produced is not to preclude an agenda given by the researcher. It is simply to see the realization of the researchers' agenda as an irremediably local achievement of the participants in a specific interview interaction.

We appreciate Tourangeau's point that making the interview more like a conversation could add problems of its own. To what extent features of "ordinary" conversation interact negatively or positively with the goals of a survey and how such interaction can be modified (e.g., in interviewer training) are all issues that need to be investigated. Our analysis should be understood as a very preliminary move in the direction that Schegloff calls a general inquiry into the survey interview as a form of talk-in-interaction. As he points out, the survey interview is and will continue to be a specific form of speech-exchange system, one that transforms in systematic ways the basic structure of ordinary conversation. The point, as he also makes clear, is that there is much about that distinctive form of talk-in-interaction that we have yet to understand. Among the questions that we try to raise is just what might be the difference between "bias" (bringing to the interaction some evidence of one's own point of view) and "clarification" (attempting to arrive at a specific understanding of the point of view of the question's designer). For example, as we begin to understand phenomena like the preference for agreement in conversation (see Sacks 1987), we can begin to investigate how interviewers might be trained not to ask questions in ways that imply agreement. Our analysis is a call for such investigations, not a proposal for unreflective abandonment of the structure of the interview. We attempt, as Fienberg understood, to raise "major methodological questions whose answers potentially might change the practice of the traditional survey interview" (p. 241).

Additional References

Jordan, B., Henderson, A., and Tatar, D. (1989), *Interaction Analysis: Foundations and Practice*, Palo Alto, CA: Xerox Palo Alto Research Center.

Lave, J. (1988), *Cognition in Practice: Mind, Mathematics, and Culture in Everyday Life*, Cambridge, U.K.: Cambridge University Press.

Sacks, H. (1987), "On the Preferences for Agreement and Contiguity in Sequences in Conversation," in *Talk and Social Organization*, eds. G. Button and J. R. E. Lee, Clevedon, U.K.: Multilingual Matters.

14

The Focused Interview[1]

Robert K. Merton & Patricia L. Kendall

For several years, the Bureau of Applied Social Research has conducted individual and group interviews in studies of the social and psychological effects of mass communications – radio, print, and film. A type of research interview grew out of this experience, which is perhaps characteristic enough to merit a distinctive label – the "focused interview."

In several respects the focused interview differs from other types of research interviews which might appear superficially similar. These characteristics may be set forth in broad outline as follows:

1. Persons interviewed are known to have been involved in *a particular concrete situation*: they have seen a film; heard a radio program; read a pamphlet, article, or book; or have participated in a psychological experiment or in an uncontrolled, but observed, social situation.
2. The hypothetically significant elements, patterns, and total structure of this situation have been previously analyzed by the investigator. Through this *content analysis* he has arrived at a set of hypotheses concerning the meaning and effects of determinate aspects of the situation.
3. On the basis of this analysis, the investigator has fashioned an *interview guide*, setting forth the major areas of inquiry and the hypotheses which locate the pertinence of data to be obtained in the interview.
4. The interview itself is focused on the *subjective experiences* of persons exposed to the preanalyzed situation. The array of their reported responses to this situation enables the investigator
    a) To test the validity of hypotheses derived from content analysis and social psychological theory, and
    b) To ascertain unanticipated responses to the situation, thus giving rise to fresh hypotheses.

Source: *American Journal of Sociology*, vol. 51, 1946, pp. 541–457.

From this synopsis it will be seen that a distinctive prerequisite of the focused interview is a prior analysis of a situation in which subjects have been involved.

To begin with, foreknowledge of the situation obviously reduces the task confronting the investigator, since the interview need not be devoted to discovering the objective nature of the situation. Equipped in advance with a content analysis, the interviewer can readily distinguish the objective facts of the case from the subjective definitions of the situation. He thus becomes alert to the entire field of "selective response." When the interviewer, through his familiarity with the objective situation, is able to recognize symbolic or functional silences, "distortions," avoidances, or blockings, he is the more prepared to explore their implications. Content analysis is a major cue for the detection and later exploration of private logics, personal symbolisms, and spheres of tension. Content analysis thus gauges the importance of what has not been said, as well as of what has been said, in successive stages of the interview.

Finally, content analysis facilitates the flow of concrete and detailed reporting of responses. Summary generalizations, on the other hand, inevitably mean that the informant, not the investigator, in effect provides the interpretation. It is not enough for the interviewer to learn that an informant regarded a situation as "unpleasant" or "anxiety-provoking" or "stimulating" – summary judgments which are properly suspect and, moreover, consistent with a variety of interpretations. He must discover precisely what "unpleasant" denotes in this context; what further feelings were called into play; what personal associations came to mind; and the like. Failing such details. the data do not lend themselves to adequate analysis. Furthermore, when subjects are led to describe their reactions in minute detail, there is less prospect that they will, intentionally or unwittingly, conceal the actual character of their responses; apparent inconsistencies will be revealed; and, finally, a clear picture of the total response emerges.

The interviewer who has previously analyzed the situation on which the interview focuses is in a peculiarly advantageous position to elicit such detail. In the usual depth interview, one can urge informants to reminisce on their experiences. In the focused interview, however the interviewer can, when expedient, play a more active role: he can introduce more explicit verbal cues to the stimulus pattern or even *re-present* it, as we shall see. In either case this usually activates a concrete report of responses by informants.

Uses of the Focused Interview

The focused interview was initially developed to meet certain problems growing out of communications research and propaganda analysis. The outlines of such problems appear in detailed case studies by Dr. Herta Herzog, dealing with the gratification found by listeners in such radio programs as daytime serials and quiz competitions.[2] With the sharpening of objectives, research interest centered on the analysis of responses to particular pamphlets, radio programs, and motion pictures. During the war Dr. Herzog and the senior author of the present paper were assigned by several war agencies to study the psychological effects of specific morale-building devices. In the course of this work the focused interview was progressively developed to a relatively standardized form.

The primary, though not the exclusive, purpose of the focused interview was to provide some basis for *interpreting* statistically significant effects of mass communications. But, in general, *experimental studies of effects* might well profit by the use of focused interviews in research. The character of such applications can be briefly illustrated by examining the role of the focused interview at four distinct points:

1. Specifying the effective stimulus
2. Interpreting discrepancies between anticipated and actual effects
3. Interpreting discrepancies between prevailing effects and effects among subgroups – "deviant cases"
4. Interpreting processes involved in experimentally induced effects

1. Experimental studies of effect face the problem of what might be called the *specification of the stimulus*, i.e., determining which x or pattern of x's in the total stimulus situation led to the observed effects. But, largely because of the practical difficulties which this entails, this requirement is often not satisfied in psychological or sociological experiments. Instead, a relatively undifferentiated complex of factors – such as "emotional appeals," "competitive incentives," and "political propaganda" – is regarded as "the" experimental variable. This would be comparable to the statement that "living in the tropics is a cause of higher rates of malaria"; it is true but unspecific. However crude they may be at the outset, procedures must be devised to detect the causally significant aspects of the total stimulus situation. Thus Gosnell conducted an ingenious experiment on the "stimulation of voting," in which experimental groups of residents in twelve districts in Chicago were sent "individual nonpartisan appeals" to register and vote.[3] Roughly equivalent control groups did not receive this literature. It was found that the experimental groups responded by a significantly higher proportion of registration and voting. But what does this result demonstrate? To *what* did the experimental group respond? Was it the nonpartisan character of the circulars, the explicit nature of the instructions which they contained, the particular symbols and appeals utilized in the notices, or what? In short, to use Gosnell's own phrasing, what were "the particular stimuli being tested"?

According to the ideal experimental design, such questions would, of course, be answered by a series of successive experiments, which test the effects of each pattern of putative causes. In practice not only does the use of this procedure in social experimentation involve prohibitive problems of cost, labor, and administration; it also assumes that the experimenter has been successful in detecting the pertinent aspects of the total stimulus pattern. The focused interview provides a useful near-substitute for such a series of experiments; for, despite great sacrifices in scientific exactitude, it enables the experimenter to arrive at plausible hypotheses concerning the significant items to which subjects responded. Through interviews focused on this problem, Gosnell, for example, could probably have clarified just what elements in his several types of "nonpartisan" materials proved effective for different segments of his experimental group.[4] Such a procedure provides an approximate solution for problems heretofore consigned to the realm of the unknown or the speculative.[5]

2. There is also the necessity for *interpreting* the effects which are found to occur. Quite frequently, for example, the experimenter will note a *discrepancy* between the observed effects and those anticipated on the basis of other findings or previously formulated theories. Or, again, he may find that one subgroup in his experimental population exhibits effects which differ in degree or direction from those observed among other parts of the population. Unless the research is to remain a compendium of unintegrated empirical findings, some effort must be made to interpret such "contradictory" results. But the difficulty here is that of selecting among the wide range of *post factum* interpretations of the deviant findings. The focused interview provides a tool for this purpose. For example:

> Rosenthal's study of the effect of "pro-radical" motion-picture propaganda on the socioeconomic attitudes of college students provides an instance of *discrepancy between anticipated and actual effects*.[6] He found that a larger proportion of subjects agreed with the statement "radicals are enemies of society" *after* they had seen the film. As is usually the case when seemingly paradoxical results are obtained this called forth an "explanation": "This negative effect of the propaganda was probably due to the many scenes of radical orators, marchers, and demonstrators."

Clearly *ad hoc* in nature, this "interpretation" is little more than speculation, but it is the type of speculation which the focused interview is particularly suited to examine, correct, and develop. Such interviews would have indicated how the audience actually responded to the "orators, marchers, and demonstrators"; the author's conjecture would have been recast into theoretical terms and either confirmed or refuted. (As we shall see, the focused interview has, in fact, been used to locate the source of such "boomerang effects" in film, radio, pamphlet, and cartoon propaganda.[7])

> In a somewhat similar experiment, Peterson and Thurstone found an unexpectedly small change in attitudes among high-school students who had seen a pacifist film.[8] The investigators held it "... probable

that the picture, 'Journey's End,' is too sophisticated in its propaganda for high school children."

Once again, the plausibility of a *post factum* interpretation, would have been enhanced, and entirely different hypotheses would have been developed had they conducted a focused interview.[9] How did the children conceive the film? To what did they primarily respond? Answers to these and similar questions would yield the kind of data needed to interpret the unanticipated result.

3. We may turn again to Gosnell's study to illustrate the tendency toward *ad hoc* interpretations of *discrepancies between prevailing effects and effects among subgroups* ("deviant cases") and the place of focused interviews in avoiding them.

> Gosnell found that, in general, a larger proportion of citizens registered or voted in response to a notice "of a hortatory character, containing a cartoon and and several slogans" than in response to a "factual" notice, which merely called attention to voting regulations. But he found a series of "exceptions," which invited a medly of *ad hoc* hypotheses. In a predominantly German election district, the factual notice had a greater effect than the "cartoon notice" – a finding which at once led Gosnell to the supposition that "the word 'slacker' on the cartoon notice probably revived war memories and therefore failed to arouse interest in voting." In Czech and Italian districts the factual notices also proved more effective; but in these instances Gosnell advances quite another interpretation: "the information cards were more effective than the cartoon notices probably because they were printed in Czech [and Italian, respectively] whereas the cartoon notices were printed in English." And yet in a Polish district the factual notice, although printed in Polish, was slightly *less* effective than the cartoon notice.[10]

In short, lacking supplementary interviews focused on the problem of deviant group responses, the investigator found himself drawn into a series of extremely flexible interpretations instead of resting his analysis on pertinent interview data. This characteristic of the Gosnell experiment, properly assessed by Catlin as an exceptionally well-planned study, is, a fortiori, found in a host of social and psychological experiments.

4. Even brief introspective interviews as a supplement to experimentation have proved useful for discerning the *processes involved in experimentally induced effects*. Thus Zeigarnik, in her well-known experiment on memory and interrupted tasks, was confronted with the result that in some cases interrupted tasks were often forgotten, a finding at odds with her modal findings and her initial theory.[11] Interviews with subjects exhibiting this "discrepant" behavior revealed that the uncompleted tasks which had been forgotten were experienced as failures and, therefore, were subjectively "completed." She was thus

able to incorporate this seeming contradiction into her general theory. The value of such interpretative interviews is evidenced further in the fact that Zeigarnik's extended theory, derived from the interviews, inspired a series of additional experiments by Rosenzweig, who, in part, focused on the very hypotheses which emerged from her interview data.

> Rosenzweig found experimentally that many subjects recalled a larger percentage of their successes in tasks assigned them than of their failures.[12] Interviews disclosed that this "objective experimental result" was bound up with the emotionalized symbolism which tasks assumed for different subjects. For example, one subject reported that a needed scholarship depended "upon her receiving a superior grade in the psychology course from which she had been recruited for this experiment. Throughout the test her mind dwelt upon the lecturer in this course: 'All I thought of during the experiment was that it was an intelligence test and that he [the lecturer] would see the results. I saw his name always before me.'"

Without such supplementary data, the hypothesis of repression which was introduced to interpret the results would have been wholly conjectural.

This brief review is perhaps sufficient to suggest the functions of the focused interview as an adjunct to experimental inquiry, as well as in studies of responses to concrete situations in everyday life.

Objectives and Procedures

A successful interview is not the automatic product of conforming to a fixed routine of mechanically applicable techniques. Nor is interviewing an elusive, private, and incommunicable art. There are recurrent situations and problems in the focused interview which can be met successfully by communicable and teachable procedures. We have found that the proficiency of all interviewers, even the less skilful, can be considerably heightened by training them to recognize type situations and to draw upon an array of flexible, though standardized, procedures for dealing with these situations.

In his search for "significant data," moreover, the interviewer must develop a capacity for continuously evaluating the interview as it is in process. By drawing upon a large number of interview transcripts, in which the interviewer's comments as well as the subjects' responses have been recorded, we have found it possible to establish a set of provisional criteria by which productive and unproductive interview materials can be distinguished. Briefly stated, they are:

1. *Nondirection*: In the interview, guidance and direction by the interviewer should be at a minimum.

2. *Specificity*: Subjects' definition of the situation should find full and specific expression.
3. *Range*: The interview should maximize the range of evocative stimuli and responses reported by the subject.
4. *Depth and personal context*: The interview should bring out the affective and value-laden implications of the subjects' responses, to determine whether the experience had central or peripheral significance. It should elicit the relevant personal context, the idiosyncratic associations, beliefs, and ideas.

These criteria are interrelated, they are merely different dimensions of the same concrete body of interview materials. Every response can be classified according to each of these dimensions: it may be spontaneous or forced; diffuse and general or highly specific; profoundly self-revealing or superficial; etc. But it is useful to examine these criteria separately, so that they may provide the interviewer with guide-lines for appraising the flow of the interview and adapting his techniques accordingly.

For each of these objectives, there is an array of specific, effective procedures, although there are few which do not lend themselves to more than one purpose. We can do no more here than indicate the major function served by each technique and merely allude to its subsidiary uses.[13] And since these procedures have been derived from clinical analysis of interview materials rather than through experimental test, they must be considered entirely provisional. Because, in the training of interviewers, it has been found instructive to indicate typical errors as well as effective procedures, that same policy has been adopted in this paper.

The Criterion of Nondirection

The value of a nondirective approach to interviewing has become increasingly recognized, notably in the recent work of Carl Rogers and of Roethlisberger and Dickson.[14] It gives the subject an opportunity to express himself about matters of central significance to him rather than those presumed to be important by the interviewer.[15] That is, in contrast to the polling approach, it uncovers what is on the subject's mind rather than his opinion of what is on the interviewer's mind. Furthermore, it permits subject's responses to be placed in their proper context rather than forced into a framework which the interviewer considers appropriate. And, finally, the informant is ordinarily far more articulate and expressive than in the directed interview.[16]

Direction in interviewing is clearly incompatible with eliciting unanticipated responses. Private definitions of the stimulus situation are rarely forthcoming when directive techniques are used. By their very nature, direct questions presuppose a certain amount of structuring by the interviewer. Direct questions, even though they are not "leading" in character, force subjects to focus their attention on items and issues to which they might not have responded on their own initiative. (This is a basic limitation of those questionnaires or schedules which provide no opportunity for subjects to express a lack of concern with items on which they are questioned.) For instance, informants who had seen a documentary film dealing with the war in Italy were asked: "Did you feel proud or annoyed when you saw how the Americans were helping in the reconstruction of Naples?" A directed question of this type at once prejudices the possibility of determining just how the subjects structured the film. The film might have been experienced impersonally as merely "interesting information." The question implies that Americans were actually taking part in the reconstruction, although some informants found the film vague on this point. Even had the subjects recognized that Americans were engaged in reconstruction, they may have learned only from the question that others were also engaged in the same work. Their replies reflected some of these implications and suggestions, which had colored their own interpretation of the film and ruled out the possibility of indicating misapprehensions. A single direct question inadvertently supplies many biasing connotations.

Nondirective techniques sometimes prove ineffective in halting irrelevant and unproductive digressions, so that the interviewer seemingly has no alternative but to introduce a direct question. But in a focused interview the limits of relevance are largely self-defined for the subject by the concrete situation. Not only are digressions less likely to occur, but, when they do occur, they are more easily dealt with by nondirective references to the concrete situation. In other words, the focal character of the experience results in a maximum yield of pertinent data through nondirective procedures.

Procedures. – The interrelations of our criteria at once become evident when we observe that nondirection simultaneously serves to elicit depth, range, and specificity of responses. For this reason the tactics of nondirection require special consideration.

The unstructured question. – Unstructured questions are intentionally couched in such terms that they invite subjects to refer to virtually any aspect of the stimulus situation or to report any of a range of responses. By answering a query of this type, the subject provides a crude guide to the comparative significance of various aspects of the situation.

In the focused interview, then, an unstructured question is one which does not fix attention on any specific aspect of the stimulus situation or of the response; it is, so to speak, a blank page to be filled in by the subject. But questions have varying degrees of structure. Several levels of structure may be distinguished as a guide to the interviewer.

1. *Unstructured question (stimulus and response free)*
   What impressed you most in this film?
   or
   What stood out especially in this radio program?
   (This type of query leads the subject, rather than the interviewer, to indicate the foci of attention. He has an entirely free choice. Not only is

he given an opportunity to refer to any aspect of the stimulus pattern, but the phrases "impressed you" and "stood out" are sufficiently general to invite reports of quite varied types of responses.)

2. *Semistructured question*

   Type A: *Response structured, stimulus free*

   What did you learn from this pamphlet which you hadn't known before?

   Type B: *Stimulus structured, response free*

   How did you feel about the part describing Jo's discharge from the army as a psychoneurotic?

   (There is obviously increased guidance by the interviewer in both types of query, but the informant still retains considerable freedom of reply. In Type A, although restricted to reports of newly acquired information, he is free to refer to any item in the pamphlet. In Type B, conversely, he is confined to one section of the document but is free to indicate the nature of his response.)

3. *Structured question (stimulus and response structured)*

   Judging from the film, do you think that the German fighting equipment was better, as good as, or poorer than the equipment used by Americans?

   or

   As you listened to Chamberlain's speech, did you feel it was propagandistic or informative?

   (Through questions of this type the interviewer assumes almost complete control of the interview. Not only does he single out items for comment, but he also suggests an *order of response* which he assumes was experienced. This leads to an oral questionnaire rather than a free interview.)

Although the fully unstructured question is especially appropriate in the opening stages of the focused interview, where its productivity is at a peak, it is profitably used throughout the interview. In some instances it may be necessary for the interviewer to assume more control at later stages of the interview, if the other criteria – specificity, range, and depth – are to be satisfied. But even in such cases, as we shall see, moderate rather than full direction is fruitful; questions should be partially rather than fully structured.

Imposing the interviewer's frame of reference. – At some points in almost every protracted interview, the interviewer is tempted to take the role of educator or propagandist rather than that of sympathetic listener. He may either interject his personal sentiments or voice his views in answer to questions put to him by subjects. Should he yield to either temptation, the interview is then no longer an informal listening-post or "clinic" or "laboratory" in which subjects spontaneously talk about a set of experiences, but it becomes, instead, a debating society or an authoritarian arena in which the interviewer defines the situation.

By expressing his own sentiments the interviewer generally invites spurious comments or defensive remarks, or else inhibits certain discussions altogether. Any such behavior by the interviewer usually introduces a "leader effect," modifying the informant's own expression of feelings. Or should the interviewer implicitly challenge a comment, the informant will often react by defensively reiterating his original statement. The spontaneous flow of the interview halts while the subject seems to maintain his ego-level intact by reaffirming his violated sentiments. In the following example the interviewer has supplied the logical implications of an expressed point of view and then has, in effect, asked whether the subject is willing to abide by these implications.

> INTERVIEWER: You say we should make a democracy out of Germany. In a democracy, the people have the right to choose their own leaders …
> (Note the didactic formulation in terms of *textbook definitions*. The attitudinal and affective implications of the subject's statement – the material looked for in a focused interview – have been ignored. Instead, the interview becomes an exercise in semantics.)
> INTERVIEWER: Supposing we were to set up a democracy and then they wanted to choose Hitler for president?
> (Here the interviewer has made invidious use of the *logical* implications of the respondent's comments. Translated, this statement reads: "Surely you can't mean this; this is a wholly indefensible position.")
> SUBJECT NO. 1: *Wait a minute.* What Hitler done he took children and we should take and mobilize this group and teach them democracy, have a constitution like the United States and make democrats out of them.
> (Note the defensive and controversial nature of the phrase: "Wait a minute." The informant's self-esteem leads him to a defensive reiteration of his original view. And, grimly pursued to his last line of retreat by the interviewer, he wards off further attack by an explosive monosyllable.)
> INTERVIEWER: And they wouldn't want to choose a leader like Hitler?
> SUBJECT NO. 1: No!

Whether the subject nominally agrees or disagrees with the interviewer's sentiments, their expression often inhibits further elaboration of comments. What is intended to draw out the informant serves only to cut off a channel of expression. Witness the following example:

> SUBJECT NO. 2: In America a man has the privilege of living in a democracy where, even though he may be of the middle or lower class, he may still reach for and attain positions of high office, whereas in England, the upper class or monied people selfishly hold onto the positions of leadership, never giving the middle or lower class an opportunity to gain such positions. For instance, *a coal miner could never hope to attain a position of high office.*

INTERVIEWER: What about David Lloyd George: *wasn't he a coal miner?*
SUBJECT NO. 2: Yes, I guess that's true.

(What the interviewer hoped to accomplish by his challenge is not at all clear. Whatever his intentions, however, the only apparent result is the abrupt silencing of a subject, who, just a moment before, had been highly articulate.)

The interviewer's introduction of his own opinions and sentiments into the discussion, then, seriously prejudices that free flow of expression which nondirection seeks to achieve.

On occasion, it will be the subject who seeks out the interviewer's attitudes or feelings by directing toward him such questions as "How do you feel about ...?" or "Do you think that ...?" This attempted reversal of roles is particularly likely to occur at just those points in the interview when continued self-exploration by the subject would be most revealing. These questions frequently reflect emotional blockage. The subject may be reluctant to explore his own feelings because they are painful or embarrassing or because they are so amorphous that he cannot easily put them into words. By directing questions to the interviewer, then, he diverts attention from himself. He hopes, at times, that the answer will provide the "correct" formulation for his own vague feelings. In other words psychological groping finds its grammatical expression in the form of a question.

Should the interviewer respond to the manifest content of these questions, however, he at once structures the stimulus material and, in this way, introduces the problems reviewed in the preceding section. It is incumbent upon the interviewer to avoid responding to the nominal meaning of many such questions posed by subjects. Although there is no way of curbing the expression of sentiments except through self-discipline, fairly specific procedures have been developed for dealing fruitfully with such questions.

In general, the interviewer should *counter a question with a question, thus converting the implied content of the informant's question into a cue for further discussion.* In doing so, he indicates that he understands the problem and is sympathetically awaiting further elaboration by the informant. This sort of stimulation is often all that the informant needs to continue his self-exploration. The following instance illustrates this technique for leading a subject to develop his own views:

SUBJECT NO. 5: Did the Germans think that the girl was working with them?
INTERVIEWER: *You mean it wasn't clear* whether she was working with the Germans or not?
SUBJECT NO. 5: That's right. You remember when ...
(Rather than answer the informant's question which would reduce the possibility of ferreting out the way in which he structured this phase of a film the interviewer responds to the *implied* meaning of the question:

"You mean it wasn't clear ...?" This provided an opportunity for the subject to indicate the film sequences which led to his confusion.)

The interview guide. – The interview guide, containing typical questions, areas for inquiry, and hypotheses based on the content analysis, is indispensable to the focused interview. It tends to make for comparability of data obtained in different interviews by insuring that they will cover much the same range of items and will be pertinent to the same hypotheses. The guide does, however, lend itself to misuse. Even when the interviewer recognizes that it is only suggestive, he may come to use it as a fixed questionnaire, as a kind of interviewing strait jacket.

The interviewer may intrude questions from his guide before it is clear that the informant has, in fact, been concerned with the matter to which the question refers. *Forcing a topic* in this way typically leads to an abrupt break in the continuity and free flow of the interview. The informant is brought up short by a question which does not apply to his immediate experience and for which, therefore, he has no ready answer. His self-explorations cease, and he often responds by a series of questions designed to have the interviewer "define his terms" or otherwise provide clues to the expected answer.

Or the interviewer may cleave too closely to the wording of questions set up in the interview guide, rather than pursuing the implications of an informant's remarks. Though it is convenient for the interviewer not to have to improvise all questions in the course of the interview, predetermined questions may easily become a liability; for, if the interviewer recognizes in the respondent's comment an allusion to an area of inquiry previously defined in the guide, he is likely to introduce one of the type questions contained in the guide. This is all well and good if the question happens to be appropriate in the given case. But unproductive interviews are those cluttered with the corpses of fixed, irrelevant queries; for often the interviewer, equipped with fixed questions dealing with the given topic, does not listen closely or analytically to the subject's comments and thus fails to respond to the cues and implications of these comments, substituting, instead, one of the routine questions from the guide. If the interviewer is primarily oriented toward the guide, he may thus readily overlook the unanticipated implications of the subject's remarks.

By listening to the implied content of what is said, the interviewer can the more readily improvise fruitful questions. He will recognize, for example, the familiar tendency of subjects to raise questions which cloak their own private feelings. For instance, informants, who were at the time undergoing military training, initially hesitated to express the anxiety provoked by having seen a film of American prisoners on Bataan:

SUBJECT NO. 9: How about *a man* being interested in a picture, but not liking it? It might rub him the wrong way, even though he finds himself interested in it.

INTERVIEWER: Do you have a particular film in mind?

(By listening to the implied content, the interviewer detects the possibly projective nature of the informant's question. He can then test this provisional hunch by utilizing a counterquestion to convert the discussion into a personal report. Instead of continuing to talk in the abstract terms of "*a man*," the informant comes to betray his own feelings.)

SUBJECT NO. 9: That part where they showed some of the wounded soldiers there on Bataan. I don't care to see that kind of stuff, although it was interesting in a way ... [And then, temporarily reverting to a projective formulation] *The public* might have a reaction to that if they were exposed to it. Although some of them realize that under battle conditions men must lose their lives or be wounded. *Some people* would say, "Look at that," and it would lower their morale.

SUBJECT NO. 5: The main thing was, I think that most of the fellows got a realization that it might be them ...

The Criterion of Specificity

In the study of real life rather than, say, in nonsense-syllable experiments in rote memory, there is all the greater need for discovering the meaning attributed by subjects to elements, aspects, or patterns of the complex situation to which they have been exposed. Thus army trainees, in one such study, reported that "the scene of marching Nazi soldiers" in a documentary film led them to feel anxious about their ability to withstand the German army. This report does not satisfy the canon of specificity. Anxiety may have been provoked by the impression of matchless power symbolized by massed armies by the "brutal expressions" on their faces to which the commentary referred; by the elaborate equipment of the enemy; by the extensive training seemingly implied by their maneuvers. Without further specification, there is no basis for selecting among the several possible interpretations.

In stressing specificity, we do not at all imply that subjects respond to each and every element of the total situation as a separate and isolated item. The situation may be experienced "as a whole" or as a complex of configurations. Individual patterns may be perceived as figures against a background. But we cannot rest with such facile formulations; we have yet to detect the "significant wholes" to which response has occurred, and it is toward the detection of these that the criterion of specificity directs the interviewer's attention. It is only in this way that we are led to findings which can be generalized and which provide a basis for predicting selective responses.[17] Inquiry has shown that, as a significant whole, brief scenes in a motion picture, for example, have evoked different responses, quite apart from the fact that seeing-a-film-in-conjunction-with-two-thousand-others was *also* a "configurative experience." But without inquiring into specific meanings of significant details, we surrender all possibility of determining the effective stimuli patterns. Thus our emphasis on "specificity" does not express allegiance to an "atomistic," as contrasted with a "configurational," approach; it serves only to orient the interviewer toward searching out the significant configurations. The fact of selective response is well attested; we must determine what is differentially selected and generalize these data.

Procedures. – We have found that specificity of reporting can be obtained through procedures in which the interviewer exercises a minimum of guidance.

It seems difficult, if not impossible, to recapture highly specific responses. Interviews on experiences of the immediate or remote past, of course, involve the problem of losses and distortions of memory. Extensive experimentation and clinical study have shown the importance of such lapses and modifications in recalled material.[18] The focused interview is, of course, subject to this same liability but not, perhaps, to the same extent as diffuse interviews; for there are certain procedures in the focused interview which facilitate the accurate report of the initial experience, which aid accounts of the "registration" of the experience rather than a distorted, condensed, elaborated, or defective report based on unaided recall.

Retrospective introspection. – These procedures are all designed to lead subjects to adopt a particular mental set – which may be called "retrospective introspection." (Of course, just as the unstructured question is essential at all stages and for all objectives of the focused interview, so retrospective introspection is more than a device for facilitating specificity of reports. It is a mood which must be maintained throughout the interview if a wide range of depth responses is to be obtained.)

Mere retrospection, without introspection, usually produces accounts of what was remembered and does not relate these to significant responses. Introspection without retrospection, on the other hand, usually leads the informant to report his reactions after they have been reconsidered in the interval between the event and the interview, rather than his experience at the time he was exposed to the stimulus situation. To minimize this problem, procedures have been developed to expedite retrospective introspection by *re-presenting* the stimulus situation so far as possible.[19] They seek to approximate a condition in which subjects virtually *re-experience* the situation to aid their report of significant responses and to have these linked with pertinent aspects of it. Re-presentation also serves to insure that both interviewer and subject are referring to the same aspects of the original situation.

The most immediate means of re-presenting documentary material is to exhibit "stills" from a motion picture, to play back sections of a transcribed radio program, or to have parts of a pamphlet re-read. Although such devices do not fully reproduce the original situation, they markedly aid the subject in recapturing his original response in specific detail. Such re-presentations do have the defect of interrupting the smooth, continuous flow of the interview, at least for a moment. If they are used frequently, therefore, the interview is likely to deteriorate into a staccato series of distinct inquiries. The best procedure, then, is to combine occasional graphic re-presentations with more frequent verbal cues. But, except for the closing stages of the interview, such cues should be introduced only after subjects have spontaneously referred to the materials in point.

Each re-presentation, whether graphic or verbal, calls for reports of specific reaction. Otherwise, subjects are likely to take the representation as an occasion for merely exhibiting their memory. Questions soliciting these reports take somewhat the following form:

> Now that you think back, what were your reactions to that part of the film?

Whatever the exact wording of such questions, they have several features in common. The interviewer alludes to a retrospective frame of reference: "Now that you think back ..." He refers to introspection: "What were your reactions (or feelings, or ideas, etc.) ...?" And, finally, he uses the past tense: "What *were* your reactions ...?" This will lead the subject to concentrate on his original experience. Emphasis on such details as the components of this type of question may seem to be a flight into the trivial. Yet experience shows that omission of any of them lessens the productiveness of replies.

Explicit references to stimulus situation. – To elicit specificity, the interviewer combines the technique of re-presentation with that of the unstructured question. A typical situation requiring further specification occurs when the subject's report of his responses has been *wholly unlinked* to the stimulus-situation. Repeatedly, we see the necessity for establishing such linkages, if observed "effects" are to be adequately interpreted. Thus tests in 1943 showed that documentary films concerning the Nazis increased the proportion of subjects in experimental groups who believed that Germany had a stronger army than the United States. Inasmuch as there was no explicit indication of this theme in the films, the "effect" could have been interpreted only conjecturally, had it not been for focused interviews. Subjects who expressed this opinion were prompted to indicate its source by questions of the following type:

> Was there anything in the film that gave you that impression?

It soon became evident that scenes which presumably stressed the "regimentation" of the Nazis – e.g., their military training from an early age – were unexpectedly taken as proof of their exceptionally thorough training, as the following excerpts from interviews indicate:

> It showed there that their men have more training. They start their men – when they are ready to go to school, they start their military training. By the time they get to our age, they are in there fighting, and they know as much as the man who has been in our service eight or nine years.

> By the looks of them where they took the boys when they were eight and started training them then, they had them marching with drums and everything and they trained them for military service when they were very young. They are well trained when they are grown men.

Thus the search for specificity yielded a clue to the significant scenes from which these implications were drawn. The interpretation of the experimental effect rests on the weight of cumulative evidence drawn from interviews and not on mere conjecture.

This case serves to bring out the need for progressive specification. If the subject's report includes only a *general* allusion to one or another part of the film, it is necessary to determine the particular *aspects* of these scenes to which he responded. Otherwise, we lose access to the often *unanticipated symbolisms* and private meanings ascribed to the stimulus situation. A subject who referred to the "regimentation of the Nazis" exemplified in "mass scenes" is prompted to indicate the particular items which led to this symbolism:

What about those scenes gave you that impression?

It develops that "goose-step parades" and the *Sieg Heil!* chorus are taken as symbols of regimentation:

> When it showed them goose-stepping out there; it numbed their mind. It's such a strain on their mind and body to do that. Just like a bunch of slaves, dogs – do what they're told.

It will be noted that these questions refer explicitly to the document or situation which is at the focus of the interview. We have found that, unless the interviewer refers to "scenes in this film," "parts of this radio program," or "sections of this pamphlet," the subjects are likely to shift toward an expression of generalized attitudes or opinion. Indispensable as such auxiliary data may be, they do not take the place of reports in which responses are linked to the test situation. Yet it is only with difficulty that the inexperienced interviewer is weaned from his embarrassment over the seeming monotony of repeated references to the stimulus situation. Preferring variety of phrase to productiveness of interview, he becomes elliptical and resorts to implicit allusions. The ease with which this leads subjects to shift to generalized opinions is brought out in the following excerpt:

> SUBJECT NO. 8: The German people were armed, but they covered it up. We didn't know about it.
> INTERVIEWER: Why didn't we know? [Note the absence of any reference to the film and the subject's immediate flight into a conjecture entirely unrelated to the film.]
> SUBJECT NO. 2: *I imagine* their country was so well policed …

Specificity not only enables the investigator to ferret out meanings of different phases of the stimulus situation; it also enables him to discover differential responses to the "same" phases of that situation. Differences in prior predispositions lead subjects to "perceive" quite different aspects of the same content. Thus, Anglophobes responded to film scenes of the Dunkirk evacuation by seizing solely upon the self-interest of the British:

> The evacuation of Dunkirk showed me that the British *could* do it, if they have to. They showed they could do it and were brave enough to do it *in the case where it was Britain they were fighting for.* They didn't start fighting until they got awful close to home.

But those with favorable or neutral attitudes toward the British noted that some French soldiers were also rescued:

> It shows courage; you mustn't give up. These fellows were practically doomed, and up comes England and salvages them, saves the greatest number of them. The English did a marvelous job ... fighting their way to the coast, evacuated the whole army *and the French.*

Specific evidence of such selective perception enables the investigator to interpret the occurrence or absence of effects rather than accepting these as brute data or resorting to conjecture, unbuttressed by evidence.

In general, specifying questions should be explicit enough to aid the subject in relating his responses to determinate aspects of the stimulus situation and yet general enough to avoid having the interviewer structure it. This twofold requirement is best met by unstructured questions, which contain explicit references to the stimulus material.

The Criterion of Range

The criterion of range refers to the coverage of pertinent data in the interview. Since any given aspect of the stimulus situation may elicit different responses and since each response may derive from different aspects of the stimulus situation, it is necessary for the interviewer to uncover the range both of response and of evocative stimuli. Without implying any strict measure of range, we consider it adequate if the interview yields data which

a) Confirm or refute the occurrence of responses *anticipated* from the content analysis
b) Indicate that ample opportunities have been provided for the report of *unanticipated* reactions; and
c) Suggest *interpretations* of findings derived from experiments or mass statistics.

Procedures. – The tactics considered up to this point have been found useful at every stage of the interview. But the procedures primarily designed to extend range do depend, in some measure, on the changing horizons of the interview: on the coverage already obtained, on the extent to which subjects continue to comment spontaneously, and on the amount of time available. The interviewer must, therefore, be vigilant in detecting transitions from one stage of the interview to another, if he is to decide upon procedures appropriate for widening range at one point rather than at another. He will, above all, utilize these procedures when informants prove inarticulate.

The central tactical problem in extending range consists in effecting transitions from one area of discussion to another. In the early stages of the interview, such transitions follow easily from the intermittent use of general unstructured questions. But, as the interview develops, this type of question no longer elicits fresh materials. Subjects then require assistance in reporting on further foci of attention. From this point, the interviewer introduces new topics either through transitions suggested by subjects' remarks or, in the final stages, by the initiation of topics from the interview guide which have not yet been explored. The first of these procedures utilizes *transitional questions*, the second, *mutational questions*.

Subject transitions. – It is not enough to say that shifts to a new area of discussion should be initiated by the subject. The interviewer who is possessed of what Murray has called "double hearing" will soon infer from the context of such shifts that they have different functions for the informant and call for different tactics by the interviewer.

Of the several reasons for shifts engineered by the informant, at least three should be considered.

1. The topic under discussion may be peripheral to the subject's own interests and feelings, so that he turns to one which holds greater significance for him. In talking about the first topic, he manifests no affect but merely lack of interest. He has little to say from the outset and exhibits boredom, which gives way to heightened interest as he moves on to a new topic.
2. The informant may have tailed at length about a given subject, and, having exhausted what he has to say, he moves the interview into a new area. His behavior then becomes very much the same as in the preceding instance.
3. He may seek to escape from a given area of discussion precisely because it is imbued with high affective significance for him, and he is not yet prepared to verbalize his feelings. This is betrayed by varying signs of resistance – prolonged pauses, self-corrections, tremor of voice, unfinished sentences, embarrassed silences, half-articulate utterances.

On the basis of such behavioral contexts, the interviewer provisionally diagnoses the meaning of the informant's transition and proceeds accordingly.

If he places the transition in the third category, he makes a mental note to revert to this critical zone at a later stage of the interview.

If, however, the transition is either of the first two types, he may safely abandon the topic unless it arises again spontaneously.

Interviewer transitions. – Generally preferable though it is to have the transitions effected by the subject, there will be occasions, nonetheless, when the interviewer will have to bring about a change in topic. When one topic is exhausted, when the informant does not spontaneously introduce another, and when unstructured questions no longer prove effective, the interviewer must introduce transitional questions if he is to tap the reservoir of response further. He may introduce a *cued* transition, or, as the interview progresses and he accumulates a series of items which require further discussion, he may effect a *reversional* transition.

In a *cued* transition, the interviewer so adapts a remark or an allusion by an informant as to ease him into consideration of a new topic. This procedure has the advantage of maintaining the flow of the interview.

Cued transitions may require the interviewer to exercise considerable ingenuity. In the following case, avowedly cited as an extreme, even bizarre, example, the informant was far afield from the radio program under discussion, but the interviewer ingeniously picked up a cue and refocused the interview on the program:

> SUBJECT NO. 1: The finest ingenuity in Germany that you ever saw. They are smart. But I think this: I don't think when this World War is over that we won't have another war. We will. We have had them since Cain killed Abel. As long as there are two human beings on this earth, there's going to be a war.
> INTERVIEWER: *Talking about Cain,* he could be called something of a small-time gangster, couldn't he? Do you happen to remember anything about gangsters being brought out at any point in this program?
> SUBJECT NO. 1: Dillinger. That was where ...
>
> (Here, although the interviewer's association was more than a little far fetched, it served its purpose in bringing the informant back to a consideration of the radio program. Had the interviewer simply changed the subject, he would have indicated that he thought the informant's remarks irrelevant, with a consequent strain on rapport. As it was, the cued transition led the informant to develop at length his structuring of a specific section of the program. When the time for the interview cannot be extended indefinitely, the cued transition enables the curbing of patent digressions, without prejudice to rapport.)

Reversional transitions are those effected by the interviewer to obtain further discussion of a topic previously abandoned, either because the subject had avoided it or, in a group interview, because someone had moved on to a new theme.

Whenever possible, the reversional question is cued, i.e., related to the topic under discussion. It can, for instance, take this form:

> That suggests something you mentioned previously about the scene in which ... What were your feelings at that point in the picture?

When it does not seem possible to relate the reversional query to the present context, a "cold" reversion may be productive:

> INTERVIEWER: A little while ago, you were talking about the scenes of bombed-out school houses, and you seemed to have more ideas on that. How did you feel when you saw that?
> SUBJECT NO. 2: I noticed a little girl lying under a culvert – it made me ready to go fight then. Because I have a daughter of my own, and I knew how I would feel if anything like that happened to her ...

This latter type of reversional query is used infrequently, however, and only in instances where it seems likely that the informant has "warmed up" to the interviewing situation sufficiently to be articulate about the topic he had avoided earlier.

Mutational questions. – Toward the close of the interview, there may still remain important points to be covered. Failing an opportunity for a cued transition, the interviewer may have to introduce a mutational question, which contains an explicit reference to previously unmentioned area:

> How did you feel about that part of the talk which dealt with the use of drugs in an X-ray examination?

Ideally, there should be no occasion for mutational questions. The more skilfully the interviewer uses unstructured questions, the more alert he is to cues, the more carefully he notes items to which he should revert, the less need for mutational questions. And their use should be kept at a minimum; for, as soon as the interviewer introduces a query of this kind, he selects a focus of attention which may have little saliency for the informant.

But mutational questions should be avoided for an additional reason. The interviewing novice (who uses them more frequently) often develops a feeling of desperation as he approaches the close of the interview with a long list of topics still to be discussed. In his anxiety to obtain some response – any response – he breaks out with a rash of questions in the desperate hope that at least one will strike a responsive chord.[20] His efforts are not unlike those of the young child who, having planted a seed, digs it up at hourly intervals to see how much it has grown – and they are just as productive. Consider the following examples taken from our dustbin of conspicuous errors:

How did you like the combination of these various types of music in one program? Was the selection of numbers a wise one? Did it interest you? Would it make you listen to it if you were home?

Do you remember the map showing just how Germans operated in France and the explanation by an intelligence officer? Do any of the rest of you remember that part of the film? Did you find yourselves pretty well bored by that kind of discussion, or do you feel you learned something from it? If you had your choice, would you want that to be in the film or cut out?

Engulfed in this deluge of questions and discouraged by the apparent request to answer all, the informant ordinarily succeeds in answering none. The flurry of queries destroys the atmosphere necessary for a successful interview, as the interviewer is cast in the role of an inquisitor, charged with anxiety and not interested in the informant, except as a source of needed data.

In general, then, mutational questions should be used only as a last resort, and, when there is no alternative, they should be phrased as generally and unspecifically as possible.

Overdependence on the interview guide. – As we have seen, misuses of the interview guide may endanger the nondirective character of the interview; they may also impose serious limitations on the range of material obtained.

The interviewer may confine himself to the areas of inquiry set forth in the guide and choke off comments which do not directly bear upon these areas. This may be termed the *fallacy of arresting comment.* Subjects' remarks which do not fall within these pre-established areas of interest may be prematurely and spuriously interpreted as "irrelevant," thus arresting what is at times the most useful type of interview material: the unanticipated response.

> INTERVIEWER: Well, now what about the first part of the film? You remember, they had photographs of the German leaders and quotations from their speeches ...
> SUBJECT NO. 10: I remember Goering, he looked like a big pig. That is what that brought out to me, the fact that if he could control the land, he could control the people.
> SUBJECT NO. 7: He is quite an egotist in the picture.
> INTERVIEWER: Did you get any impression about the German people from that?
>
> (Here the interviewer introduces a section of the film for discussion. Before he has finished his remarks, an informant volunteers his impression. No. 7 then begins his interpretation of the section. Both remarks suggest that the informants have "something on their minds." Being more attentive to his interview guide than to the implications of the informants' remarks, the interviewer by-passes the hints which might have added further to the range of the interview. He then asks

the question, from his guide, which he had probably intended to ask in the first place.)

Excessive dependence on the interview guide increases the danger of *confusing range with superficiality*. The interviewer who feels obligated to conform closely to the guide may suddenly discover, to his dismay, that he has covered only a small portion of the suggested areas of inquiry. This invites a rapid shift from topic to topic, with a question devoted to each. In some cases the interviewer seems scarcely to listen to the responses, for his questions are in no way related to previous comments. Comments elicited by this rapid fire of questions are often as superficial and unrevealing as those obtained through a fixed questionnaire. The quick "once-over" technique wastes time: it diverts respondents from their foci of attention, without any compensating increase in the interviewer's information concerning given areas of inquiry. In view of the shortcomings of rapid shifts in discussion, we suggest the working rule: *Do not introduce a given topic unless a sustained effort is made to explore it in some detail.*

The Criterion of Depth

Depth, as a criterion, involves the elaboration of affective responses beyond limited reports of "positive" or "negative," "pleasant" or "unpleasant," reactions. The interviewer seeks to obtain a maximum of *self-revelatory comments concerning how the stimulus material was experienced.*

The depth of reports in an interview varies, not everything reported is on the same psychological level.[21] The depth of comments may be thought of as varying along a continuum. At the lower end of the scale are mere descriptive accounts of reactions which allow little more than a tabulation of "positive" or "negative" responses. At the upper end are those reports which set forth varied psychological dimensions of the experience. In these are expressed symbolisms, anxieties, fears, sentiments, as well as cognitive ideas. A main task of the interviewer, then, is *to diagnose the level of depth by which his subjects are operating at any given moment and to shift that level toward whichever end of the "depth-continuum" he finds appropriate to the given case.*

The criterion of maximizing depth – to the limited extent possible in a single focused interview – guides the interviewer toward searching out the *personal context* and the *saliency* of responses.

It is a central task of the focused interview to determine how the prior experiences and predispositions of respondents relate to their structuring of the stimulus situation.[22]

Personal and social contexts provide the links between the stimulus material and the responses. It is through the discovery of such contexts that variations in the meaning ascribed to symbols and other content are understood; that the ways in which the stimulus material is imported into the experience world of subjects are determined; and that the self-betrayals and self-revelations which clarify the covert significance of a response are elicited. Thus, in the following excerpt, it becomes clear that social class provided the context for heightened identification with the British portrayed in a documentary film.

> INTERVIEWER: In what way does this picture make you feel closer [to the British]?
> SUBJECT NO. 6: I don't come from such a well-to-do family as Mrs. Miniver's. Hers was a well-to-do family, and that picture didn't show anything of the poor families. But this one brought it closer to my class of people, and you realize we are all in it and everybody gets hurt and not just the higher class of people.

The criterion of depth also sensitizes the interviewer to variations in the saliency of responses. Some responses will be central and invested with affect, urgency, or intense feelings; others will be peripheral, of limited significance to the subject. The interviewer must elicit sufficiently detailed data to discriminate the casual expression of an opinion, which is mentioned only because the interview situation seems to call for it, from the strongly motivated response which reaches into central concerns of the informant. It appears that the atmosphere of an expressive interview allows greater opportunity for degrees of saliency to be detected than the self-ratings of intensity of belief which have lately been incorporated into questionnaires and attitude scales. But, unless the interviewer is deliberately seeking out depth responses, he may not obtain the data needed to distinguish the central from the peripheral response.

Procedures. – In following up the comments of subjects, the interviewer may call for two types of elaboration. He may ask the subjects to describe what they observed in the stimulus situation, thus inviting fairly detached, though significantly selective, accounts of the content. Or he can ask them to report how they *felt* about the content. Both types of elaboration are useful, but, since the latter more often leads to depth responses, it is preferable in a fairly brief interview. Consequently, we sketch only those tactics which lead to the second type of elaboration.

Focus on feelings. – It has been found that subjects move rather directly toward a report of depth responses when the follow-up questions contain key words which refer explicitly to a *feeling context*. Focusing on a fairly recent, concrete experience, subjects usually become progressively interested in exploring its previously unverbalized dimensions, and, for the most part, no elaborate detour is needed to have them express their sentiments. But the context for such reporting must be established and maintained. Thus the interviewer should phrase a question in such terms as "Hew did you *feel* when …?" rather than imply a mere mnemonic context by asking "What do you *remember* about …?"

Illustrations are plentiful to show how such seemingly slight differences in phrasing lead respondents from an impersonal description of content to reports of their emotional responses to this content.

INTERVIEWER: Do you happen to remember the scenes showing Warsaw being bombed and shelled? What stood out about that part of the film?
SUBJECT NO. 1: The way people didn't have any shelter; the way they were running around and getting bombed ...

(The interviewer's "What stood out?" has elicited only an abbreviated account of the film content. He might have proceeded to follow this line of thought – elaborations of the objective events, further details of the squadrons of bombers, and so on. But this would have been comparatively unproductive, since the interviewer is primarily concerned with what these scenes *meant* to the informant. Therefore, he shifts attention to the response level and at once elicits an elaborate report of feeling, which we reproduce in part.)

INTERVIEWER: How did you feel when you saw that?
SUBJECT NO. 1: I still can't get worked up over it yet [1942], because in this country you just can't realize what war is like over there. I'm talking for myself. I know I couldn't fight at the present time with the viciousness of one of those people. I could shoot a man before he'd shoot me, knowing he was going to shoot me. But I couldn't have the viciousness I know those people have ...

Restatement of implied or expressed feelings. – Once the feelings context has been established, further elaboration will be prompted by the occasional restating of the feelings implied or expressed in comments. This technique, extensively developed by Carl Rogers in his work on psychotherapeutic counseling, serves a twofold function. By so rephrasing emotionalized attitudes, the interviewer implicitly invites progressive elaboration by the informant. And, second, such reformulations enhance rapport, since the interviewer thus makes it clear that he fully "understands" and "follows" the informant, as he proceeds to express his feelings.[23]

Comparative situations. – In certain cases the interviewer can use the partially directive technique of suggesting meaningful comparisons between the test situation and parallel experiences which the subjects are known, or can be presumed, to have had. Such comparisons of concrete experiences aid the verbalization of affect. The suggested comparison is designed not so much to have subjects draw objective parallels (or contrasts) between the two experiences as to serve as a release for introspective and affective responses.

Witness the following excerpt from an interview with inductees, who had implied that they were viewing a documentary film of Nazi military training within the context of their own current experience:

INTERVIEWER: Do you suppose that we Americans train our men in the same way [i.e., comparison with Nazi training as shown in film]?
SUBJECT NO. 6: They train them more thoroughly.
SUBJECT NO. 2: The way we are rushed through our training over here, it doesn't seem possible.

> Subject No. 1: That's what enters my mind about the training we are getting here. Of course, a lot of talk exists among the fellows that as soon as training is over, we're going into the fight. I don't know any more about it than they do. The training we're going to get right here is just our basic training and if we get shipped across, I can't see that we'd know anything about it except marching and doing a little left flank and right flank and a few other things like that …
>
> (The suggested comparison provided an apt opportunity for the subjects to go on to express their anxieties about going overseas unprepared for combat. The interviewer was then able to ascertain the specific scenes in the film which had further provoked these anxieties.)

It should be emphasized, however, that this procedure is effective only when the experience drawn on for comparison is known to be centrally significant to the subject and if the comparison flows from the interview. Otherwise, comparisons, far from facilitating depth responses, actually disrupt the continuity of the interview and impose an alien frame of reference upon the informant. In such instances the interviewer becomes a target for hostility: he is asked to define his terms, state the purpose behind his question, and the like.

Conclusion

Social scientists have come to abandon the spurious choice between qualitative and quantitative data; they are concerned rather with that combination of both which makes use of the most valuable features of each.[24] The problem becomes one of determining *at which points* he should adopt the one, and at which the other, approach.

The passing references made to the chief functions of the focused interview can perhaps be best summarized by indicating how such qualitative materials have been integrated with quantitative data. When the interview precedes the experimental or statistical study, it is used as a *source of hypotheses*, later submitted to systematic test. A study of the social psychology of mass persuasion exemplified in a war-bond drive on the radio provides a case in point.[25]

> In the preliminary phases of this study, focused interviews were conducted with 100 persons who had heard a "marathon" war-bond drive by a radio "celebrity," Kate Smith, whose broadcasts at fifteen-minute intervals during a period of seventeen hours resulted in $39,000,000 bond pledges. Analysis of the interviews indicated that the public image of Smith as a "patriot nonpareil" played an important role in the process of persuasion and, further, that this image was, in turn, the result of "propaganda of the deed," i.e., of publicized *acts* rather than *verbal claims*. The marathon bond drive itself was an instance of such

propaganda, as the interviews revealed. To test this interpretation, a polling interview with a representative sample was conducted to determine the comparative currency of the Smith-as-patriot image among those who had and had not heard the marathon bond drive. By keeping constant listeners' relationships to Smith – "fans," "occasional listeners," and nonlisteners – the hypothesis was confirmed. Among all three groups it was found that exposure to the marathon served to increase the frequency of the Smith-as-patriot image which entered into the process of persuasion. In this instance the focused interview was used to develop hypotheses, the mass schedule to check them at strategic points.

In other cases the procedure has been reversed. The focused interview has served *to interpret previously ascertained experimental findings*. In one experimental study of a documentary film, an effect was found which ran counter to all expectations.

The basic theme of the film, iterated and reiterated throughout, held that Britain fought and won the crucial "Battle of Britain" *alone*, thus securing a precious year in which the United States could prepare. Nevertheless, the film produced the boomerang effect of significantly increasing the proportion of those who felt that Britain would have been conquered had it not been for our Lend-Lease supplies at the time (despite the commentator's reminder that our aid was then little "more than a trickle"). Focused interviews were conducted with sample audiences to determine, among other things, the sources and process of this boomerang effect. The interviews found that audiences responded selectively; they magnified a single ten-second clip of a few crates stamped "from the U.S.A." being unloaded on a London dock. This scene was taken to symbolize American aid and, to all intents and purposes, an American victory. Just as ethnocentrism leads subjects to perceive American stamps as larger than foreign stamps of equal size, so part of the audience seized upon and magnified the only scene in the entire film which referred to an American achievement.

Such interview evidence not only provides grounds for interpreting an otherwise unintelligible experimental result but also helps design a further experimental check on the interpretation by appropriate revisions of the film.

These brief illustrations must suffice to indicate the auxiliary role of the focused interview as an instrument of research. It is hoped that, with increasing use, its procedures will be substantially improved and its applications greatly extended.

Notes

1. This article will be identified by the Bureau of Applied Social Research, Columbia, University, as Publication No. A-55. We are indebted to Dr. Samuel A. Stouffer

and Dr. Carl I. Hovland for permission to draw upon materials for the Research Branch, Information and Education Division, Army Service Forces. To Miss Marjorie Fiske and Miss Eva Hofberg, colleagues in the bureau, we are grateful for assistance in the preparation of material.

2. "What Do We Really Know about Day Time Serial Listeners?" in Paul F. Lazarsfeld and Frank N. Stanton (eds.), *Radio Research, 1942–43* (New York: Duell, Sloan & Pearce, 1944).

3. Harold F. Gosnell, *Getting Out the Vote: An Experiment in the Stimulation of Voting* (Chicago: University of Chicago Press, 1927).

4. Significantly enough, Gosnell did interview citizens in several election districts who received notices. However, he apparently did not focus the interviews in such fashion as to enable him to determine the significant phases of the total stimulus pattern; see his summary remark that "interviews ... brought out the fact that [the notices] had been read with interest and that they had aroused considerable curiosity." And note his speculation that "part of the effect [of the mail canvass] may have been due to the novelty of the appeal" (*op. cit.*, pp. 29, 71). Properly oriented focused interviews would have enabled him to detect the points of "interest," the ineffectual aspects of the notices, and differences in response of different types of citizens.

5. The same problem arises in a more complicated and difficult form when the experimental situation is not a limited event but an elaborate complex of experiences. Thus Chapin studied the gains in social participation which can be attributed "to the effects of living in the [public] housing project." As he recognized, "improved housing" is an unanalyzed "experimental" situation: managerial policies, increased leisure, architectural provision for group meetings, and a host of other items are varying elements of the program of "improved housing" (see F. S. Chapin, "An Experiment on the Social Effects of Good Housing," *American Sociological Review*, V [1940], 868–79).

6. Solomon P. Rosenthal, "Change of Socioeconomic Attitudes under Radical Motion Picture Propaganda," *Archives of Psychology*, No. 166, 1934.

7. Paul F. Lazarsfeld and Robert K. Merton "Studies in Radio and Film Propaganda," *Transactions of the New York Academy of Sciences, Series II* VI (1943), 58–79; Robert K. Merton and Patricia Kendall "The Boomerang Effect – Problems of the Health and Welfare Publicist." *Channels* (National Publicity Council), Vol. XXI (1944); and Paul F. Lazarsfeld and Patricia Rendall, "The Listener Talks Back," in *Radio in Health Education* (prepared under the auspices of the New York Academy of Medicine) (New York: Columbia University Press, 1945).

8. Ruth C. Peterson and L. L. Thurstone, *Motion Pictures and the Social Attitudes of Children* (New York: Macmillan Co., 1933).

9. On the problems of *post factum* interpretations see R. K. Merton, "Sociological Theory," *American Journal of Sociology*, L (1945), esp. 467–69.

10. *Op. cit.*, pp. 60, 64, 65, 67.

11. B. Zeigarnik, "Das Behalten erledigter und unerledigter Handlungen," *Psychologische Forschung*, IX (1927), 1–85.

12. Saul Rosenzweig, "The Experimental Study of Repression," in H. A. Murray, *Exploration in Personality* (Oxford University Press; 1938), pp. 472–90.

13. This paper is based upon an extensive manual of procedures for the focused interview. It is our hope that it represents an addition, however slight, to the growing number of critical self-examinations of method by sociologists and psychologists which lead to closer scrutiny of prevailing procedures. We refer to works such as Carl R. Rogers, *Counselling and Psychotherapy* (New York: Houghton Mifflin Co., 1942); John Dollard, *Criteria for the Life History* (New Haven: Yale University Press, 1935); Gordon

W. Allport, *The Use of Personal Documents in Psychological Science* (New York: Social Science Research Council, 1942); Louis Gottschalk, Clyde Kluckhohn, and Robert Angell, *The Use of Personal Documents in History, Anthropology, and Sociology* (New York: Social Science Research Council, 1945); and Florence Kluckhohn, "The Participant-Observer Technique in Small Communities," *American Journal of Sociology*, XLVI (1940), 331–43.

14. Rogers, *op. cit.*, pp. 115–28; F. J. Roethlisberger and W. J. Dickson, *Management and the Worker* (Cambridge: Harvard University Press, 1938), chap. xiii.

15. Thus meeting the objection raised by Stuart A. Rice: "A defect of the interview for the purposes of fact-finding in scientific research, then, is that the questioner *takes the lead*. That is, the subject plays a more or less passive role. Information or points of view of the highest value may not be disclosed because the direction given the interview by the questioner leads away from them. In short, data obtained from an interview are as likely to embody the preconceived ideas of the interviewer as the attitudes of the subject interviewed" (S .A. Rice [ed.], *Methods in Social Science* [Chicago: University of Chicago Press, 193I], p. 561).

16. Rogers (*op. cit.*, p. 122), reporting an unpublished study by E. H. Porter, states that in ten directive interviews, the interviewer talked nearly three times as much as the subject. In nine non-directive interviews, on the other hand, the interviewer talked only half as much as the subject.

17. An overcondensed case illustrates this point. Following a series of tests of documentary films, the hypothesis was advanced that audiences retain items of information presented in the form of "startling facts" of the type exploited by the Ripley "Believe-It-or-Not" column. Such items have attention value; they stand out as a figure against the ground. They have diffusion value, readily becoming part of the currency of small talk ("Did you know that …?"). And they have confidence value: they are "cold facts," as idiom so aptly puts it. On the basis of such tentative formulations, which await more theoretical phrasing, it was predicted that a "startling fact" – namely, that the first American casualty in this war occurred as early as 1940 – would be one of the most notable informational effects of a documentary film. This proved to be the case, with a differential of 36 per cent between the experimental and the control groups. Without focused interviews, the differential effects of different phases of such a complex situation as a forty-minute film would be difficult to anticipate.

18. See the survey by David Rapaport, *Emotions and Memory* (Baltimore: Williams & Wilkins Co., 1942).

19. A mechanical device, the Lazarsfeld-Stanton Program Analyzer, has been developed to serve much the same purpose with certain kinds of test materials (for a detailed description of the Analyzer and its operation see Tore Hallonquist and Edward A. Suchman, "Listening to the Listener," in Lazarsfeld and Stanton [eds.], *op. cit.*).

20. The inexperienced interviewer, beset by social anxiety, often reacts in the same way to the silences which occasionally follow unstructured questions. He is insensitive to the "pregnant silence." Instead of remaining silent himself for a minute or modifying his original question, he may bombard the subject with questions. This only makes the informant more inarticulate and discourages whatever comments might have been forthcoming.

21. See Roethlisberger and Dickson, *op. cit.*, pp. 276–78.

22. Two kinds of personal context typically find expression in the focused interview. The one is the *idiosyncratic context*, highly personalized experiences which are likely to occur rarely even within a relatively homogeneous group (e.g., the American subject who remarks: "… it reminds me of the way I felt when my brother came back

from the war after he had been reported dead. We were living in Russia and ..."). The other is the *role context*, experiences which are common for persons occupying a given status. Which of these types of context is of greatest concern to the interviewer depends, of course, on the purposes of his study.

23. Carl Rogers, *Counseling and Psychotherapy* and "The Non-directive Method for Social Research," *American Journal of Sociology*, L (1945), 279–83.

24. See Paul F. Lazarsfeld, "The Controversy over Detailed Interviews – an Offer for Negotiation," *Public Opinion Quarterly*, VIII (1944), 38–80 and Paul Wallin, "The Prediction of Individual Behavior from Case Studies," in Paul Horst (ed.), *The Prediction of Personal Adjustment* (New York: Social Science Research Council, 1941).

25. Robert K. Merton, Alberta Curtis, and Marjorie Fiske, *Mass Persuasion* (New York: Harper & Bros., in press).

15

The Focussed Interview and Focus Groups: Continuities and Discontinuities

Robert K. Merton

No one can be more surprised at my being here than I. Four years ago, I wrote myself a "self-emancipation proclamation," a one-page statement asserting that I would not again accept any invitation from any source to write a book, edit a book, write a paper, write a review article – or give a public lecture (unless it so happened that I had already written or edited that book, written that paper or review article, or assembled notes for the public lecture). Yet here I am. But what was one to do when an admired student of long ago turns out to be the president of the New York chapter of the professional organization that one's lifelong collaborator at Columbia had helped to found? (You will instantly recognize both allusions: the one to Alan Meyer, the other to Paul Lazarsfeld.) That did not provide many degrees of freedom. However, in accord with the spirit of that self-emancipating proclamation, I did prevail upon the organizers of this session to bill me unmistakably as indulging only in impromptu remarks.

However, that doesn't mean that I've done no homework at all. I had to do some, or remain wholly silent. The truth of the matter is that there can't be many people in the field of social science and certainly none in the related field of marketing research who know less about focus groups than I. If there are, that spells trouble. So it was that when Alan broached the subject of focus groups to me, he enlisted my curiosity at once. It had been only a little while ago that Pat Kendall and I had learned of the widespread use of focus groups in marketing research. Perhaps we had been reading the "wrong" books and the "wrong" journals. At any rate, when this development was lately called to our attention and when the techniques employed in focus-group research were said to derive from our work some 40 years ago on the focussed

Source: *Public Opinion Quarterly*, vol. 51, no. 4, 1987, pp. 550–566.

interview of groups (Merton and Kendall, 1946; Merton, Fiske, and Kendall, 1956), my own curiosity about that development began to mount. Still, I did little to gratify that curiosity at the time. Other research questions and problems were occupying my attention. And as the literary philosopher Kenneth Burke once observed (in a memorable fashion that I like to describe as the Burke theorem): "A way of seeing is also a way of not seeing – a focus upon object A involves a neglect of object B." (That maxim, by the way, is clearly one to be remembered in the use of focussed interviews and focus groups.)

So it was that when Alan Meyer invited me to speak to this assembly about that subject, I couldn't resist the multiple temptations he had put before me. But now I want to translate Alan's invitation into the cognitive terms, which he may not recognize, that helped bring me here. This, then, is my interpretation of what he was saying; his subtext and my reconstruction of what was contained in that invitation: "Here is a grand opportunity to meet with a group of accomplished and informed social researchers, many of them your old friends, drawn partly from the universities and partly from that world of marketing research to which Paul Lazarsfeld introduced you half a century ago. Here is an opportunity also to combine a newly emerging interest in the origins and rapid growth of focus-group research with your lifelong interest in identifying various patterns in the emergence and transmission of knowledge, particularly in the diffusion of knowledge from one socio-cultural world to another. How are ideas conveyed and how are they modified in the course of diffusion? What can be learned about patterns of change in the diffusion of innovations from science into practice? And so on. Having devoted a great part of your life to studies in the sociology of science – though, unlike Paul Lazarsfeld, rather less to the sociology of social science – you now have an opportunity to reflect aloud, to speculate, about this sort of thing in connection with the emergence and growth of focus-group research." The impromptitude of this occasion holds for the specific subject; the underlying questions I want to address are enduring and not very well understood ones; surely not well understood by me and, privately I suspect, not by many others.

I am therefore indebted to Judith Langer for having brought me up-to-date on the state of the art of focus-group research in the space of the past few minutes. My partly prepared impromptu remarks will be based largely on what I've just heard and on some documents I found lurking in ancient files. Those files are essential since I don't take much stock in vagrant memories – that is, memories without visible means of documentary support. The files provide factual checks on memories of how the focussed interview as concept-and-procedure started for me.

Prelude to the Focussed Interview

It all started in my first inadvertent work session – a thoroughly unplanned work session – with Paul Lazarsfeld back in November 1941. That story has been told in print several times (Hunt, 1961; Lazarsfeld, 1975:35-37; De Lellio, 1985:21-24), but never in tracing the seedbed of the focussed interview. I retell it here in that new context.

To begin with, Paul and I had never heard of one another before coming to Columbia. We had not only not read one another; we had literally never heard of one another. (Actually, that reciprocal ignorance is not as strange as it may seem. After all, Paul had come from one way of life; I, from quite another. Substantively speaking, we had quite different interests and even a posteriori, there is little a priori reason to suppose that our interests would ever converge and overlap.)

But back to November 1941, when Paul, as the elder of us, invited the Mertons to dinner. In what I was to discover was typical Pauline fashion, upon our arrival Paul met us at the door and said something like this: "Bob, I have wonderful news for you. I've just gotten a call from the O.F.F. in Washington [that was the Office of Facts and Figures which was the predecessor of the Office of War Information which in turn was, I believe, the predecessor of the Voice of America]. They want me to do some tests of responses to several radio morale programs. So here's a great opportunity for you. Come with me to the studio to see how we test audience response."

Thus it was that Paul dragged me into the strange world of radio research – back in those early days, unknown to just about everyone and surely so to me. I knew that Paul headed up something called the Office of Radio Research but knew nothing about its work. So off we went and then it was that I saw a strange spectacle. Do try to see it through my then naive eyes and remember that your present sophistication is the legacy of almost half a century of evolving inquiry. I enter a radio studio for the first time, and there I see a smallish group – a dozen, or were there twenty? – seated in two or three rows. Paul and I take our places as observers at the side of the room as unobtrusively as we can; there is no one-way mirror or anything of that sort. These people are being asked to press a red button on their chairs when anything they hear on the recorded radio program evokes a negative response – irritation, anger, disbelief, boredom – and to press a green button when they have a positive response. For the rest, no buttons at all. I soon learn that their cumulative responses are being registered on a primitive polygraph consisting of the requisite number of fountain pens connected by sealing wax and string, as it were, to produce cumulative curves of likes and dislikes. That primitive instrument became known as the Lazarsfeld-Stanton program analyzer. Thereafter, we observe one of Paul's assistants questioning the test-group – the audience – about their "reasons" for their recorded likes and dislikes. I begin passing notes to Paul about what I take to be great deficiencies in the interviewer's tactics and procedures. He was not focussing sufficiently on *specifically* indicated reactions, both individual and aggregated. He was inadvertently guiding responses; he was not eliciting spontaneous expressions of earlier responses when segments of the radio program were being played back to the group. And so on and so on. For although this is a new kind of interview situation for me, I am not unfamiliar with the art and craft of interviewing. For one thing, I had spent more time than I care to remember during the summer of 1932 when I was a graduate student at Harvard, helping to keep myself alive by working on a WPA project devoted to interviewing just about all the hoboes and homeless men and women that could be located in the Boston area. Having had the experience of interviewing under those sometimes strenuous conditions, this situation strikes me as providing almost privileged access to people's states of mind and affect.

At any rate, after the interview is over, Paul asks me: "Well, what did you think of it?" I proceed to express my interest in the general format and to reiterate, at some length, my critique of the interviewing procedure. That, of course, is all Paul had to hear. As I was to learn over the years was altogether typical of him, he promptly co-opts me.[1] "Well, Bob, it happens that we have another group coming in for a test. Will you show us how the interview should be done?" That was not a defensive-aggressive question, as you might mistakenly suppose it was. Rather, that was our Paul, founding Director of the Office of Radio Research (as of other university-linked organizations dedicated to social research), engaged in preliminary co-optation. I allow as how I will try my hand at it – and thus began my life with what would eventuate as the focussed group-interview.

Judith Langer spoke of the promptitude these days with which focus-group data are acquired and the promptitude with which qualitative reports based on those data are prepared. That's not entirely unfamiliar. I recall Paul inducing me to work on a distinctly preliminary analysis of those interview materials during the next days, the weekend. The report was in the Office of Facts and Figures within a week. That, remember, was in November 1941. Then came December 7th, and the war which held little nationalistic meaning but much moral significance for many of us back then. Not very much later and for some time during the war, I found myself serving as the liaison research person between the Columbia group and what had been established by the United States Army in October of that year as the Research Branch of what was successively known as the Morale Division, then the Special Services Division, and finally as the Information and Education Division. (The movement toward euphemisms had plainly begun.) The Research Branch was directed on its research (not administrative) side by the ingenious and practiced social researcher Sam Stouffer (who would eventually see to it that a distillation of the field studies conducted during World War II would appear in the form of the four volumes of *The American Soldier*).[2] Looking anew at volume 1, I note that Paul and I are both listed as "consultants," although in the event, Paul contributed infinitely more than I in that capacity, especially through his early formulation of latent structure analysis (which appears in volume 4, devoted to methodological innovations by or for the Research Branch).

A bit more about the early phase in the genesis and growth of the focussed group-interview. For a time, I found myself interviewing groups of soldiers in Army camps about their responses to specific training films and so-called morale films – some of them designed by Frank Capra and other directors of that calibre. In the course of that experience and later in work at the Bureau of Applied Social Research (which had evolved from the Columbia Office of Radio Research), there developed the set of procedures which came to be known as the focussed interview. As Sam Stouffer noted in his preface to volume 4, those procedures were not reported there because, by agreement with him and his associate Carl Hovland, they had been published several years before in the paper by Pat Kendall and myself (Merton and Kendall, 1946).

As early as 1943, also, we were putting focussed interviews to use with individuals as well as groups. A prime case in point is the study of a "radio marathon," then a wholly new historical phenomenon, which promised to provide a "strategic research site" for investigating the collective behavior and social contexts of mass persuasion (Merton, Fiske, and Curtis, [1946] 1971). During a period of 18 hours, the pop singer Kate Smith, widely perceived as a charismatic patriot-figure, spoke a series of prepared texts on 65 occasions, eliciting the then unprecedented total of $39 million in war-bond pledges. We conducted focussed interviews with 100 New Yorkers who had listened to part or, in some cases, to all [!] of the Smith broadcasts, both those listeners who had responded by pledging a war bond and those who had not. These interviews were conducted with listeners individually in their homes, not collectively in a radio studio. In the absence of the program analyzer to provide points of departure, the interviews were focussed upon the broadcast texts which we had subjected to an intensive content analysis. The resulting qualitative materials did much to help shape the interpretation of the quantitative data, based upon polling interviews with a representative sample of about a thousand New Yorkers. It was the focussed-interview data that led to identification of a public distrust related to a sense of anomie – in which "common values were being submerged in a welter of private interests seeking satisfaction by virtually any means which are effective" (p. 10). Analysis of these data led us also to a social phenomenon: "in place of a sense of *Gemeinschaft* – genuine community of values – there intrudes *pseudo-Gemeinschaft* – the feigning of personal concern with the other fellow in order to manipulate him the better" (p. 142); in still other words, "the mere pretence of common values in order to further private interests" (p. 144) (Merton, 1975:83; Cohen, 1975; Beniger, 1987).

The focussed interview of individuals did not exhibit certain assets and liabilities of the focussed interview of small groupings. (I say "groupings" since these were not, of course, *groups* in the sociological sense of having a common identity or a continuing unity, shared norms, and goals.) Still, interaction among the members of such pro tem contrived groups evidently served to elicit the elaboration of responses just as it may have contaminated individual responses by making for observable convergence of them. Correlatively, the individual interviews based on prior content-analysis of the matters under examination clearly allowed for more intensive elucidation by each person while not providing for the introduction of new leads stimulated by others.

Years later, Harriet Zuckerman adapted and developed this tactic of interviews with individuals focussed on the prior analysis of "texts" in her study of an ultra-elite, Nobel laureates in science (Zuckerman, 1972, 1977: App. A). There, the content being analyzed in detail to provide foci for the interview was of course far more complex and wide-ranging than in the studies of mass-communication behavior. It involved, for example, identifying hypothetically key events and sequences in the biographies of the laureates, provisional identification of their sociometric networks at various phases of their careers, the spottting of their successes and failures in research, and patterned sequences identified in their bibliographies. As Zuckerman noted, this was a kind of "focussed interview," one that provides for analysis and interpretation rather than only for chronicle (as is typically the case with "oral histories").

But back to the focussed interview with groups. This is plainly not the occasion for a systematic account of its essential features as a research tool. However, should you be able to find a copy of *The Focused Interview* – to my dismay, the publisher insisted on dropping one of the *s*'s in *focussed* – you will find a full account of component procedures and the rationale for each of them. But you are not apt to locate a copy. That book, published by The Free Press in 1956 after two editions had been published by the Bureau of Applied Social Research in mimeographed form, is thoroughly out of print. In fact, this copy, which I located for this evening, contains a card from my secretary of the mid-1970s which reads: "This is the only copy we have in the office."[3] You might turn instead to the more accessible paper by Pat Kendall and myself, published in the *American Journal of Sociology* ten years before the book (Merton and Kendall, 1946).

In light of all this, you will not be surprised to learn that what I've heard about focus-group research thus far tonight, and the little reading I've done on the subject, resonates. At least, in its bold outlines, the disciplined use of focus-group data has an amiable congruence with what we were trying to do with the focussed interview back then. However, I was struck by certain features of Judith Langer's summary of the *uses* of focus-group materials nowadays. These seem to contrast strongly with the ways in which we had been making use of focussed-interview materials. You will recall my having referred to work with Sam Stouffer and the Research Branch which had involved focussed group-interviews. That work was in conjunction with Carl Hovland, who headed up the Experimental Section of the Research Branch. Carl, who was on leave from Yale during the war, was possibly the most accomplished experimental psychologist ever to work on the effects of social communication; many of you may not know him since he died in 1961 at the age of 49, but he is remembered admiringly and affectionately by those of us who knew him well. Now, Carl was the one designing and directing controlled experiments on the responses of soldiers to those training and "morale" films. One would think that the experimental use of test and control groups would be taken to provide a sufficient design for identifying the effects of the films. But Carl wisely recognized that this was not so. It could not provide the specific qualitative information we were able to provide through our focussed interviews. That information moved beyond the *net effects* of "the films" – a most complex set of evocative stimuli – to identify, at least provisionally, the elements and configurations of that complex experience which might have led to those effects. The quantitative experimental design enabled one to determine the aggregate effects but provided no clues to *what it was about the film's content* that might have produced the observed effects. The focussed interview was designed to provide such materials – it identified, provisionally and subject to checks through further quantitative experimental research, the aspects of situational experience leading to the observed outcomes. This was so either in investigating a particular concrete experience, as in the case of responses to a particular film or radio program, or a recurrent experience, which, I take it, is often the research focus of focus-group research these days.

Our qualitative adjuncts to the experimental design soon convinced that brilliant designer of experiments Carl Hovland that both kinds of data were required for sound conclusions: the rigor of the controlled experiment had its costs since it meant giving up access to the phenomenological aspects of the real-life experience and invited mistaken inferences about the sources of that experienced response; the qualitative detail provided by the focussed group-interview in turn had its costs since it could lead only to new hypotheses about the sources and character of the response which in turn required further quantitative or, in this case, further experimental research to test the hypotheses.

From what I have read and heard, I gather that much of focus-group research today as a growing type of market research does not involve this composite of both qualitative and quantitative inquiry. One gains the impression that focus-group research is being mercilessly misused as quick-and-easy claims for the validity of the research are not subjected to further, quantitative test. Perhaps the pressures of the marketplace for quick-and-easy – possibly, for quick and relatively inexpensive – research make for this misuse of focus groups. That misuse – the term seems a smidgen less harsh than "abuse" – consists in taking merely plausible interpretations deriving from qualitative group interviews and treating them as though they had been shown to be reliably valid for gauging the *distributions* of response.

Shannon's fundamental theory of communication reminds us that calculated redundancy has its uses by enlarging the probability that the message will get through. So I say redundantly and emphatically that, for us, qualitative focussed group-interviews were taken as sources of new ideas and new hypotheses, not as demonstrated findings with regard to the extent and distribution of the provisionally identified qualitative patterns of response. Those ideas and hypotheses had to be checked out by further survey research (or in the case of the Research Branch studies, by further experimental research). The point is that limited qualitative research cannot in principle deal with the distribution and extent of tentatively identified patterns. (Medicine had to discover that clinical observations were no substitute for epidemiological investigation.) I can report to you that some of the hypotheses derived from focussed interviews during our collaborative work with Carl Hovland did *not* check out upon further inquiry. The point is, of course, that there is no way of knowing in advance of further quantitative research which plausible interpretations (hypotheses) will pan out and which will not.

Focussed Interview and Focus Groups:
Continuities and Discontinuities

I've been asked to speak to the subject of continuities between the focussed interview and the current use of focus groups. I believe that there are both continuities and discontinuities. I have the impression that there is rather more intellectual continuity than explicitly recognized historical continuity. After all, *The Focused Interview* sold only a few thousand copies, for the most part in the 1950s, I believe, and then went out of print. We have no evidence on the distribution of those copies – say, as between academics and market researchers. Looking into files, which over the years have proved to be a continuing source of serendipitous[4] and therefore surprising finds, I discover a long-forgotten reference to a letter in the mid-1970s. It testifies that there was some direct and identifiable continuity which was then recognized by research people in the world of commerce. Rather than paraphrase that letter, I'll transmit this archival tracer intact, thanks to my home Canon photocopier which allows me to canonize this document (without possible error):

> Benson & Benson, Inc.
> P.O. Box 269
> Princeton, N.J. 08540
> June 17, 1976

Professor Robert K. Merton
Fayerweather Hall
Columbia University
New York, N.Y. 10027

Dear Professor Merton:

Over the years we have derived considerable use from our copy of the second edition of *The Focussed Interview – A Manual.* As you undoubtedly are aware, focussed group interviewing has become widespread in commercial circles and is eliciting interest in the academic and non-profit research sectors. Oddly enough, little has been written on the subject in systematic fashion, and, in nearly every case, that which has apparently should not have been. We have urged other researchers to refer to the *Manual,* but invariably have been told that copies simply are not to be found. In other words, we apparently possess one of the last known copies of the *Manual,* and, understandably, are reluctant to lend it out.

Now, we are starting to receive queries for Xerox copies.

Our copy carries no copyright and the Introduction suggests the report is in the public domain.

We would like to reprint the manual and offer it for sale to interested researchers at about $10–$12 per copy, plus postage. We think it is only fair that we consult with you on this first. We would propose to offer the authors a 15% royalty on each copy sold. Payment would be made semi-annually....

Sincerely,
Robert Bezilla
Executive Vice President

Now, like a longtime qualitative researcher, I want to take you briefly through a part of this document which testifies to continuity between academe and the marketplace. Note that it begins by referring to "our copy of ... *The Focussed Interview – A Manual."* That must refer to the second mimeographed edition put out by the Columbia Bureau of Applied Social Research rather than the far more widely circulated letterpress edition published by The Free Press in 1956. This I infer from the spelling of the word *Focussed* in the title, a spelling I have always preferred and therefore adopted in the two Bureau editions but one, as I've said, which The Free Press (as before it, the editor of the *American Journal of Sociology*) had unwarrantably but forcibly diminished to *Focused.* Thus, the two-essed *Focussed* serves as a marker of the earlier editions. Note too that by 1976, the executive vice president of Benson & Benson is reporting that "focussed [n.b.] group interviewing has become widespread in commercial circles and is eliciting interest in the academic and non-profit sectors." If his impression was sound, this suggests – somewhat to my startle now and perhaps back in 1976 – that the pattern of focussed group-interviewing had expanded to the point of eliciting enlarged interest in the academic world where it had originated. Not to continue with a line-by-line gloss, I remark only now on the intrinsic decency of Robert Bezilla of Benson & Benson in suggesting a royalty to the authors should he be allowed to reprint the manual; this, mind you, even though he (mistakenly) assumed that the work was in the public domain.

You may be curious about what happened in response to that generous offer to reprint, as indeed I am. But nothing in my archival files allows me to say, from which I conclude that nothing of consequence happened.

That is one indication of direct continuity between academia and the marketplace. I gather that during the passage from Morningside Heights to Madison Avenue the focussed interview has undergone some sea changes of the kind I've been in a position only to hint at: the quick would-be conversion of new plausible insights into demonstrable gospel truths. As I say, I'm not really qualified to speak to this point since I've seen next to nothing of current focus-group research at close range. But I note the following observation by Leo Bogart (1984:82):

> In the 1970s, another type of qualitative research rapidly moved to the forefront: the so-called focus group interview in which a half-dozen to a dozen people are assembled and engaged in a discussion. (The term *focus group* is a barbarism that confused sociologist Robert K. Merton's technique of an unstructured but "focused" interview – in which a skillful interrogator keeps the respondent's attention from wandering off the subject at hand – and the traditional sociological technique of talking to a homogeneous or related group of people who stimulate each other under the interviewer's practiced guidance.)* A group interview can be conducted with little more expense than an intensive interview with one individual, but since everyone in the group gets counted, a respectable number of respondents can be toted up in the sample.
>
> The most beguiling aspect of focus groups is that they can be observed in action by clients and creative people hidden behind a one-way mirror. Thus, the planners and executors of advertising can be made to feel that they are themselves privy to the innermost revelations of the consuming public. They *know* what consumers think of the product, the competition, and the advertising, having heard it at first hand. The trouble is that people who can be enticed into a research laboratory do not always represent a true cross-section of potential customers. A cadre of professional respondents are always ready to volunteer, and loud-mouths can dominate and sway the discussion. While useful and provocative ideas emerge from groups just as they do from individual qualitative interviews, it is dangerous to accept them without corroboration from larger-scale survey research.

So much for critical observations on some present-day practices in focus-group research. Now back for a few moments to the archives. Roaming through my files of that full generation ago – and you recall what Ortega y Gasset, Karl Mannheim, and Julián Marías had to say about the social reality and dynamics of generations – I have come upon a long-forgotten letter to Jeremiah Kaplan, the founding president of The Free Press, telling how the mimeographed editions of *The Focussed Interview* came to be transformed into the printed edition. Having shared this letter with my coauthors, Marjorie Fiske and Pat Kendall, I now include it in what is fast becoming an archive-based though still fragmentary account of the evolution of the focussed group-interview as prelude to the evolving focus-group mode of research.

[Mr. Jeremiah Kaplan
The Free Press]
8 August 1955

Dear Jerry,

... The news of the moment in this: I have set myself a quota, during these comfortable vacation-days, of so many pages a day for rewriting the Focused Interview. Now that a week has gone by and I am still on schedule, I am quite confident that it will be completed by the time I return. Since my secretary is away next week, there will be a little delay in typing this new version but the ms. will definitely be ready for the printer by the end of the month....

Item 1: This is a complete *re-writing*: scarcely five sentences in a chapter remain intact. Nevertheless, it is not, in any significant sense, a new *edition*; there is next to nothing by way of new material (except for a little based on focused interviews on the diaries of medical students) and little by way of new ideas. I've tried only to eliminate the worst horrors of exposition in the earlier printings and, for the rest, to make it clear, if not fascinating. It seems to me, therefore, that it should not be designated as a new edition, but as the Third Re-printing (rewritten), so that no excessive claims seem to be implied. I hope you agree. (I'll explain the nature of the rewriting in the preface.)

Item 2: As you know, this is a short book – it will run to about 230 ms. pages (including about 25 single-spaced pages of an analytical table of contents which was found useful in the Bureau 'editions'). I wouldn't like to have the book be too expensive: it is all straight text, no tables or charts, and should be easy to set in type. At the same time, I hope that Sid can design it so that it isn't too crowded. Can you let me have your thinking on price and design? ...

Yours,

[Robert K. Merton]

As can be seen, by the mid-1950s the essential concept of the focussed interview and its basic procedures with their stated rationales had become stabilized. Indeed, these did not evolve further at the Columbia Bureau. So it was that this interlinear rewriting of the Manual, which took place on the sands of Ocean City (and thus perhaps introduced a new idiom, by-the-sea-change), became the version that could diffuse and evidently did diffuse into various research sectors, notably it seems into the sector of market research.

Intellectual Diffusion and Obliteration by Incorporation

That particular pathway of diffusion into the marketplace was neither intended nor, as I recall, anticipated. Speaking for myself, I thought of the focussed interview as a generic research technique, one that could be and would be applied in every sphere of human behavior and experience, rather than largely confined to matters of interest in market research. As for the actual paths of diffusion taken by the focussed interview, I cannot say. No case study of that diffusion has been made. Perhaps a study utilizing the now available resources of citation analysis coupled with interview or questionnaire inquiries among representative samples of different populations of social researchers would provide some understanding of the extent and directions of that diffusion of a modest, delimited, and readily identifiable innovation as well as the kinds and determinants of diverse kinds of changes in it as it spread to one or another research sector. Not, mind you, that the diffusion of this technique warrants such a study because of its research importance but only because it seems to have some of the elements of a strategic research site[5] for investigation of the diffusion of intellectual innovations – and that, as many of you know, was a subject of deep interest in the Columbia Bureau of Applied Social Research back in the 1960s, as you'll recall from the path-breaking study by Jim Coleman, Elihu Katz, and Herb Menzel (1966). And as you could not know, that interest has been brilliantly renewed on Morningside Heights by Ronald S. Burt (1987) in his reanalysis of the Coleman–Katz–Menzel data.

So much for an excursion into the serious, systematic study of the diffusion of innovations. Here, in the concluding moments of these remarks, I can only turn to the archives which once again yield a bit of pertinent evidence – evidence which bears witness that the focussed interview was not confined to academe or the marketplace but, at least once, found its way into the sphere of religion, viz.:

> Board of Education
> The United Methodist Church
> Division of the Local Church
> September 18, 1969

Dr. Robert K. Merton
Department of Sociology
Columbia University
New York, New York 10027

Dear Dr. Merton:

We are conducting a major study of the state of the church school of The United Methodist Church and would like to make use of the focused interview technique which you have described in the book by that title.

I am having difficulty locating additional copies of the book and am wondering if you could direct me to a supplier from whom we might purchase copies for use in our training sessions. Up to this time the only copies we have been able to discover are those which are in several libraries.

Your help in this matter will be greatly appreciated.

Cordially yours,
Warren J. Hartman

Back now to a few more bits of documentary evidence on the continuity from the focussed interview as a mode of social and psychological inquiry to the focus group. I turn to the fairly recent past and the virtual present for a few qualitative indicators of that continuity. In 1976, precisely 30 years after Pat Kendall's and my first publication on the focussed interview, an introduction in a book entitled *Qualitative Research in Marketing* by Danny Bellenger, Kenneth Bernhardt, and Jack Goldstucker (published by the Chicago Marketing Association) virtually begins by reporting that "Merton, Fiske, and Kendall distinguish the focus group as following these criteria" and then proceeds to quote the paragraph on "The Nature of the Focused Interview" that opens our book. Here you will note a diagnostic conflating of the focussed interview and the focus group, at least a terminological conflation. We never used the term "focus group" – at least, not as I recall – but apparently these authors on marketing research saw the focus group as so fully derivative as to have us setting down criteria for focus groups. To be sure, we repeatedly examine the values and limitations of using focussed interviews in groups rather than independently with later aggregated individuals and that might be a basic theme in the continuity-cum-change.

Recognition of the accent on that theme is found in a fairly recent article just drawn to my attention that was published in *Information Technology and Libraries* (December 1983). Introducing a research program for library users and on-line public access catalogs (OPACS), it has occasion to refer to "focused-group interviews" and goes on to say (p. 381) that "complete descriptions of the focused-group interview method and analysis are given in Merton, Fiske and Kendall's manual on the method."

Early on in these remarks – so long ago that you are not apt to remember – I hazarded the impression that there was more "intellectual continuity" between the focussed interview and focus groups than "explicitly recognized historical continuity." The distinction between the two kinds of continuity is one that has long seemed basic to me in trying to understand patterns in the historical transmission of knowledge. For in the course of time, ideas which are taken up and utilized or developed become so much a part of current knowledge, both explicit and tacit, that their sources and consequently the lines of intellectual continuity get increasingly lost to view. I have identified this phenomenon in the transmission of knowledge as "obliteration by incorporation (OBI)": "the obliteration of the sources of ideas, methods, or findings by their incorporation in currently accepted knowledge."[6] At the outset, the source of a particular idea or method is known and identified by those who make use of it. In due course, however, users and consequently transmitters of that knowledge who are thoroughly familiar with its origins come to assume that this is also true of their readers. Preferring not to be obvious or to insult their reader's assumed knowledgeability, they no longer refer to the *original* source. And since, in all innocence, many of us tend to attribute a significant idea, method, or formulation to the author who introduced us to it, the equally innocent transmitter sometimes becomes identified as the originator. Thus it is that in the successive transmission of knowledge, repeated use of it may erase all but the immediately antecedent "source," thus producing what I described in *On the Shoulders of Giants* (Merton, 1965:218–219ff.) as a historical palimpsest (or palimpsestic syndrome) in which the *original* source is not only obliterated but replaced by the intermediary between source and recipient of that knowledge.

Without doing the requisite research, I cannot presume to say how much of the seeming discontinuity between the focussed interview and its modified (and, I take it, sometimes abused) version in the form of focus groups is actually another instance of obliteration by incorporation. But that some OBI has occurred can be inferred from a recent article by two professors of sociology at the University of California–Riverside, David L. Morgan and Margaret T. Spanish (1984), which describes "focus groups" as "a relatively new research tool" (p. 253). If the focussed interview has experienced even occasional obliteration by incorporation in the originating field of sociology, one is inclined to suppose that it is all the more (a fortiori) likely to have occurred in other fields into which it had diffused.

And now a final word, stemming once again from the marketplace, but one which, much to my pleasure, recognizes that the focussed interview is not at all confined to market research. Indeed, in light of its use by religious and other eleemosynary institutions, it might even be described as ecumenical. But perhaps more telling is a review of *The Focused Interview* appearing in the October 1956 issue of *The Journal of Marketing*. Understandably, the review is oriented to its probable readers in remarking that the book "should be of particular value to the student and practitioner of marketing research." Good enough; more qualitative evidence of diffusion from academe to the marketplace. But much more in point for the original concept of the focussed interview as a generic rather than substantively restricted research tool is the concluding declaration in the review that "This manual should be read by those who are attempting to understand the problems involved in subjective or motivation research in whatever field it may lie." Precisely so. Useful for marketing research, to be sure, but not only for marketing research. Rather, a set of procedures for the collection and analysis of qualitative data that may help us gain an enlarged sociological and psychological understanding in whatsoever sphere of human experience.

Notes

* Paul F. Lazarsfeld and Frank Stanton first combined these techniques in the radio Program Analyzer. Groups of people pressed buttons to record their moment-by-moment responses to what they heard. The interviewer, examining the tape, questioned them as to why they reacted as they did. CBS still uses this technique to evaluate television programs.

1. In his passion to get all problems he thought important solved, Paul made it an enduring practice to co-opt associates of every kind to work on them – students, of course, but also colleagues of varied stripe: young and old; near and far; social scientists, logicians, mathematicians, statisticians, and philosophers. This pattern of disinterested co-optation has been beautifully recaptured in print by two of our students from those ancient days of the 1940s and 50s: James S. Coleman (1980) and David L. Sills (1987).

2. Samuel A. Stouffer *et al.*, The American Soldier: Adjustment During Army Life. Samuel A. Stouffer *et al.*, The American Soldier: Combat and Its Aftermath; Carl I. Hovland, Arthur A. Lumsdaine, and Fred D. Sheffield, Experiments on Mass Communication; Samuel A. Stouffer *et al.*, Measurement and Prediction. Princeton: Princeton University Press, 1949.

3. I've just found evidence, in the form of a letter from the executive vice president of Benson & Benson Inc. written a dozen years ago, that the book was out of print at least by then. However, I'll postpone reporting that until later since it provides me with a bridge between the focussed interview and focus groups which I had forgotten until I came upon the letter.

4. In this printed version of my talk I refer to an unpublished monograph by Robert K. Merton and Elinor Barber (1958). It treats the social and cultural contexts of the coinage of the word *serendipity* in the 18th century; the climate of relevant opinion in which it first saw print in the 19th; the diverse social circles of litterateurs, physical and social scientists, engineers, lexicographers, and historians into which it diffused; the changes of meaning undergone in the course of diffusion, and the ideological uses to which it has been variously put. I rather doubt that the diffusion of the focussed interview is ready for a comparable analysis.

5. The concept of strategic research site is elucidated somewhat in Merton, 1987.

6. The phenomenon of OBI is noted in Merton, 1968, and in other writings since. This summary is drawn from Merton, 1979; see also Garfield, 1977.

References

Beniger, James R. (1987) "Personalization of mass media and the growth of pseudo-community." *Communication Research* 14:352–371.
Bogart, Leo (1984) *Strategy in Advertising*. 2d ed. Chicago: Crain Books.
Burt, Ronald S. (1987) "Social contagion and innovation: Cohesion versus structural equivalence." *American Journal of Sociology* 92:1287–1335.
Cohen, Harry (1975) 'Pseudo-*Gemeinschaft*: A problem of modern society." *Western Sociological Review* 5:35–46.
Coleman, James S. (1980) "Paul F. Lazarsfeld: The substance and style of his work." Pp. 153–174 in Robert K. Merton and Matilda White Riley (eds.), *Sociological Traditions from Generation to Generation: Glimpses of the American Experience*. Norwood, NJ: Ablex Publishing Corp.

Coleman, James S., Elihu Katz, and Herbert Menzel (1966) *Medical Innovation: A Diffusion Study.* Indianapolis: Bobbs-Merrill.

De Lellio, Anna (1985) "Intervista a Robert K. Merton: Le aspettative sociali di durata." *Rassegna Italiana di Sociologia* 26:3–26.

Garfield, Eugene (1977) "The 'obliteration phenomenon' in science – and the advantage of being obliterated!" Pp. 396–398 in Eugene Garfield, *Essays of an Information Scientist,* vol, 2. Philadelphia: ISI Press.

Hunt, Morton (1961) "'How does it come to be so?': A profile of Robert K. Merton." *The New Yorker,* 28 January.

Lazarsfeld, Paul F. (1975) "Working with Merton." Pp. 35–66 in Lewis A. Coser (ed.), *The Idea of Social Structure.* New York: Harcourt Brace Jovanovich.

Merton, Robert K. [1965] (1985) *On the Shoulders of Giants.* New York: Harcourt Brace Jovanovich.

—— (1968) *Social Theory and Social Structure.* New York: The Free Press.

—— (1975) "On the origins of the term: pseudo-*Gemeinschaft.*" *Western Sociological Review* 6:83.

—— (1979) Foreword to Eugene Garfield, *Citation Indexing: Its Theory and Application in Science, Technology, and Humanities.* New York: John Wiley.

—— (1987) "Three fragments from a sociologist's notebooks: Establishing the phenomenon, specified ignorance, and strategic research materials." *Annual Review of Sociology* 13: 1–28.

Merton, Robert K., and Elinor Barber (1958) "The travels and adventures of serendipity: A study in historical semantics and the sociology of science." Manuscript.

Merton, Robert K., with Marjorie Fiske and Alberta Curtis [1946] (1971) *Mass Persuasion.* New York: Harper and Bros. Reprint, Westport, CT: Greenwood Press.

Merton, Robert K., Marjorie Fiske, and Patricia L. Kendall (1956) *The Focused Interview.* New York: The Free Press.

Merton, Robert K., and Patricia L. Kendall (1946) "The focused interview." *American Journal of Sociology* 51:541–557.

Morgan, David L., and Margaret T. Spanish (1984) "Focus groups: A new tool for qualitative research." *Qualitative Sociology* 7:253–270.

Sills, David L. (1987) "Paul F. Lazarsfeld, 1901–1976: A biographical memoir." Pp. 251–282 in *National Academy of Sciences, Biographical Memoirs.* Washington: The National Academy Press.

Zuckerman, Harriet (1972) "Interviewing an ultra-elite." *Public Opinion Quarterly* 36:159–175.

—— (1977) *Scientific Elite: Nobel Laureates in the United States.* New York: The Free Press.

16

The Group Interview

E. S. Bogardus

In the newer fields of social research, the personal interview is achieving a place of increasing scientific importance. Its role in bringing fundamental attitudes to the surface for scientific scrutiny is secure. But the deeper it penetrates social attitudes the slower and more expensive it becomes as a method of research.

Hence, as the individual intelligence tests are being supplemented by group tests, so the individual interview is being supplemented by the group interview. The latter is developing not so much as a complete substitute for the former, but as a substitute for the less personal part. A large amount of valuable work in connection with personal interviews can be accomplished by the group interview, leaving to personal interviews only the most vital phases.

In the group interview it is possible to make preliminary explanations of principles and methods, to answer important questions in the presence of all that might normally be thought of by only a few, and to develop a general interest in research. Group discussion brings out points that otherwise would remain obscure. Group enthusiasm may arouse an interest in research work on the part of many persons who otherwise would never become concerned.

Moreover, preliminary data of importance can be secured by the group interview. By having experiments worked out and mimeographed, a hundred or more persons may willingly work at them together for an hour at a time. The group interest is sufficient to obtain results from persons who normally would consider the project tedious and who would not respond.

In the Race Relations Survey,[1] it was possible to secure from groups formal materials, such as the names of persons who have had race relations experiences, who have first-hand knowledge of race problems, and of persons who would be of especial help in securing data. A considerable amount of exploration work can be done in this way, such as the securing of "leads," and the gathering of "card catalogue" materials.

Actual investigation may be started in the group interview. In studying social distances, a one-page experiment (Document I) was worked out relative to recording cordial, antipathetic, and neutral reactions. After a brief explanation the members of the group were asked to classify each race. The list was read slowly, keeping pace with the persons sitting on the front row. As the first feeling reactions were desired and not the second and the more cognitive and rationalized, the experiment worked well. Then, other items of the experiment were carried out. Finally, one question was given to be written out thoughtfully and returned in two days. This question suggested that each person choose one of the races toward which he felt the greatest aversion and write out all his experiences, direct and hearsay, together with his emotional reactions thereto. This brought splendid results. Most important of all it laid capital foundations for personal interviews, which dealt with points not already treated in the written materials. Certain persons were at once discovered who could write good life histories; others were located who might become good research interviewers.

Document I: Social Distance

Races Alphabetically Arranged

1.	Armenian	21.	Jew-German
2.	Bulgarian	22.	Jew-Russian
3.	Canadian	23.	Korean
4.	Chinese	24.	Mexican
5.	Czecho-Slovak	25.	Mulatto
6.	Dane	26.	Negro
7.	Dutch	27.	Norwegian
8.	English	28.	Portuguese
9.	Filipino	29.	Pole
10.	French	30.	Roumanian
11.	French-Canadian	31.	Russian
12.	Finn	32.	Croatian (Jugo-Slav)
13.	German	33.	Scotch
14.	Greek	34.	Scotch-Irish
15.	Hindu	35.	Spanish
16.	Hungarian	36.	Syrian
17.	Indian (American)	37.	Swedish
18.	Irish	38.	Turk
19.	Italian	39.	Welsh
20.	Japanese		

Races Arranged by Social Distance

I	II	III
Cordial Feeling	*Neutral Feeling*	*Antipathetic Feeling*
------------------------------	------------------------------	------------------------------
------------------------------	------------------------------	------------------------------
------------------------------	------------------------------	------------------------------
------------------------------	------------------------------	------------------------------
------------------------------	------------------------------	------------------------------
------------------------------	------------------------------	------------------------------
------------------------------	------------------------------	------------------------------
------------------------------	------------------------------	------------------------------

In the first column list the races toward which you feel friendly; in the second column list the races toward which you have any neutral feeling, due perhaps to not knowing the races in question; and in the third column list the races toward which you feel any antipathy.

Then examine the three columns and put a cross in front of the races in the "cordial feeling" column toward which you feel the most cordial. Put a cross in front of the races in the "antipathy column" toward which you feel the most antipathy. Put a cross in front of the races in the "neutral feeling" column which you know least about.

In another group interview (Document II) in which a similar method was followed, and in still another type of group interview (Document III) a more difficult task was essayed – that of arousing the interest of each individual in writing his racial life history – the results surpassed expectations.

Document II: Changes in Opinion

(Races Alphabetically Arranged as in Document I)

1. What races do you feel farther away from than ten years ago?
2. Describe freely your experiences and actual racial contacts with each of the leading races which feel farther away from you now than formerly.
3. What races do you feel closer to than ten years ago?
4. Describe freely your experiences and actual racial contacts with each of the leading races which you feel closer to than formerly.

Document III: Personal Race-Relations History

In place of a library assignment, write out your race-relations history in narrative form. Do not *generalize*, but describe *experiences*. As stimuli to this letter-writing narrative process the following questions are set down. They are not to be answered in order or categorically, but are simply to be turned to as stimuli for further thinking.

In narrating experiences and memories it is well "to let one's self go," describing the feelings and emotions that one had; it is also important to describe the expressions of the "other fellow's" feelings and emotions. Special attention to the gestures of other persons involved, even facial expressions – of pleasure, disgust, fear, anger, – are important. The spirit that one is in when writing a letter to an intimate friend is perhaps most important of all.

I. First Contacts and Backgrounds

1. What incidents or circumstances happened in the play experiences of your childhood that helped to fix your attitudes toward any race?
2. What experiences did either of your parents have with members of any race whom they employed? With whom they had business dealings?
3. What school experiences or impressions do you recall concerning the children of other races?
4. What races was your father descended from? Your mother?

II. Conflicts and Accommodation

1. In what ways were you *shocked* by what you saw or heard then, or since, about the members of other races?
2. What books did you read, then or since, that fixated your attitudes in any way racially? Explain.
3. What public speakers, ministers, lecturers, missionaries, or others influenced you racially then, or since, and how?
4. What experiences have you had in befriending the members of any other race? With what results?
5. What members of any other race have ever taken advantage of you, and how?
6. What motion pictures have you seen which helped to fix your racial attitudes in any way?
7. What newspapers have you read which have played a part in influencing your racial opinions? How?
8. What magazines or scientific journals have influenced you for or against any race? How?

9. How have your opinions been influenced by discussion?
10. Has your sympathy been aroused for any group under discussion by what seemed the unjust and unfair charges made against them? Explain.
11. Has your antipathy been intensified by what seemed to be the biased character of the arguments advanced in their defense? Explain.

III. Narratives

1. Choose the race for which you have the greatest antipathy and describe the experiences under which your antipathy originated.
2. Choose the race (outside your own) toward which you feel the most cordial and describe the experiences under which that cordiality of feeling originated.

Another type of group interview was developed in the Boys' Work Survey[2]; boys' attitudes and opinions concerning motion pictures were obtained. Several public school teachers co-operated. The best results were obtained from an English class in which the teacher (one who enjoyed the confidence of her class) assigned as a normal written exercise in English the general theme of "Leisure Time Activities" and then the following questions were suggested as a guide to the discussion. The class period was utilized in this way.

1. What are your most interesting activities outside of school hours?
2. Explain in detail why attending movies comes high or low on your list.
3. Are the movies more or less interesting than they were a year ago ?
4. Describe the parts you like to see best.
5. When and under what conditions did you first become interested in the movies?
6. What else besides the picture interests you? Give illustrations.

Valuable hints were secured in this way. The group interview indicated that certain boys should be personally interviewed. The method illustrates well a phase of the exploration principle. Some of the answers, to be sure, were stereotyped; some were written particularly for the teacher's benefit; and some children made disparaging remarks in answer to one or more of the questions – all of which were valuable as disclosing the attitudes of the respective boys.

In the Boys' Work Survey the *discussion type of group interview* was tried out. Fourteen group interviews were arranged with as many different types of boys' welfare leaders. Each leader called a meeting of ten to twenty representative persons of experience in his field or under his supervision who were working with boys. Each group interview was held at a time suitable to the particular group – one at 10 a.m., four at 12 o'clock, two at 4 p.m., four at 6 p.m., and three at 7:30 p.m. Each lasted two or three hours. The list is as follows:

> Playground directors
> Y. M. C. A. boys' directors
> Catholic boys' workers
> Jewish boys' workers
> Colored boys' workers
> Special school principals
> School attendance officers
> Probation officers
> Juvenile police officers
> Neighborhood conference
> Social research workers
> Conference of boys
> Scout masters
> Social workers

Each group was addressed briefly by the director of the Survey on the nature of the problem, on how the community is becoming interested in boys, and how the experiences of successful boys' workers might be of help in the development of a greater community interest in boys and in boys' welfare agencies. Some of the experiences that other boys' workers have reported were related. The nature of social research as being confidential, similar for example to medical research, was made clear. Some of the questions upon which information of an experience nature rather than of an opinion nature were desired, were mentioned, and then, 3 x 5 slips of papers were passed around upon which these questions, usually four in number, had been neatly typed. Each person was asked to feel free to present any data that any one or all of these questions suggested to him. The questions follow:

Topics for Group Discussion

1. What are your biggest problems in working with boys in this city? What do you worry about most?
2. What would you say are *their* biggest problems ? What do they worry about?
3. What do you do for boys that they respond to best? How do you affect changes in their attitudes toward life?
4. What changes in methods of working with boys have you made since you first became interested in them? (Experiences rather than opinions are valuable.)

Any one who would volunteer was asked to start out, and then others in succession followed in order around the circle. The interview was usually held around a table and informality was encouraged. Sometimes a person would take the questions too objectively, that is, like a questionnaire, and give simply "yes" or "no" answers. The discussion immediately went on to the next person, and then later the person who had fallen into the questionnaire habit would usually become interested and relate valuable experiences.

Each group, representing one type of boys' work, was composed, as a rule, of men who were well acquainted, even addressing each other by their nick-names. The only "new" person present would be the interviewer who, however, was known by name at least to the group and who had little difficulty ordinarily in establishing rapport.

The methods pursued in securing mental release were similar to those of the personal interview, namely, consideration, gradation, identification, and indirect interrogation. Questions in the form of declarative remarks were introduced occasionally. Frequently the remark of the one speaking would stimulate four or five others to want to talk at once and to tell their experiences. Often several would try to talk simultaneously. It was not uncommon for at least one man in each group to "get started," and to tell so much that others would feel called upon to respond in explanation, and for the first person to stop suddenly with an exclamation: "I'm afraid I've said too much." Each person in referring to the questions before him would always make statements which would call for further explanation and for interpretation. In watching for significant statements of this character, and in showing a special interest in these, the person in charge of the group interview can be instrumental in having new points brought out. Often a statement of one member starts new trains of thought in the minds of several others present.

One of the main values of the group interview is that there are always persons present who disclose themselves as possessors of data of a too personal nature to be told except in a personal interview. Practically every group interview was followed by significant personal ones, and thus functioned as an explorational enterprise, uncovering valuable source materials.

Moreover, in the excitement which a group interview may reach, and particularly in the counter statements made by one person in answer to another's disclosure, data will be brought to the surface that a personal interview would not likely touch at all. At nearly every group interview a question would elicit contradictory replies from two or more present. At once each would feel called upon to defend his position and in so doing would draw upon his store of reserve experiences in surprising ways. As a result of group discussion, certain persons present developed new points that had not previously occurred to them, and which probably would not have been secured in a personal interview. Creative group discussion is a superior technique.

One of the most interesting group interviews was held at a branch library in an industrial and business district where boys were numerous and troublesome. It was a boys' conference – 45 being present. After brief explanatory remarks including new play facilities that were going to be brought to the neighborhood, the boys were asked to tell what they would like to have in that neighborhood which they do not have, and later in the discussion, were asked to tell why so many boys were getting into trouble there. Of course the older and more troublesome boys were not present, but there were in attendance boys who "ran with" the older boys, the "gangs" as it were, and who on the other hand had a sense of larger responsibility. At first the statements of the boys were brief and valueless but presently one boy made a statement which the others challenged, and at once five boys were on their feet. In fact the main difficulty during the last half of the meeting was to keep only one boy talking at a time. The boys repeatedly made statements that would be challenged, and would be followed by explanations. The frankness of boys was never more evident than at this conference. Problem parents, problem teachers, gang raids, the police, community disinterest – all these came in for discussion. Restless energy seeking expression in unorganized and disorganized ways wherever organized procedure is not adequately provided sums up the findings of this interview.

Note-taking is a special problem at the discussion type of group interview. In itself it has a strong inhibitory effect, and yet, the conversation as it moves back and forth from individual to individual is so shifting that it is almost impossible to recall fully afterward. The solution that proved best was for the interviewer to keep a few of the slips of paper in his hand upon which the four questions had been typed and given to each one present. It was feasible to jot down from time to time among these questions the necessary "catchwords."

The success of the group interview depends in part on the relation of the leader to the group. If he is one whom all know and have confidence in and who is scientific and considerate in methods of presentation, good results may be expected. If he is relatively unknown and arbitrary, then nothing of value will result. If the chairman is a teacher and the group is a class – in a university, a lodge, a labor union, a church, then he has definite claim on the membership for work. If the relationship is such that the chairman ordinarily makes "assignments," then the "group interview" may naturally be substituted for an assignment. The greater the continuity of the relationship between leader and group the better the group interview results. Where a group has simply been called together for the purpose of the interview, failure is likely to occur.

A group of persons in early maturity respond to a group interview more satisfactorily than older persons who have too many "reserve mechanisms." In a group interview with an audience of mature, public spirited leaders, it was found that they were more intent on "passing resolutions" than on digging up data scientifically; they were especially slow in disclosing their own experiences in any worth while way.

It is best to plan the group interview so that it can be completed while all are present. To allow the ordinary group to work out materials at home and "mail them in" produces only partially successful results. Other things intervene. The chief exception to this rule is found in the "continuity" groups, such as "classes" where a written-out statement of experience may be substituted for other work, or a "life-history" for a "term" paper.

In all group interviews the "experimental materials" need to be tried out carefully beforehand on one's self and collaborators. It is a gross waste of time and energy to submit an incompletely worked out project to a large group. Too much emphasis cannot be put on working out projects with exceedingly great care beforehand.

Notes

1. Of the Pacific Coast, 1923–25.
2. Of Los Angeles, 1925.

17

Studying Intergroup Relations Embedded in Organizations

Clayton P. Alderfer & Ken K. Smith

Introduction

Research in organizational behavior is frequently either "basic research," in which the aim is to increase general knowledge of human behavior in organizations, or "action research," in which the goal is to solve problems of specific organizations. While this division has resulted in fruitful advances, it has also tended to keep the separate schools from mutually beneficial exchanges. For example, the various "social technologies" used in action research might be utilized to generate basic-research data that are unavailable through more traditional research methods (Alderfer, 1977c). The purpose of this paper is to explain how action methods can enhance basic research on intergroup relations embedded in organizations.

Our approach addressed three related issues: (1) the theoretical nature of group and intergroup relations in organizations; (2) the methods researchers employ to study group and intergroup phenomena; and (3) the kind of data, and therefore the nature of understanding, that results from the methods employed. We assume that these three issues are related as shown in Figure 1.

In the diagram, methodology has a somewhat more central position than it is often given. Normally methodologists and philosophers of social science give primary attention to the dialogue between theory (abstraction) and data (concrete events); they often invoke the hypothetico-deductive method or some modification of it (Kaplan, 1964; Marx, 1965; Blalock, 1971). Frequently, they do not relate methodological tactics to the phenomena under study. But there is precedent within physical science and social science for relating methodology to the phenomena under study. Within physical science

Source: *Administrative Science Quarterly*, vol. 27, no. 1, 1982, pp. 35–65.

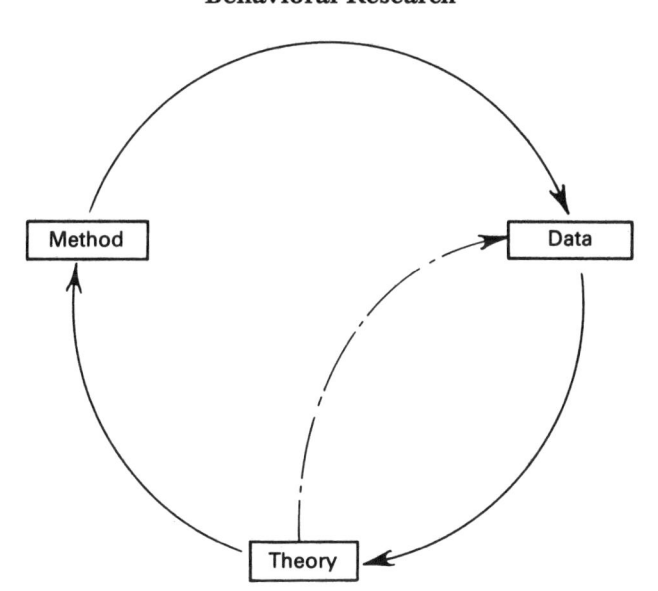

Figure 1: Interrelationships Among Theory, Method, and Data in Behavioral Research

there has been discussion of the importance of technological inventions in the development of theory (Conant, 1952; Kuhn, 1962). Reflecting on measurement problems in social science, Webb *et al.* (1966) suggested that, while some instruments we think of as "definitional" in physics reflect theoretical achievements, many measures in social science lack theoretical foundation.

Within behavioral science there is a tradition of research on research transactions. Among participant observers, there is an established body of literature that documents the researcher's role and the behavioral dynamics emanating from that role (Whyte, 1955; Adams and Preiss, 1960). Survey researchers have conducted systematic studies on the effects of interviews and of the interviewer's behavior on the respondent's answers (Hyman *et al.*, 1954). Experimental social psychologists have examined experimenter effects (Rosenthal, 1966; Rosenthal and Rosnow, 1968). Research in these three traditions documents the method's effect on the phenomena being studied. We want to point out that, despite their differences in method, these three areas all concerned the interpersonal relationship between investigator and respondent. It has been suggested (e.g., by Becker, 1967; Argyris, 1968; Sieber, 1973; Schuman and Hatchett, 1974; Douglas, 1976) that group and intergroup forces might affect research transactions, but no conceptual statements or methodological procedures have been available to help us deal explicitly with group and intergroup dynamics in field settings. This paper offers such statements and procedures and relates them to intergroup theory.

Our primary aim in this paper is to explain concretely what the theory → method → data cycle implies for the conduct of research about intergroup relations and organizations. In comparison with more conventional social research, we emphasize the significance of data collection methods. Techniques developed from experiential group dynamics and action research and modified for organizational research are central in this study. Of particular importance are the links between the theory of the phenomena being studied and the behavior of investigators who must interact with the phenomena in order to study it. We assume that researchers cannot escape entanglement with the phenomena they study. Our particular purpose here is to specify how one might reason about intergroup relations and organizations in order to study them more intensively and comprehensively than has been possible previously.[1]

We hope also to provide bases on which readers can assess the contribution of our orientation to research with organizations. Our core argument is that methodology provides access to specific kinds of data that call in turn for further elaboration of intergroup theory. We present data from two studies, both to illustrate the phenomena that the methods can reveal and to demonstrate how replication is accomplished. In total, this paper both describes and exemplifies the cycle of Figure 1.

An attitude toward research and learning, captured by two quotations, underlies this orientation. The first pertains to the relationship between the actions of investigators and their impulses to develop new theory. Joan Bazar, after reviewing Jay Haley's wide-ranging contributions, noted, "Haley, by this point realized that he had a set of procedures looking for a theory" (Bazar, 1979:6). The culture of social research rarely encourages researchers to act imaginatively in order to open new arenas in their thinking. The second quotation pertains to the quality of the relationship between investigators and respondents, too often called subjects, a term that tells careful listeners what investigators feel about the people who help them do their work. Erik Erikson (1964:229) provides the second proposition: "I have put it this way: one can study the nature of things by doing something *to* them, but one can really learn something about the essential nature of living beings only by doing something *with* them or for them" (emphasis his). Together these two propositions provide a sense of the underlying value position of this paper. We believe investigators can develop better theories about human behavior and organizations if they change their traditional research roles and if this change reflects a noncollusive respect rooted in mutual exchange between respondents and researchers.

The Nature of Groups and Intergroup Relations in Organizations

Understanding intergroup relations in organizations is a complex problem, the study of which can be traced to some of the earliest work in organizational behavior (Alderfer, 1977a; Alderfer *et al.*, 1982). Participant observer studies of intergroup relations in organizations were reported by Sayles and

Strauss (1953), Whyte (1955), Sayles (1958), Dalton (1959), Crozier (1964), and Strauss (1962, 1964). Social psychologists working in an experimental tradition have been especially influenced by Sherif and Sherif's (1969) series of field experiments and by Blake, Shepard, and Mouton's (1964) studies and application to managerial behavior. Tajfel (1970) carried out an extensive series of experiments on the effects of "group membership" (social categorization) on social perception and behavior, and Billig (1976) has recently written a book on the social psychology of intergroup relations. New interest in intergroup dynamics in organizations has also been stimulated by applied behavioral scientists who have attempted to use research results to change organizations (Burke, 1972; Lewicki and Alderfer, 1973; Alderfer and Brown, 1975; Alderfer, 1977b; Berg, 1977; Nadler, 1978; Alderfer *et al.*, 1980). The difficulties associated with doing field research on intergroup relations in organizations have been well documented in the methodological literature, but, until now, these difficulties have not been analyzed by explicit use of intergroup theory (cf. Kahn and Mann, 1952; Adams and Preiss, 1960; Becker, 1967; Merton, 1972; Kidder and Stewart, 1975).

The present section defines groups in organizations, gives a general framework for explaining intergroup dynamics in organizations, and explains the specifically methodological concept of microcosm group. These concepts provide the theoretical framework for reasoning about methodological procedures. In part, the ideas build upon well established concepts (e.g., ethnocentrism), and in part they represent departures from existing positions.

Groups in Organizations

Within the social psychology literature, there is no shortage of definitions of groups, but there is also no clear consensus among those who propose them (Cartwright and Zander, 1968). Because these definitions have largely depended on work done in laboratories by social psychologists studying internal properties of groups, they are limited in recognizing the external properties of groups. A definition of "groups in organizations" gives a more balanced attention to both internal and external properties (Alderfer, 1977a: 230):

A human group is a collection of individuals (1) who have significantly interdependent relations with each other, (2) who perceive themselves as a group by reliably distinguishing members from nonmembers, (3) whose group identity is recognized by nonmembers,[2] (4) who, as group members acting alone or in concert, have significantly interdependent relations with other groups, and (5) whose roles in the group are therefore a function of expectations from themselves, from other group members, and from nongroup members.[3]

This conceptualization of a group makes every individual member into a group representative whenever he or she deals with members of other groups, and it treats every transaction among individuals as, in part, an intergroup event (Rice, 1969; Smith, 1977).

Intergroup Relations in Organizations

Every organization consists of a large number of groups, and every organizational member represents a number of these groups when dealing with other people in the organization. The groups in an organization can be divided into two broad classes: identity groups and organizational groups. An identity group may be thought of as one whose members share some common biological characteristic (such as sex), have participated in equivalent historical experiences (such as migration), are subjected currently to certain social forces (such as unemployment), and as a result have similar world views. When people enter organizations, they bring along their identity groups, which are based on variables such as ethnicity, sex, age, and family.[4] An organizational group may be conceived of as a group whose members share approximately common organizational positions, participate in equivalent work experiences, and consequently have similar organizational views. Organizations assign members to organizational groups according to division of labor and hierarchy of authority. One critical factor in intergroup relations in organizations is that membership in identity groups is not independent from membership in organizational groups. Certain organizational groups tend to be filled by members of particular identity groups. In the United States, for example, positions in upper management tend to be held by older white males, and certain other positions tend to be held by females and minorities (Loring and Wells, 1972; Purcell and Cavanagh, 1972).

Both identity groups and organizational groups fit the five criteria of the definition of a human group. First, there are significant interdependencies between identity-group members because of their common historical experiences and between organizational group members because of their equivalent work or organizational experiences. Second, members of either group can reliably distinguish themselves from nonmembers on the basis of common historical experience or common location in the organization. However, the precision of this identification process depends on the permeability of group boundaries, which refers to the ease with which boundaries can be crossed and members can enter and leave groups. This applies equally to the next characteristic. Third, nonmembers are able to recognize members. The fourth and fifth aspects of the definition are highly linked when applied to identity and organizational groups. When they relate to individuals from other groups, group members may be more or less aware of the extent to which they are acting as, or being seen as, group representatives. Each person belongs to a number of identity groups and organizational groups. At any moment he or she may be a member of a large number of these groups simultaneously. The group that is made focal at a particular moment will depend on the representation from other groups and on what issues are critical in the current intergroup exchanges. A white person in a predominantly black organization, for example, can rarely escape representing white people in some way, no matter what her or his preference is. But if that white person is in a predominantly white organization, he or she will probably be seen as representing instead some other group, such as a particular hierarchical level. Rarely are individuals "just people" when they act in organizations. When there are no other group representatives present, individuals may experience themselves as "just people" in the context of their own group membership, but this will quickly disappear when the individual is placed in a multiple group setting. How group members relate to each other within their groups, as a function of their own and others' expectations, is highly dependent on the nature of the intergroup forces active at that time.

Research on intergroup relations has identified a number of characteristics of intergroup relations that do not depend on the particular groups or the specific setting where the relationship occurs (Sumner, 1906; Coser, 1956; Blake, Shepard, and Mouton, 1964; Sherif and Sherif, 1969; Levine and Campbell, 1972; Van den Bergh, 1972; Deutsch, 1973; Kidder and Stewart, 1975; Billig, 1976; Alderfer, 1976a, 1980b). These include:

1. *Group boundaries.* Both physical and psychological group boundaries determine group membership. Transactions among groups are regulated by variations in the permeability of the boundaries (Alderfer, 1977b).

2. *Power differences.* The types of resources that can be obtained and used differ among groups (Lasswell and Kaplan, 1950). The variety of dimensions on which there are power differences and the degree of discrepancy among groups influence the degree of boundary permeability among groups.

3. *Affective patterns.* The permeability of group boundaries varies with the polarization of feeling among the groups, that is, it varies with the degree to which group members associate mainly positive feelings with their own group and mainly negative feelings with other groups (Sumner, 1906; Coser, 1956; Levine and Campbell, 1972).

4. *Cognitive formations, including "distortions."* As a function of group boundaries, power differences, and affective patterns, groups tend to develop their own language (or elements of language, including social categories), condition their members' perceptions of objective and subjective phenomena, and transmit sets of propositions – including theories and ideologies – to explain the nature of experiences encountered by members and to influence relations with other groups (Sherif and Sherif, 1969; Blake, Shepard, and Mouton, 1964; Tajfel, 1970; Billig, 1976).[5]

5. *Leadership behavior.* The behavior of group leaders and representatives reflects boundary permeability, power differences, affective patterns, and cognitive formations of their group in relation to other groups. The behavior of group representatives, including formally designated leaders, is both cause and effect of the total pattern of intergroup relations in a particular situation.

Concept of Microcosm Groups

As researchers, we can ask what methodologies are available for observing and studying intergroups in action. One technique directly derivable from intergroup theory is to create an organizationally based group in which representatives of the salient groups are present. This is called a microcosm group. In order for it to be a real group, the microcosm group must have an organizationally valid task. The most appropriate task for the microcosm group, which is created for research purposes, is to shape and monitor the research process on behalf of the organization as a whole. The task may include regulating the boundaries between the researcher and the organization, managing power differences between research and organizational processes, monitoring affective patterns, correcting cognitive distortions, and making the research activity beneficial for both the organization and the researchers.

The concept of microcosm group follows directly from the definition of groups in organizations and from the characteristics of intergroup relations in organizations. Using the proposition that all individuals are group representatives, the microcosm group may be designed to show the relations among the groups in or among organizations through the interpersonal relationships of its members (Alderfer, 1977b). The boundary permeability, power differences, affective patterns, cognitive formations, and leadership behavior found in the microcosm group may then be interpreted, in part, as mirroring the analogous dynamics of the larger organization. (Searles, 1955; Steele, 1975; Cooper, 1976; Doehrman, 1976; Sachs and Shapiro, 1976; Alderfer, 1976b, 1977b; Alderfer *et al.*, 1982).

Since the purpose of creating a microcosm group is to have a structure that will allow observation of particular intergroup relationships within or among organizations, it is necessary that the membership of the microcosm group be such that, first, the definitional requirements of a group in general are met, and, second, the critical intergroup processes within the group can be observed. For example, if an organization is experiencing interracial conflict, the microcosm group should include the major parties of the conflict in sufficient numbers and in balanced proportion so that no one subgroup of group representatives feels its perspective is significantly simplified or obscured. Or, if labor management issues are prominent, then representatives of these groups should be included in the microcosm group in the same way. No single microcosm group, however, can adequately reflect all possible intergroup relations in an organization. Researchers and members of the organization must decide together which group relations are of primary interest and must then compose the microcosm group accordingly.

Methods for Intergroup Research

According to the three-step process for conducting research, methods and procedures may be derived from theoretical propositions and may also represent experiential tests of the concepts in action. In this section, we specify six steps that can be taken to conduct intergroup research with organizations: (1)

preliminary interviews, (2) microcosm group formation, (3) group and intergroup interviews, (4) organic questionnaire development and pretesting, (5) questionnaire administration, and (6) feedback to the microcosm groups. Research generally proceeds in this order, but it may not be possible or desirable to complete all six steps, depending on the circumstances of the investigation, especially on the condition of the organization and the nature of the intergroup relations.

Preliminary Interviews

The researcher first conducts a series of interviews with individuals who are members of the groups that might be studied. These preliminary interviews consist of both open-ended questions that give the researcher information about group and intergroup life in the system and specific questions designed to elicit the names of individuals who would be able to provide complementary perspectives.

When intergroup dynamics are alive in a system (it is rare when they are not), simple questions tend to produce very rich responses, providing that the researcher can assure confidentiality and develop mutual respect between researcher and respondent. This process can be begun in meetings held before the interviews, in which potential respondents can meet the researcher and hear about the purpose of the study.

The preliminary interviews rapidly educate the researcher about the intergroup issues in the system. The researcher is then able to shape the content of future questions, understand important information about power relations of the groups being studied, and thereby set parameters for composing a microcosm group.

Microcosm-Group Formation

Parameters for microcosm groups are developed through negotiation between researchers and organizational members. It must be determined, in general, whether organizational groups or identity groups or both are to be the primary focus of the study. Then it must be determined which specific intergroup relations are to be investigated. Since the most information will be available about the set of intergroup relations around which the microcosm group is formed, the microcosm group's membership should be chosen both to heighten and to keep manageable the salient intergroup processes.

Decisions about establishing the membership may be made by the researcher, or the researcher may choose to rely upon existing norms in the system to form the group. Microcosm group members should be volunteers who want to engage in the research enterprise. Volunteering is important because the kind of motivation necessary to make this method work effectively cannot be reduced solely by one's peers through election, by one's boss through the chain of command, or by one's knowledge of the researchers' prestige.

As a general rule, a microcosm group should not have more than twelve members, or the effects of size will interfere with members' ability to interact face-to-face. The formation of microcosm-group boundaries is helped if the existence of the group is made public. To keep the group boundaries permeable, provision should be made both for interaction between the microcosm group and other organizational units, and for periodic rotation of members. If there are significant power differences among the groups being studied, then the numbers of people from each group should not merely mirror the organization conditions. The people from each subgroup within the microcosm group will influence the behavior, cognition, and feelings of the group members, and significant numerical imbalances will result in a suppression of important intergroup data (cf. Kanter, 1977). Dominant groups will control the information available from less dominant groups, or the less dominant groups will withhold information out of fear of retaliation by the more dominant groups. Depending on the potency of the power differences, it may be appropriate to include approximately equal numbers of people from each group, or to include more members from the less powerful groups. The composition of the microcosm group may change during the research, depending on the duration of the study. If an adequate power balance is achieved within the microcosm group, then events in the group will provide insights about effective patterns, cognitive formations, and leadership behavior in the particular intergroup relationship that is being studied. These insights are largely unavailable by any other systematic means.

In the theory of intergroup relations in organizations, group boundaries, power differences, affective patterns, cognitive formations, and leadership behavior are interdependent variables. Thus, forming a microcosm group changes the group boundaries of the parent system. Also, adjusting the proportional representation in a group so that it is different from the proportions of the larger system is a change. Another change occurs when investigators take leadership roles in the transactions between organizational members and data collectors. These are but three examples of how the process of studying an organization using intergroup methods changes the organization. The first two exemplify changes that are unique to the present methodology, but the third is shared with virtually all methods of social research. In general, studying an organization means changing it, however unintended or slight the change may be. The methods described here make the process of this change more explicit than do more conventional methods, and they provide a theory that can be used to reason about the changes and to balance the costs and benefits of various types of changes.

The philosopher Berkeley posed what seemed in his time to be an imponderable philosophical problem. If a tree fell in a forest and no one was present to hear the noise, was sound associated with the falling tree? In Berkeley's time, there were no tape recorders. If we now imagine all forests populated with tape recorders, what was once primarily a philosophical problem becomes much more of a technical problem. A similar point applies to designing microcosm groups for organizational research. If the research problem implies that the power dynamics of the system may keep certain affective patterns and cognitive formations suppressed unless the subgroup proportions in the microcosm group are adjusted, the methodology provides a means to do this. According to the theory, the adjustment in proportions will produce data about cognition and affect that are otherwise unobtainable, but it will change organizational behavior in the process. Intergroup methodology gives access to information otherwise unavailable, but it does so only within limits of uncertainty similar to those posed by Heisenberg in his quantum mechanics (Cline, 1965: 169-171; Alderfer and Brown, 1975: 212-214).

In using this microcosm-group methodology, we recognize that researchers also represent a variety of groups. Intergroup theory assumes that researchers, like members of the organization, have their own biases due to their set of relevant group experiences. Correction for the biases, a fundamental principle for all scientific investigation, is, therefore, a matter not of striving for objectivity but of providing a means for complementary and conflicting biases to be observed and understood. The microcosm group is one potent means of revealing the alternative cognitive formations not only among organizational members but also between organizational members and researchers.

Group and Intergroup Interviews

After the microcosm group is formed and its role in the research is clear to all members, or when it becomes clear that a microcosm group cannot be formed, the intergroup issues in the system can be explored in depth and detail by means of group and intergroup interviews. Interviews begin with microcosm-group members and, if it is necessary to broaden or deepen understanding of particular phenomena, they extend to others in the system. In this way, data from the microcosm group may be complemented by data obtained from other individuals and groups, or lack of a microcosm group can be corrected.

The group interviewer must not only be concerned about her or his relationship with the respondents, but must also be concerned about the respondents' relationships to each other and about the intergroup forces operating on these relationships. All three of these relationships will influence the data.

The optimal number of people for a group interview is six to eight, a size that is large enough to induce effects of group dynamics and small enough to minimize competition for air time. The simplest form of group interview brings together people with a common identity group or organization group but without a hierarchical relationship to one another. The group interviewer opens the session by explaining the purposes of the session, the basis for composing the group, the problem of confidentiality, and how she or he hopes the group will work together.

The group interview poses special problems of confidentiality. In the individual interview, the interviewer can guarantee confidentiality and the respondent must only decide whether he or she can trust the professional integrity of the interviewer. In a group interview, the willingness of each respondent to observe confidentiality must be determined as well. To deal with this problem, the group interviewer should address the issue at the beginning of the session and ask the people whether they would be willing to agree to treat what will be said in the interviews confidentially. Generally, respondents are quite willing to make and keep this agreement. If a respondent is unwilling, the interviewer should thank the respondent for her or his honesty and then point out to the others that they should answer the questions, bearing in mind that the material may not be treated confidentially. Making the issue explicit also alerts respondents to the possibility that some of their peers may make the commitment but may not keep it.

The group interview may aid or impede learning about feelings and cognitions. For each question, there is the possibility that everyone in the group will answer and thus indicate the degree of consensus and dissensus. By hearing the responses of someone else, respondents may be stimulated to say things that they either would not think of or would not be willing to share in an individual interview. Some people, however, become uncomfortable in a group situation. They may say nothing at all, or they may attempt to answer every question decisively and thereby discourage others from giving their views. The group interviewer can manage this situation by saying that she or he is interested in hearing from all who wish to speak, wants to learn about points of agreement and disagreement, and does not require the group to reach agreement on any issue. If the group develops a pattern of allowing only a few people to speak, the group interviewer can comment on the pattern without naming names, and can remind the group that he or she is interested in hearing from everyone who wishes to speak.

The group interviewer can also observe the behavior of respondents. When the group is composed of people who share a common fate in the organization (e.g., tellers in a bank, or black male managers), then the interview provides data on the internal dynamics of the group. When an intergroup interview is composed of approximately equal numbers from each of two groups, the interview provides data about the external as well as the internal relations of the groups.

An intergroup interview is a more complex behavioral phenomenon than is a group interview. Depending on the intergroup relationship being studied, it might be appropriate to have a team of interviewers instead of an individual interviewer. For example, if the intergroup context were based on race, the interviewing team should consist of one member from each race. It might also be appropriate for various members of a research team to conduct group interviews according to the team member's group memberships.

A group or intergroup interview is similar to a microcosm-group meeting, except that the microcosm group typically represents more than two groups, meets repeatedly, and expresses changing relations among groups in the system over time. A group or intergroup interview is analogous to a carefully focused snapshot, and a microcosm group is analogous to a moving picture.

Nevertheless, in designing and conducting both intergroup interviews and microcosm groups, researchers should understand and apply intergroup theory.

Organic Questionnaire Development and Pretesting

An organic questionnaire is a questionnaire that is drawn up with regard to the language and culture of the group to which it will be administered (Alderfer and Brown, 1972). In contrast, a standardized questionnaire is one that is administered to diverse groups without regard to their languages and cultures. The organic questionnaire is based on the ideas and feelings uncovered during the preliminary individual interviews, during microcosm-group sessions, and during group and intergroup interviews. The organic questionnaire consists of a series of statements made by organizational members that respondents rate according to one or more of the standard response scales. An organic questionnaire provides a means for groups in a system to have their perspectives in their own language incorporated into the research. This methodological technique recognizes and incorporates the different cognitive formations characteristic of intergroup life.

The chief advantage of the organic questionnaire over standardized questionnaires is that it enhances the involvement of respondents and decreases the psychological distance between researchers and respondents. The major disadvantage is that the organic questionnaire is expensive, since a unique questionnaire must be developed for each intergroup study. Using an organic questionnaire also has epistemological implications. The methodology does not permit researchers to accumulate empirical generalizations based on administration of the same instrument in diverse settings. Replicability and generalizability of findings depend instead on the repeated use of the full intergroup research process.

The microcosm group plays an important role by pretesting each organic questionnaire after it is drafted. Members of the group complete the questionnaire and discuss their reactions. These discussions are inevitably valuable for improving the instrument so that it will clearly permit respondents from diverse groups to express their views. In several experiences with organic instruments, we have learned how blind standard instruments can be to local cultural conditions. In one case, for example, we found that each of several work groups had no single name that was known in all other groups. These many named groups had to be listed on the questionnaire by several names so that they could be recognized by the members of all other groups. This phenomenon is what one would expect from intergroup theory, but it is largely unrecognized by most people who use standard questionnaires.

Questionnaire Administration

Questionnaires are most effectively administered in sessions containing about 20 people. By intergroup theory, a relevant microcosm-group member should be present to help verify the history of the research process and answer questions from members of their own groups. A questionnaire is a transaction across group boundaries between a researcher who is an outsider and respondents who are insiders. All the forces that are present in any intergroup transaction, and that lead to the transmission of distorted information, will be present in a questionnaire session. The presence of microcosm-group members in the session makes the boundary between researcher and organization more permeable. Microcosm-group members have contributed ideas to the instrument, taken the questionnaire themselves, and helped to improve it as an effective means for people to report organizational conditions. They understand what the instrument is trying to measure, and they will have determined whether they can trust the researcher. Their communication of these impressions helps the research transaction.

The exact role of microcosm-group members in questionnaire sessions should be subject to negotiation. There may even be situations in which microcosm-group members should not attend questionnaire sessions (cf. Alderfer *et al.*, 1980) because of particular intergroup dynamics. In general, however, each questionnaire session is a unique intergroup event, the design of which can be significantly improved through the participation of the microcosm group.

Feedback to the Microcosm Group

The microcosm group can be very helpful in developing concepts that enrich the meaning of the data that has been gathered. The principles and technologies of data feedback (Chesler and Flanders, 1967; Miles *et al.*, 1969; Argyris, 1970; Heller, 1970; Brown, 1972; Alderfer and Holbrook, 1973; Nadler, 1977; Alderfer, 1980a) should be used to shape the way the data are shared with the microcosm group. For some data, it is appropriate that the microcosm group first be broken into its smaller identity or organizational subgroups and then be given the data. For other data, it is appropriate that all microcosm-group members examine the data simultaneously so that the forces operating through the intergroup representation are made apparent. In early stages of the feedback process, participants invariably focus on their concern about the validity of the data (Neff, 1965). Researchers, too, must be concerned about the validity of their findings. In later stages, both respondents and investigators become concerned with what the findings indicate about the phenomena being studied.

The microcosm group provides a safe and contained setting in which to explore fruitfully the validity and the meaning of the data. Should conflicts arise, commitments made among members during the formation of the microcosm group can help members understand and manage the conflicts constructively.

The microcosm group's struggling with the research findings may help generate insights about how the data expresses unexplored group boundaries, organizational power relationships, identity group and organizational group memberships, subtle differences in cognitive formations, and covert affective patterns. Knowledge of these variables will significantly help in the development of theories and concepts that extend beyond easily observable data.[6]

Variations in Use of Specific Techniques

Although six steps in the intergroup research process are specified here, all six are not always appropriate for every study. Prevailing intergroup conditions may make it too costly to form a microcosm group. The alternative would be for researchers to develop a series of relationships with individuals who represent the various groups in the system but who never meet as a group (Alderfer, 1976a). Even if the microcosm group can be formed, group and intergroup interviews may not be necessary if the system is not excessively complex. If the microcosm group cannot be formed, then group and intergroup interviews may provide the best approximation to the knowledge that would have been available from the microcosm group. The responses to the organic questionnaire can be studied with a more efficient quantitative analysis of intergroup variables than can be applied to either behavioral observations or interviews. However, even a questionnaire specifically tailored to the organization may not be appropriate if a substantial proportion of the respondents are illiterate, or if the activity of composing organic items would be experienced as a severe threat by some units in the system. The six steps provide a logical sequence for generating data about intergroup relations in and among organizations. The degree to which the full sequence should or could be used depends on the intergroup relations being studied.

The major gain from using this methodology is that the quality of data and the depth of understanding of intergroup dynamics in organizations are increased. When using this methodology, researchers have access to information that is usually not uncovered when using more conventional methods. In contrast with other methods, this one permits a thoroughness of exchange between investigators and respondents that gives both an opportunity to correct biases. This results in a more comprehensive theoretical understanding of organizations. Researchers become more familiar with the underlying dynamics of the systems they study, and they become more aware of the effects of their own group memberships on their functioning as investigators. People who use these methods tend to become more aware of the limitations of conventional methods in producing data, an insight that develops from understanding the impact of intergroup relations on organizational dynamics.

But these gains do not come without costs. Investigators cannot achieve this greater depth of understanding without having greater skill in working with human systems and without taking more time to establish and maintain relationships with respondents. Intergroup methods also call for a greater commitment from participating groups and organizations. If the investigators should prove to exploit the respondents, both parties will tend to learn the effects sooner and face the consequences more completely. When using these methods, both investigators and respondents become more powerful in relation to one another and can therefore help or hurt each other more than when more conventional methods are used. Thus both the technical and ethical demands on investigators who use these methods are substantial.

Illustrative Studies

The methodology described in this paper has been used in several empirical studies. Those investigations have provided an empirical basis for sharpening the conceptualization of the method, for testing the method's utility in a variety of contexts, and for generating advances in a general theory of intergroups in organizations. This section describes two of these studies and provides illustrative results.

The two studies were selected to parallel the distinction between organizational groups and identity groups in intergroup theory. Study 1 dealt primarily with the functional and hierarchical dimensions of organizational groups. Study 2 pertained to identity-group dynamics in race relations between black managers and white managers. A fuller account of the microcosm group and its role in the two studies is provided elsewhere (Alderfer, 1977a; Alderfer *et al.*, 1980).

Three theoretical issues were examined in each study. These issues were not selected a priori; they arose during the use of intergroup methods. The first issue is the nature and quality of daily work-based interpersonal relationships among individuals who belonged to different groups. Studies of this issue indicated how intergroup forces influence work relations among organizational members. The second issue is how the group members experience and perceive the effects of outside groups on their work relations. An examination of this issue showed how additional groups within the organization influence the dynamics of the primary intergroup relationship, and it provided part of an empirical basis for understanding "intergroup context." The third issue concerns elements of the dynamics of power in each intergroup relationship. The data provided from a study of this issue showed the effects of social-system dynamics on the intergroup relations.

These issues span three levels of analysis. The first issue focuses on relationships among *individuals* who represent different task groups. The second examines the effect of exogenous groups on the primary intergroup relationship being examined. The third shows the effects of a larger *social system* on the intergroup relationship in question.

Study 1: Task Groups on a Workflow

This study examined the intergroup dynamics among task groups in the 250-person Drawing Division of a large corporation. The major task of the Drawing

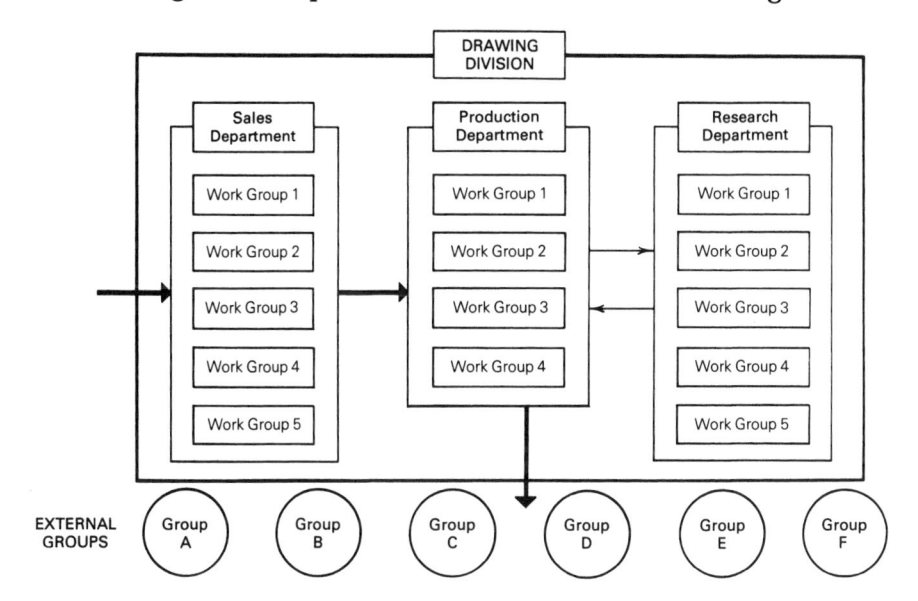

Figure 2: Simplified Workflow Schematic for Setting

Division was to produce the engineering drawings needed to install electronic equipment. A large proportion of the customer requests that came to the division were routine and could be filled from the division files, which contained standard prints. The division was also responsible for the orders that required custom designs.

The division had three major departments, which here we call Sales, Production, and Research. Each department was further divided into work groups that included labor and management. Sales had approximately 74 employees in five work groups; Production had about 123 employees in four work groups; and Research had about 53 employees in five work groups. Routine orders were received by the Sales Department, which verified or clarified all necessary information and then passed the orders to Production. Production then obtained the appropriate drawings and sent them to the Manufacturing Division, a group outside the division which was responsible for making the equipment. Nonroutine orders involved the Research Department. If the Production Department did not have an appropriate drawing on file, it would contact the Research Department which would create the drawing. Production would add a copy of the new drawing to its files and pass the drawing on to the Manufacturing Division. To accomplish their tasks, it was necessary for Drawing-Division members to interact with a variety of other divisions in addition to the Manufacturing Division. Figure 2 diagrams a simplified workflow of the system.

A microcosm group was developed. It included eight people from labor and three from management, and all major work groups were represented. There were five women and six men; of the total, two were black, and nine were white. Both union and management endorsed the study.

Table 1: Mean Percentage of Employees Summed across Work Groups within Each Department Requiring Contact with Other Departments*

Department Reporting Contact	Department Requiring Contact[†]		
	Sales	Production	Research
Sales	55	26	8
Production	26	40	28
Research	12	19	34

* Means were computed by summing across the percentages computed for each work group within the department.
[†] The interaction between department reporting contact and department requiring contact was highly significant (analysis of variance, $p < .001$). Main effects were not significant.

The first phase of the analysis was to determine how much interaction among the various groups was necessary for people to do their work. The organic-questionnaire item designed to measure contacts among members of groups inside the Drawing Division was: "Listed below are the names of all work groups within the Drawing Division, subdivided by department. Place an 'X' in front of those work groups with whom you must relate in order to do your work."

The results are presented in Table 1. The pattern is very clear. In each department, contact was highest among members of internal work groups and next highest among members of the departments immediately adjacent

Table 2: Mean Percentage of Employees Summed across Work Groups within Each Department Requiring Contact with Outside Departments

Outside Department Receiving Contact*	Department Requiring Contact		
	Sales	Production	Research
A[†]	18	40	42
B[‡]	18	39	50
C[‡]	61	29	52
D	65	62	52
E[‡]	42	8	8
F[‡]	26	29	60

* This list was composed by taking the three most frequently contacted groups for each department.
[†] χ^2 for difference among departments, $p < .05$.
[‡] χ^2 for difference among departments, $p < .001$ Note: In this and in subsequent tables, the χ^2 statistic is used to compare distributions of responses between groups. Percentages are reported in the tables to aid interpretation of the data.

STUDYING INTERGROUP RELATIONS EMBEDDED IN ORGANIZATIONS 303

on the workflow. Members of departments at the beginning and end of the workflow reported the least amount of contact with each other.

The organic-questionnaire item designed to measure contact with groups outside the Drawing Division was: "Listed below are the names of a large number of work groups outside the Drawing Division with whom members of the division must work. Place an 'X' in front of the names of those departments with which you must work."

Table 2 presents the results of this measure. Of the six most frequently contacted groups outside the division, only one does not show a statistically significant difference across the three departments within the division. The other five external groups had many contacts with one or two departments inside the division. These results suggest that most work groups interacted with Department D and that each department had a unique pattern of relations with other external groups.

Respondents were next asked to rate the quality of the contacts between groups inside and groups outside the division. Scales consisting of three items were used. For the measure of "task" variables, respondents were asked to rate the accuracy, timeliness, and completeness of their work. For the measure of "relationship" variables, respondents were asked to rate the way another group's supervision interacts with the respondent's group, the way

Figure 3: Mean Perceived Severity of Task and Relationship Problems for Inside and Outside Groups

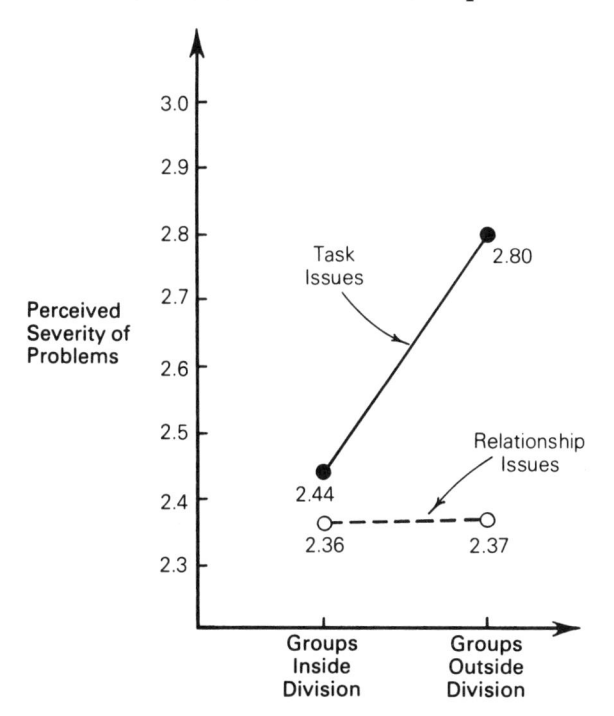

supervision of the respondent's group interacts with the other group, and the ability of the other group to understand the problem of the respondent's group. The respondents were asked to rate their reaction to each of these items on a five-point scale in which 5 was "always a problem." Respondents rated the groups inside and the groups outside the division with whom they had to interact most in order to do their work.

Figure 3 shows the mean severity of problems from the inside and outside groups as perceived by individuals in the division as a result of analysis of variance. Groups inside the division were associated with less severe problems then were groups outside the division ($p < .05$), and task issues were associated with more severe problems than were relationship issues ($p < .001$). There was a significant interaction between group location and type of problem ($p < .001$). The difference in severity between task problems and relationship problems was greater for groups outside the division than for groups inside the division.

These results show the effects of task-group forces being expressed in the interpersonal relationships between people in different locations in the work flow.

The Drawing Division brought together two different professional disciplines. The Sales Department was identified with customer service. Its objective was to meet customer needs at the lowest possible cost. The Production Department and the Research Department were identified with engineering. Their objective was to develop the best possible technical solution for customer problems. Although the existence of the Drawing Division testified to the need for bringing the two professional disciplines together, the interviews revealed that the major political struggle in the division was due to members' perceptions of discrimination between the disciplines with regard to allocation of scarce resources (i.e., people, pay, promotions) at both the division and corporate levels.

Four items were designed to assess members' perceptions of favoritism toward particular groups:

1. In the division, groups oriented toward customer service occupy a position of favor relative to other groups.
2. In the corporation as a whole, engineering occupies a position of favor relative to other groups.
3. In the division, groups oriented toward engineering occupy a position of favor relative to other groups.
4. In the corporation as a whole, groups oriented toward customer service occupy a position of favor relative to other groups.

Respondents answered these items using a six-point scale that ranged from "strongly agree" to "strongly disagree"; there was no midpoint on the scale. Mean perceived degree of favoritism was derived from the sums of items 1 and 4 for customer service and 2 and 3 for engineering. Figure 4

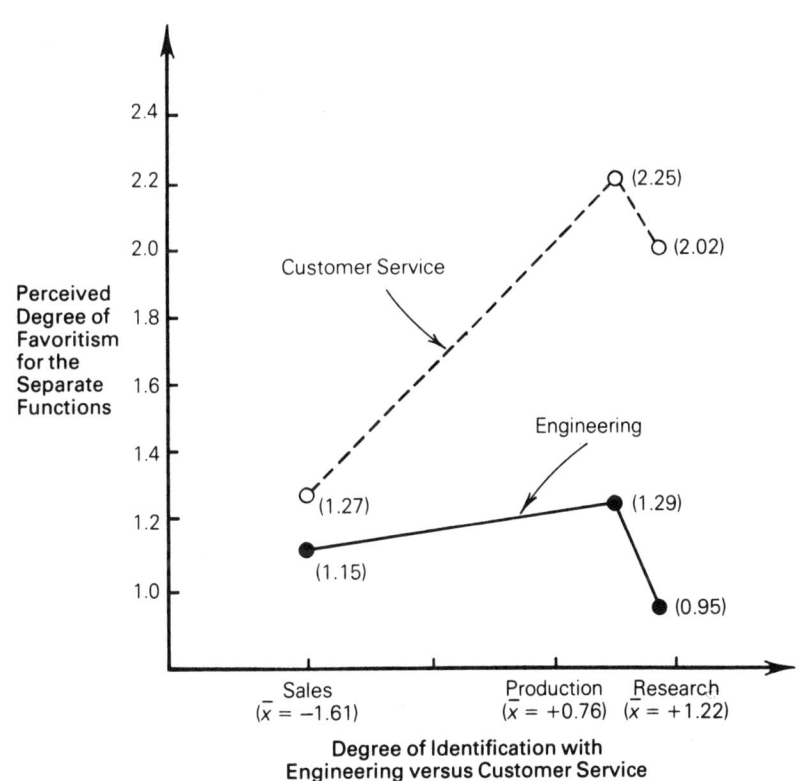

Figure 4: Mean Perceived Favoritism for Sales and Engineering by District Groups

[Figure 4: A graph plotting Perceived Degree of Favoritism for the Separate Functions (y-axis, ranging from 1.0 to 2.4) against Degree of Identification with Engineering versus Customer Service (x-axis). Three district groups are plotted: Sales ($\bar{x} = -1.61$), Production ($\bar{x} = +0.76$), and Research ($\bar{x} = +1.22$). Customer Service line (dashed): values 1.27, 2.25, 2.02. Engineering line (solid): values 1.15, 1.29, 0.95.]

Note: The placement of the three district groups on the horizontal axis was determined by the difference between the group's score on identification with engineering minus its score on identification with customer service.

shows the results of analysis of variance. Customer service was perceived to be more favored than engineering ($p < .001$). There was also an interaction between department and discipline such that customer service was perceived to be substantially more favored than engineering by Production and Research than by Sales ($p < .01$).

Figure 5 shows the means of the four separate items based on an analysis of variance, with data from the three departments pooled. As the level of analysis changes from division to corporation, the perceived advantage of customer service over engineering increases ($p < .01$). This shows that organizational power based outside the division affects how the work groups perceive each other.

This workflow study showed that intergroup effects operated at the three levels of analysis, the interpersonal, the exogenous groups (division), and the social system (corporation). At each level, there were effects that we had not

Figure 5: Mean Perceived Favoritism for Sales and Engineering at Division and Corporate Levels

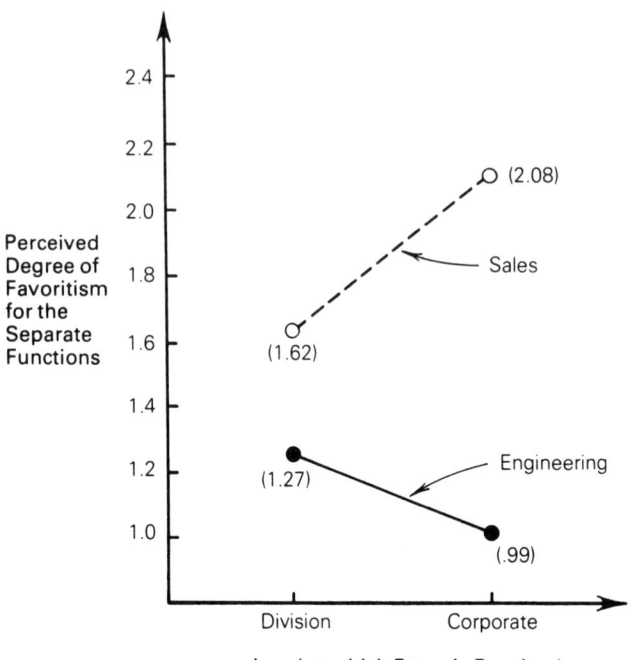

[Figure 5: Line graph with y-axis "Perceived Degree of Favoritism for the Separate Functions" ranging from 1.0 to 2.4, and x-axis "Level at which Favor is Received" showing Division and Corporate. Sales line (dashed) rises from (1.62) at Division to (2.08) at Corporate. Engineering line (solid) falls from (1.27) at Division to (.99) at Corporate.]

seen before. Of special importance were the notable nonlinear differences between more micro- and more macro-units.

Data on task and relationship issues are common in small group studies, but almost no attention has been paid to the intersection of these issues in intergroup research. The effects of exogeneous groups on the dynamics of intergroup relations on a common workflow have not been considered in any research literature known to us. The effects of larger-system forces on the perceptions by work-group members of resource allocation also have not been discussed in the empirical literature, to our knowledge, although these findings are clearly related to other studies of power in organizations (Pfeffer and Salancik, 1974; Pfeffer and Moore, 1980).

Study 2: Race Relations in Management

This was a study of the approximately 2,000 managers of a 13,000-person business corporation, here named the XYZ Company. Microcosm-group members included six black managers and six white managers. The group represented four levels of management and a variety of departments and geographical locations. In each race, there were equal numbers of men and women. The research team consisted of a black female and a white female, and a black male and a white male.

The procedures used in the first study were followed in this study. All black managers in the company, and a 30-percent random sample of the white managers, were invited to attend organic-questionnaire sessions. Of the 815 managers invited, 676 attended (an 83-percent response rate) and completed the same questionnaire. Managers attended questionnaire sessions with others of the same race and sex and, when possible, of the same management level. This particular design was evolved as a result of conversations between the research team and the microcosm group. Three hundred fifty-one white males, 185 white females, 61 black males, and 79 black females completed the questionnaire.

Table 3 presents items describing qualities of face-to-face race relations as perceived by the four race/sex groups. A higher percentage of blacks than of whites reported that they had serious conversations about race, both with members of their own race and with members of the other races. Each racial group reported that members of the other group socialized more with each other than with members of the other race, and each racial group tended to see this pattern as weaker in its own group than in the other group. On balance, blacks evaluated the quality of one-to-one black–white relationships more nega-

Table 3: Perceptions of Face-to-Face Relations among Black Managers and White Managers

Questionnaire Items and Responses	White males	White females	Black males	Black females
I have serious conversations about racial issues with XYZ* people of my own racial background.† (Often, very often)	7	6	54	51
I talk about race relations with XYZ people who are of a different race than mine.† (Often, very often)	7	11	21	17
Blacks socialize mainly with other blacks regardless of job level.† (Strongly agree, agree, mildly agree)	84	82	77	70
Whites socialize mainly with other whites regardless of job level.† (Strongly agree, agree, mildly agree)	84	71	89	81
Good one-on-one black–white relationships are common in XYZ.† (Strongly agree, agree, mildly agree)	74	84	40	59

Percentage Responding Positively

* XYZ is a fictitious name for the corporation.
† Differences among race–gender groups $p < .01$ by χ^2.
Note: Percentages are used in Tables 3, 4, and 5 to show clearly the potency of race effects on intergroup perceptions. Task group effects, while statistically significant, were not as "obviously" potent.

tively than did whites. These data show intergroup forces being expressed in the interpersonal relationships between black and white organizational members.

In the next stage of this study, influences of group-level issues on the racial intergroups in the XYZ Company were addressed. While working with the microcosm group, the research team discovered the existence of two "interest groups" that affected race relations among XYZ managers. The first was the Black Managers' Association, and the second was the Foremen's Club. Each of these organizational groups had a formal structure, met regularly by itself, and had a legitimized basis for periodic meetings with top management in the company. Although the Foremen's Club did not formally restrict its membership to white people, it recruited very few black members. People could remember only one black officer in the club, and he "did not last long," as one white person said in an interview. The Black Managers' Association did restrict its membership to black people, although there was a running debate among the members as to whether this was a good policy. The Black Managers' Association regularly invited white managers to their meetings when their presence was relevant to particular topics the group was exploring.

Table 4: Perceptions of "Interest Group" Dynamics Among Black Managers and White Managers

Questionnaire Items	White Foremen's Club Members	White Foremen's Club Nonmembers	Black BMA Members	Black BMA Nonmembers
The Foremen's Club works to improve working conditions for its members.†	86	65	75	82
The Black Managers' Association works with top management to solve racial problems in XYZ.	84	77	81	66
The Foremen's Club is essentially a social organization.†	85	78	57	63
The Black Managers' Association is essentially a social organization.†	43	45	34	53
The Foremen's Club is essentially a racist organization.†	23	16	53	51
The Black Managers' Association is essentially a racist organization.†	64	45	16	25

*Represents responses of those answering "strongly agree," "agree," or "mildly agree."
† Differences among membership categories $p < .01$, χ^2 test.

There was debate in both groups concerning the degree to which the group existed primarily for social activities. Membership in the Foremen's Club was restricted to people at the first (lowest) level of management, but the Black Managers' Association was open to black managers at all levels. Most members of the Black Managers' Association were nevertheless first-level managers, because most black managers were at that level.

Table 4 presents a series of items on the organic-questionnaire that pertain to the two organizations. Analyses were based on comparisons between members and nonmembers of both organizations across racial groups. Black managers were substantially more likely to see the Foremen's Club as "racist" than were whites (either members or nonmembers). White managers were substantially more likely to see the Black Managers' Association as "racist" than were blacks (members or nonmembers). The Foremen's Club was seen more often as a "social organization" than was the Black Managers' Association by both black and white managers, although this view was less common among black managers. Members of either organization were more likely than were nonmembers to see their organization solving organizational problems.

In sum, the data show evidence of effects of racial-identity groups on the perceptions of both groups. There is also evidence that both blacks and whites in the organization saw the two groups in significantly different terms.

Microcosm-group members suggested that allocation of organizational resources between black and white managers should be examined particu-

Table 5: Perceptions of Promotion Dynamics Among Black Managers and White Managers

Questionnaire Items and Responses	White males	White females	Black males	Black females
Personnel Committees view white males as a proven commodity.[†]	33	49	86	88
The way Personnel Committees are set up within XYZ, it is almost impossible for blacks to reach upper management.[†]	4	10	72	73
Despite EEO targets for blacks, competent whites will be promoted at XYZ.	81	88	97	95
Despite racial discrimination, competent blacks will be promoted at XYZ.	95	94	64	66
Qualified whites are promoted more rapidly than equally qualified blacks.[†]	4	7	62	53
Qualified blacks are promoted more rapidly than equally qualified whites.[†]	82	75	13	12

Percentage Responding Positively*

* Represents responses of those answering "strongly agree," "agree," or "mildly agree."
[†] Differences among membership categories $p < .01$ χ^2 test.

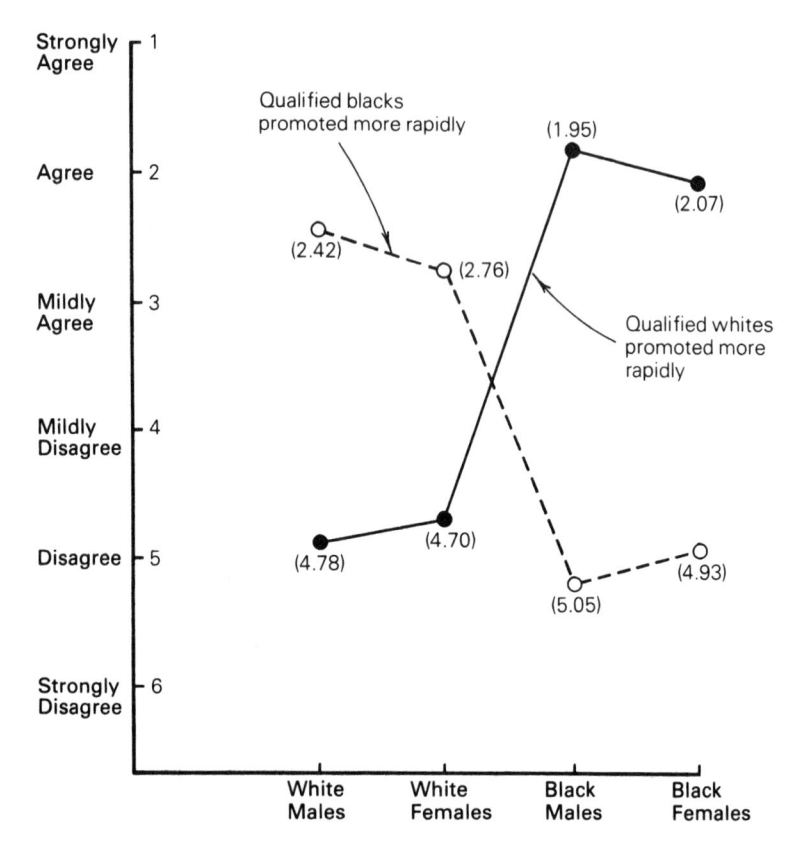

Figure 6: Mean Perceived Promotion Advantage for Blacks and Whites

- Strongly Agree — 1
- Agree — 2
- Mildly Agree — 3
- Mildly Disagree — 4
- Disagree — 5
- Strongly Disagree — 6

Qualified blacks promoted more rapidly: (2.42) White Males, (2.76) White Females, (1.95) Black Males, (2.07) Black Females

Qualified whites promoted more rapidly: (4.78) White Males, (4.70) White Females, (5.05) Black Males, (4.93) Black Females

larly with respect to promotions. The troubling issue for both black and white managers was how the organizational forces came together to favor one group over the other for advancement in the system. Table 5 presents a series of items pertaining to this issue. Black managers thought that Personnel Committees – the groups in the XYZ Company that made promotion decisions – greatly favored whites over blacks. A high proportion of managers from both races thought that competent people from both races would be promoted, but each racial group tended to believe that a larger number of competent members of the other race would be promoted. Each group thought that the other had a decided advantage on rates of promotion. Whites saw the advantage of blacks arising from affirmative action, and blacks saw the advantage of whites deriving from numerical control of influential positions and committees.

The last two items in Table 5 were subjected to analysis of variance in order to test for interaction between identity-group membership and perceived favoritism for either racial group.

Figure 6 shows the highly significant ($p < .001$) interaction. The results in this figure are similar to those in Figure 4.

In summary, the race study, like the task-group study, showed intergroup effects operating at three different levels (interpersonal, interest group, and systemic) and provided unique findings relevant to each level. A special theme cutting across data from each level was the presence of both parallel and nonparallel perceptions between the racial groups. Both black groups and white groups reported that they socialized mainly with their own group and that the other group behaved more in this way than their own group. But blacks had decidedly more negative evaluations of black–white interactions than whites did. The Black Managers' Association and the Foremen's Club were both seen as racist by members of the "out group" relevant to each organization. But the Foremen's Club was seen as more of a "social" organization than the Black Managers' Association by both blacks and whites. Blacks and whites both thought their own groups were at a disadvantage in the competition for promotions in the corporation. But the two racial groups differed in their perceptions of how the Personnel Committees operated in the organization.

Toward a Concept of Embedded Intergroups in Organizations

The task-group study and the race-relations study both used the intergroup methodology. The same ideas from intergroup theory underlay the methodological procedures in both studies, although the major actions and instruments differed between studies because the intergroup problems and organizational context differed.

Information about interpersonal dynamics, about interest-group dynamics, and about tensions due to systemic allocation of resources was gained in both studies. The levels of analysis emerged through intergroup methodology. All three levels of analysis can be readily related to the concept of groups in organizations and to the propositions about intergroups in organizations that were stated in the theoretical portion of this paper. The findings concerning these three levels of analysis confirm the utility of the methodology already described. They also, in our minds, indicate the need for additional concepts. First, the differences in patterns of perception between groups of apparently equivalent function and power were more complex than a consideration of simple ethnocentrism would lead one to predict. Second, the presence of statistical interaction among different levels of organizational analysis suggests a need for a means to think about hierarchical intergroup effects. "Hierarchical" is used to mean both the inclusion of one level of analysis in another level and the domination of one group by another. We use the term "embedded intergroups" to characterize the phenomenon we are about to discuss. The argument proceeds from here in two steps. First, we explain why the data from the two studies reported here show limitations of the familiar concept of ethnocentrism. Second, we define and explain the concept of embedded intergroup relations.

Limitations of Ethnocentrism as a Concept

In one line of research on intergroup relations especially familiar to social psychologists, the effects of inequalities between groups have either been minimized or ignored, in large part because the research methods have isolated the intergroup processes from the context, or the researchers have failed to account for their own representative roles (e.g., Blake, Shepard, and Mouton, 1964; Sherif and Sherif, 1969; Burke, 1972). Other schools have given the hierarchical relations among groups a prominent place in their theoretical statements (Van den Bergh, 1972; Billig, 1976; Smith, 1977; Brown, 1978). The concept of embedded intergroups falls into this second class. Both the task-group study and the race-relations study show marked hierarchical intergroup effects, and power differentials are evident in the way group members assessed their own advantages and disadvantages in the allocation of resources by the organization.

In the task-group study, customer service was found to dominate engineering at the corporation level, but at the division level, engineering dominated customer service. Nevertheless, even at the division level, customer service was seen as favored over engineering. Perhaps, even though engineers outnumbered and outranked customer-service people in the division, corporate values were being infused into the division to such a degree that even the smaller and less influential customer service groups were perceived by other groups to be dominant and were more valued. Moreover, we speculate that the immediate threat of seizure of internal power by the engineers may have led the customer-service people to deny their own relative advantage, lest they be seen as "uppity" and be treated less favorably locally for their relative success in the broader corporate context. If our speculation is correct, then the trend for customer services to be seen as more favored within the Drawing Division would have been even more pronounced than indicated by our data. These data make sense if we look at them as the expression of one intergroup conflict embedded in another, larger intergroup conflict in which the dominant external group overdetermined the perceptions of the internal intergroup dynamics. A similar but more extreme pattern may be observed in the race-relations study. Both black and white groups reported that members of their own groups were disadvantaged in promotion. For blacks, this belief was based on the composition of corporate Personnel Committees, which were overwhelmingly white; for whites, it was tied to their interpretation of the company's response to government pressures for affirmative action. The central problem is then to understand not only the relative power of the group in its immediate intergroup setting, but also to appreciate the dominance structure of groups in larger intergroup contexts.

STUDYING INTERGROUP RELATIONS EMBEDDED IN ORGANIZATIONS   313

Figure 7: Embedded Intergroup Analysis for Task Groups

Figures 7 and 8 illustrate the application of our embedded intergroup analysis to the task-group study and the racial-group study. Each diagram shows how the intergroup pattern would look to an individual looking "upward" from a primary group. As shown in Figure 7, individual members of the Sales Department would see a division managed by members of the other group and a corporation led by members of their own group. Individual

Figure 8: Embedded Intergroup Analysis for Racial Groups

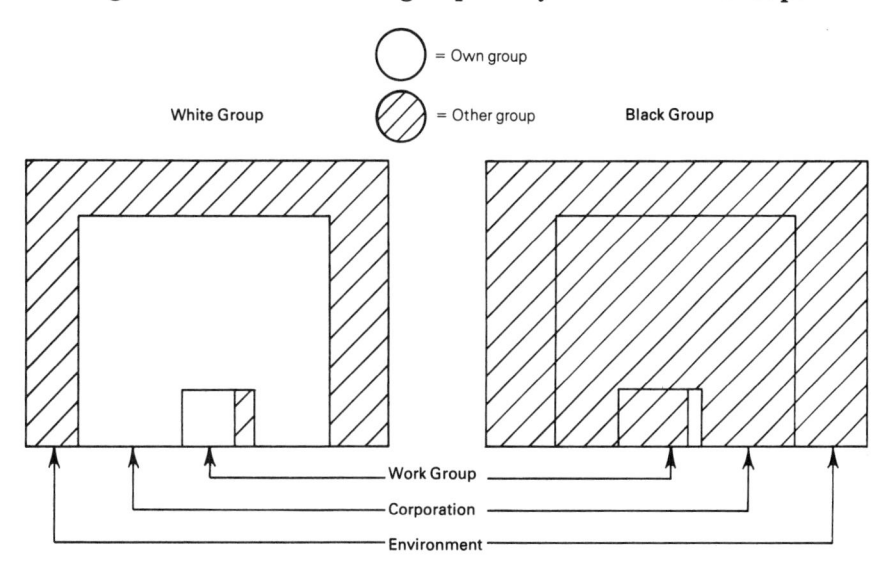

members of both the Production and the Research departments would see a division led by members of their own group and a corporation led by members of the other group. As shown in Figure 8, individual whites see the corporation managed by members of their own group and an external environment controlled by blacks. Individual blacks see the corporation led by members of the other group, and the environment dominated by the other group.

Each of the four intergroup relations is unique, but when we apply the concept of embeddedness to them, all the findings become explainable in a coherent way. It is necessary, however, to consider several levels of analysis. The embedded intergroup concept provides a guiding principle for drawing together micro- and macro-phenomena into a coherent whole.

One multilevel variable of particular interest in these studies was the tendency for group members to exaggerate their own disadvantage in explainable ways. Intergroup dynamics operate at multiple levels, and the perceptions of groups at any particular level tend to be shaped by phenomena at higher levels, such that perceived disadvantage at a higher level tends toward denial of advantage at lower levels. Moreover, the higher the level at which the disadvantage is perceived, the more severe the denial at lower levels.

Both studies showed the effects of outside groups on the intergroup dynamics. The Sales, Production, and Research Departments belonged to the same division, but each work group had its own set of external contacts. Thus, the relations among the three departments inside the division were influenced by their unique exchanges with groups outside the division. In the race study, there were both black and white interest groups that had special roles in the organization. These special groups served their members by negotiating with senior management and by sponsoring social activities. Despite their similar roles, the two groups were differently perceived by members and nonmembers. With the aid of the embedded concepts, these varying perceptions become more understandable. The Black Managers' Association was seen by both blacks and whites as more influential and less social than the Foremen's Club. This difference in consensual perception of the two groups reflects the difference between black and white embeddedness in the XYZ Company, as shown in Figure 8.

The embedded nature of organizational groups also affects face-to-face relations. This was most clearly evident in the race study. Blacks and whites thought that each group socialized primarily with its members, but those interactions were not thought to be the same for both groups. Blacks reported more discussion about racial issues, both within their own group and outside it, than whites did. This pattern is related to the different patterns of embedding encountered by blacks and by whites in the predominantly white XYZ Company. Members of the minority group are forced to deal with intergroup issues and to come to grips with their relationships in intergroup terms. Members of the majority group can overlook group forces and can attempt to explain their relationships mainly in terms of the individuals involved.

The embedded-intergroup concept in organizations further explains a number of considerations not accounted for by researchers using the more familiar notion of ethnocentric relations between ingroups and outgroups. The task-group study showed differential effects of ethnocentrism depending on whether respondents were reporting on task aspects or on relationship aspects of their intergroup dynamics. The race study indicated that, although blacks and whites showed similar ethnocentric patterns with respect to informal socializing, the two groups reported quite different patterns in their conversations about race relations. We suggest that these patterns would be reversed if whites were a minority in a predominantly black organization. The race study also showed ethnocentric patterns in perceptions of "racism" in the Foremen's Club and the Black Managers' Association. The data having to do with perceived allocation of resources identify conditions in which groups seem motivated to minimize or to invert usual ethnocentric tendencies. In both studies, groups tended to minimize their advantage or emphasize their disadvantage – a marked contrast to the usual ingroup–outgroup pattern in which groups see themselves favorably and others unfavorably. Embedded intergroup analysis provides a way to understand and explain these phenomena, while the more classical ethnocentric perspectives by themselves do not.

As a consequence of the findings from the two studies and their interpretation, the theory of group and intergroup relations in organizations should be modified to include the concept of embedded intergroup relations.

The Concept of Embedded Intergroup Relations

Embeddedness refers to interpenetration across levels of analysis; it concerns how system and subsystem dynamics are affected by suprasystem events, and vice versa (Miller, 1978). Relations among identity groups and among organizational groups are shaped by how these groups and their representatives are embedded in the organization and also by how the organization is embedded in its environment. The effects of embeddedness may be observed on individual members, on the dynamics within identity groups and organizational groups, and on the intergroup transactions among diverse identity groups and organizational groups.[7]

Effects of embeddedness derive from power differences among groups across levels of analysis. "Congruent" embeddedness means that power differences at the system level are reinforced by those at the subsystem and the suprasystem levels. "Incongruent" embeddedness means that power differences at the system level differ from those at other levels. The relations among groups are more complex under incongruent embeddedness than under congruent embeddedness. Affective patterns, cognitive formations, and leadership behavior will be less consistent and less ethnocentric, within a level and among levels, under incongruent embeddedness than under congruent embeddedness. In particular, incongruently embedded groups will be inclined to minimize their advantages and emphasize their disadvantages in order to prevent loss of power.

Conclusion

The theory → method → data → theory cycle has now been completed. We employed the conception of groups-in-organizations to analyze methodology and demonstrated the full use of intergroup methods in two empirical studies. Both studies produced data relevant to three levels of analysis (interpersonal, group, and organizational) and identified findings that called for further explanatory concepts to account for embedded intergroup effects in organizations. Previously, the study of intergroup effects in organizations had been restricted to differences between what were generally viewed as nonoverlapping groups. The idea of analyzing intergroup relations within a hierarchy has been suggested by other writers, but there has been no empirical evidence demonstrating the interactive effects of the multiple levels (Rice, 1969; Billig, 1976; Smith, 1977; Brown, 1978).

The concept of intergroup relations embedded in organizations is important whenever intergroup effects may shape research results. Rosenthal (1966: 374–379), for example, suggested minimizing human contact to control the impact of experimenter behavior on subjects. In intergroup theory, the efficacy of this procedure for minimizing bias depends on how group memberships are presented in the minimal contact transaction. A video tape of a white experimenter giving instructions to a black subject in a predominantly white college in the United States, for example, would not be viewed as the experimental equivalent of a video tape of a black experimenter giving instructions to a white subject in the same college. Similarly, participant observers in field settings do not escape intergroup forces simply because they enter the territory and culture of their respondents. Intergroup theory emphasizes that the participant observer will be perceived as a group representative by respondents. Therefore, however data are gathered by participant observers, their quality and meaning will be shaped by the relations between the groups represented by the observer and the groups being studied. Finally, the standardized questionnaire, the tool of so much of social research, is not so standardized, according to intergroup theory. What appears to be a universal instrument when viewed by an investigator inside her or his research group is seen as a culture-bound document imposed on other groups, when viewed from an intergroup perspective.

Intergroup theory has implications in the training of researchers. If every research transaction is an intergroup event, and all data collected are subject to intergroup forces, then researchers must learn to understand and manage their own group representations. Evidence has been published by both black and white scholars showing that acceptance of this proposition does not rest on intellectual arguments alone (e.g., Merton, 1972; Cedric X, 1973) Intergroup theory assumes that researchers and research teams are subject to the same forces in their own work as are the people they study. The traditional goal of objectivity, by which investigators separate themselves from the phenomena they study, should be replaced by a notion that calls on researchers to search for their own biases and then to build compensatory mechanisms into their research procedures. Accordingly, the list of necessary research skills expands to include the awareness of one's various group memberships, the knowledge of how these affiliations affect research with people from different groups, and the capacity to use these effects to obtain a deeper and more complete understanding of organizational phenomena.

Finally, the theory of group and intergroup relations developed above can be used to reconceptualize many topics in traditional organizational research. Much of the leadership literature, for example, focuses on the internal dynamics of small groups and gives far less attention to the dynamics of leaders representing their own groups to other groups (e.g., Vroom and Yetton, 1973; Fiedler, Chemers, and Mahar, 1976; Hollander, 1978). Intergroup theory both implies that such a picture of leadership is significantly incomplete and calls attention to relationships among leaders as peers and to relationships between leaders and superordinates, as well as to relationships between leaders and followers. Much of the leadership literature does not recognize identity groups. Intergroup theory identifies the limited generality of this work and suggests that more diverse investigators studying more diverse kinds of groups would significantly alter ideas about this subject. Similar comments apply to other topics such as small group dynamics, organization structure, leadership succession, organizational selection, socialization, and promotion. This conceptual development has been begun elsewhere (Alderfer, 1977a).

Notes

* We wish to acknowledge research support from the Office of Naval Research Contracts N00014-67-A 0097 0017 and N00014-79-C-0626; feedback on earlier drafts from David Berg, Kathy Kram, Connie Gersick, Valerie Simmons, David Morgan; and clerical support from Roberta Sutkowski and Marie Avitable.

1. Even though the formal presentation begins with theory for the sake of intellectual clarity, the actual process of discovery began with a series of methodological adventures described in Alderfer (1971) and Alderfer and Brown (1975). These methods were initially rooted in the invention of the social technology of experiential learning in groups (cf. Bion, 1961; Bradford, Gibb, and Benne, 1964; Rice, 1965; Gibbard, Hartman, and Mann, 1974; Cooper and Alderfer, 1978; Alderfer and Cooper, 1980). The experiential group was independently developed in several places and served a variety of theoretical traditions. Anthony (1971) provides a history of these developments.

2. The term "recognized" is used here in a psychological rather than a legal sense. A surreptitious group may lack legal recognition but still engage in intergroup transactions. These transactions could not occur without a psychological recognition of the group by members and nonmembers.

3. This concept of group differs from the notion of reference group used by Merton (1968) and others in its emphasis on behavior, on active (not just fantasized) interdependence among members, and on group representational functions. It is closest to the concept proposed by Rice (1969).

A recent book by Alvin Zander, *Groups at Work* (1977), represents the efforts by an accomplished scholar of group dynamics to set a new agenda for research on groups in organizations. Zander is concerned with living groups in organizations, but his definition – "a group is a collection of individuals who are interdependent to some degree" (Zander, 1977: 6) – retains the inward focus characteristic of laboratory social psychology to which Zander himself has contributed greatly. Many of the problems Zander addresses in his book, such as recruitment, secrecy, group embarrassment, and meetings have intergroup explanations, but his analysis is almost wholly focused on internal dynamics.

4. Identity-group membership covers a variety of "individual difference" variables as defined by industrial psychologists. "Individual differences" are based on variables such as ethnicity, race, sex, age, religion, and family and are only in part individual differences; they are largely group differences. The terms "identity group" and "organizational group" are not equivalent to the more familiar terms "informal group" and "formal group", although there is some overlap in the phenomena they attempt to explain. (1) The formal–informal distinction is usually tied to events that arise from happenings in organizations. According to this view, one does not become a member of an "informal" group until one has become a member of the organization. Membership in an identity group predates and postdates membership in organizations. It is unlikely that research people will belong to an informal group in an organization they are studying, but it is virtually guaranteed that they will belong to identity groups that exist also in the organization. (2) The horizontal dimension of formal groups does help to define one kind of organization group, but until very recently there was little tendency for scholars to use intergroup concepts to analyze the vertical dimension of organizations (see Brown, 1978, for a major step in this direction).

5. There are some potentially interesting connections between intergroup theory's way of dealing with cognitive formations and the proposals of attribution theory (Frieze, Bar-Tel, and Carroll, 1979). The important distinction might turn on explaining stereotyping. McGillis (1979: 274), for example, talked about "stereotypical expectancies," defined as "traits attributed to a group member simply because of a person's membership in a group." The "simply" is important because it suggests normatively that group membership should not be a basis for attributing characteristics. Intergroup theory posits that groups naturally "teach" their members about their own and other groups. In intergroup theory, prejudice and discrimination are not disposed of by attempting to eliminate or ignore group differences. Instead these differences are recognized and accepted and ways are found to negotiate among groups with minimal damage to group or individual interests.

6. The microcosm group is also used in action research and in bringing about organizational change. This additional role is very important to motivate microcosm-group members, and it may be essential for the method to work effectively. All known uses of microcosm groups include action research. When action research is part of the contract between researcher and organization, the microcosm group also plays a key role in the design and conduct of data feedback to the entire organization. See Alderfer *et al.* (1980) and Alderfer (1977b) for a case describing the role of the microcosm group in organization-wide feedback.

7. The writer who has come closest to suggesting such a concept is Rice (1969), who proposed that intergroup theory can be used to explain phenomena at different levels of analysis. The term subsystem, system, and supra system are from Miller (1978), who gives only minimal attention to intergroup dynamics in his treatment of living systems.

References

Adams, Richard N., and Jack J. Preiss, eds. 1960. *Human Organization Research.* Homewood, IL: Dorsey.
Alderfer, Clayton P. 1971. "The effect of individual, group, and intergroup relations on a management development program." *Journal of Applied Psychology*, 55: 302–311.
———. 1976a. "Boundary relations and organizational diagnosis." In H. Meltzer and F. W. Wickert (eds.), *Humanizing Organizational Behavior*: 109–133. Springfield, IL: Thomas.
———. 1976b. "Change processes in organizations." In Marvin D. Dunnette (ed.), *Handbook of Industrial and Organizational Psychology*: 1591–1638. Chicago: Rand–McNally.
———. 1977a. "Group and intergroup relations." In J. R. Hackman and J. L. Suttle (eds.), *Improving Life at Work*: 227–296. Santa Monica, CA: Goodyear.
———. 1977b. "Improving organizational communication through long-term intergroup intervention." *Journal of Applied Behavioral Science*, 13: 193–210.
———. 1977c. "Organization development." *Annual Review of Psychology*, 28: 197–225.
———. 1980a "The methodology of organization diagnosis." *Professional Psychology*, 11: 459–468.
———. 1980b "Consulting to underbounded systems." In C. P. Alderfer and Cary L. Cooper (eds.), *Advances in Experiential Social Processes*, 2: 267–295. London: Wiley.
Alderfer, Clayton P., Charleen J. Alderfer, Leota Tucker, and Robert C. Tucker. 1980. "Diagnosing race relations in management." *Journal of Applied Behavioral Science*, 16: 135–166.
Alderfer, Clayton P., and L. Dave Brown. 1972. "Designing an empathic questionnaire for organizational research." *Journal of Applied Psychology*, 56: 456–460.
———. 1975. *Learning from Changing.* Beverly Hills, CA: Sage.
Alderfer, Clayton, P., L. Dave Brown, Robert E. Kaplan, and Ken K. Smith. 1982. *Group Relations and Organizational Diagnosis.* New York: Wiley (forthcoming).
Alderfer, Clayton P., and Cary L. Cooper, eds. 1980. *Advances in Experiential Social Processes*, vol. 2. London: Wiley.
Alderfer, Clayton, P., and John Holbrook. 1973. "A new design for survey feedback." *Education and Urban Society*, 4: 437–464.
Aldrich, Howard E. 1979. *Organizations and Environments.* Englewood Cliffs, NJ: Prentice-Hall.
Anthony, E. J. 1971. "The history of group psychotherapy." In H. I. Kaplan and B. J. Sadock (eds.), *Comprehensive Group Psychotherapy*: 4–31. Baltimore, MD: Williams and Wilkens.
Argyris, Chris. 1968. "Some unintended consequences of rigorous research." *Psychological Bulletin*, 70: 185–197.
———. 1970. *Intervention Theory and Method.* Reading, MA: Addison-Wesley.
Bazar, Joan. 1979. "Jay Haley." *APA Monitor*, 10 (11): 6.
Becker, Howard S. 1967. "Whose side are we on?" In W. J. Filstead (ed.), *Qualitative Methodology*: 15–26. Chicago: Markham.

Berg, David N. 1977. "Failure at entry." In P. Mirvis and D. N. Berg (eds.), *Failures in Organization Development and Change*: 33–56. New York: Wiley.
Billig, M. 1976. *Social Psychology and Inter-group Relations*. London: Academic Press.
Bion, W. R. 1961 *Experiences in Groups*. New York: Basic Books.
Blake, Robert R., Herbert Shepard, and Jane Mouton. 1964. *Managing Intergroup Conflict in Industry*. Houston, TX: Gulf.
Blalock, Hubert M., Jr., ed. 1971 *Causal Models in the Social Sciences*. Chicago: Aldine.
Bradford, Leland, Jack Gibb, and Kenneth Benne. 1964. *T-Group Theory and Laboratory Method*. New York: Wiley.
Brown, L. Dave. 1972. "Research action: Organizational feedback understanding and change." *Journal of Applied Behavioral Science*, 8: 697–711.
———. 1978 "Toward a theory of power and intergroup relations." in C. L. Cooper and C. P. Alderfer (eds.), *Advances in Experiential Social Processes*, 1: 161–180. London: Wiley.
Burke, W. Warner. 1972 "Managing conflict between groups." In J. Adams (ed.), *Theory and Method in Organizational Development: An Evolutionary Process*: 255–268. Arlington, VA: National Training Laboratory.
Cartwright, Dorwin, and Alvin Zander. 1968. *Group Dynamics*, 3rd ed. Evanston, IL: Row-Peterson.
Cedric X (Clark). 1973. "The role of the white researcher in black society: A futuristic look." *Journal of Social Issues*, 29: 109–118.
Chesler, Mark, and M. Flanders. 1967 "Resistance to research and research utilization: The death and life of a feedback attempt." *Journal of Applied Behavioral Science*, 3: 469–487.
Cline, Barbara. 1965 *Men Who Made a New Physics*. New York: Crowell.
Conant, James B. 1952. *Modern Science and Modern Man*. New York: Doubleday.
Cooper, L. 1976. "Mirroring: One vehicle to organizational clarity." *International Journal of Social Psychiatry*. 22, 1039–1045.
Coser, Lewis A. 1956. *The Functions of Social Conflict*. Glencoe, IL: Free Press.
Cooper, Cary L., and C. P. Alderfer, eds., 1978 *Advances in Experiential Social Processes*, vol.1. London: Wiley.
Crozier, Michel. 1964 *The Bureaucratic Phenomenon*. Chicago: University of Chicago Press.
Dalton, Melville. 1959. *Men Who Manage*. New York: Wiley.
Deutsch, Morton. 1973. *The Resolution Conflict*. New Haven, CT: Yale University Press.
Doehrman, M. J. 1976. "Parallel processes in supervision and psychotherapy." *Bulletin of the Menninger Clinic*, 40: 3–104.
Douglas, Jack D. 1976. *Investigative Social Research: Individual and Team Field Research*. Beverly Hills, CA: Sage.
Erikson, Erik. 1964 *Insight and Responsibility*. New York: Norton.
Fiedler, Fred E., M. M. Chemers, and L. Mahar. 1976. *Improving Leadership Effectiveness: The Leader Match Concept*. New York: Wiley.
Freize, I. R., D. Bar-Tel, and John S. Carroll. 1979. *New Approaches to Social Problems*. San Francisco: Jossey-Bass.
Gibbard, Graham S., J. J. Hartman, and R. D. Mann. 1974. *Analysis of Groups*. San Francisco: Jossey-Bass.
Heller, Frank A. 1970. "Group feedback analysis as a change agent." *Human Relations*, 23: 319–333.
Hollander, Edwin P. 1978. *Leadership Dynamics*. New York: Free Press.
Hyman, Heubert, W. J. Cobb, J. J. Feldman, C. W. Hart, and C. H. Stember 1954. *Interviewing in Social Research*. Chicago: University of Chicago Press.

Kahn, Robert L., and F. Mann 1952. "Developing research partnerships." *Journal of Social Issues*, 8: 4–10.
Kanter, Rosabeth M. 1977. *Men and Women of the Corporation.* New York: Basic Books.
Kaplan, Abraham. 1964. *Conduct of Inquiry.* San Francisco: Chandler.
Kidder, L. H., and V. M. Stewart. 1975. *The Psychology of Intergroup Relations: Conflict and Consciousness.* New York: McGraw-Hill.
Kuhn, Thomas S. 1962. *The Structure of Scientific Revolutions.* Chicago: University of Chicago Press.
Lasswell, Harold, and A. Kaplan. 1950. *Power and Society.* New Haven, CT: Yale University Press.
Levine, Robert A., and D. T. Campbell. 1972. *Ethnocentrism.* New York: Wiley.
Lewicki, Roy J., and Clayton P. Alderfer. 1973. "The tensions between research and intervention in intergroup conflict." *Journal of Applied Behavioral Science,* 9: 424–449.
Loring, R., and T. Wells. 1972. *Breakthrough: Women into Management.* New York: Van Nostrand-Reinhold.
Marx, Melvin. 1965. "The general nature of theory construction." In M. Marx (ed.), *Theories in Contemporary Psychology:* 4–46. New York: MacMillan.
McGillis, Daniel. 1979. "Biases and jury decision-making." In I. R. Freize, D. Bar-Tel, and John S. Carroll (eds.), *New Approaches to Social Problems:* 265–284. San Francisco: Jossey-Bass.
Merton, Robert K. 1968. *Social Theory and Social Structure.* New York: Free Press.
——. 1972. "Insiders and outsiders." *American Journal of Sociology,* 78: 9–47.
Miles, Matthew B., H. A. Hornstein, D. M. Callahan, P. H. Calder, and R. S. Schiavo. 1969. "The consequences of survey feedback: Theory and evaluation." In W. G. Bennis, K. B. Benne, and R. Chin (eds.), *The Planning of Change:* 457–468. New York: Holt, Rinehart & Winston.
Miller, James G. 1978. *Living Systems.* New York: McGraw-Hill.
Nadler, David A. 1977. *Feedback and Organization Development Using Data-based Methods.* Reading, MA: Addison-Wesley.
——. 1978 "Consulting with labor and management: Some learnings from quality-of-work-life projects." In W. Warner Burke (ed.), *The Cutting Edge: Current Theory and Practice in Organization Development:* 262–277 LaJolla, CA: University Associates.
Neff, Frank. 1965. "Survey research: A tool for problem diagnosis and improvement in organizations." In A. W. Gouldner and S. M. Mitler (eds.), *Applied Sociology:* 23–38. New York: Free Press.
Pfeffer, Jeffrey, and G. R. Moore. 1980. "Power in university budgeting: A replication and extension." *Administrative Science Quarterly,* 25: 637–653.
Pfeffer, Jeffrey, and Gerald R. Salancik. 1974. "Organizational decision making as a political process." *Administrative Science Quarterly,* 19: 135–151.
Purcell, T. V., and G. F. Cavanagh. 1972. *Blacks in the Industrial World.* New York: Free Press.
Rice, A. K. 1965. *Learning in Groups.* London: Tavistock.
——. 1969. "Individual, group, and intergroup processes." *Human Relations,* 22: 565–584.
Rosenthal, Robert. 1966. *Experimenter Effects in Behavioral Research,* New York: Appleton-Century-Crofts.
Rosenthal, Robert, and R. L. Rosnow, eds. 1968. *Artifact in Behavioral Research.* New York: Academic Press.
Sachs, D. M., and S. H. Shapiro. 1976. "On parallel processes in therapy and teaching." *Psychiatric Quarterly,* 45: 394–415.

Sayles, Leonard. 1958. *Behavior of Industrial Work Groups.* New York: Wiley.

Sayles, Leonard R., and G. Strauss. 1953. *The Local Union: Its Place in the Industrial Plant.* New York: Harper and Brothers.

Schuman, Howard, and S. Hatchett. 1974. *Black Racial Attitudes: Trends and Complexities.* Ann Arbor, MI: Survey Research Center.

Searles, Harold F. 1955. "The informational value of the supervisor's emotional experiences." *Psychiatry*, 18: 135–146.

Sherif, Musafir, and C. Sherif. 1969. *Social Psychology.* New York: Harper & Row.

Sieber, Samuel D. 1973. "The integration of fieldwork and survey methods." *American Journal of Sociology*, 78: 1335–1359.

Smith, Ken K. 1977. "An intergroup perspective on individual behavior." In J. R. Hackman, E. E. Lawler, and L. W. Porter (eds.), *Perspectives on Behavior in Organizations*: 359–372. New York: McGraw-Hill.

Steele, Fritz. 1975. *Consulting for Organizational Change.* Amherst, MA: University of Massachusetts Press.

Strauss, George. 1962. "Tactics of the lateral relationship: The purchasing agent." *Administrative Science Quarterly*, 7: 161–187.

——. 1964. "Workflow frictions, interfunctional rivalry, and professionalism: A case study of purchasing agents." *Human Organization*, 23: 137–149.

Sumner, William G. 1906. *Folkways.* New York: Ginn.

Tajfel, H. 1970. Experiments in intergroup discrimination. *Scientific American*, 223: 96–102.

Van den Bergh, Pierre. 1972. *Intergroup Relations: Sociological Perspectives.* New York: Basic Books.

Vroom, Victor H., and Philip W. Yetton. 1973. *Leadership and Decision-making.* Pittsburgh: University of Pittsburgh Press.

Webb, E. J., D. T. Campbell, R. D. Schwarts, and L. Sechrest. 1966. *Unobtrusive Measures: Nonreactive Research in the Social Sciences.* Chicago: Rand-McNally.

Whyte, William F. 1955. *Street Corner Society.* Chicago: University of Chicago Press.

Zander, Alvin. 1977. *Groups at Work.* San Francisco: Jossey-Bass.

18

Focus Groups

David L. Morgan

Introduction

Although some form of group interviewing has undoubtedly existed for as long as sociologists have been collecting data (e.g. Bogardus 1926), the past decade has produced a remarkable surge of interest in group interviews generally and focus groups in particular. Much of this interest first surfaced in the mid-1980s. In 1987, Robert Merton published remarks that compared his pioneering work on "focused interviews" (Merton & Kendall 1946) with marketers' uses of the focus group, while John Knodel and his collaborators (Knodel *et al* 1987) published a summary of their focus group research on demographic changes in Thailand. The next year produced two book-length treatments of focus groups by social scientists (Krueger 1988/1994, Morgan 1988). This initial burst of interest was followed by other texts (Stewart & Shamdasani 1990, Vaughn *et al* 1996), a reissuing of Merton *et al*'s original manual (Merton *et al* 1956/1990) an edited collection of more advanced material (Morgan 1993a), and at least two special issues of journals (Carey 1995, Knodel 1995).

The current level of interest in focus group interviews is evident from searches of *Sociological Abstracts, Psychological Abstracts*, and the *Social Science Citation Index*. All of these sources show a steady growth in research using focus groups, indicating that well over a hundred empirical articles using focus groups appeared in refereed journals during 1994 alone. These searches also show interesting patterns in the use of focus groups. In particular, a content analysis of the materials from *Sociological Abstracts* revealed that over 60% of the empirical research using focus groups during the past decade combined them with other research methods, although the proportion of studies that rely solely on focus groups has been increasing in recent years.

Source: *Annual Review of Sociology*, vol. 22, 1996, pp. 129–152.

Hence, this review pays attention to uses of focus groups both as a "self-contained" method and in combination with other methods. Before examining the uses of focus groups, however, I examine how focus groups are related to group interviews in general.

Focus Groups and Group Interviews

This chapter defines focus groups as a research technique that collects data through group interaction on a topic determined by the researcher. This definition has three essential components. First, it clearly states that focus groups are a research method devoted to data collection. Second, it locates the interaction in a group discussion as the source of the data. Third, it acknowledges the researcher's active role in creating the group discussion for data collection purposes.

While this definition is intentionally quite broad, each of its three elements does exclude some projects that have occasionally been called focus groups. First, focus groups should be distinguished from groups whose primary purpose is something other than research; alternative purposes might be: therapy, decision making, education, organizing, or behavior change (although focus groups that are primarily for data collection may have some of these outcomes as well). Second, it is useful to distinguish focus groups from procedures that utilize multiple participants but do not allow interactive discussions, such as nominal groups and Delphi groups (these techniques are reviewed in Stewart & Shamdasani 1990). Finally, focus groups should be distinguished from methods that collect data from naturally occurring group discussions where no one acts as an interviewer. The distinction here is not whether the group existed prior to the research, but whether the researcher's interests directed the discussion, since focus groups are often conducted with existing groups (Morgan 1989).

Lying behind this effort to define focus groups is the fundamental question of whether focus groups should be distinguished from other types of group interviews. In one camp are those who use an inclusive approach that treats most forms of group interviews as variants on focus groups. In another camp, however, are those who use an exclusive approach that treats focus groups as a narrower technique not to be confused with other types of group interviews. One version of the exclusive approach, which is particularly common in marketing research (Greenbaum 1988, 1993, McQuarrie 1996), is a statement that focus groups must meet some specified set of criteria, typically that they consist of structured discussions among 6 to 10 homogeneous strangers in a formal setting. The problem with this approach is that it fails to demonstrate any advantages of either limiting the definition of focus groups to studies that meet these criteria or excluding group interviews that deviate from them.

In contrast to such unthinking reliance on an exclusive definition of focus groups, Frey & Fontana (1991) have created a typology that locates focus groups as one among several categories of group interviews. The typology includes some that the present definition already distinguishes from focus groups (nominal and Delphi groups and observations of naturally occurring groups), and some (brainstorming groups and field interviews in naturally occurring settings) that the current definition would treat as variations on focus groups. (See Khan & Manderson 1992 for a similar but more anthropologically based typology). One way to assess the usefulness of a typology such as Frey & Fontana's is to ask if it can determine whether a particular group interview is or is not a focus group. According to the dimensions that define their typology, group interviews are something other than focus groups if they: (i) are conducted in informal settings; (ii) use nondirective interviewing; or (iii) use unstructured question formats. Yet applied demographers such as Knodel (1987, 1995) have held focus group interviews throughout the world and have concluded that they can be adapted to a wide variety of settings and culture practices. Similarly, social science texts on focus groups (Krueger 1993, Morgan 1988, Stewart & Shamdasani 1990) describe ways to conduct focus groups with more or less directive interviewing styles and more or less structured question formats, depending on the purposes of the particular project. It would thus, in actual practice, be quite difficult to apply Frey & Fontana's typology to determine whether any given group interview was or was not a focus group.

In the long run, the question of whether sociologists should use a more inclusive or exclusive definition of focus groups will depend on which approach maximizes both the effective application of available techniques and the innovative development of new techniques. For the present, this remains an open question. Consequently, this chapter follows an inclusive approach that treats focus groups as a set of central tendencies, with many useful variations that can be matched to a variety of research purposes.

Current Uses for Focus Groups

This review necessarily concentrates on the uses of focus groups by sociologists. Still, it should be obvious that focus groups, like other qualitative methods, are used across a wide variety of different fields. Other disciplines in which focus groups are relatively widespread include communication studies (Albrecht *et al* 1993, Staley 1990), education (Brotherson & Goldstein 1992, Flores & Alonzo 1995, Lederman 1990), political science (Delli Carpini & Williams 1994, Kullberg 1994), and public health (Basch 1987). Outside of academia, focus groups are well known to be popular in marketing (Goldman & McDonald 1987, Greenbaum 1993), where they have been used for everything from breakfast cereals (Templeton 1987) to political candidates (Diamond & Bates 1992). This acceptance in applied marketing has not, however, carried over to the academic field of marketing (McQuarrie 1990), although there does seem to be a trend toward more methodological research in this field (McDonald 1993, Nelson & Frontczak 1988).

Given the breadth of possible applications of focus groups and group interviews, it is hardly surprising that they have found uses in many of the specialty areas that interest sociologists, including: aging (Knodel 1995, Duncan & Morgan 1994), criminology (Sasson, 1995), medical sociology (Morgan & Spanish 1985, McKinlay 1993), political sociology (Gamson 1992), social movements (Cable 1992), and the sociology of work (Bobo et al 1995). In addition, many applications of focus groups do not fit within the neat, traditional boundaries of sociology's subdisciplines. For example, Shively's (1992) study of how American Indians and Anglos responded to cowboy movies used focus groups within a cultural studies framework; Jarrett's (1993, 1994) work on low-income, African American women combined elements of family sociology, inequality, and race and ethnicity; and Pinderhughes' (1993) investigation of racially motivated violence mixed elements of urban sociology, criminology, and race relations.

Despite this wide-ranging interest in focus groups, they have found more currency within several specific areas of sociological interest. In particular, marketing's legacy of using focus groups to hear from consumers has carried over into their use in the development and evaluation of programs ranging from substance abuse (Lengua et al 1992) to curricular reform (Hendershott & Wright 1993). Program development efforts use focus groups to learn more about the potential targets of these programs in order to reach them more effectively. This use often occurs under the explicit rubric of "social marketing", which applies tools such as focus groups to socially valued goals, as in Bryant's (1990) program to encourage breast feeding among low-income women. On the program evaluation side, focus groups have become an important tool in qualitative evaluation research, including not only post-program evaluation, but also needs assessment and strategic planning (Krueger 1994).

Two specific research areas where the applied use of focus groups has had a major and continuing link to sociology are family planning and HIV/AIDS. The application of focus groups to research on fertility first emerged in the early 1980s (e.g. Folch-Lyon et al 1981). These studies typically sought a better understanding of knowledge, attitudes, and practices with regard to contraception in the Third World; in particular, advocates of a social marketing approach to contraceptives (Schearer 1981) argued that focus groups could supplement the kind of attitudinal data that surveys produced. Since that time, focus groups have been an important source of data on fertility and family planning preferences around the world, as in the work of Ward et al (1991) in Guatemala, Honduras, and Zaire, or Knodel et al (1987) in Thailand. This established application in the study of sexual behavior also led to the use of focus groups in research on the spread of HIV, both in the Third World (Irwin et al 1991) and the West (Kline et al 1992, Pollak et al 1990).

An important theme that reappears in many of these uses of focus groups is their ability to "give a voice" to marginalized groups. For example, in early HIV/AIDS research (Joseph et al 1984), epidemiologists used focus groups to gain a better understanding of at-risk groups with whom they had little prior experience, such as gay and bisexual men. Focus groups have thus been used in many applied settings where there is a difference in perspective between the researchers and those with whom they need to work. Others have argued, however, that the value of focus groups goes well beyond listening to others, since they can serve as either a basis for empowering "clients" (Magill 1993, Race *et al* 1994) or as a tool in action and participatory research (Hugentobler *et al* 1992, Padilla 1993). Similarly, feminist researchers have noted the appeal of focus groups because they allow participants to exercise a fair degree of control over their own interactions (Nichols-Casebolt & Spakes 1995, Montell 1995).

Uses in Combination with Other Methods

As noted at the outset of this review, a content analysis of *Sociological Abstracts* revealed that a majority of the published research articles using focus groups combined them with other methods. Further examination of the specific combinations of focus groups with other methods showed that the most frequent pairings were with either in-depth, individual interviews or surveys. Between these two, the use of focus groups with individual interviews is the more straightforward, since both are qualitative techniques. (This does not, however, imply that the two methods are interchangeable; the following section contains a comparison of individual and group interviews.) Investigators' reasons for combining individual and group interviews typically point to the greater depth of the former and the greater breadth of the latter (Crabtree *et al* 1993). For example, individual interview studies have used follow-up group interviews to check the conclusions from their analyses and to expand the study populations included in the research (Irwin 1970). This strategy has the advantage of getting reactions from a relatively wide range of participants in a relatively short time. In a complementary fashion, focus group studies have used follow-up interviews with individual participants to explore specific opinions and experiences in more depth, as well as to produce narratives that address the continuity of personal experiences over time (Duncan & Morgan 1994). This strategy has the advantage of first identifying a range of experiences and perspectives, and then drawing from that pool to add more depth where needed. Thus, depending on the varied needs that a qualitative study has for breadth and depth, there is little difficulty in combining individual and group interviews.

While studies that bring together focus groups and surveys are one of the leading ways of combining qualitative and quantitative methods, such designs also raise a complex set of issues, since the two methods produce such different kinds of data. Morgan (1993c) presented a conceptual framework to clarify these issues by distinguishing four ways of combining qualitative and quantitative methods in general and focus groups and surveys in particular.

The four ways of combining the methods are based on which method received the primary attention and whether the secondary method served as a preliminary or follow-up study.

Thus, the first combination contains studies in which surveys are the primary method and focus groups serve in a preliminary capacity. Survey researchers typically use this design to develop the content of their questionnaires. Because surveys are inherently limited by the questions they ask, it is increasingly common to use focus groups to provide data on how the respondents themselves talk about the topics of the survey. Although this practice has long been common in marketing research, systematic publications in this area did not appear until social scientists renewed their interest in focus groups (Fuller *et al* 1993 O'Brien 1993, Zeller 1993b). Still, this is an area that is just beginning to receive attention, and many issues are only now arising, such as the need to find other means of pursuing focus group insights that are not amenable to survey research (Laurie 1992, Laurie & Sullivan 1991). At present, this is easily the most common reason for combining focus groups and surveys.

In the second combination, focus groups are the primary method while surveys provide preliminary inputs that guide their application. Studies following this research design typically use the broad but "thin" data from surveys to assist in selecting samples for focus groups or topics for detailed analysis. With regard to sampling, Morgan & Zhao (1993) and O'Connor *et al* (1992) both used surveys of medical records to divide a larger population into different "segments" that they then compared using separate sets of focus groups. With regard to analysis, Morgan (1994) and Shively (1992) both illustrated the use of findings from a brief preliminary survey with focus group participants to guide the more detailed interpretive analysis of the data from the group discussions. Compared to the first combination, studies that use surveys as a secondary method to assist focus group research are relatively rare.

The third combination once again uses surveys as the primary method, but the focus groups now act as a follow-up that assists in interpreting the survey results. One increasingly common use for qualitative follow-up methods, including focus groups, is to recontact survey respondents for illustrative material that can be quoted in conjunction with quantitative findings. More interesting from a methodological perspective are efforts to clarify poorly understood results, such as Knodel's (1987) and Wolff *et al*'s (1993) efforts to account for fertility rates and education levels in Thailand, Morgan's (1989) investigations of the ineffectiveness of social support among recent widows, and Harari & Beaty's (1990) deeper probing of surface similarities in the survey responses of black workers and white managers in South Africa under apartheid. Among the four combinations, these designs are the second most frequent, but they have yet to receive any systematic methodological attention.

The final combination of surveys and focus groups uses focus groups as the primary method and surveys as a source of follow-up data. One such application would examine the prevalence of issues or themes from the focus groups. For example, Nichols-Casebolt & Spakes (1995: 53) followed up their focus groups by locating secondary data from surveys that showed policy makers "the scope of the problems associated with the issues identified by the participants." Another possibility would be to survey a large number of sites to determine where the results from a more limited focus group study might be most immediately transferable. But studies that employ designs from this fourth combination are easily the rarest of this set. One likely reason that those who conduct focus group studies seldom do smaller follow-up surveys is their desire to avoid any implication that quantitative data are necessary to "verify" the results of the qualitative research. In other words, the issues that accompany combining methods from different "paradigms" (Lincoln & Guba 1985) involve not just technical considerations, but epistemological and political issues as well (Bryman 1988). Still, the current popularity of work from the first combination, where focus groups aid in developing surveys, demonstrates the potential value of combining focus groups with quantitative methods. It thus seems likely that research using various combinations with surveys will continue to be not only one of the major uses of focus groups but also one of the most practical ways of bringing together qualitative and quantitative methods.

How Focus Groups Compare to Other Sociological Methods

Despite the increasingly widespread use of focus groups as a method within sociology and the other social sciences, virtually all this work has occurred in the past ten years. This "newcomer" status has encouraged comparisons between focus groups and the various traditional methods in each of these areas but researchers have offered two very different reasons for comparing methods. One reason for comparing focus groups to more familiar methods has been to determine whether the two methods produce equivalent data. According to this view, focus groups are most useful when they reproduce the results of the standard methods in a particular field. A different reason for comparing focus groups to existing methods has been to locate the unique contributions that each can make to a field of studies. According to this view, focus groups are most useful when they produce new results that would not be possible with the standard methods in a particular field. There is an obvious paradox here, as focus groups cannot produce results that are simultaneously the same as and different from results of familiar techniques. Unfortunately, the failure to recognize these divergent goals has limited the cumulative knowledge from studies that compare focus groups to other methods. Nonetheless, these comparisons are useful for summarizing the strengths and weaknesses of focus groups.

Comparisons to Surveys

In one of the earliest reports of a major social science application of focus groups, Folch-Lyon *et al* (1981) also included a detailed comparison to a survey on the same topic. This study investigated attitudes toward contraception in Mexico using two independent research teams. One team conducted 44 focus groups with some 300 participants, while the other did household surveys with over 2000 respondents. Overall, the authors had little difficulty in matching the investigation of their substantive topics across the two methods, their results showed an overwhelming convergence. As Stycos (1981) pointed out, however, most of Folch-Lyon *et al*'s judgments about the convergence between the two methods were based on subjective assessments of the correspondence of the findings; fortunately, more recent efforts have used more systematic comparisons.

Ward *et al* (1991) compared survey and focus group results from three studies on family planning in Guatemala, Honduras, and Zaire. For each of their three studies, they matched topic areas where methods contained similar questions, and they judged results from the two methods to be similar when "they would lead to the same conclusions" (p. 272). Based on explicit comparisons across a total of 60 variables, they found that the results from the two methods were: (i) highly similar for 30% of the variables; (ii) similar, but focus groups provided more information for 42% of the variables; (iii) similar, but surveys provided more information for 17%; and (iv) dissimilar for 12% of the variables. The biggest difference found between the methods was the ability of the focus groups to produce more in-depth information on the topic at hand.

In another systematic comparison of survey and focus group results, Saint-Germain *et al* (1993) reported on two studies of the barriers to breast cancer screening services for older Hispanic women in the southwestern United States. To assess the comparability of the results, the authors rank-ordered a list of barriers according to how often survey respondents had experienced each, and then they compared this to a rank-order of how often each barrier was mentioned in the focus groups. Saint-Germain *et al*'s conclusions (1993: 363) matched those of Ward *et al*: "The findings of the focus group interviews, in most cases, confirmed the findings of the previous population surveys. In many cases, the focus group interviews went beyond the information obtained in the survey, amplifying our understanding of the various facets of barriers to breast cancer screening and specifying more exactly how some of the barriers work in practice."

Although each of these studies emphasized the convergence of the results from focus groups and surveys, a consistent set of differences did occur in all three studies. First, the survey interview setting limited what respondents said about sensitive topics, in comparison to what they revealed in focus groups. Second, the differences in response options meant that surveys were better able to elicit yes/no answers about specific behaviors and experiences, even though the forced-choice format of the survey items limited what respondents could say on general attitude areas, in comparison to the more open-ended discussions in the focus groups. Finally, Ward *et al* explicitly noted that all of these comparisons used only the variables that occurred in both studies, thus downplaying the fact that the surveys typically covered many more topics than did the focus groups. There was thus a key tradeoff between the depth that focus groups provided and the breadth that surveys offered.

Comparisons to Individual Interviews

Fern's (1982) work on the relative productivity of individual interviews and focus groups was one of the very few methodological studies that involved a head-to-head comparison between the two methods. Using an "idea generation" task, Fern compared focus groups to an equivalent number of aggregated responses from individual interviews (i.e. "nominal groups"). He determined that each focus group participant produced only 60% to 70% as many ideas as they would have in an individual interview; he also had raters judge the quality of ideas from the two methods, and again an advantage appeared for individual interviews. These results clearly argue against the notion that focus groups have a "synergy" that makes them more productive than an equivalent number of individual interviews. Instead, the real issue may well be the relative efficiency of the two methods for any given project. For example, Fern's results suggest that two eight-person focus groups would produce as many ideas as 10 individual interviews. As Crabtree *et al* (1993) have pointed out, however, a number of logistical factors, such as location of the interviews, the mobility of the participants, the flexibility of their schedules, would determine which study would actually be easier to accomplish.

The major issue in studies of individual and group interviews has not, however, been the number of ideas they generate, but the comparability of the results they produce. Wight (1994) reported one of the rare studies on this issue. The study involved both group and individual interviews with the same adolescent males concerning their sexual experiences, and systematic variation in which of the two types of interviews was done first. Wight concluded that the greatest number of discrepancies occurred between reports of boys who participated in individual interviews first and then in focus groups, while boys who started in group interviews gave similar accounts in subsequent individual interviews. Kitzinger (1994a, b) reported that the conclusions about the results from her study on HIV issues validated those of Wight's, although she also found that the difference between individual and group interviews was limited to heterosexual males. Kitzinger thus argued against a generalized effect of groups on conformity, and she called for more attention to how such processes are affected by the group's composition, the topic, the relationship of the interviewer to the group, and the general context of the interview.

Kitzinger (1994b: 173) also reached the more general conclusion that, "Differences between interview and group data cannot be classified in terms of validity versus invalidity or honesty versus dishonesty .... The group data documenting macho or sexual harassing behaviour is no more 'invalid' than that showing the research participants' relatively acceptable behaviour in interview settings." It thus seems a safe conclusion that, if one searches, one is bound to find differences in how some interviewees talk about some topics in individual versus group interviews. For those cases where we are interested only in a specific social context, this interest will determine which form of data is more valid. In general, however, the existence of differences between what is said in individual and group interviews is as much a statement about our culture as our methods, and this is clearly a research topic of interest in its own right.

Strengths and Weaknesses of Focus Groups

One benefit of comparing focus groups to other methods is a more sophisticated understanding of the strengths and weaknesses of focus groups. For example, rather than just listing exploratory research as a strength of focus groups, it is now necessary to note that individual, nominal interviews can be a more effective technique for idea generation (Fern 1982) and that surveys can be more effective for determining the prevalence of any given attitude or experience (Ward *et al* 1992). Comparisons to other methods have thus led to the conclusion that the real strength of focus groups is not simply in exploring what people have to say, but in providing insights into the sources of complex behaviors and motivations (Morgan & Krueger 1993).

Morgan & Krueger also argued that the advantages of focus groups for investigating complex behaviors and motivations were a direct outcome of the interaction in focus groups, what has been termed "the group effect" (Carey 1994, Carey & Smith 1994). An emphasis on the specific kinds of interactions that occur in focus groups is also an improvement over vague assertions that "synergy" is one of their strengths. What makes the discussion in focus groups more than the sum of separate individual interviews is the fact that the participants both query each other and explain themselves to each other. As Morgan & Krueger (1993) have also emphasized, such interaction offers valuable data on the extent of consensus and diversity among the participants. This ability to observe the extent and nature of interviewees' agreement and disagreement is a unique strength of focus groups. A further strength comes from the researcher's ability to ask the participants themselves for comparisons among their experiences and views, rather than aggregating individual data in order to speculate about whether or why the interviewees differ.

The weaknesses of focus groups, like their strengths, are linked to the process of producing focused interactions, raising issues about both the role of the moderator in generating the data and the impact of the group itself on the data. With regard to the role of the moderator, Agar & MacDonald (1995) used discourse analysis to compare the conversations between interviewers and interviewees in a single focus group and a set of individual interviews They concluded that the dynamics of the individual interviews put more burden on the informants to explain themselves to the interviewer, while the moderator's efforts to guide the group discussion had the ironic consequence of disrupting the interaction that was the point of the group. Saferstein (1995) also used discourse analysis to make a similar point about moderator control in a comparison of focus groups and naturally occurring talk at a job site. In particular, he noted that it is the moderator, rather than the ongoing work of the group, that determines the agenda and form of the discussion. Both of these articles directly questioned the assertion that focus groups mimic a conversation among the participants, and each independently suggested that a meeting would be a better analogy due to the control exercised by the moderator.

Although the issues that Agar & MacDonald (1995) and Saferstein (1995) raised are of most concern with more directive styles of moderating, there is no denying that the behavior of the moderator has consequences for the nature of the group interviews. But the issue of interviewer effects is hardly limited to focus groups, as is shown in work from both survey research (Fowler & Mangione 1990) and individual interviewing (Mischler 1986). All of these issues point to the importance of understanding the range of variation that is possible across different styles of moderating, a range discussed in the following section.

In terms of weaknesses that are due to the impact of the group on the discussion itself, Sussman *et al* (1991) used a design from small group research and administered questionnaires before and after focus groups to find out if the discussions changed the participants' attitudes. They found the predicted "polarization" effect – attitudes became more extreme after the group discussion. The magnitude of this effect was small, however, as it accounted for only 4% of the variance in attitude change; this may be significant in an analysis of variance, but it is not likely to skew the results of most focus group research. Nonetheless, the point is well taken that we know little about how group members affect each other, and research designs from the social psychological study of small groups can offer useful tools for investigating this issue.

A final weakness due to the impact of the group on its participants concerns the range of topics that can be researched effectively in groups. Because group interaction requires mutual self-disclosure, it is undeniable that some topics will be unacceptable for discussion among some categories of research participants. At present, however, assertions about this weakness of focus groups are based more on intuition than data, since there are no empirical investigations of the range of topics or participants that either can or cannot be studied with group interviews. In particular, claims that focus groups are inappropriate for "sensitive topics" seem to ignore the widespread use of group interviewing to study sexual behavior in all forms. Further, the growing use of focus groups with cultural minorities and marginalized groups suggests that experience is the best predictor of where focus groups will and will not work. Fortunately, several of the researchers who have worked with sensitive topics and minority groups have written about their use of focus groups in these settings (Jarrett 1993, 1994, Hoppe *et al* 1995, Hughes & DuMont 1993, Kitzinger 1994a, b, Zeller 1993a), and only time will tell how widely these techniques apply to other topics and populations.

Research Designs for Sociological Applications of Focus Groups

As the previous sections demonstrate, sociologists and other social scientists have used focus groups in many ways for many purposes. Yet, if there are many ways of doing focus groups, then how does a practicing researcher make choices between doing focus groups one way versus another? And how does an outside reviewer determine whether a focus group project was done in a proper and effective fashion? The emerging consensus is that these issues can be resolved through an emphasis on research design in focus groups.

An emphasis on research design has advantages both for the field of focus groups as a whole and for individual investigators. For the field of focus groups, Morgan (1992a) has argued that an emphasis on research design would generate explicit principles that would replace the "rules of thumb" that have guided past practice. Thus, rather than simply asserting that focus groups should consist of structured discussions among 6 to 10 homogeneous strangers in a formal setting, an emphasis on research design would systematically investigate the implications of conducting more structured versus less structured discussions, of using smaller versus larger groups, etc. For the individual investigator, such research design principles would provide a means for linking the purposes of the research and the specific procedures that best achieve these purposes. For example, in his research on the political consciousness of ordinary citizens, Gamson (1992) first noted that his procedures departed from the prevailing rules of thumb when he used loosely moderated groups of four to six familiar acquaintances who met at one of the participants' homes; he then justified each of these design decisions by stating why it would produce data better suited to his purposes.

In considering the set of issues involved in designing focus group research, it is useful to distinguish between decisions that apply to the research project as a whole (i.e. project-level design issues), and those that apply to the conduct of a particular group (i.e. group-level design issues). While decisions at the project level specify the kinds of data that the focus groups should produce, group-level design decisions largely determine how to conduct the groups in order to produce such data. In particular, many of the group-level decisions are related to issues of group dynamics that help to ensure a productive discussion.

Project-Level Design Issues

Standardization

As a project-level design issue, standardization addresses the extent to which the identical questions and procedures are used in every group. At one extreme would be an emphasis on "emergence" that lets the questions and procedures shift from group to group in order to take advantage of what has been learned in previous groups. At the other extreme, a project could begin by determining a fixed set of questions and procedures that would apply throughout. Of course, standardization is actually a matter of degree, and even standardized designs allow minor variations that accommodate the unique aspects of each group, in order to avoid what Merton *et al* (1990) called the fallacy of adhering to fixed questions.

Although nothing like a census of focus group designs among sociologists exists, it is quite clear that the majority of these research projects have used a fixed research design that relied on a consistent set of predetermined questions and procedures. This tendency toward standardized research designs has not gone unexamined. Orosz (1994) has argued that this aspect of focus groups is inconsistent with many of the key tenets of qualitative research, while Brotherson & Goldstein (1992) made the case for pursuing standardization within an emergent research design. According to the present argument for making decisions according to research design principles, whether to standardize the questions and procedures in a focus group project should not be based on past tradition, within either the more standardized practices of focus group researchers or the less standardized approach favored by practitioners of other qualitative methods. Instead, it should be based on a conscious assessment of the advantages and disadvantages of standardization with regard to the goals of a particular project.

The great advantage of standardization, and its most common justification is the high level of comparability that it produces across groups. This comparability is particularly valuable when the goal of the research is to compare the responses of different categories of participants (see the discussion of segmentation in the next section). As Knodel (1993) pointed out, standardization has the particular advantage of facilitating the analysis of focus groups by allowing for direct comparisons of the discussions from group to group. The obvious disadvantage of standardization is that one must live with whatever questions and procedures were chosen prior to entering the field, which would be inimical to many truly exploratory applications of focus groups.

Morgan (1993c) has described two types of designs that combine the advantages of more standardized and more emergent designs (see Morgan 1992b for a partial application of these procedures). The first such design breaks the project into phases that move from less standardized to more standardized groups. This has the advantage of allowing the early groups in the project to take a more exploratory approach, which then serves as the basis for developing a later set of standardized questions and procedures grounded in the data themselves. The second compromise design organizes the questions in each group according to a "funnel" pattern that begins with a fixed set of core questions and then proceeds to a variable set of specific issues. This has the advantage of maintaining comparability across groups for the first part of each discussion but allowing the later section of each group to vary according to the emergent needs of the research.

Sampling

Focus group research reveals its historical association with marketing research by using the term "segmentation" to capture sampling strategies that consciously vary the composition of groups. This use of segmentation to create groups that consist of particular categories of participants is a long-standing practice, as illustrated by Folch-Lyon *et al*'s (1981) study on family planning, where they composed groups that were as homogeneous as possible by sex, age, marital status, contraceptive use, socioeconomic status, and geographical location. The most obvious kinds of segmentation capture something about the research topic itself. For example, if gender differences were of interest, then one might conduct separate groups of men and women, or an evaluation study might segment the groups into more frequent and less frequent users of the program in question.

Segmentation offers two basic advantages. First, it builds a comparative dimension into the entire research project, including the data analysis. For example, Folch-Lyon *et al* (1981) analyzed their data according to the categories described above and found the most wide-ranging differences between groups of men and women, with some additional differences between groups in rural and urban areas. Second, segmentation facilitates discussions by making the participants more similar to each other. For example, even if the behavior of men and women does not differ greatly on a given topic, discussion still may flow more smoothly in groups that are homogeneous rather than mixed with regard to sex. The same logic applies to dividing groups according to the age, race, or social class of the participants, although the value of segmenting to facilitate a free-flowing discussion obviously depends on the research topic.

The obvious disadvantage of segmentation is that it can greatly multiply the number of groups. As Knodel (1993) pointed out, it is seldom wise to run just one group per segment, since what one learns about that segment is confounded with the group dynamics of that unique set of participants. As Knodel also noted, however, using multiple segmentation criteria can produce acceptable designs that have only one group "per cell" in the overall design as long as there are multiple groups in each separate segment (e.g. there may be several groups of women, several rural groups, and several groups of older participants, but only one group of older, rural women). Even so, using multiple segmentation criteria can easily lead to projects that involve large numbers of focus groups, like the 44 groups conducted by Folch-Lyon *et al* (1981).

Number of Groups

The most common rule of thumb is that most projects consist of four to six focus groups. The typical justification for this range is that the data become "saturated" and little new information emerges after the first few groups, so moderators can predict what participants will say even before they say it (Zeller 1993b). Morgan (1992a) has suggested that diversity in either the participants or the range of topics to be covered will increase the number of groups necessary to achieve saturation. For example, Kitzinger wished to hear about views on AIDS from a wide range of different populations and thus conducted 52 groups, while Gamson (1992) wanted each of his groups to give their opinions on four different political issues and thus conducted 37 groups in order to produce enough discussion on each topic.

As the previous section noted, using multiple segments will increase the number of groups needed, which is a special case of diversity in the study population. Projects that use a lower level of standardization will also typically need more groups, since this produces more variation in the topics that are raised group to group. The connection between the number of groups and issues of standardization and segmentation raises the question of how different aspects of research design for focus groups intersect – a topic addressed at the end of this section.

Group-Level Design Issues

Level of Moderator Involvement

The presence of a moderator is one of the most striking features of focus groups. Groups in which the moderator exercises a higher degree of control are termed "more structured," and Morgan (1992a) has called attention to two senses in which a group can be more structured. First, it can be more structured with regard to asking questions, so that the moderator controls what topics are discussed (e.g. directing attention away from what are deemed less important issues). Second, it can be more structured with regard to managing group dynamics, so that the moderator controls the way that the participants interact (e.g. trying to get everyone to participate equally in the discussion). Both of these aspects of moderator involvement can be elements of the research design.

With regard to the moderator's involvement in asking questions, a less structured discussion means that the group can pursue its own interests, while a more structured approach means that the moderator imposes the researcher's interests, as embodied in the questions that guide the discussion. A key factor that makes groups more or less structured is simply the number of questions. Thus, if the average focus group lasts 90 minutes, and the moderator has the responsibility for covering a great many questions during that time, then the moderator will be heavily involved in controlling the group's discussion. Unfortunately, there is currently little consensus about what constitutes a more structured or less structured approach to questioning. For example, Lederman (1990: 123) characterized a guide that contained five broad questions as "quite structured," while Byers & Wilcox (1991: 65) termed a guide with 17 specific questions "relatively unstructured."

One possible cause for this confusion is the failure to distinguish between structure that controls questioning and structure that controls group dynamics. In managing group dynamics, a less structured approach allows participants to talk as much or as little as they please, while a more structured approach means that the moderator will encourage those who might otherwise say little and limit those who might otherwise dominate the discussion. Although most marketing approaches to focus groups (e.g. Greenbaum 1993) have typically advocated a more structured control of group dynamics, many social science approaches have explicitly favored a less directive style of interviewing (e.g. Krueger 1994, Merton *et al* 1990). Morgan's (1988) instructions for how to conduct "self-managed" groups, in which the moderator does not even sit at the same table as the participants, probably represent the extreme in social science advocacy of less structured approaches to group dynamics.

In general, marketing researchers, more than social science researchers, prefer research designs with high levels of moderator involvement that impose more structure with regard to both asking questions and managing group dynamics. Morgan (1988) has suggested that this reflects a difference between the marketing goal of answering questions from an audience of paying customers and the social science goal of generating new knowledge for an audience of peer reviewers. To the extent that this broad generalization does hold, it is a nice illustration of the general principle that research designs should follow from research goals. This conclusion – that approaches to moderating should be linked to research goals – is strongly supported by one of the few instances of systematic research that evaluates differences in moderator style (McDonald 1993). Further, it implies that arguments about whether moderators should use a more or less structured approach are meaningless unless one specifies the goals of the research.

Group Size

The number of participants who are invited to a focus group is one element of the research design that is clearly under the researcher's control. Morgan (1992a) reviewed the bases for determining group size, concluding that smaller groups were more appropriate with emotionally charged topics that generated high levels of participant involvement, while larger groups worked better with more neutral topics that generated lower levels of involvement. On the one hand, a smaller group gives each participant more time to discuss her or his views and experiences on topics in which they all are highly involved. On the other hand, a larger group contains a wider range of potential responses on topics where each participant has a low level of involvement. In addition, small groups make it easier for moderators to manage the active discussions that often accompany high levels of involvement and emotional topics, whereas large groups are easier to manage when each participant has a lower level of involvement in the topic.

This last point once again raises an issue that involves the intersection of two different design principles: group size and moderator involvement. Although it is generally the case that design dimensions cannot be considered in isolation from each other, current knowledge about how design issues impinge on each other is limited to a few obvious considerations. In addition to the linkage between group size and moderator involvement, earlier portions of this section noted connections between standardization and sample segmentation, and between the number of groups and both standardization and segmentation. There is thus an increasing but still limited stock of knowledge about how design issues go together. This limitation is understandable, given that most of the explicit investigations of research design in focus groups have come from social scientists and consequently reflect only a decade or so of activity.

Data Quality Concerns

The basic goal in specifying research designs for focus groups is to ensure that the research procedures deliver the desired data. Despite the best research designs, however, things can still go wrong due to poor planning or the inappropriate implementation of otherwise optimal designs. Krueger (1993) and Morgan (1995) have both noted that data quality depends on a number of factors, including whether the researcher locates enough participants, selects appropriate samples, chooses relevant questions, has a qualified moderator(s), and uses an effective analysis strategy.

Standards for reporting on research procedures are one practical step to improve the quality of focus group research. At present, the reporting of focus group procedures is a haphazard affair at best. Based on the studies reviewed for this chapter, the following is one effort to develop such standards. First, to learn the overarching context for the research, readers should know whether a standardized set of questions and procedures applied throughout the project. Then, most basically, readers should know the number of groups conducted and the size range of these groups. There should also be information on the group composition, including relevant background data on the participants. In particular, when groups are divided into different sample segments, there should be information on the basis for this sampling strategy and the number of groups per segment. Regardless of whether the study used segmentation, it is important to report the sources for locating participants and other information about recruitment procedures. In terms of the interview itself, thorough summaries of the question content are needed; surprisingly, many current publications say very little about the questions that were asked. Similarly, most current reports say little about moderating, and useful information would include concrete descriptions of the degree of structure that the moderator(s) imposed, how many moderators were used, and what their training and qualifications were. Finally, ethical issues need to be discussed, and, although the field as a whole has been slow to address ethical concerns in focus group research, there now is at least one discussion of this topic (Smith 1995).

This kind of information would aid not only reviewers in judging the quality of the research design and procedures but also other researchers in adapting these practices into future work. For both of these purposes, it would be highly desirable for research reports to go beyond merely presenting factual information to including justifications for the more crucial design decisions. This process of making public the basis for our decisions about why to do focus groups one way and not another is a vital step in the growth of our field.

Future Directions for Focus Groups

The steady increase in the use of focus groups over the past decade clearly demonstrates that sociologists and other social scientists have found them to be a useful and practical method for gathering qualitative data. The leading role that sociologists have played in this field has been most evident in methodological research on focus groups, which has given sociologists a major influence on both their current uses and future directions. In terms of future directions, a group of social science researchers participated in focus groups, funded in part by the American Sociological Association that led to a statement on "Future Directions for Focus Groups" (Morgan 1993b). Not surprisingly, several of the specific topics considered there have been echoed here, such as the need to set standards for focus groups and the need to further define the strengths and weaknesses of the method.

The major theme raised in the focus group discussions on future direction was the need to do more research on focus groups as a method, and several of the studies reviewed here provide concrete examples of how to accomplish this. For example, both Agar & MacDonald (1995) and Saferstein (1995) demonstrate the value of discourse analysis for investigating interactions between moderators and participants. Sociologists who have experimented with discourse analysis (e.g. Gamson 1992) have concluded that the time and expense spent in producing such data have little value for substantive analyses of what was said in groups. Yet, methodological analyses of how things are said in focus groups may well be a more profitable use of these tools. Another potentially useful technique from another field is Sussman *et al*'s (1991) application of procedures from small group research. As Morgan & Krueger (1993) note, however, it is important not to confuse the standard decision-making paradigm in small groups research with the data gathering goals of focus groups. One particularly promising aspect of the Sussman *et al* procedures is the post-group questionnaire, and other focus group researchers (Pies 1993, Swenson *et al* 1992) have used this technique to investigate not only the impact that the discussion had on the participants, but also their feelings about the discussion, including the extent to which they were able to share their true opinions on the topics they discussed. One final promising technique for methodological research on focus groups is McDonald's (1993) use of an archive of focus group transcripts to investigate how differences in project goals were linked to differences in moderator style. Unfortunately, qualitative researchers have been slower in archiving their work than their quantitative counterparts; still, the opportunity to compare the qualitative procedures of multiple investigators across multiple topics would be an exciting opportunity that should not be limited to focus groups.

Data analysis is another topic for future work on focus groups. To date, most discussions of how to analyze focus groups have occurred within broader discussions of the method (e.g. Knodel 1993), and only one article is specifically dedicated to analysis of issues (Bertrand *et al* 1992). Although it is true that many of the analytic issues in focus groups are the same as in other qualitative methods, it is also true that focus groups raise some unique issues, such as the ongoing debate about the circumstances under which the unit of analysis should be the groups, the participants, or the participants' utterances (Carey & Smith 1994, Gamson 1992, Morgan 1995). In addition, focus groups offer some special opportunities for the application of computer technologies in the analysis of qualitative data (Javidi *et al* 1991).

Beyond such strictly methodological concerns, there are also promising new uses for focus groups. The most notable of these involves researchers who are more actively engaged with the participants and their concerns. In an earlier section, this was summarized as an increasing interest in focus groups among those who pursue goals such as empowerment or approaches such as action and participatory research. Underlying many of these efforts is a desire to break down the division between using groups as a means for gathering data and as a means for educating, mobilizing, or intervening with participants. This matches a widespread concern in the social sciences about the artificiality of the division between researchers and those who are researched. This issue is especially relevant for focus groups, since they have been widely touted (e.g. Morgan & Krueger 1993) as a means for helping to bridge the gap between those in authority and the people they control.

One question about focus groups that has remained unasked, however, is why they have reemerged with such popularity at this particular time. One segment of our future work on focus groups should thus go beyond practical concerns with the method itself to ask about their place within the history of sociology – especially since this is the discipline that is self-consciously charged with the study of humans in groups. Part of the present popularity of focus groups may indeed be due to their unique advantages for addressing such contemporary issues as empowerment and diversity. Whether this is true or not, it is clear that focus groups are both being shaped by the directions that our discipline is taking and playing a role in shaping those directions.

References

Agar M, MacDonald J. 1995. Focus groups and ethnography. *Hum. Organ.* 54: 78–86.

Albrecht TL, Johnson GM, Walther JB. 1993. Understanding communication processes in focus groups. See Morgan 1993a, pp. 51–64.

Basch CE. 1987. Focus group interview: an underutilized research technique for improving theory and practice in health education. *Health Educ. Q.* 14: 411–48.

Bertrand JE, Brown JE, Ward VM. 1992. Techniques for analyzing focus group data *Eval. Rev.* 16: 198–209.

Bobo L, Zubrinsky CL, Johnson JH, Oliver ML. 1995. Work orientation, job discrimination, and ethnicity: a focus group perspective. *Res. Sociol. Work* 5: 45–55.

Bogardus ES. 1926. The group interview *J. Appl. Sociol.* 10: 372–82.

Brotherson MJ, Goldstein BL. 1992. Quality design of focus groups in early childhood special education research. *J. Early Interv.* 16: 334–42.

Bryant CA. 1990. The use of focus groups in program development. *Natl. Assoc. Pract. Anthropol. Bull.* 39: 1–4.

Bryman A. 1988. *Quality and Quantity in Social Research.* London: Unwin Hyman.

Byers PY, Wilcox JR. 1991. Focus groups: a qualitative opportunity for researchers. *J. Bus. Comm.* 28: 63–78.

Cable ES. 1992. Women's social movement involvement: the role of structural availability in recruitment and participation processes. *Sociol. Q.* 33: 35–50.

Carey MA. 1994. The group effect in focus groups: planning, implementing and interpreting focus group research. In *Critical Issues in Qualitative Research Methods,* ed. J Morse, pp. 225–41. Thousand Oaks, CA: Sage.

——. 1995. Issues and applications of focus groups. *Qual. Health Res.* 5: 413–530 (Special issue).

Carey MA, Smith M.1994. Capturing the group effect in focus groups: a special concern in analysis. *Qual. Health Res.* 4: 123–27.

Crabtree BF, Yanoshik MK, Miller WL, O'Connor PJ. 1993. Selecting individual or group interviews. See Morgan 1993a, pp. 137–49.

Delli Carpini MX, Williams B. 1994. The method is the message: focus groups as a method of social, psychological, and political inquiry. *Res. Micropolit.* 4: 57–85.

Diamond E, Bates S. 1992. *The Spot: The Rise of Political Advertising on Television.* Cambridge, MA: MIT Press. 3rd ed.

Duncan MT, Morgan DL. 1994. Sharing the caring: family caregivers' views of their relationships with nursing home staff. *The Gerontologist* 34: 235–44.

Fern EF. 1982. The use of focus groups for idea generation: the effects of group size, acquaintanceship, and moderator on response quantity and quality. *J. Mark Res.* 19: 1–13.

Flores JG, Alonso CG. 1995. Using focus groups in educational research. *Eval. Rev.* 19: 84–101.

Folch-Lyon E, de la Macorra L, Schearer SB. 1981. Focus group and survey research on family planning in Mexico. *Stud Fam. Plan.* 12: 409–32.

Fowler FJ, Mangione TW. 1990. *Standardized Survey Interviewing*. Thousand Oaks, CA: Sage.

Frey JH, Fontana A. 1991. The group interview in social research. *Soc. Sci. J.* 28: 175–87. See also Morgan 1993a, pp. 20–34.

Fuller TD, Edwards JN, Vorakitphokatorn S, Sermsri S. 1993. Using focus groups to adapt survey instruments to new populations: experience from a developing country. See Morgan 1993a, pp. 89–104.

Gamson WA. 1992. *Talking Politics*. Cambridge, UK Cambridge Univ. Press.

Goldman AK, McDonald SS. 1987. *The Group Depth Interview: Principles and Practice*. Englewood Cliffs, NJ: Prentice Hall.

Greenbaum TL. 1988/1993. *The Practical Handbook and Guide to Focus Group Research*. Lexington, MA: Lexington. Rev. ed.

Harari O, Beaty D. 1990. On the folly of relying solely on a questionnaire methodology in cross-cultural research. *J. Manage. Issues* 2: 267–81.

Hendershott A, Wright S. 1993. Student focus groups and curricular review. *Teach. Sociol.* 21: 154–59.

Hoppe MJ, Wells EA, Morrison DM, Gillmore MR, Wilsdon A.1995. Using focus groups to discuss sensitive topics with children. *Eval. Rev.* 19: 102–14.

Hugentobler MK, Israel BA, Schurman SJ. 1992. An action research approach to workplace health: integrating methods. *Health Educ. Q.* 19: 55–76.

Hughes D, DuMont K. 1993. Using focus groups to facilitate culturally anchored research. *Am. J. Community Psychol.* 21: 775–806.

Irwin J. 1970. *The Felon*. Englewood Cliffs, NJ: Prentice Hall.

Irwin K, Bertrand J, Mibandumba N, Mbuyi K, Muremeri C et al. 1991. Knowledge, attitudes and beliefs about HIV infection and AIDS among healthy factory workers and their wives, Kinshasa, Zaire. *Soc. Sci. Med* 32: 917–30.

Jarrett RL. 1993. Focus group interviewing with low-income, minority populations: a research experience. See Morgan 1993a, pp. 184–201.

———. 1994. Living poor: family life among single parent, African-American women. *Soc. Probl.* 41: 30–49.

Javidi M, Long LW, Vasu ML, Ivy DK. 1991. Enhancing focus group validity with computer-assisted technology in social science research. *Soc. Sci. Comput. Rev.* 9: 231–45.

Joseph JG, Emmons CA, Kessler RC, Wortman CB, O'Brien K, et al. 1984. Coping with the threat of AIDS: an approach to psychosocial assessment. *Am. Psychol.* 39: 1297–302.

Khan ME, Manderson L. 1992. Focus groups in tropical diseases research. *Health Policy Plan.* 7: 56–66.

Kitzinger J. 1994a. The methodology of focus groups: the importance of interaction between research participants. *Sociol. Health Illn.* 16: 103–21.

———. 1994b. Focus groups: method or madness. In *Challenge and Innovation: Methodological Advances in Social Research on HIV/AIDS*, ed. M Boulton, pp. 159–75. New York: Taylor & Francis.

Kline A, Kline E, Oken E. 1992. Minority women and sexual choice in the age of AIDS. *Soc. Sci. Med* 34: 447–57.

Knodel J. 1993. The design and analysis of focus group studies: a practical approach. See Morgan 1993a, pp. 35–50.

———. 1995. Focus group research on the living arrangements of elderly in Asia. *J. Cross-Cult. Gerontol.* 10: 1–162 (Special issue).
Knodel J, Chamratrithirong A, Debavalya N. 1987. *Thailand's Reproductive Revolution: Rapid Fertility Decline in a Third-World Setting.* Madison, WI: Univ. Wisc. Press.
Krueger RA. 1993. Quality control in focus group research. See Morgan 1993a, pp. 65–85.
———. 1988/1994. *Focus Groups: A Practical Guide for Applied Research.* Thousand Oaks, CA: Sage. 2nd ed.
Kullberg JS. 1994. The ideological roots of elite political conflict in post-Soviet Russia. *Eur. Asia Stud.* 46: 929–53.
Laurie H. 1992. Multiple methods in the study of household resource allocation. In *Mixing Methods: Qualitative and Quantitative Research* ed. J Brannen, pp. 145–68. Brookfield, VT: Avebury.
Laurie H, Sullivan O. 1991. Combining qualitative and quantitative data in the longitudinal study of household allocations. *Sociol. Rev.* 39: 113–30.
Lederman LC. 1990. Assessing educational effectiveness: the focus group interview as a technique for data collection. *Commun. Educ.* 39: 117–27.
Lengua LJ, Roosa MW, Schupak-Neuberg E, Michaels ML, Berg CN, Weschler LF. 1992. Using focus groups to guide the development of a parenting program for difficult-to-reach, high-risk families. *Fam. Relat.* 41: 163–68.
Lincoln YS, Guba EG. 1985. *Naturalistic Inquiry.* Thousand Oaks, CA: Sage.
Magill RS. 1993. Focus groups, program evaluation, and the poor. *J. Sociol. Soc. Welfare* 20: 103–14.
McDonald WJ. 1993. Focus group research dynamics and reporting: an examination of research objectives and moderator influences. *J. Acad. Mark. Sci.* 21: 161–68.
McKinlay JB. 1993. The promotion of health through planned sociopolitical change: challenges for research and policy. *Soc. Sci. Med.* 36: 109–17.
McQuarrie EF 1990. Review of: Morgan, *Focus Groups as Qualitative Research*, and McCracken, *The Long Interview. J. Mark. Res.* 13: 114–17.
McQuarrie EE 1996. *The Market Research Toolbox.* Thousand Oaks, CA: Sage.
Merton RK. 1987. The focused interview and focus groups: continuities and discontinuities. *Public Opin. Q.* 51: 550–66.
Merton RK, Fiske M, Kendall PL. 1956/1990. *The Focused Interview.* New York: Free Press. 2nd ed.
Merton RK, Kendall PL. 1946. The focused interview. *Am. J. Sociol.* 51: 541–57.
Mischler KG. 1986. *Research Interviewing: Context and Narrative.* Cambridge, MA: Harvard Univ. Press.
Montell FB. 1995. *Focus group interviews: a new feminist method.* Presented at Annu. Meet. Am. Sociol. Assoc., Washington, DC.
Morgan DL. 1988. *Focus Groups as Qualitative Research.* Thousand Oaks, CA: Sage.
———. 1989. Adjusting to widowhood: do social networks really make it easier? *Gerontologist* 29: 101–7.
———. 1992a. Designing focus group research. In *Tools for Primary Care Research*, ed. M Stewart, et al, pp. 177–93. Thousand Oaks, CA: Sage.
———. 1992b. Doctor caregiver relationships: an exploration using focus groups. In *Doing Qualitative Research in Primary Care: Multiple Strategies*, ed. B Crabtree, W Miller, pp. 205–30. Thousand Oaks, CA: Sage.
———. 1993a. *Successful Focus Groups: Advancing the State of the Art.* Thousand Oaks, CA: Sage.
———. 1993b. Future directions for focus groups. See Morgan 1993a, pp. 225–44.

——. 1993c. *Focus groups and surveys.* Presented at Annu. Meet. Am. Sociol. Assoc., Pittsburg, PA.

——. 1994. *Seeking diagnosis for a family member with Alzheimer's disease.* Presented at Annu. Meet. Am. Sociol. Assoc., Los Angeles, CA.

——. 1995. Why things (sometimes) go wrong in focus groups. *Qual. Health Res.* 5: 516–22.

Morgan DL, Krueger RA. 1993. When to use focus groups and why. See Morgan 1993a, pp. 3–19.

Morgan DL, Spanish MT. 1985. Social interaction and the cognitive organisation of health-relevant behavior. *Sociol. Health Illness* 7: 401–22.

Morgan DL, Zhao PZ. 1993. The doctor–caregiver relationship: managing the care of family members with Alzheimer's disease. *Qual. Health Res.* 3: 133–04.

Nelson JE, Frontczak NT. 1988. How acquaintanceship and analyst can influence focus group results. *J. Advert.* 17: 41–48.

Nichols-Casebolt A, Spakes R 1995. Policy research and the voices of women. *Soc. Work Res.* 19: 49–55.

O'Brien KJ. 1993. Improving survey questionnaires through focus groups. See Morgan 1993a, pp. 105–17.

O'Connor PJ, Crabtree BF, Abourizk NN. 1992. Longitudinal study of a diabetes education and care intervention. *J. Am. Board Fam. Practice* 5: 381–87.

Orosz JF. 1994. *The use of focus groups in health care service delivery: understanding and improving the health care experience.* Presented at Qual Health Res. Conf., Hershey, PA.

Padilla R. 1993. Using dialogical methods in group interviews. See Morgan 1993a, pp. 153–66.

Pies C. 1993. *Controversies in context: ethics, values, and policies concerning NORPLANT.* PhD thesis. Univ. Calif, Berkeley.

Pinderhughes H. 1993. The anatomy of racially motivated violence in New York City: a case study of youth in southern Brooklyn. *Soc. Probl.* 40: 478–92.

Pollak M, Paicheler G, Pierret J. 1992. AIDS: a problem for sociological research. *Curr. Sociol./La Sociol. Contemp.* 40: 1–134.

Race KE, Hotch DF, Packer T. 1994. Rehabilitation program evaluation: use of focus groups to empower clients. *Eval. Rev.* 18: 730–40.

Saferstein B. 1995. *Focusing opinions: conversation, authority, and the (re)construction of knowledge.* Presented at Annu. Meet. Am. Sociol. Assoc., Washington, DC.

Saint-Germain MA, Bassford TL, Montano G. 1993. Surveys and focus groups in health research with older Hispanic women. *Qual. Health Res.* 3: 341–67.

Sasson T. 1995. Crime *Talk: How Citizens Construct a Social Problem.* Hawthorne, NY: Aldine.

Schearer SB. 1981. The value of focus group research for social action programs. *Stud. Fam. Plan.* 12 407–8.

Shively JE. 1992. Cowboys and Indians: perceptions of Western films among American Indians and Anglos. *Am Sociol. Rev.* 57: 725.

Smith MW. 1995. Ethics in focus groups: a few concerns. *Qual. Health Res.* 5: 478–86.

Staley CS. 1990. Focus group research: the communication practitioner as marketing specialist. In *Applied Communication Theory and Research,* ed. D O'Hair, G Kreps, pp. 185–201. Hillsdale, NJ: Erlbaum.

Stewart DW, Shamdasani PN. 1990 *Focus Groups: Theory and Practice.* Thousand Oaks, CA: Sage.

Stycos JM. 1981. A critique of focus group and survey research: the machismo case. *Stud Fam. Plan.* 12: 450–56.

Sussman S, Buyton D, Dent CW, Stacy AW, Flay BR. 1991. Use of focus groups in developing an adolescent tobacco use cessation program: collective norm effects. *J. Appl. Soc. Psychol.* 21: 1772–82.

Swenson JD, Griswold WF Kleiber PB. 1992. Focus groups: method of inquiry/intervention. *Small Groups Res.* 23: 459–74.

Templeton JF. 1987. *Focus Groups: A Guide for Marketing and Advertising Professionals.* Chicago: Probus.

Vaughn S, Shumm JS, Sinagub S. 1996. *Focus Group Interviews in Education and Psychology.* Thousand Oaks. CA: Sage.

Ward VM, Bertrand JT, Brown LF. 1991. The comparability of focus group and survey results *Eval. Rev.* 15: 266–83.

Wight D. 1994. Boys' thoughts and talk about sex in a working class locality of Glasgow. *Sociol. Rev.* 42: 702–37.

Wolff B, Knodel J, Sittitrai W. 1993. Focus groups and surveys as complementary research methods: a case example. See Morgan 1993a, pp. 118–36.

Zeller RA. 1993a Focus group research on sensitive topics: setting the agenda without setting the agenda. See Morgan 1993a, pp. 167–83.

——. 1993b. Combining qualitative and quantitative techniques to develop culturally sensitive measures. In *Methodological Issues in AIDS Behavioral Research*, ed. D Ostrow, R Kessler, pp. 95–116. New York: Plenum.

19

The Methodology of Focus Groups: The Importance of Interaction Between Research Participants

Jenny Kitzinger

Introduction

Focus groups are group discussions organised to explore a specific set of issues such as people's views and experiences of contraception (Barker and Rich 1992, Zimmerman *et al.* 1990), drink-driving (Basch *et al.* 1989), nutrition (Crokett *et al.* 1990) or mental illness (Grunig 1990). The group is 'focused' in the sense that it involves some kind of collective activity – such as viewing a film, examining a single health education message or simply debating a particular set of questions. Crucially, focus groups are distinguished from the broader category of group interviews by 'the explicit use of the group interaction' as research data (see Merton 1956 and Morgan 1988: 12).

There is nothing new about focus groups. They are first mentioned as a market research technique in the 1920s (Basch 1987; Bogardus 1926) and were used by Merton in the 1950s to examine people's reactions to wartime propaganda (Merton *et al.* 1956). In fact it is Merton who is often credited with developing the 'focused interview' with groups. (Although he never actually used the term 'focus group' and would beg to differ from some contemporary uses of the technique) (see Merton 1987).

Group discussions in their widest sense have continued to be popular as a method of data collection throughout the 1970s and 80s within particular niches. For example, group methods are often used within 'communication research' such as in the evaluation of health education material, and in film and television reception studies (Frazer 1987, Philo 1990, Schlesinger *et al.* 1992, Corner 1990). Such methods are also popular in studies designed to explore people's experiences of services such as health screening and in action research projects involving grass-roots participation (Gregory and McKie 1991, Watts and Ebbutt 1987). However, group work has not been systematically developed as a research technique within social science in general and although group interviews have often implicitly informed research they are rarely acknowledged as part of the process (see Frey and Fontana 1991: 177). Even when group work is explicitly included as part of the research it is often simply employed as a convenient way to illustrate a theory generated by other methods or as a cost-effective technique for interviewing several people at once. Reading some such reports it is hard to believe that there was ever more than one person in the room at the same time. This criticism even applies to many studies which explicitly identify their methodology as 'focus group discussion' – in spite of the fact that the distinguishing feature of focus groups is supposed to be the use of interaction as part of the research data. Reviewing over 40 published reports of 'focus group studies' I could not find a single one concentrating on the conversation between participants and very few that even included any quotations from more than one participant at a time. This article attempts to redress the balance through a detailed examination of the interactions between the research participants on the AIDS Media Research Project.

The AIDS Media Research Project: Why Focus Groups were Used and How they were Selected

The AIDS Media Research Project was a three-pronged study of the production, content and effect of media messages about AIDS (see Beharrell 1993, Miller and Williams 1993, Kitzinger 1990). Focus groups were used to examine the 'effect' element in this equation – to explore how media messages are processed by audiences and how understandings of AIDS are constructed. We were interested not solely in what people thought but in *how* they thought and *why* they thought as they did. We were also concerned to examine how diverse identities and social networks might impact upon research participants' perceptions of AIDS and their reactions to the media coverage. Such research objectives necessitated the use of in-depth work and we opted for group work because of our interest in the social context of public understandings.

We conducted a total of 52 different discussions, comprising 351 participants. The bulk of these sessions were conducted by the author, others were run by colleagues on the project: Peter Beharrell, David Miller and Kevin Williams. Each group consisted of, on average, 6 research participants and the discussion lasted approximately 2 hours and was tape-recorded. All participants also completed individual questionnaires.[1] This represents a far more extensive use of focus groups than any other study which I have located to date. Many 'focus group studies' rely on no more than 4 or 5 groups, and this may be a perfectly adequate number when working with particular populations. In our case, however, the sample covered a wide range of different 'populations' in England, Scotland and Wales and the groups were selected in order to explore diversity, rather than in order to establish any kind of 'representativeness'. The sample included so-called 'general population' groups such as five women whose children attended the same play group, a team of civil engineers working on the same site, and six members of a retirement club. It also included some groups who might be expected to have particular perspectives on AIDS – groups such as prisons officers, male prostitutes, IV drug-users and lesbians.

We chose to work with pre-existing groups – clusters of people who already knew each other through living, working or socialising together. We did this in order to explore how people might talk about AIDS within the various and overlapping groupings within which they actually operate. Flatmates, colleagues, family and friends – these are precisely the people with whom one might 'naturally' discuss such topics, at least in passing, and these are major sites of 'collective remembering' (see Middleton and Edwards 1990). Although the practice of using existing friendship groups is discouraged by standard market research texts such wariness seemed unjustified in our case. By using pre-existing groups we were sometimes able to tap into *fragments* of interactions which approximated to 'naturally occurring' data (such as might have been collected by participant observation). The fact that research participants already knew each other had the additional advantage that friends and colleagues could relate each other's comments to actual incidents in their shared daily lives. They often challenged each other on contradictions between what they were *professing* to believe and how they actually behaved (e.g. 'how about that time you didn't use a glove while taking blood from a patient?' or 'what about the other night when you went off with that boy at the disco?').

Above all it is useful to work with pre-existing groups because they provide one of the social contexts within which ideas are formed and decisions made. Khan and Manderson recommended the explicit use of such informal as well as formal 'focus groups' for anthropological research into understandings of health and illness in village settings. They worked with groups composed, for example, of a woman, her daughter, daughter-in-law and unrelated immediate neighbours. 'Such natural clusterings of people' they point out, 'represent, in a loose fashion, the resources upon which any member of the group might draw [...] [for] information and advice. This is a group that may weave or repair nets together, while watching over children and discussing the events of the previous day. It is precisely this natural social network which provides the scripting for the management of an illness event – what to do with a child with bloody diarrhoea, for example; or how to nurse high fever; or who to call in the case of threatened miscarriage' (Khan and Manderson 1992:60). In the same way such 'natural clusterings' at work, social events or in the home (along with the mass media) provide part of the 'scripting' for people's response to AIDS in Britain.

It would be naive, however, to assume that group data is by definition 'natural' in the sense that it would have occurred without the group having been convened for this purpose. It is important to note that although, *at times*, the focus groups may approximate to participant observation the focus groups are artificially set up situations. Rather than assuming the group session unproblematically and inevitably reflects 'everyday interactions' (although sometimes it will) the group should be used to encourage people to engage with one another, verbally formulate their ideas and draw out the cognitive structures which previously have been unarticulated.[2]

Running the Focus Group Sessions – Maximising Interaction Between Participants

Perceiving the research session as a forum within which ideas could be clarified rather than simply as a 'natural event' influenced the ways in which we chose to run the groups. Sessions were conducted in a relaxed fashion with minimal intervention from the facilitator – at least at first. This allowed the facilitator to 'find her feet' and permitted the research participants to set the priorities. However, the researcher was never passive. Trying to maximise interaction between participants could lead to a more interventionist style: urging debate to continue beyond the stage it might otherwise have ended, challenging people's taken for granted reality and encouraging them to discuss the inconsistencies both between participants and within their own thinking.

The facilitator also employed several group exercises. At the start of the session, for example, participants were asked to play 'the news game' which involved dividing into two small 'teams' and writing their own news bulletin using a pre-selected set of photographs taken from actual TV news bulletins. Later they were presented with a pack of cards bearing statements about who might be 'at risk' from AIDS and asked, as a group, to sort the cards into different piles indicating the degree of 'risk' attached to each 'type of person'. Such exercises involve people in working together with minimal input from the facilitator and encourage participants to concentrate on one another (rather than on the group facilitator) during the subsequent discussion. The card game also encourages everyone to talk as each participant reads out a statement in turn and the material existence of the cards seemed to embolden some people. Seeing the card physically placed under the 'wrong' category makes the dissenting individual twitch – often they have reached out and moved the card even before they have been able to articulate their dissent. Once having done so the onus is upon them to explain their reasoning. Transferring key statements onto large cards which have to be placed in different piles by the research participants is a useful technique which can be adapted to many different situations. For example, I have used the 'card game' with peace campaigners (asking them to sort statements about gender and violence into different 'agree'–'disagree' categories); old people in residential care (assigning degree of importance to different statements about the quality of their care) and with midwives (describing how they saw their professional role). The cards can carry statements about opinions, descriptions of people, accounts of events or even pictures. The categories into which these cards are to be sorted may range from degree of agreement or importance, to the perceived health risk attributed to a certain activity. The 'cards' can even be advertisements – with the group being asked to order them according to different criteria – such as 'offensiveness' or 'effectiveness'. The final layout of the cards is not important – it is the process of getting there which is revealing.

Such exercises not only provided invaluable data from each group but allow for some cross-comparisons *between* groups. Each discussion session has its own dynamic and direction – when it comes to analysis it is extremely useful to have a common external reference point such as that provided by the card game or the use of vignettes (Khan and Manderson 1992). At the very least such exercises served as a 'party game': 'warming up' participants and encouraging them to engage with one another. Unfortunately some people, of course, do not like party games and at worst such games could make people feel uncomfortable and reminded some research participants of school lessons!

Whether or not we were always successful our intentions were to encourage interaction between research participants as much as possible. When group dynamics worked well the co-participants acted as co-researchers taking the research into new and often unexpected directions and engaging in interaction which were both complementary (such as sharing common experiences) and argumentative (questioning, challenging, and disagreeing with each other). The following discussion explores the advantages of focus groups under these two headings of 'complementary' and 'argumentative' in order to examine how both the *similarities* between group participants, and their individual *differences*, contribute to the data collection process.

Complementary Interactions: The Importance of the Shared Culture

Group work is invaluable for 'grounded theory development – focusing on the generation rather than the testing of theory and exploring the categories which the participants use to order their experience' (Glazer and Strauss 1967). How do researcher participants think about 'risk', for example, and what criteria do they use to evaluate the threat posed by HIV (Irwin *et al.* 1991), hazardous waste (Desvousges and Smith 1988) or the factors influencing one's susceptibility to heart attack (Morgan 1988).

Group work ensures that priority is given to the respondents' hierarchy of importance, *their* language and concepts, *their* frameworks for understanding the world. In fact, listening to discussions between participants gives the researcher time to acclimatise to, for example, their preferred words for speaking about sex and prevents the researcher from prematurely closing off the generation of meaning in her own search for clarification. Take the following exchange between two research participants within one group:

> *LL1*: I remember an AIDS advert with a huge tombstone thing
> *LL2*: Oh, you mean the advert where they abseil down
> *LL1*: That's right, the one that looks like a Benson and Hedges cigarette advert [Lesbians, group 1]

The exchange between the research participants not only allows the researcher to understand which advertisement they are talking about but to gather data on their shared perception of that image.

The fact that group participants provide an audience for each other encourages a greater variety of communication that is often evident within more traditional methods of data collection. During the course of the AIDS project group participants argued, boasted, made faces at each other, told stories and on one occasion, sang songs. Group work is characterised by teasing, joking and the kind of acting out that goes on among peers. For example, some participants acted out the 'look' of an 'AIDS carrier' (contorting their faces, squinting and shaking) and others took evident delight in swapping information about the vast quantities of saliva one would need to drink before running any risk of infection. (You'd need to swallow 'six gallons', 'eight gallons', 'ten gallons' or 'bathe in it while covered in open sores'.) Brainstorming and loose word association was a frequent feature of the research sessions. In several groups any attempt to address the risks HIV poses to gay men were drowned out by a ritual period of outcry against homosexuality:

> *ITM*: Benders, poufs
> *ITM*: Bent bastards
> *ITM*: Bent shops
> *ITM*: they're poufs, I mean I don't know how a man could have sex with another man it's..
> *ITM*: It's disgusting […]
> *ITM*: Ah, Yuk!

A certain amount of similar 'brain-storming' accompanied discussion of the idea that 'AIDS comes from Africa':

> *ITF*: Look at all the famine over there, all the disease coming off the dead cows and all that, they die and all that
> *ITM*: Dirtiness
> *ITM*: Filthy
> *ITF*: Blackness
> *JK*: Blackness? what about it?

ITM: It's black
ITF: Black, Blackness, it's black, that's what I mean it's dirty
ITM: It's just disgusting. [Young people in intermediate treatment]

These sorts of interactions can make groups seem unruly (both at the time and when attempting to analyse the data) but such 'undisciplined' outbursts are not irrelevant or simply obstructive to the collection of data about what people 'know'. On the contrary, the enthusiasm with which some people acted out 'the look of an AIDS carrier' vividly demonstrates the voyeuristic fascination of 'the Face of AIDS' and the way in which some media images are reproduced, reinforced and reiterated through social interaction. The relish with which people swapped information about the vast quantities of saliva needed to pose any risk of infection highlights the potency of the 'yuk' factor in helping them to recall certain 'facts' about AIDS and suggests the potential of harnessing peer communication. The outcry provoked by any mention of homosexuality and the loose word-association about 'blackness' reveal an essential element in how people think about AIDS among gay men or in Africa. They form part of why some people believe that gay men (and lesbians) are inherently vulnerable to HIV or why they so readily accept that Africa is a hotbed of HIV infection (Kitzinger and Miller, 1992.)[3] Tapping into such variety of communication is important because people's knowledge and attitudes are not entirely encapsulated in reasoned responses to direct questions. Everyday forms of communication such as anecdotes, jokes or loose word association may tell us *as much*, if not *more*, about what people 'know'. In this sense focus groups 'reach the parts that other methods cannot reach' – revealing dimensions of understanding that often remain untapped by the more conventional one-to-one interview or questionnaire.

In addition to the advantages discussed above focus groups facilitate the collection of data on group norms. Often a particular phrase will mobilise an assertion of group consensus. A group of mothers, for example, discussing whether they had the 'right' to know if another child in the play group had the virus asserted that 'you think of your own first'. It was this phrase, and these sort of sentiments, which seemed to capture their consent and resulted in nods of agreement round the group and assertions that 'that's right' and 'of course'. Indeed, it was often the strength of the collective reaction that highlighted the specific context within which the research participants experienced AIDS information. When I asked one group of young women whether they had ever come across the advice that they could 'try sex which avoids penetration' they responded with initial bemusement followed by spontaneous protest: 'If you really wanted to prevent it everyone would end up locked in their house', 'It's sort of saying don't bother having sex, don't bother even going out in the first place', 'It's [saying that sex is] a lost cause!' [School students].

This apparently unanimous agreement underlined the extent to which young heterosexual women may experience such safer sex recommendations in terms of prohibitions. Advice to avoid penetration is seen as yet more constraints on, and attempts to control their sexual expression. They do not perceive it as an invitation to explore other avenues of pleasure as suggested by some optimistic health educators and feminist writers. Their rejection of non-penetrative sex drew attention both to the style and context of such safer sex advice and to what Fine calls 'the missing discourse of desire' (Fine 1988). This is not to say that on an individual level these women might not find most pleasure in what they would call 'foreplay' – a 'subjective' experience that might be more easily tapped by interview – but the very lack of public discourse about this contributes to the difficulties women face when attempting to establish the validity of such experiences or to secure safer sexual practices with men.

The downside of such group dynamics is, of course, that the group may censor any deviation from group standards – inhibiting people from talking about certain things. Observation of how group members interacted certainly highlighted the potential stigma some groups attached to 'knowing too much' about AIDS. In several groups if one person revealed detailed information about how HIV was transmitted they were met with suspicion and cries of 'How come you know so much about this?' Ironically, in the context, ignorance can, it seems, earn more respect than interest or knowledge – a fact which, in itself, is important to confront. There were also certain items of personal information which research participants on the AIDS project were sometimes prepared to confide to the researcher – in person or via their questionnaire – but were not prepared to reveal to the group as a whole (e.g. being gay, having been raped, or having a bisexual husband). When using groups it is important to consider what information may be censored by particular group compositions. 'Minority' (female/black/gay) voices are muted within 'majority'/'general population' groups.

However, it should not be assumed that groups, by definition, are inhibiting relative to the supposed 'privacy' of an interview situation. In fact, depending on their composition groups can sometimes actively facilitate the discussion of otherwise 'taboo' topics because the less inhibited members of the group 'break the ice' for shyer participants or one person's revelation of 'discrediting' information encourages others to disclose. For example, when one group member revealed that needles were often left lying around in her block of flats another woman said that she experienced the same problem. She added that she would not usually volunteer such information because: 'you don't want folk to know it goes on in your bit' and it is not the sort of information you reveal to an 'outsider' [Residential group]. In another case the researcher was unable to persuade one woman to explain what she was thinking, and it was only the timely intervention of her friends that helped to clarify what was going through her mind. The extract reproduced below occurred after the researcher had shown the group an image from a particular advertisement. One participant, Gail, had immediate associations with the image – associations which I was at a loss to understand. However her friends, Tessa and Brenda caught on very quickly to what she was thinking and helped her to articulate it:

JK: Can any of you imagine what this means? What the slogan underneath might be?

Gail: [bursts out laughing, hides head in hands, suddenly Tessa joins in]

Gail: I'll say nothing! Oh, Brenda don't make me laugh

JK: Are you making up fantasy slogans for it in your head?

Gail: No, no, no! [pause]

JK: Can you imagine what it might say? [laughter, followed by silence]

JK: Gail, please tell me!

Gail: No, no, no [laughter] don't make me laugh

JK: Please!

Gail: I don't know

JK: Would you be happier writing it down?

Gail: No! [all laugh] It just makes me think of things ...

Tessa: What, are you thinking of? Oral sex?

Gail: Yes, that's right! [Cleaners]

Not only do co-participants help each other to overcome embarrassment but they can also provide mutual support in expressing feelings which are common to their group but which they might consider deviant from mainstream culture (or the assumed culture of the researcher). This may be particularly important when working with those who are oppressed or marginalised such as, in our case, drug users, and male prostitutes. Some writers seem to assume that focus groups are inappropriate for researching 'sensitive' topics or when working with 'sensitive' research populations but in fact the opposite may be true.[4] It is worth noting that focus groups have successfully been used to elicit data from people who are perceived by researchers as, by definition, 'difficult subjects' e.g. 'difficult-to-reach, high-risk families' (Lengua et al. 1992) and 'high apprehensives' who are anxious about communicating (Lederman 1983).[5] Not only does safety in numbers make some people more likely to consent to participate in the research in the first place ('I wouldn't have come on my own') but being with other people who share similar experiences encourages participants to express, clarify or even to develop particular perspectives. Groups may be particularly useful when one wishes to gain access to critical comments from groups such as pregnant women, who tend to be 'grateful' and complementary about the services on offer. Some researchers have noted that group discussions can quickly become 'a collective "moan session"' as 'conversation seemed to feed on the climate of depreciation created' (Watts and Ebbutt 1987:31) and Geis and his colleagues, in their study of the 'lovers of AIDS victims', found that: 'The group meeting experience evoked more angry and emotional comments about the medical community than did the individual interviews ... perhaps the synergism of the group "kept the anger going" and allowed each participant to reinforce another's vented feelings of frustration and rage ...' (Geis et al. 1986:48). Group work is invaluable in enabling people to articulate experiences in ways which break away from the clichés of dominant cultural constructions. This may be particularly important for medical sociologists who are often working with people who share stigmatised or 'taboo' experiences (e.g. bereavement, mental illness, infertility, cancer).

To sum up, many authors write as if the impact of the group on the expression of individual points of view is a purely negative, inhibiting or distorting factor. In so far as such criticisms are accurate, they need not be seen as a problem. Even if the group does 'censure' certain types of information this does not invalidate the data from the group session: people do not operate in a social vacuum, knowing what is (and is not) expressed in a group context may be as important as knowing what is expressed in a confidential, one-to-one interview. (And if one wishes to explore this further one can, of course, use a *combination* of such methods). In any case it is unjustified to make such generalisations about group work. Most authors who draw such conclusions are actually making assumptions on the basis of working with only one type of group configuration (such as groups comprised entirely of strangers, or 'family units' or work colleagues). Our research, conducted with a variety of group types, makes such assumptions impossible. The AIDS Media project data demonstrate that groups may actually *facilitate* the expression of difficult or taboo experiences. Instead of generalising about the effect of 'groups' we need to pay close attention to the *composition* of groups and how the characteristics of any *particular* group may influence what is said. We can then explore what this tells us about social pressures and the construction and the communication of knowledge.

Argumentative Interactions: The Importance of Difference

The group process however, is not only about consensus and the articulation of group norms and experiences. Differences between individuals within the group are equally important and, in any case, rarely disappear from view. Regardless of how they are selected, the research participants in any one group are never entirely homogeneous. Participants do not just agree with each other; they also misunderstand one another, question one another, try to persuade each other of the justice of their own point of view and sometimes they vehemently disagree.

During the course of the group the facilitator can explore such differences of opinion and encourage the participants to theorise about why such diversity exists. In our 'pre-existing groups' people were sometimes surprised to discover how differently they thought about some things especially when the group otherwise appeared relatively homogeneous (e.g. by gender, race, and class). Such unexpected dissent led them to clarify why they thought as they did, often identifying aspects of their personal experience which had altered their opinions or specific occasions which had made them re-think their point of view. Had the data been collected by interviews the researcher might have been faced with 'armchair' theorising about the causes of such difference but in a focus group these can be explored 'in situ' with the help of the research participants.

The difference between participants also allows one to observe not only how people theorise their own point of view but how they do so in relation to other perspectives and how they put their own ideas 'to work'. This process in itself clarifies what people are saying. In both questionnaires and in individual interviews it is easy to assume that someone is giving the 'right' answer for the right reason. However, diversity within a group ensures that people are forced to explain the reasoning behind their thinking just as much when they give the 'right' answer as when they give the wrong one. For example, in several groups research participants asserted that 'you can *not* tell by looking who has HIV'. However, when challenged by other members of the group, several people justified this point of view by saying that it was simply impossible to distinguish between someone who has HIV anti-body positive and someone who looked ill for some other reason (such as having flu or 'ordinary' cancer).

Close attention to the ways in which research participants tell stories *to one another* also prevents the researcher from assuming that she knows 'the meaning' of any particular anecdote or account. During the course of the group session the researcher witnesses how such stories actually operate in a given social setting, how they are mobilised in social interaction, what ideological work they are employed to achieve. For example group members often enthusiastically shared tales about the 'vengeful AIDS carrier' who sleeps with an unwitting stranger and departs leaving the message: 'Welcome to the AIDS club'. A health educator commenting on this phenomena suggested that such tales could do more for the prevention of HIV transmission than all the health education campaigns put together (*Guardian* 30.10.91). If such stories do serve such functions it is certainly not all they do: in our 'general population' groups such tales were *not* often used to advise people to take precautions during sex with anyone – instead they were used to justify identifying and isolating 'AIDS carriers'.

People's different assumptions are thrown into relief by the way in which they challenge one another, the questions they ask, the evidence people bring to bear on an issue, the sources they cite, and what arguments seem to sway the opinion of other members of the group. When analysing the script of a group discussion it is well worth having special coding categories for certain types of interaction between participants such as 'question', 'cited sources', 'deferring to the opinion of others' and 'changes of mind'. When one person tells an anecdote or relates the plot of a TV programme, what line of questioning do the other members of the group pursue in order to decide, for instance, whether a particular person described in a story really is an 'innocent' victim of AIDS? When one participant describes an occasion when they think they might have put themselves at risk – what queries are raised by the co-participants or how do they seek to reassure their friend? When an argument breaks out, what sort of evidence seems to 'work' in influencing the opinion of others? And what is going on when people appear to change their minds in response to information or theories presented by co-participants. For example in one group there was a great deal of initial scepticism about the view that HIV was created in a laboratory but a story told by one of the other members of the group shifted the consensus:

> *PP*: My-holier-than-thou mother-in-law to put it politely, keeps informing me that it was a man-made disease.
> *PP*: Well my brother works in a lab [...] in America and when that all came out that it was a man-made virus I wrote and asked him and his letter was censored, what he answered to me was all blanked out [...] That made me think, "aye, it is a man-made thing, there's something in that. Why should they blank out his letter?" [...]
> *JK*: What do the rest of you think of this story?
> *PP*: It makes it more probable
> *PP*: It makes me think it could be the way it started
> *PP*: There must be something [Women with children attending same playgroup]

This interaction was typical of many of the 'turning points' in the groups. People commonly appeared to change their minds in responce to 'personal' evidence based on anecdotes or the perceived behaviour of professionals rather than information from leaflets or advertisements and there was a clear 'hierarchy of credibility' in operation between different types of sources (mothers-in-laws coming rather low down on the list in Western culture!).

Finally, one can also observe how language and forms of speech may facilitate or inhibit communication. For example there is a theory that if people's vocabulary does not contain the term 'HIV' they may be unable to comprehend the distinction between the symptom-free state of being HIV antibody positive and the diagnosis of AIDS. This did not prove to be the case. Data from the AIDS Media Research Project show that people could understand the distinction without possessing the accurate medical language (and vice versa). However there was some evidence to suggest that if people do not have (or do not *use*) different words to identify HIV and AIDS they may have difficulty communicating the distinction to others. This is clearly illustrated by one brief extract from a tangled dispute between Alec (who knows the difference between being a 'carrier' and 'actually having the disease') and Kenny:

> *Alec*: You can be a carrier or you can actually have the disease. [...]
> *Kenny*: How can you carry something and not have it. Say you're carrying a shopping bag – you've got it.
> *Alec*: It could be someone else's. You're just carrying it and you can pass it on to someone else. [...] A picture that I saw on the TV, she was a carrier she gave it to her baby, she didn't actually have it.

Kenny: How can you give somebody something that you've not got?
Alec: You're carrying a shopping bag, but it might not be actually your shopping bag.
Kenny: How can you give somebody something if you've not got it, for God's sake man, wake up, come off the mind expanding drugs please Alec. [School students]

The debate quickly became confused by the lack of linguistic specificity. Both boys resort to terms such as 'carrying it' and 'having it' and the discussion became hopelessly side-tracked by an inappropriate metaphor. This is actually a condensed extract of a much lengthier interchange between the two boys – they were unable to resolve their differences and the debate ended with a scornful Kenny declaring: 'I'm not arguing any more'. Such interactions help researchers to identify the precise influence of particular words or phrases and are invaluable when attempting to design or improve health education or other intervention strategies.[6]

Conclusion

Focus groups do not easily tap into individual biographies or the minutiae of decision making during intimate moments, but they do examine how knowledge and, more importantly, ideas both develop, and operate, within a given cultural context. As such focus groups are perfect for 'filling in the gaps' so often exposed by KAP surveys and are ideal for inductive approaches aimed at generating concepts and hypotheses which, as Mullen and Reynolds point out, may have far more potential for health education research, theory and practice than the dominant deductive models (Mullen and Reynolds cited in Basch 1987:435).

To sum up, this paper has argued for the overt exploitation and exploration of interactions in focus group discussion. There are, it has been suggested, 10 main advantages to be gained from the interaction between participants. Such interaction:

- highlights the *respondents'* attitudes, priorities, language and framework of understanding
- encourages a great variety of communication from participants – tapping into a wide range and form of understanding
- helps to identify group norms
- provides insight into the operation of group/social processes in the articulation of knowledge (e.g. through the examination of what information is censored or muted within the group)
- Can encourage open conversation about embarrassing subjects and facilitate the expression of ideas and experiences that might be left underdeveloped in an interview

Through detailed attention to the interaction between different members of the group a researcher can:

- explore differences between group participants in situ with them and, because participants reflect upon each other's ideas, ensure that the data is organic/interconnected.
- use the conflict between participants in order to clarify why people believe what they do. Examine the questions that people ask one another in order to reveal their underlying assumptions and theoretical frameworks.
- explore the arguments people use against each other, identify the factors which influence individuals to change their minds and document how facts and stories operate in practice – what ideological work they do.
- analyse how particular forms of speech facilitate or inhibit peer communication, clarify or confuse the issue (in ways directly relevant to improving communication).

This article is *not* arguing that the group data is either more or less 'authentic' than data collected by interviews; instead it is based on the premise that 'all talk through which people generate meaning is contextual, and that the contexts will inevitably somewhat colour the meaning' (Dahlgren 1988: 292). It is a predictable sign of the dominance of the interview paradigm that when researchers have found differences between data collected by interviews and group discussion they have sometimes blithely dismissed the latter as 'inaccurate'. Hoijer, for example, is one of the few authors critically to address both interviews and group discussions. She used both techniques in her study of audience understandings of television programmes. However, at one point she states that 'Comparing interpretations and opinions expressed individually with what is later said in a group discussion, there are always several cases of diversion. In fact, too many to permit taking *the group discussion* as a valid basis for audience interpretations and reactions' (Hoijer 1990:34, my emphasis).

But difference between interview and group data can not be classified in terms of 'honesty' and 'dishonesty' or 'truth' versus 'falsehood'. Comparing the effects of different methodologies when talking to heterosexual men about sex, for example, some researchers have noted that these research participants are more likely to express macho attitudes (with a male researcher) or to sexually harass (a female researcher) in group settings than in individual interviews (Wight in press; Green *et al.* in press). The group data documenting macho or sexual harassing behaviour is no more 'invalid' than that showing the research participants' relatively acceptable behaviour in interview situations. Instead of disregarding data from group settings we need to acknowledge the different types of discourses that may be expressed in the 'private' and 'public' arena, or with peers versus with an interviewer. The fact that particular groups facilitate the articulation of particular kinds of perspectives can then be consciously addressed and the importance of that context can be considered.

We are none of us self-contained, isolated, static entities; we are part of complex and overlapping social, familial and collegiate networks. Our personal behaviour is not cut off from public discourses and our actions do not happen in a cultural vacuum whether that is negotiating safer sex, sharing needles, attending for a smear test or going 'queer bashing'. We learn about the 'meaning' of AIDS (or sex, or health or food or cigarettes) through talking with and observing other people, through conversations at home or at work; and we act (or fail to act) on that knowledge in a social context. When researchers want to explore people's understandings, or to influence them, it makes sense to employ methods which actively encourage the examination of these social processes in action.

Acknowledgements

I would like to thank my colleagues – Peter Beharrell, David Miller, Kevin Williams – and the grant holders – Mick Bloor, John Eldridge, Sally Macintyre and Greg Philo – for their contributions to this paper. I would also like to acknowledge the support of the funding body – the Economic and Social Research Council, grant no. XA44250006 and to thank Kay Weaver for lively debate on this issue.

Notes

1. The questionnaire provided data on each participant's attitudes and beliefs prior to the group discussion – allowing for some comparison between initial, individual responses and later group responses (for a discussion of the differences see Kitzinger, in press). Completion of questionnaires also helped to maximise subsequent debate and to encourage research participants to express their own point of view because, as other authors have noted, 'the process of writing things down reinforces a person's commitment to contributing them to the group, even in the face of apparent disapproval' (Morgan 1988, 58, Greenbaum 1987).

2. This paper does not address the relative merits of focus groups as opposed to participant observation. Although I was informally involved with some of the groups prior to the start of sessions (e.g. joining them in preparing a meal or sitting through the end of their business meeting) I do not have any way of systematically comparing such methods from this study. I agree with Morgan, however, when he suggests that focus groups are particularly suited to the study of attitudes and cognition whereas participant observation may be more appropriate for studies of social roles and formal organisations (Morgan 1988, 17).

3. Such racist and heterosexist comments raise ethical dilemmas for any researcher. These may be particularly acute for the group facilitator if such comments are directed at other members of the group and take the form of bullying or intimidation. Such ethical problems can be addressed through (a) thinking about the composition of the groups prior to running any such sessions and (b) using dissent within the group to challenge and debate such attitudes. Looking through the transcripts it is also clear

that, on a few occasions, I simply intervened to silence discussion, or at least 'move it along' because of my own discomfort with what was being said or the perceived discomfort of other members of the group.

4. I suspect that gender is one of the factors influencing both researchers' and research participants' reactions to group work. Women, unlike most men, have a well established tradition of sharing 'personal' information with other women and it is no coincidence that many self help and therapeutic techniques, not to mention consciousness raising, are based on group work. Many so-called 'personal' topics have been very successfully explored by female researchers through group discussions with women (see, for example, Haug, 1983).

5. Group work can, however, discriminate against people with communication disabilities. Working on a study of residential care for the elderly I excluded at least one potential group participant on the basis that it required my full attention, and frequent repetition, to follow what he was saying and he became extremely agitated when I failed to understand. It was also clear within the subsequent focus groups that if each person had a different disability this could compound each of their communication difficulties. For example, deafness, dementia and partial paralysis made it difficult for three members of one group to sustain any sort of conversation with each other, although each could communicate with me. On the other hand it was also true that some of the old people who might have been unable to sustain a one-to-one interview were able to take part in the group contributing intermittently. Even some apparently 'unresponsive patients' eventually responded to the lively conversations generated by their co-residents. Considerations of communication disabilities should not rule out group work, but must be considered as a factor.

6. Medical sociologists and health educationalists often emphasise the importance of 'peer communication' and the 'community environment' and it is clear that group-based intervention programs may be more effective than those targeted at individuals (see Basch, 1987 pp 412–3). It is this understanding that has led some researchers to argue that focus groups are 'indispensable to translating behavioural theories into effective prevention programs in a given setting' (Valdiserri 1989). Uncovering people's own 'models of rationality' and understanding their perspective 'is integral to achieve a key goal of health education – empowerment – and focus group interviews are an appropriate method for understanding and developing sensitivity toward those we serve' (Basch 1987, 436).

References

Barker, G. and Rich, S. (1992) Influences on adolescent sexuality in Nigeria and Kenya: findings from recent focus-group discussions, *Studies in Family Planning*, 23, 199–210.

Basch, C., Decicco, I. and Malfetti, J. (1989) A focus group study on decision processes of young drivers: reasons that may support a decision to drink and drive, *Health Education Q.*, 16, 389–96.

Basch, C. (1987) Focus group interview: an underutilized research technique for improving theory and practice in health education, *Health Education Q.*, 14, 411–8.

Bogardus, E. (1926) The group interview, *J. Applied Sociology*, 10, 372–82.

Beharrell, P. (1993) AIDS and the British Press, in Eldridge, J. (ed) *Getting the Message*, London: Routledge, 210–252.

Corner, J., Richardson, K. and Fenton, N. (1990) Nuclear Reactions: Forms and Response in Public Issue, *Television, A Media Research Monograph 4*. London: John Libbey.

Crockett, S., Heller, K., Merkel, J. and Peterson, J. (1990) Assessing beliefs of older rural Americans about nutrition education: Use of the focus group approach, *J. American Dietetic Association*, 90, 563–7.

Dahlgren, P. (1988) What's the meaning of this? Viewers' plural sense-making of TV news, *Media, Culture and Society*, 10, 285–301.

Desvousges, W.H. and Smith, V.K. (1988) Focus groups and risk communication: the 'science' of listening to data, *Risk Analysis*, 8, 479–84.

Frazer, E. (1987) Teenage girls' reading of Jackie, *Media Culture and Society*, 9, 407–25.

Frey, J. and Fontana, A. (1991) The group interview in social research, *Social Science J.*, 28, 175–87.

Fine, M. (1988) Sexuality, schooling and adolescent females: the missing discourse of desire, *Harvard Educational Rev.*, 58, 29–53.

Geis, S., Fuller, R. and Rush, J. (1986) Lovers of AIDS victims: psychosocial stresses and counselling needs, *Death Studies*, 10, 43–53.

Glazer, B. and Strauss, A. (1967) *The Discovery of Grounded Theory*. Chicago: Aldine.

Green, G., Bernard, M., Barbour, R. and Kitzinger, J. (in press) Who wears the trousers? sexual harrassment in the interview setting, *Women's Studies International Forum*.

Greenbaum, T. (1987) *The Practical Handbook and Guide to Focus Group Research*. Lexington, M.A.: Lexington Books.

Gregory, S. and Mckie, L. (1991) The smear test: listening to women's views, *Nursing Standard*, 5, 32–6.

Grunig, L. (1990) Using focus group research in public relations, *Public Relations Review*, 1, 36–49.

Haug, F. (1983) *Female Sexualization: a collective work of memory*. London: Verso.

Hoijer, B. (1990) Studying viewers' reception of television programmes: theoretical and methodological considerations, *European J. Communication*, 5, 29–56.

Irwin, K. *et al.* (1991) Knowledge, attitudes and beliefs about HIV infection and AIDS among healthy factory workers and their wives, Kinshasa, Zaire, *Social Science and Medicine*, 3, 917–30.

Khan, M.E. and Manderson, L. (1992) Focus groups in tropical diseases research, *Health Policy and Planning*, 7, 56–66.

Kitzinger, J. (1990) Audience understanding of AIDS media messages: a discussion of methods, *Sociology of Health and Illness*, 12, 319–35.

Kitzinger, J. and Miller, D. (1992) 'African AIDS': the Media and Audience Beliefs. In Aggleton, P., Davies, P. and Hart, G., *AIDS: Rights, Risk and Reason*. London: Falmer Press, 28–52.

Kitzinger, J. (1993) Understanding AIDS: researching audience perceptions of Acquired Immune Deficiency Syndrome. In Eldridge, J. (ed) *Getting the Message*. London: Routledge, 271–304.

——. (in press) Focus Groups: method or madness? In Boulton, M. (ed) *Challenge and Innovation: Methodological Advances in AIDS Research*. London: Falmer Press.

Kreuger, R. (1988) *Focus Groups: A Practical Guide for Applied Research*. London: Sage.

Lederman, L. (1983) High Apprehensives talk about communication apprehension and its effects on their behaviour, *Communication Quarterly*, 31, 233–7.

Lengua, L. *et al.* (1992) Using focus groups to guide the development of parenting program for difficult-to-reach, high-risk families, *Family Relations*, 4, 163–8.

Mayone Stycos, J. (1981) A critique of focus group and survey results: the machismo case, *Studies in Family Planning*, 12, 450–6.

Merton, R. *et al.* (1956) *The Focused Interview: A Report of the Bureau of Applied Social Research.* Columbia University.

Merton, R. (1987) The focussed interview and focus group: continuities and discontinuities, *Public Opinion Quarterly*, 51, 550–66.

Middleton, D. and Edwards, D. (1990) *Collective Remembering.* London: Sage.

Miller, D. and Williams, K. (1993) Negotiating HIV/AIDS information: agendas, media strategies and the news. In Eldridge, J. (ed) *Getting the Message.* London: Routledge, 12–44.

Morgan, D. (1988) *Focus Groups as Qualitative Research.* London: Sage.

Philo, G. (1990) *Seeing and Believing.* London: Routledge.

Schlesinger, P., Dobash, R., Dobash, R. and Weaver, K. (1992) *Women Viewing Violence.* London: BFI.

Validisem, R. (1989) *Preventing AIDS: the Design of Effective Programs.* London: Rutgers University Press.

Watts, M. and Ebbutt, D. (1987) More than the sum of the parts: research methods in group interviewing, *British Educational Research J.* 13, 25–34.

Wight, D. (in press) Boys' thoughts and talk about sex in a working class locality of Glasgow, *Sociological Review.*

Zimmerman, M. *et al.* (1990) Assessing the acceptability of NORPLANT implants in four countries: findings from focus group research, *Studies in Family Planning*, 21, 92–103.

20

Focus Groups and Ethnography

Michael Agar & James MacDonald

Focus groups are sociological methods (Merton and Kendall 1946) that developed in advertising and marketing, but have recently mushroomed into a widely used method of social research. As anthropologists, we view this development with some skepticism. Our intuition is that a few hours with a few groups guarantees only that the "quality" in "qualitative" will go the way of fast food. At the same time, the senior author recently heard reports from several members of a national epidemiological panel that showed how focus groups turned quantitative researchers into fascinated listeners to human voices. Even if focus groups accomplish nothing else this result alone suggests that they be taken seriously.

It is clear that focus groups are here to stay; it is also clear that they play an important role in the politics of social research that any anthropologist would support. We decided to explore how an interest in focus groups could be developed into a more elaborate interest in ethnographic research. What we want to show in this article is that there are two answers. First, ethnography provides broader frames of interpretation in terms of which focus group details take on added significance. Second, ethnographic methods of transcript analysis add depth to an understanding of what actually occurred in a particular focus group session.

In this article, then, we take a focus group and justify these two answers. We were handed an excellent opportunity for the exercise. Over several months we collaborated on a study of adolescent LSD users. Based on several ethnographic interviews with former users and parents, as well as news clippings and other written materials, we'd put together a report on what we'd found (MacDonald and Agar 1994). We decided to do a focus group, with adolescents we hadn't interviewed, to check the role a focus group might play vis-à-vis other ethnographic data.

Source: *Human Organization*, vol. 54, no. 1, 1995, 78–86.

The key characteristic of focus groups, according to Morgan's *Focus Groups as Qualitative Research*, is "the explicit use of the group interaction to produce data and insights that would be less accessible without the interaction found in a group" (1988:12). The difference, when compared to an interview, is that the focus group members talk with each other in addition to the interviewer. The difference, when compared with participant observation, is that the group is talking about a topic introduced by a moderator rather than one they generated in a natural situation.

Krueger, in his *Focus Groups: A Practical Guide for Applied Research*, says that: "a focus group can be defined as a carefully planned discussion designed to obtain perceptions on a defined area of interest in a permissive, nonthreatening environment" (1988:18). The contradiction between "carefully planned" and "permissive" contains the same contrast that Morgan lays out when he talks of the groups as both "controlled" and "naturalistic." Even at this definitional level, some interesting problems appear, problems that will surface in the detailed look at transcripts to come.

This isn't the only hint of complications. For example, a focus group works to the extent that group members discuss the topic among themselves. But there is an outsider, the moderator, and probably an observer as well, who are responsible for the group and the topics to be discussed. Too much moderator control prevents the group interaction that is the goal; too little control, and the topics might never be discussed.

As another example, a "frequent goal" of a focus group is to "conduct a group discussion that resembles a lively conversation among friends or neighbors" (Morgan 1988:22). At the same time, the general strategy is to make up the group out of "strangers." But it is not automatic that a group of strangers will have a "lively conversation" about anything. In fact, a judgment as to whether a conversation occurred, lively or not, is a delicate matter that calls for some close analysis of transcripts.

Before we talk about such issues, we need to tell the story of our focus group. To prepare for our focus group meeting, the two authors met and listed six topical "foci" – what Krueger calls the "questioning route" – issues that were pivotal in the original report. We decided that we both would moderate, and would talk with each other during the session as well, our goal being to reduce the role of the lone, authoritarian moderator figure – a naive goal, as it turned out. We rehearsed the opening lines, tossed the tape recorders into the car, and drove to the meeting that we had been reassured would be ready to go – even more naive, as you'll see shortly.

In summary, the youths did talk about the topics we introduced, and what they said supported and complicated what we'd found in our analysis. But, as conversational analysts would have predicted, the structure of a focus group sets constraints on the interaction. Turns are usually short, moderator control is inevitable, a few group members dominate, and group formation sets up constraints on what can be said. And, as ethnographers would have predicted, only the prior qualitative work made interpretation of focus group results possible. Without that prior work, a naive adult would have learned that a lot of kids were using LSD, that the situation was much more complicated than he/she had thought, but little else. Such a lesson in itself has some value, since it is important to demonstrate that the kids had something interesting and intelligent to say about their drug use. The addition of broader ethnographic context and more detailed transcript analysis, however, offers more.

The Group

The story of the formation of our focus group is a comedy of errors. We'd done our earlier ethnographic analysis with former LSD users in a treatment program and planned to do the group with the young clients as well. The program staff – we want to be clear on this important point – were praised by our interviewees, supported and encouraged our study, and spent time to help us out. At the same time, they are incredibly overworked, underpaid, mental health professionals with more kids to take care of than they can reasonably handle, given budget cuts, increasing demands for their services, and the LSD "boom" in the metropolitan suburb where they work.

From our selfish research point of view, they didn't make the preparations for the group that we'd expected. We'd asked for a group of former LSD users, young people we hadn't interviewed before, for a session to last from one-and-a-half to two hours. "No problem," we were told. The date was set.

On that appointed day we arrived in the waiting room and talked with a group member. He had no idea who we were or what was about to happen. We met the counselor at the time the group was to have started, and he said he'd tell the participants what we wanted to do and say they could leave if they wanted. After he finished his discussion and we set up the equipment, he told us several of them would have to leave at seven, which left us roughly forty-five minutes of time.

The two authors entered the meeting room. The young people filed in, counselor in tow. He told them, sympathetically and accurately, who we were and what we wanted to do. Three of them walked out. We were left with four stiffly seated youths who looked at us and the recording equipment as if they were in one of the circles of hell – not the ninth, but close.

Both authors, as they discussed at length after the event, felt like the situation was at this point already a disaster. But we pressed on. No sooner had we started than the counselor walked in with another participant, one who, he said "needed to be in this group." The young man had no idea what was going on. His words are featured in an example to come, but for a long time he simply sat silently and stared at the tape recorder. With our group of five participants and two moderators, we launched off into the focus group.

The group history taught us two things. First, a focus group that started off under what we might generously call less than perfect circumstances produced something of value, though the value derived from its relationship to other ethnographic work. In retrospect this is no surprise, because even disasters – maybe especially disasters – count as ethnographic data.

Second, and most important for the focus group literature, every focus group has a story behind it. Where is it? Why isn't it routinely reported in focus group accounts? Certainly the literature we've consulted emphasizes how critical the selection of group members is. And certainly we violated the "strangers" rule, since the youth all knew each other. But we suspect that many focus groups are drawn together through networks, that they are products of institutional processes that powerfully shape them. Such histories belong in the focus group data for, without them, it's difficult to evaluate the scope of what was learned.

Robitussin

One of the issues we'd tackled in the earlier report, logically enough, was, "why do kids use LSD?" We thought we'd come up with some answers, some good ones, from the kids' point of view. Needless to say, we'd listed this as topic A in our focus group plan.

What follows is an excerpt from an early portion of the group. Some conventions of transcriptions need to be explained, since they are done in a style developed in conversational analysis.

Punctuation signals tone – a period is the "I'm done" falling tone; a comma is a rising "more to come;" a question mark signals the rising question intonation.

Pauses are indicated in several ways. An "=" signals a run-on, without the usual pause; a "+" indicates a longer than expected pause; if the pauses are longer than two seconds, the actual length is indicated in parentheses.

A colon after a sound indicates that the sound was stretched out, given how that speaker usually speaks; underlining means that a particular word was emphasized, through stress and/or volume, more so than what was expected.

The "//" marks indicate where two speakers overlapped.

Transcriptions can be much more detailed than this, and in some cases the use of the conventions is a close judgment call. But the conventions do allow us to ground some interpretations in ways that typical focus group transcripts don't.

Here is the transcript. "MA" is the first author; "JM" is the second author; the other initials label the participants. The numbers indicate where we are on the tape according to the counter on the recorder. We should note that turns 9 through 16 are an aside – C accidentally called T ("Ted") by his real name rather than the pseudonym he'd chosen.

074.
1 MA. why do people use lsd. = what's the advantages. = what do they get out of it. why //
2 T.   //can can you compare it to robitussin?
3 MA. can I compare it to ro-can you compare it to // robitussin.
4 T.   // yeah
5 MA. (2.6) can you compare it – are you sayin // it's . . .
6 T.   // no . . . .
7 C.   // it's totally different J.
8 T. no, // it's no:t.
9 C.   // I mean T. (laugh)
10 MA. (laugh) Ted. that's Ted over there // Ted Koppel, We have Ted
11 C.   // yeah. (laugh)
12 MA. Koppel // here.
13 C.   // yeah.
14 T. Ted Nugent.
15 C. Ted Nugent. (laugh)
16 MA. Ted Nugent. +
17 T. no you you can't compare it to like I – you know I mean you can't compare lsd with like robitussin. +
18 C. they're two totally different things T.
19 T. not recess-well // they're two totally different things but
20 N.   // . . . . . same thing
21 T. they do the // same thing.
22 C.   // well yeah but it's still different. (2.7)
23 MA. you te-you te-you tell-this is news. Talk-tell me some more.
24 JM. how well how do they do the same thing?
25 T. you don't know about robitussin?
26 MA. I know what it is, sure. But // uh
27 T.   // you drink like a whole bottle of it, it'll make you like + tri:p, see trai:ls and everything. +
28 MA. huh.
29 T. it'll really mess you up.
30 C. (laugh)
31 MA. lesson number one. (laugh)
32 T. . . . heres done robitussin? You done robitussin?
33 J. only when it was safe.
(several laugh)
(3.19)
34 C. robo:, stay away from that. uch.
35 MA. So some folks would do would do // like
36 T.   // mm hmm. lot of people, if they can't get their hands on acid they'll do // robitussin
37 MA.   // they'll do robitussin.
38 N. just go steal robitussin.

39 MA. for Christ's sake. huh.
40 C. (laugh)
41 MA. du:h. I had no idea. And what is – so: what is it about those two. I mean let's s:ay for a sec those are equivalent. what's – why do why do people – what is it doing for em. what's – is it the trails? is it – what. what are – what // what's the story, what's the
42 T.   // um hmm. . . .
43 MA. drive, what's the what's the interest?
44 T. the loss of + being able to think straight.
45 MA. sorry?
46 T. the loss of being able to think straight, feeling like a moron, I dunno.
47 MA. I do that for a livin.
48 C. (laugh)
cough
(4.8)
49 JM. so, m – is that i:t? Is that all there is about acid? (5.2)
50 C.   // m:
51 ?   // u:h
52 JM. // what – I mean + why would anyone m:ess with acid. robitussin you can get it at the drugstore.
53 T. well everyt – everytime I guess you do acid you you do + it's – you know you don't have // the same exact thing over again, like
54 C.   // cause it doesn't – right.
55 T. when you get drunk, usually, you get drunk on the same thing it's gonna be – you're gonna get drunk the same way. if you do acid everything's + you know everytime you do acid something happens – different is gonna happen.
56 MA. huh. does that corres – does that make sense to the //
57 T.   //cause all acid's different. all beer or whatever stuff like that, robitussin's ma:de the sa:me. 122

This passage occurred early in the group discussion. Neither MA nor JM, after several interviews, had come across the use of Robitussin, a legally available cough medicine, as an LSD substitute. One interviewee had mentioned Robitussin casually, in passing, but neither of us picked it up as a significant topic worth further exploration.

There's a reason Robitussin popped up as an issue early on, an obvious one upon later reflection. T, who introduced the topic, turned out to dominate the first phase of the group discussion. The pattern was already clear in this brief segment. T had never used LSD, though he had used Robitussin. T established his expertise, his right to talk, by pushing Robitussin onto the floor. He tried to dominate the talk by pushing his other topics onto the floor for the rest of the session. But whatever the personal motivation of one group member, the fact remains. The focus group immediately produced a surprise that nothing in our previous research had revealed. The possible use of

Robitussin, "Robo" as C called it, as a substitute for LSD is a piece of the contemporary drug puzzle we hadn't known much about.

We think this is one place where focus groups shine. Through group interaction, we learn that something we hadn't noticed before is a significant issue for drug-experienced young people. This lively group interaction is obviously something that can't happen in an individual interview. Turns 17 through 22 show one stretch where three youths engage the issue, as do 32 through 38, though with moderator comments in that segment as well. The structure of pauses and overlaps makes its lively nature explicit.

From the way the group takes up the topic, it is clear that something significant is going on, something significant to *them*. A new piece of the territory is revealed. The focus group won't tell you where it fits in with other parts of the landscape, nor will it tell you much about how the new territory looks, but it will tell you that it's there.

One reason why the information will be sketchy lies in the interactional structure of the group. (A second reason, the shared knowledge of group members, is discussed later.) What kind of structure is a focus group? It is somewhere between a *meeting* and a *conversation*. A meeting has a manager, someone who introduces topics and allocates turns to speakers, a person called the "moderator" in the case of focus groups. A conversation is a looser structure, with turns and topics up for grabs among people with equal rights to the floor.

As a *meeting*, the focus group is called by somebody, for a reason. To the extent that group members participate, they look to the moderator to start it, guide it, and stop it. Going in we had in mind strategies to minimize our controlling role, because we felt that some earlier focus group transcripts we'd looked at showed too much control by the moderator. With a method that featured group interactions, we thought the moderator should keep his nose out of it whenever possible.

We might as well have started to drive by deciding it wasn't such a good idea to steer. Trace the initials down the left side of the transcript and see how long it takes until an "MA" or "JM" appears. Notice that at the pauses at 5, 22, 33, and 50, pauses that go beyond the two second limit that indicates that the silence has stretched on longer than usual (Chafe 1979), a moderator jumps in to fill in the dead air space with a comment or question. It was our group and everyone knew who was responsible for it.

Group members looked to us to guide where it was we wanted to go. This is evident in 2, where T introduces a topic by asking a question of the moderator, and throughout in the way the moderators' questions are taken seriously, that is, where the participants work to figure out some kind of response.

What this pattern means is that, to some extent, the raison d'être of focus groups is contradicted by their structure. Their great strength, says the literature, is that they allow group members to interact in ways that they would ordinarily do out there in their daily lives. But a conversation over coffee isn't the same as a meeting in a group. Conversations don't have alien moderators with questions on their mind that, for whatever reason, the group has decided to take seriously and to which they orient their discussion.

So, focus groups are, in part, meetings. In meetings, the manager runs things and asks questions and the participants respond. Our job, in this sample transcript, was to pursue the question, "Why do kids use LSD?" Suddenly "Robo" came up – it even had a nickname, a sure sign of its centrality. But we couldn't drop everything and scatter into a discussion of "Robo." We didn't know enough to ask questions yet. Given the group's disagreement, we didn't even know if it truly had a strong connection to LSD. We hadn't had time to digest the surprise, a surprise evident in MA's moderator turns at 23, 28, 31, 39, and 41. We had a limited amount of time and several topics to cover.

Another reason why focus group information is sketchy has to do with the *conversation* rather than the meeting aspect. In American conversations, turns are typically short, and a couple of members usually dominate. In this transcript, a pattern emerges that characterizes much of what was to come. At first T dominates; C comments here and there; the rest of the group wait in the background, and, when they do talk, it is often so light that the recorder barely picks it up. About two-thirds of the way through the group discussion the pattern changes. T struggles with J for domination and loses. J, a former heavy LSD user, takes over due to more personal experience with the designated topic, as will be shown in a section to come. Shortly after that struggle T leaves the group. By and large this conversational structure defines how the group goes.

What we're getting here in the example transcript are short verbal bursts from two group members out of five. This is not the focus group dream, which envisions all members speaking with each other elaborately so that outsiders can get a sense of the details of their world. The focus group is, in part, a conversation, and conversations have dominant members and brief turns at talk. In an individual interview, the lone interviewee is dominant, with all the time he or she needs to develop a line of thought.

The focus group is an ambiguous beast, both meeting and conversation. The two moderators took different ways through the ambiguity. MA took on a more conversational role. The problem here is that moderator formulations and comments can be taken as conclusive, ending the flow of talk, rather than as invitations to continue the topic, as would be the case in actual conversations. JM plays a more directive role by asking questions. The problem here is that questions can highlight the authority of the moderator and place youths in a performing and evaluative mode.

In some cases such strategies work. But an excellent example of how *both* strategies can disrupt interaction appears at the end of the transcript. In 48 MA makes a self-deprecating statement as a group participant. C laughs, as she often does, but other than that the comment produces almost five seconds of dead time, a massive pause given the usual two second limit. JM comes next with a question, one that implies that the youths haven't told us enough, and this strategy results in another five second pause. The two moderator strategies represent conversation and meeting at their extremes. The long pauses show that neither "pure" strategy worked smoothly in this particular case. On the other hand, JM's question does elicit an important bit of validation of the earlier study.

This passage shows the focus group at its best. We learned something new and confirmed something old. The group context enables both types of results, since the reactions of others signal whether statements are significant from the group's point of view, and it is the group point of view that is the goal of ethnographic research. At the same time, the passage shows how the structure of focus groups, both as meeting and as conversation, limits the amount of information and sets up contradictory expectations for the moderator. The group offers evaluations of significance, something you don't get in individual interviews. But the individual interview opens large spaces for an individual voice to articulate the texture of his or her world, something that seldom happens in a focus group.

The Quiet Ones

There *were*, however, a couple of moments in the focus groups that approached the nature of individual interviews. One moment in particular is worth showing, since it makes explicit how one voice was silent and why.

Earlier, we mentioned that one young man was brought in late to the group. He was told he "needed to be in this group" by the counselor. He had no idea what was going on and, for the most part, sat quietly while the others, usually T and C and the moderators, talked. His consciousness of the tape popped up at 283, when he agreed with something and was told that he had to talk because "We can't hear him nod on the tape." At 325 he raised his hand, and this exchange followed:

JM. no no no no, you're not (laugh) supposed to raise // your
J.   // I'm sorry who are these tapes for?
JM. hand. just talk. What?
J. who are these tapes for?
JM. oh you don't // know this stuff?
      T.   // for your parents
MA. C. (laugh)
327

There follows a discussion of the study, who's paying for it, and who'll hear the tapes, a discussion that we don't reproduce here. Finally, at 345, JM asks J a direct question. J, it turns out, is the only group member with extensive LSD experience, and he launches into the kind of things we had heard in the interviews, fending off T's rude attempt to gain the floor along the way, rude because he interrupts mid-clause rather than at what the conversational analysts call a "possible completion point." We mentioned this struggle in the preceding section, when we noted that shortly after his loss of the floor, T left the group.

1 JM. and what's your experience.
2 J. oh it's nothing like what they all s – I mean + when I dosed it was like + my eyes were open, right, I could see, right, I saw – I could see everything. + it wasn't that I was seeing little men or seeing chairs moving, I was just awake, you know I could + I I could smell the flowers you know. I was just alive, I mean I wasn't like in a . . . . //
3 T.   // wa-you could smell the flo:wers even like they're ten feet away?
4 J. I'm not saying like that. = I'm saying the air was fresh.
   //I was appreciating the world more, and uh, I don't know,
5 T. //oh
6 J. and people that were nice seemed nicer and people that were rude seemed ruder and everything was just clear and straight ahead, // and everything was real honest and flat out and
7 MA. // huh
8 J. you could really understand the way everything worked, and you were just – your eyes were like opened, you know, you could you could understand, I mean it was just a good feeling just to have everything laid out fo:r you, and to under – to know to know the way things are and to understand the way things are, and like, you know and you could say, well that person has a little good in them, and that person doesn't have any good. I mean, you know, you can you know look at the trees and take nature in, ..., it's groo:vy, //I mean, but you know, that's like the past, ...
9 C.   // (light laugh)
10 J. . . . . . worry about it. I'll say, ...
11 MA. That's a nice description.
12 J. Well I mean it's just
13 MA. Well that sounds that sounds real positive. I mean that kind of //clarity and appreciation and stuff like that.
14 J.   //yeah
yeah, and I mean emotions were a lot clearer and everything just everything was just + up there. just there you know. that's why + that was my experience.
15 MA. that was well said. (3.4) how about – does does that correspond with with what some of the rest of you have heard or experienced either way?
16 C. sounds right. (2.9)
17 N. some people see trails and some people + it's all different . . . .
18 J. you see, you sometimes have a little – go into a little daze for a couple of minutes. rm talking about the overall experience. I'm talking about the

overall attitude. not not really what you're seeing, but what you're thinking, what's going through your head, yeah it's not it's not I mean you might see trails, you might see things, you know, I mean that happens. but rm saying that the overall experience is just very positive heavy kind of thing, it just lifts you up, most of the times, sometimes + it doesn't, but // you
19 MA.   // uh huh
20 J. know, seven times out of ten you you go there. (4.2)
21 MA. huh (3.4)
20 JM. hhh. ss. so what kind of – this sounds great. So what kind of kids do acid?
21 T. anybody
22 C. // . . . . .
23 JM. //jocks? 381

To say that this segment contrasts with most of the meeting/conversation nature of the focus group is an understatement. J's descriptions resemble an individual interview, with other group members dropping back into an audience role. J is like most of our earlier ethnographic sample, an experienced, articulate LSD user who has positive things to say about his drug experience.

MA and JM play roles similar to those in the transcript segment we examined in the previous section. JM's question starts J into his description, and then MA plays a more participatory role with backchannel signals in 7, 19, and 21, and formulations in 11, 13, and 15. At 15, MA returns to a meeting orientation after the long pause that signals that J is finished with what he has to say, and tries to restore group interaction. C confirms J's story and N adds a superficial comment, something that bothers J and leads him into another description of how what he's saying is more elaborate than N's summary. After J finishes, a long pause, followed by another long pause after MA's backchannel, leads JM to step back into his role as questioner, a move that reinitiates the T and C pattern already shown in the previous transcript segment.

JM's question is ironic, on reflection. J opened his description, in turn 2, by saying that what he's about to tell us is "nothing like what they all say." He's telling us he's different from the other members of the group. He doesn't take LSD for some general effect, the reasons the others have given for taking LSD in earlier parts of the focus group; instead, he takes it for clarity, clarity in perception of nature and the others around him.

After JM asks his question, the discussion centers on the traditional social categories that always come up – jocks, head bangers, and the like. The irony is that J may have just taught us how to ask the question better, that the kinds of youth who use LSD don't map onto the available social categories, but rather onto the different purposes they have in mind. This, like the topic of Robitussin, counts as a new idea that came out of the focus group, one deserving of further research.

In this segment we learned the power and importance – and beauty – of a voice we almost missed hearing. J finally asked a question about the tape that made explicit the reasons for his silence, reasons we dealt with that then led him to talk. But when he talked, he took us into a segment that was more ethnographic interview than conversation/meeting interaction. Statements were no longer brief; the moderator was no longer in control. The emphasis shifted from group evaluations of topic significance to a single person's voice articulating his experience.

The segment with J leads us to another question for any focus group. Who are those silent voices in the group? Why aren't they talking? What do they have to say?

Indexed Talk

Now we would like to show how the ethnographic research we did prior to the focus group enabled interpretation of the abbreviated focus group talk in a way that led to a productive interaction between both kinds of data. For our purposes here, the results of the earlier analysis will be called *folk models* (Holland and Quinn 1987), frames of interpretation that we assume group members share, frames that we as analysts attempt to partially model. The term "folk" is used to signal that the world *of* some group of people is of interest; it is *their* point of view rather than the point of view of outsiders. "Model" is meant to suggest an analyst's construct, with the assumption that they are models *of* group members' resources, from the analyst's point of view, that help outsiders understand what they tell us.

Different relationships hold between talk and folk models during a focus group and during an ethnographic interview. In interviews talk usually *explains* the folk model; in a focus group, talk usually *indexes* it. Ethnographic interviews typically involve two people, one, the ignorant interviewer, the other, the knowing interviewee. During a successful interview the interviewer mostly listens and the interviewee mostly talks. The interviewee tries to explain things fully and make motives and actions clear to the interviewer. The folk model is made explicit through narration, exposition, and description, genres of talk we will lump together here as explanation.

This interviewer/interviewee relation can also appear in focus groups, as we showed in the previous section, when a group member, J, took the floor and explained things to the moderators. But when group members interact among themselves, they generally share folk models, so in their own interaction they can briefly refer to things known in common rather than explain them. In the words of the ethnomethodologists, the folk models are being indexed rather than explained.

Consider the example of being "fried" or showing the signs of overuse of LSD. The fact that adolescents may quit using LSD because they have taken too much was brought up during both the interviews and the focus group, but the way "being fried" was talked about was different in the two contexts. During the interviews the adolescents explained the meaning of being fried by LSD to the interviewer. (Since we're no longer analyzing interaction, the transcripts are presented in a simpler form.)

Interviewer: What made you decide to try to quit? Was it that [bad] trip?

I was tired of doing it so much, you know. I couldn't – I wasn't sleeping at all during the night. I went to school the next day, you know I'd fall asleep in classes, I was failing a lot of my classes. I couldn't sleep cause I was you know eating so much of it, I guess I just got tired of it for awhile, take a break from it.

I know people and my friends know people that were just getting good grades, actively participating in school. I mean like going to school and had nice lives. Two years later after consistent using, their lives are shit and they don't care, and that seems like a typical oh, drugs are going to waste you, but it happens sometimes, it really does.

The adolescents explained being fried during the interview; but among themselves, during the focus group, they just made reference to it. Here's an example:

MA: .... There were a lot of different reasons – possible reasons why a person would stop using LSD.
C. Brain would fry out.
T. They start getting burnt.
C. Yeah, really, remember Noah.
T. Really.
JM: What happened?
T. Burnt to a crisp.
C. Fried.
J. He can't remember his name sometimes.
C. Yeah, he is pretty bad, pretty bad.

When the general topic "possible reasons why a person would quit LSD" was introduced by the moderator, C quickly volunteered being "fried" as one possible reason. This idea was then reiterated and confirmed by T, and a shared reference, a friend known to both, was offered and accepted as an example of becoming fried and then quitting. During this exchange there were nods and sounds of agreement from other group members.

Being fried is a major reason for quitting LSD. The use of the term in the focus group, in ways that the analysis of interviews led us to expect, strongly confirms this part of the folk model, but there is no clear explanation in the focus group of what being fried actually is. A part of the folk model the authors had postulated based on a wealth of explanation in the earlier interview study was supported; but during the focus group there was no explanation, and therefore no possibility of building to that same conclusion from the focus group itself.

Another conclusion we reached after the earlier interviews was that one of the adolescent's main objectives in tripping is to transform his or her surroundings through a limited loss of control. The location, activity, social group, and drug dose of a trip are manipulated so that control can be lost without the user actually being in danger. Limited loss of control leads to a good trip, but if too much control is lost a trip can become very bad. This part of the adolescent LSD folk model was indexed many times and in many ways during the focus group interaction.

C, a non-LSD user, referred to this situation when she described how the outcome of a trip is sensitive to dose and location. Her comment specified why all trips are different:

> C. Yeah, it depends on how much you take too or where you are. It's all kind of like a mind thing.

J, the frequent LSD user, made a less obvious reference to the same idea in these interview-style elaborate comments about bad trips:

> I mean, where, if like – if like some cops start drivin by your house, I mean it's more than one, even if it is just one. You know, and you're gonna start talking to yourself, that's especially if you're like alone. If you're with a lot of people, and you know you're cool, and you know you're safe, then you just get your mind in that frame. But if you're not like by yourself, like in your house, and you're just like looking out the windows, and it's like I don't know, it's all the way you think. It's all in your mind.

An even less direct connection to control and situation is made in this comment by Cy about one aspect of an exciting trip (Cy only talked at the end of the session, after T had gone):

> Cy. Adrenalin rush. Yeah, like if the cops find you and you're like runnin away from them or somethin like that, and they're chasing you or something. Cause I had friends that had been trippin and the cops found out they were – but it was just like one lady and they outran her. They said – they said it was like a rush, you know. They like jumped through bushes. They went through like a creek and stuff. They said it was fun.

A final example implies the same folk model. It also supports another inference we drew from the interviews. We suggested that LSD requires a safe, stress-free location to produce a good trip, and that this is one reason it was so popular in affluent suburban settings.

MA. What is it about this chemical that makes it more of a white suburban drug than any, than anything else? We can't figure it out. Got any theories?

J. It's probably kind of scary dosing in like a big city. You don't have the fresh air and you don't have the trees. Big buildings, toxic stuff in the air, you know it's just all dark, and I mean I'm sure it's done in the city too, but I'm saying it's a lot more people all around you, and like a lot more phobic, you know, a claustrophobic kind of thing, closin in on you. You know there's stuff everywhere around you and stuff. I mean so its probably why people you know enjoy it more goin out a little bit, you know. That's just my theory. I've never heard that but if I were to think why.

These examples – being fried and a limited loss of control – show how focus group interaction supports a folk model constructed on the basis of qualitative interviews. The group understands the implied reference, accepts the utterances, and the talk moves on without the folk model itself ever being overtly stated.

But on other occasions, disagreements arise. The introduction of the idea that Robitussin is "just like LSD," presented in an earlier section, was an example of this situation. It created a noticeable difference of opinion. Robitussin and its similarities to LSD were neglected during the earlier ethnographic interviews. Only one person mentioned it, and that person pointed out that the two drugs are not alike.

There was never much physical feeling in it, [LSD] it was all mental and I think that's how it differs mostly with the Nyquil or Robitussin or whatever you take.

In the focus group discussion, on the other hand, the reactions of group members to each other taught us that Robitussin is a well known and significant drug. It is likely that Robo and LSD are thought of as being similar in some ways. They are similar enough for the earlier interviewee to have used their differences to help define LSD; and they are similar enough for T to assert that they are the same. But they are also different enough for the other group members to strongly disagree with T's assertion.

The "robo" segment not only verifies a part of the adolescent LSD folk model we suggested (as the "fried" and "control" segments did), it also *complicates* it. The focus group transcript shows that within a folk model that includes agreement on the significance of Robitussin, different positions are taken on what that significance in fact means. The transcript indicates variations within the folk model. This is something that the group interaction makes clearly visible, something that an individual interview can't reveal.

Another interesting discovery emerged when the focus group was compared with the earlier interviews. This discovery taught us that not all young people shared all folk models, that, in fact, some youths shared folk models with parents rather than other adolescents.

We had anticipated a group of six to eight adolescents with LSD experience. We ended up with a group of five, only two of whom had taken LSD; only one of those two, J, had extensive experience with it. The group members were similar in many ways. They were the same age, lived in the same suburban community, and all had extensive exposure to drugs. We assumed they would share similar opinions and beliefs about drugs, since they all knew the same suburban drug scene. As it turned out, some exchanges between the users and the nonusers contradicted this assumption.

In the earlier interviews we had talked only with heavy LSD users and with non-using adults. These two kinds of interviewees were dramatically different when they talked about LSD. We anticipated that we would get responses from the focus group that were similar to what we had heard from the adolescent users. The surprise was that the non-using adolescents in the focus group were sometimes closer to the adults than they were to the adolescents who had taken LSD.

When the non-users in the group talked about the kinds of kids who take LSD or how being fried can lead to quitting, their statements were like those of the users. They were, in other words, operating with the same folk model. But when the non-users described the trip experience itself, or reasons for taking LSD, they sounded more like the adults had in the earlier interviews.

The non-users all described the trip experience in a way that trivialized it, as in these examples taken from the transcript.

T. [The] tree jumped out in front of me
T. [See], like faces in the tree
T. The buildings start walking
C. [You] turn to jello.
N. [You] go to la-la land.

After listening to a number of these characterizations J, the only heavy user in the group, said, "I don't agree with what these others said." He then went on to describe his trip experiences in the semi-poetic way characteristic of the heavy users we had interviewed, a passage that was quoted at length in the previous section. He talked of how LSD transforms the world into a fascinating place where common experiences become like mythic journeys. He spoke of himself being transformed and augmented by the drug.

In the earlier interviews, we'd concluded that understanding the trip experience is the key to understanding why a person takes LSD and why they quit. The parents' interviews lacked a model of the experience and, therefore, their explanations of why kids used LSD was dramatically different from that of the youths. The non-users in the focus group were similar. Their characterizations of tripping and their disagreement with the users on the subject suggest that they viewed the trip experience differently. They resembled the adults more so than the LSD-using youths.

The non-using youths in the focus group, logically enough, also share adult models about why people trip. The non-users mentioned two motivations for LSD use most often mentioned by the adults, peer pressure and escape.

> T. Or just to do it to be social – socially do drugs. It's like a social drinker.
> MA. why do acid?
> C. To get fucked up
> N. To escape reality

These are the standard "push" explanations expressed by the adults. People are pushed into LSD use by some force outside them. Heavy LSD users give a "pull" explanation. Their explanations assume that people are drawn to tripping by the attraction of the world created through the LSD experience.

The discovery of how the youth folk models differ around the nature of a trip and reasons for use counts as another surprise, but, once again it is typical of focus group results – discovery without explanation. Clearly something is happening but there isn't enough information to explain what. But we are left with a fascinating hypothesis. Perhaps the usual social labels – preps, headbangers, and the like – aren't important in understanding who uses and why. Perhaps different folk models around reasons for use separate users from non-users, models whose social distribution we only glimpse here.

Conclusion

To sum all this up, focus groups and ethnographic research do stand in several interesting and important relationships to each other. First of all, the detailed analysis of the transcript yields more than their usual casual use in focus group summary reports. Among other things, the detailed analysis shows who was in charge, which parts were interview-like, meeting-like, and conversation-like, which topics were lively and which were flat, how well ratified topics were by the group as a whole, and who dominated and who was silent. The detailed analysis is time consuming and requires some training in conversational analysis, but we hope we've shown that the application of the method in especially significant portions of the transcript is worth the effort.

Second, we hope we've also shown that the availability of previously constructed folk models from other ethnographic data enables a richer and more significant interpretation of focus group data. In focus groups, participants should draw on shared folk models that were, in part, modelled during ethnographic analysis. Our examples show how sometimes they did and sometimes they didn't, both results being of value. In several examples, like being fried and limited loss of control, group discussion could be interpreted only because of the folk models we had constructed earlier. But in other examples, like Robitussin, the discussion suggested variations on the model, complications that further work must take into account. Finally, some discussions called into question the assumption that the youths shared the same folk model at all. In fact the line between LSD experience and lack of it suggested that non-using adolescents shared some models with another outsider group, the parents.

All of these results are interesting and useful. We might have felt discouraged during and immediately after the focus group because we were anticipating the wrong kind of results. As individuals predisposed to consider ethnographic interviews as the most important kind of data, we were looking for explanations, not indexing. We both had committed to minimizing moderator involvement, and we also wanted to build on the explanations from the earlier interviews. In other words, we went into the group thinking of it as a group ethnographic interview. We were looking for exactly the kind of material that focus groups are not designed to produce.

We overlooked the fact that the focus group was producing results, but results of a different kind. Many of our earlier analyses were being either confirmed or complicated in interesting ways. This material was not in the form of explanations but rather in the form of exchanges among group members, exchanges that indexed the folk models we had inferred from the prior ethnographic data. But without the prior folk models, we couldn't have interpreted what was being indexed.

We can't emphasize this critical relationship enough. The powerful validation and complication that we found in the focus group transcripts presupposes prior ethnographic work. In this research context, we believe the focus group can be a useful ally. Many of the users of focus groups, however, advocate them as a stand-alone method, a qualitative shortcut into the world of focus group members. As far as such an exclusive use of focus groups goes, we retain the skepticism with which we opened this article. Without prior knowledge of the folk models as a base, there's nothing to evaluate the group exchanges against, nothing in terms of which to register and interpret the surprises that occur. A focus group can show a researcher some new territory, but it can't tell you much about what it is you've just seen. Ethnography helps resolve this problem, first, by enabling a fine tuned evaluation of the focus group discourse, second, by providing the interpretive folk models necessary to understand indexed focus group talk in more significant ways.

We're not the only ones to have noticed interesting issues in focus group interaction and the ties between that interaction and more comprehensive ethnographic work (Swenson, Griswold, and Kleiber 1992; Fielding and Fielding 1986). At the same time, Owen Murdoch, an anthropology graduate student at the University of Maryland, reports that his recent review of the focus group methods literature shows that the principal issue of interest is the quantification of focus group data. We hope we've shown there's another way to think about things, one that maps more naturally onto the kind of resource that focus groups can represent.

References

Chafe, Wallace, 1979 *The Flow of Thought and the Flow of Discourse: Discourse and Syntax.* (Vol. 12: *Syntax and Semantics.*) New York: Academic Press.
Fielding, Nigel G. and Jane L. Fielding 1986 *Linking Data.* Newbury Park, CA: Sage.
Holland, Dorothy and Naomi Quinn 1987 *Cultural Models in Language and Thought.* Cambridge: Cambridge University Press.
Krueger, Richard A. 1988 *Focus Groups: A Practical Guide for Applied Research.* Newbury Park, CA: Sage.
MacDonald, James and Michael Agar 1994 What Is a Trip – and Why Take One? In *LSD: Still with Us after All These Years.* Leigh Henderson and William Gloss, eds. Pp. 20–30. New York: Lexington Books.
Merton, R. K. and R. L. Kendall 1946 The Focused Interview. *American Journal of Sociology* 51: 541–557.
Morgan, David L. 1988 *Focus Groups as Qualitative Research.* Newbury Park, CA: Sage.
Swenson, J. D., W. F. Griswold, and P. B. Kleiber 1992 Focus Groups: Method of Inquiry/Intervention. *Small Group Research* 23: 459–474.